Concise German Review Grammar

Second Edition

Jack Moeller
Oakland University

Helmut Liedloff
Southern Illinois University

In association with
Helen Lepke, *Clarion University*
Simone Berger, *Tufts University*

Houghton Mifflin Company   **Boston   Toronto**
Geneva, Illinois   Palo Alto   Princeton, New Jersey

Sponsoring Editor: Susan M. Mraz
Senior Development Editor: Barbara Lasoff
Senior Project Editor: Charline Lake
Senior Manufacturing Coordinator: Priscilla J. Bailey

Cover design by Harold Burch, Harold Burch Design, New York

Printed in the U.S.A.

Library of Congress Catalog Card Number: 94-76529

ISBN: 0-395-68875-2

1 2 3 4 5 6 7 8 9-DH-98 97 96 95 94

Contents

KAPITEL 4   Word Order ▪ Conjunctions ▪ Infinitive Phrases   43

KAPITEL 5   Nominative Case ▪ Accusative Case   63

KAPITEL 6   Dative Case   81

KAPITEL 7   Two-way Prepositions   95

KAPITEL 8   Genitive Case   108

KAPITEL 15 Special Grammatical Points   203

To the Student

INTRODUCTION

Concise German Review Grammar is designed for students who have a basic knowledge of German grammar. The book provides a complete review of the grammmar topics normally covered in beginning courses and introduces new elements as appropriate for work in intermediate courses. It can be used as a primary text for grammar review or as a reference tool.

The text is organized in a way that allows you easy access to information. Clear, concise explanations and numerous charts and examples will help you increase your mastery of German grammar. Descriptions of grammatical features are followed directly by exercises so that you can practice immediately what you have learned. Most of the exercises are in meaningful context. Each chapter also contains a summary section, **Zusammenfassung,** that has additional exercises and provides topics for compositions and for working with a partner. A Self-Test for each chapter provides you with the opportunity to review structures introduced in the chapter and enables you to ascertain which grammar points need more practice.

ORGANIZATION AND CONTENT

Organization of Chapters

Concise German Review Grammar contains 15 chapters. Each chapter consists of grammar explanations, exercises following the explanations, and a set of summarizing exercises. Most chapters are devoted to one grammatical feature (for example, dative case in *Kapitel 6);* some have several features, closely related (for example, the past tenses in *Kapitel 3:* simple past, present perfect, and past perfect). Chapters can be used in the sequence they appear in the book or in whatever sequence is most appropriate for a given class or syllabus.

Grammar Explanations

Grammatical explanations are in English so that the concepts can be clearly understood. They aim for completenessas well as conciseness. Definitions of basic grammatical terms with their German equivalents are given in the explanations as well as in Appendix B: Grammatical Terms.

Exercises

The exercises that follow the grammatical explanations are built around a theme or an everyday situation—thus helping you use form to express meaning. The use of fill-in and question/answer formats, as well as translation exercises, permits the production of whole conversations that are in "genuine" language.

Instructions are in English and models are provided throughout so that you clearly understand how to do each exercise and what type of response is expected. So that you can concentrate on the grammar point being reviewed without the distraction of unfamiliar words, the vocabulary in the exercises is limited to a basic list of 1,200 frequently used words. Occasionally, the content of an exercise requires that words be used that are not on this list; in such cases, the meanings are given in the margin. By continually using these basic words, you will gain mastery of commonly-used vocabulary—an additional advantage of this special feature.

Zusammenfassung

This summary section contains exercises, partner work, and composition topics that combine all the grammatical features of the chapter in oral and written format. The instructions are in German.

Self-Tests

Following *Kapitel 15* is a set of 15 Self-Tests—one for each chapter. The Self-Tests will help you determine whether you have understood the grammatical features introduced in the chapter and whether you can apply this understanding. An Answer Key to the Self-Tests follows the Self-Test for *Kapitel 15*. Included in the Answer Key are cross-references to the section of the chapter in which the grammatical point is explained and practiced.

Reference Section

The reference section contains five separate elements:

1. Appendix A: Grammatical Tables—a grammar summary with tables and charts and a list of strong verbs and irregular weak verbs with their principal parts;

2. Appendix B: Grammatical Terms—a list of German grammatical terms defined as briefly as possible in English and illustrated by German examples;
3. a German-English vocabulary of all words used in the text;
4. an English-German vocabulary of the words needed to do the translation exercises;
5. an index of grammatical features that enables you to look up a particular grammar point easily.

You should get in the habit of consulting the reference section to look up such grammatical features as case endings, verb forms, two-way prepositions, or verbs and prepositions with special meanings.

WORKING WITH THE TEXT

You will be familiar with most of the grammar topics in *Concise German Review Grammar.* When your instructor assigns a grammatical feature or you wish to review a particular one on your own, you should first read the presentations as a memory refresher and note any new or forgotten points. Then you should do the exercise or exercises immediately following the explanations, paying special attention to any that offer difficulty. After you have done these exercises, you should check your overall mastery of the chapter by doing the exercises and activities in the **Zusammenfassung.** As part of the review process in preparing for a chapter test on grammar, you should do the corresponding Self-Test, checking your answers against those in the Answer Key provided in your text.

ACKNOWLEDGMENTS

The authors and publisher of *Concise German Review Grammar,* Second Edition, would like to thank Simone Berger, Tufts University, for writing the Self-Tests and those grammar exercises that are new to this edition; Renate Gerulaitis, Oakland University, for her many useful suggestions; and Helen Lepke, Clarion University, and Constanze Kirmse, Goethe Institute, Munich, for their past contributions. Special thanks go to the following people for their thorough and thoughtful review of the first edition and of the manuscript for this new edition. Their comments and suggestions were invaluable during the development of the Second Edition.

Richard C. Figge, The College of Wooster, Wooster, OH
Christian W. Hallstein, Carnegie Mellon University, Pittsburgh, PA
Robert G. Hoeing, The State University of New York at Buffalo, Buffalo, NY

Ilse Hoyle, National University, Los Angeles, CA
Rachael Huener, University of Minnesota, Minneapolis, MN
John M. Jeep, Miami University, Oxford, OH
Gunhild Lischke, Cornell University, Ithaca, NY
Franziska Lys, Northwestern University, Evanston, IL
Terry Reisch, Hillsdale College, Hillsdale, MI
Claus Reschke, University of Houston, Houston, TX
Michael Schultz, New York University, New York, NY
Mary Michele Wauchope, San Diego State University, San Diego, CA
Reinhard Zollitsch, University of Maine, Orono, ME

The authors would like to thank the staff and associates of Houghton Mifflin Company for their support of the Second Edition of *Concise German Review Grammar:* Diane B. Gifford, Sponsoring Editor, for initiating the project and making it possible, and Barbara Lasoff, Senior Developmental Editor, who oversaw the project and provided valuable editorial suggestions. The authors would also like to thank Jochen Liesche, copyeditor, for his many suggestions and careful reading of the manuscript, and Julia Chitwood for overseeing the manuscript through the various phases of production with great expertise and efficiency.

Finally the authors wish to express their indebtedness to Karen Hohner for her insightful suggestions and her careful preparation of the manuscript. Only a person with her concern and expertise could have put together the various parts of the manuscript that became *Concise German Review Grammar,* Second Edition.

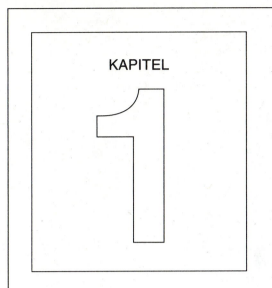

KAPITEL

Present Tense ■

Imperative ■

1 Infinitive° stems and endings

der Infinitiv

Infinitive	Stem + ending	English equivalent
arbeiten	**arbeit** + **en**	*to work*
sammeln	**sammel** + **n**	*to collect*

The infinitive is the basic form of a verb, the form listed in dictionaries and vocabularies. It is the form used with modals (see *Kapitel* 2), in the future tense (see *Kapitel* 2), and in certain other constructions (see *Kapitel* 15). A German infinitive consists of a stem plus the ending **-en** or **-n.**

Note that in this section and all other sections in this book, the examples and charts precede the description of a grammatical feature. This arrangement should enable you to visualize and understand the description more easily.

2 Basic present-tense° endings

das Präsens

	fragen	arbeiten	atmen	heißen	sammeln
ich	frag**e**	arbeit**e**	atm**e**	heiß**e**	samm(e)**le**
du	frag**st**	arbeit**est**	atm**est**	heiß**t**	sammel**st**
er/es/sie	frag**t**	arbeit**et**	atm**et**	heiß**t**	sammel**t**
wir	frag**en**	arbeit**en**	atm**en**	heiß**en**	sammel**n**
ihr	frag**t**	arbeit**et**	atm**et**	heiß**t**	sammel**t**
sie	frag**en**	arbeit**en**	atm**en**	heiß**en**	sammel**n**
Sie	frag**en**	arbeit**en**	atm**en**	heiß**en**	sammel**n**

Most German verbs form the present tense from the stem of the infinitive. Most verbs add the following endings to the stem: **-e, -st, -t, -en.**

1. The verb ending **-st** of the 2nd person singular (**du**-form) and the ending **-t** of the 2nd person plural (**ihr**-form) and 3rd person singular (**er/es/sie**-form) expand to **-est** and **-et** if:
   a. the stem of the verb ends in **-d** or **-t: arbei<u>t</u>en → du arbei<u>t</u>est, er/es/sie arbei<u>t</u>et;**
   b. the stem of the verb ends in **-m** or **-n** preceded by another consonant: **at<u>m</u>en → du at<u>m</u>est, er/es/sie at<u>m</u>et.** Exception: If the stem of the verb ends in **-m** or **-n** preceded by **-l** or **-r**, the **-st** and **-t** do not expand: **ler<u>n</u>en → du ler<u>n</u>st, er/es/sie ler<u>n</u>t.**

2. The ending **-st** of the 2nd person singular (**du**-form) contracts to -**t** if the verb stem ends in **-s, -ss, -ß, -tz,** or **-z: hei**ß**en** → **du hei**ß**t; si**tz**en** → **du si**tz**t.**

3. In many verbs with the stem ending in **-el,** the **-e** in the stem of the 1st person singular (**ich**-form) is often dropped: **samm**el**n** → **ich samml**e**.**

3   Present tense of stem-changing verbs

	tragen (a → ä)	laufen (au → äu)	nehmen (e → i)	lesen (e → ie)
ich	trage	laufe	nehme	lese
du	**trägst**	**läufst**	**nimmst**	**liest**
er/es/sie	**trägt**	**läuft**	**nimmt**	**liest**
wir	tragen	laufen	nehmen	lesen
ihr	tragt	lauft	nehmt	lest
sie	tragen	laufen	nehmen	lesen
Sie	tragen	laufen	nehmen	lesen

German verbs can be categorized as strong, weak, or irregular weak, based on how they form the past tenses. In the present tense, many strong verbs with the stem vowels **a** or **au** take an umlaut in the 2nd person (**du**-form) and 3rd person (**er/es/sie**-form): **a → ä; au → äu.** Many strong verbs with the stem vowel **e** also exhibit a vowel change in the 2nd and 3rd persons singular: **e → i** or **e → ie.** Note that **sto**ß**en** (*to push*) is the only common verb with the stem-vowel change **o → ö: du stö**ß**t, er/es/sie stö**ß**t.**

	laden	halten	raten	treten
du	lädst	hältst	rätst	trittst
er/es/sie	lädt	hält	rät	tritt

Note the forms of the stem-changing verbs that end in **-d** or **-t:**

- The ending of the 2nd person singular (**du**-form) is **-st,** not **-est.**
- **Halten, raten,** and **treten** do not add an ending in the 3rd person singular (**er/es/sie**-form): **hält, rät, tritt.**

For a list of common vowel-changing verbs, see Appendix A: 24. Some basic stem-changing verbs are given below.

a → ä	au → äu	e → i	e → ie
braten	laufen	brechen	befehlen
fahren	saufen	essen	geschehen
fallen		fressen	lesen
fangen		geben	sehen
graben		gelten	stehlen
halten		helfen	
laden		nehmen	
lassen		sprechen	
raten		sterben	
schlafen		treffen	
schlagen		treten	
tragen		vergessen	
wachsen		werfen	
waschen			

□ ————————————

A. Verben.   Restate with the cued subject.

▶ ich lese (du)
  du liest

1. ich sehe (er)
2. wir essen (du)
3. er hilft (ich)
4. sie sprechen (sie, *sg.*)
5. er nimmt (ihr)
6. ich laufe (sie, *sg.*)
7. wir fahren (du)
8. er läßt (ich)
9. sie schlafen (er)
10. ich trage (sie, *sg.*)
11. sie stößt (ihr)
12. ich rate (er)

B. Stefanies Tag.   Alex and Stefanie are talking about Stefanie's typical day. Complete their conversation with the appropriate forms of the verbs in parentheses.

1. STEFANIE: Ich _____ morgens nie lange. Um sieben _____ ich aus dem Bett. (schlafen / springen)
2. ALEX: Und dann _____ du Kaffee? (trinken)
3. STEFANIE: Ja, und ich _____ drei Brötchen zum Frühstück. Das _____ mir Energie für den ganzen Morgen. (essen / geben)
4. ALEX: _____ du mit dem Fahrrad zur Uni? (fahren)
5. STEFANIE: Ja, meistens. Oft mit meinem Freund Gerd. Er _____ immer vor Hertie. Wir _____ sofort in die Bibliothek. (warten / gehen)
6. ALEX: In der Bibliothek _____ ich euch manchmal. Ihr _____ viel dort. Ihr _____ immer am Fenster. (sehen / lesen / sitzen)
7. STEFANIE: Stimmt. Gerd _____ viel. Am Nachmittag _____ er mit dem Englischprofessor. (arbeiten / sprechen)
8. ALEX: Und was _____ dann? (geschehen)
9. STEFANIE: Dann _____ wir zusammen Kaffee, und ich _____ nach Hause. Nach so einem Tag _____ ich abends meistens zu Hause. (trinken / kommen / bleiben)

———————————— ☐

4   Haben, sein, werden, and wissen in the present tense

	haben	sein	werden	wissen
ich	habe	**bin**	werde	**weiß**
du	**hast**	**bist**	**wirst**	**weißt**
er/es/sie	**hat**	**ist**	**wird**	**weiß**
wir	haben	**sind**	werden	wissen
ihr	habt	**seid**	werdet	wißt
sie	haben	**sind**	werden	wissen
Sie	haben	**sind**	werden	wissen

The verbs **haben, sein, werden,** and **wissen** are irregular in the present tense. *Note:* The irregular forms appear in boldface in the table above.

5   Wissen vs. kennen

a. wissen

Weißt du, wie Gerds Schwester heißt?   —Nein, das **weiß** ich nicht.

The verb **wissen** means *to know something as a fact*. **Wissen** is often followed by a clause (e.g., **wie Gerds Schwester heißt**).

b. kennen

Kennst du Gerds Schwester Anna?   —Nein, ich **kenne** sie nicht.

Kennst du Berlin gut?   —Nein, ich **kenne** Berlin, aber nicht gut.

The verb **kennen** means *to be acquainted with a person, place, or thing*. Unlike **wissen, kennen** cannot be followed by a clause.

□ ————————————

C. Geburtstage.   Andrea and Michael are talking about the birthdays in their families. Complete their conversation with the correct forms of the verbs **sein, haben,** and **werden.**

1. ANDREA: Mein Bruder _____ bald Geburtstag. Und ich _____ noch kein Geschenk für ihn.
2. MICHAEL: Wann _____ sein Geburtstag? Und wie alt _____ er?
3. ANDREA: Er _____ drei Jahre jünger als ich, und ich _____ jetzt 17. Doch ich _____ im Mai 18.
4. MICHAEL: Dann _____ du ja volljährig° und darfst wählen!   *of age* _____ du noch mehr Geschwister?
5. ANDREA: Ja, zwei Schwestern. Sie _____ Zwillinge°. Sie _____   *twins* im Dezember Geburtstag und _____ dann 27.
6. MICHAEL: Dann _____ ihr aber eine große Familie! Ich _____ auch zwei ältere Schwestern. Eine arbeitet schon – sie _____ Ingenieurin. Doch die andere studiert noch. Sie _____ Ärztin.

D. Kulturelles.   The students are talking about Germany in their German class. Complete the minidialogues with the correct forms of the verbs **kennen** and **wissen.**

1. ANNA: _____ du das Buch „Die Blechtrommel" von Günter Grass?

   CHRISTINE: Nein, ich _____ es nicht, aber ich _____, daß Grass ein bekannter deutscher Autor ist.

   ANNA: Dann _____ du wahrscheinlich auch nicht, daß es eine Verfilmung des Buches gibt.

2. PATRICK: _____ ihr Frankfurt am Main? _____ ihr, daß es
dort viele Banken gibt?

   DANIEL: Nein, aber wir _____, daß Goethe dort geboren ist.
Peter _____ sogar, wo Goethes Geburtshaus ist.
Er _____ auch viele Gedichte von Goethe.

3. RICHARD: _____ ihr, daß Berlin die Hauptstadt von
Deutschland ist?

   BARBARA: Ja. Und wir _____ auch das Brandenburger Tor°   famous gate in Berlin
aus dem Fernsehen.

—————————————— □

6 | Uses of the present tense

Anna **schreibt** gerade einen Brief.   *Anna **is writing** a letter right now.*

1. The present tense is used to talk about an event taking place at the
same time that it is being described.

Anna **arbeitet** schwer. $\left\{\begin{array}{l}\textit{Anna } \textbf{works} \textit{ hard.}\\ \textit{Anna } \textbf{is working} \textit{ hard.}\\ \textit{Anna } \textbf{does work} \textit{ hard.}\end{array}\right.$

Arbeitet Gerhard auch schwer? $\left\{\begin{array}{l}\textbf{Is} \textit{ Gerhard also } \textbf{working} \textit{ hard?}\\ \textbf{Does} \textit{ Gerhard also } \textbf{work} \textit{ hard?}\end{array}\right.$

2. German verbs have one present-tense form to express what English
expresses with two or three different forms of the verb.

Jürgen **wohnt** schon lange in München.
*Jürgen **has been living** in Munich for a long time.*

Uschi **arbeitet** seit September bei dieser Firma.
*Uschi **has been working** for this company since September.*

3. The present tense in German can be used to express an action
begun in the past that continues into the present.

Lisa **macht** in einer Woche Examen.
*Lisa **is taking** her (final) exam in one week.*

Kommen Sie heute abend?
***Are** you **coming** tonight?*

4. The present tense is generally used to express an action intended
or planned for the future when an adverb of time (e.g., **in einer
Woche**) or the context makes the future meaning clear.

□——————————

E. Peter in Hamburg.   You have received a letter from your friend Peter. Tell about his experience in Hamburg by translating the following information.

1. Peter has been living in Hamburg for four weeks.
2. He's going to stay there for six months.
3. He already knows a lot of people.
4. He has a new girlfriend.
5. He has known her for a couple of weeks.
6. They're spending a lot of time together.
7. Next weekend they're going to visit her parents.

——————————— □

7	Separable-prefix verbs°	*das trennbare Verb*

mitkommen   **Kommst** du heute **mit**?   *Are you **coming along** today?*

anrufen   Ich **rufe** um sieben **an**.   *I'll **call** at seven.*

aufpassen   **Paß** bitte **auf**.   *Please **pay attention**.*

A separable-prefix verb consists of a basic verb plus a prefix that is separated from the verb under certain conditions. In independent clauses in the present and simple past tenses and in the imperative, the verb is in first or second position and the prefix is in final position.

Willst du **mitkommen?**

In the infinitive, a separable prefix is attached to the base form of the verb.

In spoken German, the stress falls on the prefix of the separable-prefix verb: **Willst du mit´kommen? Komm doch mit´.**

Separable prefixes are derived from prepositions or adverbs. Some of the most common separable prefixes are listed below:

ab	bei	her	nach	weg
an	ein	hin	nieder	zu
auf	entlang	los	vor	zurück
aus	fort	mit	vorbei	zusammen

spazierengehen   Ich **gehe** jeden Tag zwei Stunden **spazieren**.
*I **go walking** for two hours every day.*

radfahren   **Fährst** du gern **Rad?**
*Do you like **bike riding?***

Other verbs (e.g., **spazieren**) and nouns (e.g., **Rad**) can also function as separable prefixes.

☐————————

F. Kleine Konversationen.   Complete the following sentences with the expressions given in parentheses.

1. Aua! Du _____! (mir wehtun)
   Warum _____ ? (du / nicht / aufpassen)
   —Oh, Entschuldigung!
2. _____? (du / mit mir / spazierengehen)
   —Hm, ich glaube, ich _____. (lieber / radfahren°)
3. Was _____ ? (du / vorhaben / heute abend)
   —Nichts, ich _____. (vielleicht / fernsehen)
4. _____? (du / gern / Ski fahren)
   —Oh ja, sehr gern.
5. _____? (du / anziehen / dein neues Kleid)
   Es _____. (aussehen / so hübsch)
   —Das ist ein schönes Blau, nicht?
6. Ich _____. (dich / anrufen / später)
   —Gut, ich bin zu Hause.

————————— ☐

Capitalize **Rad** when separated.

8 Imperative° forms

der Imperativ

	fragen	warten	tragen	laufen	nehmen	lesen
Familiar singular:	frag(e)	wart(e)	trag(e)	lauf(e)	nimm	lies
Familiar plural:	fragt	wartet	tragt	lauft	nehmt	lest
Formal:	fragen Sie	warten Sie	tragen Sie	laufen Sie	nehmen Sie	lesen Sie

Each German verb has three imperative forms, corresponding to the three forms of address: the familiar singular imperative (**du**-form), the familiar plural imperative (**ihr**-form), and the formal imperative (**Sie**-form), which is the same for both singular and plural.

1. The familiar singular imperative is used when addressing someone to whom you would say **du**. The imperative is formed from the infinitive verb stem. An **-e** may be added to the imperative form, but it is usually omitted in colloquial German: **frag(e)**. An **-e** is also added if the verb stem ends in **-m** or **-n** preceded by another consonant: **atme, öffne**. An **-e** need not be added, however, if the verb stem ends in **-m** or **-n** preceded by **-l** or **-r**: **lern(e)**. An **-e** is added in written German if the verb stem ends in **-d** or **-t**, or **-ig**: **rede, warte, entschuldige.**

   Verbs with stems that change from **e → i** or **e → ie** retain the stem-vowel change but do not add **-e**: **nehmen → nimm, lesen → lies. Werden** is an exception: **werden → werde. Werde nicht ungeduldig.**

   Verbs with stems that change from **a → ä** do not take umlaut in the familiar singular imperative: **tragen → trag(e), laufen → lauf(e).**

   The pronoun **du** is occasionally used for emphasis or clarification: **Warum muß ich immer Kaffee holen? Geh *du* mal.**

2. The familiar plural imperative is used when addressing people to whom you would say **ihr**. It is identical to the present-tense **ihr**-form of the verb. The pronoun **ihr** is occasionally used for emphasis or clarification: **Ich habe schon so viel Kuchen gegessen. Eßt *ihr* doch mal!**

3. The formal imperative is used when addressing one or more persons to whom you would say **Sie**. It is identical to the present-tense **Sie**-form of the verb. The pronoun **Sie** is always used in the imperative and follows the verb: **Warten *Sie* bitte einen Augenblick.**

4. In written German, an exclamation point is often used after a command: **Bitte tun Sie das!**

a. imperative of separable-prefix verbs

Paß auf!   *Watch out!*

Kommen Sie bitte **mit!**   *Come along,* please.

In the imperative, a separable prefix is in last position.

b. imperative of *sein*

Familiar singular: **Sei** nicht so nervös.   *Don't **be** so nervous.*

Familiar plural: **Seid** ruhig!   ***Be** quiet.*

Formal: **Seien** Sie froh.   ***Be** glad.*

Note especially the **du**-form **sei** and the **Sie**-form **Seien Sie**.

c. *wir*-imperative

DIETER: Was machen wir heute abend?   *What'll we do tonight?*

JÜRGEN: **Gehen wir** doch mal ins Kino!   ***Let's go** to the movies!*

English imperatives beginning with *Let's* can be expressed in German with the 1st person plural present-tense form of the verb followed by the pronoun **wir**.

9 | Use of the imperative

Öffnen Sie bitte das Fenster.   *Please **open** the window.*

Rufen Sie während der Geschäftszeit **an.**   ***Call** during business hours.*

Gehen wir jetzt.   ***Let's go** now.*

Imperatives are verb forms used to express commands, instructions, suggestions, and wishes.

□ ————————

G. Reiseführer°.   You are helping a German tourist in Bonn by giving directions from the **Beethovenhalle** to the **Hauptbahnhof.**   tour guide

▶ am Fluß entlanggehen
   Gehen Sie am Fluß entlang.

1. an der Brücke nach rechts abbiegen
2. geradeaus bis zur Haltestelle laufen
3. dort auf die Straßenbahn warten
4. die 21 nehmen
5. vorher die Fahrkarte am Automaten kaufen
6. am Bahnhof aussteigen

H. Noch einmal.   Just as you finish telling the tourist how to get to the **Hauptbahnhof,** a young person asks for the same directions. Give them to her/him.

▶ am Fluß entlanggehen
   Geh am Fluß entlang.

I. Zum dritten Mal.   Repeat the directions a third time for three young people who also want to go to the train station.

▶ am Fluß entlanggehen
   Geht am Fluß entlang.

J. Machen wir es.   Construct sentences using the **wir**-imperative with the cues provided.

▶ gehen / jetzt
  Gehen wir jetzt!

1. fahren / mit dem Bus
2. besuchen / heute abend Peter und Eva
3. anrufen / sie doch
4. spazierengehen / später
5. bleiben / lieber zu Hause
6. machen / erstmal unsere Arbeit

——————————— ▢

Zusammenfassung

A. Kaffeepause.   Peter sitzt in der Bibliothek und liest. Er ist sehr müde. Sibylle kommt an seinen Tisch, und sie gehen zusammen ins Café. Setzen Sie die richtigen Verbformen ein.

In der Bibliothek:

1. SIBYLLE: _____ du oder _____ du? (schlafen / lesen)
2. PETER: Ich _____ für den Chemietest, aber ich _____ wirklich todmüde. (lernen / sein)
3. SIBYLLE: Du _____ zuviel. (arbeiten).
   _____ _____ doch ins Café, und _____ _____ einen Kaffee. (**wir**-*imperative*: gehen / trinken)

Im Studentencafé:

4. SIBYLLE: Was _____ du? (trinken)
   Ich _____ es dir. (holen)
5. PETER: _____ mir bitte einen Kaffee. (bringen)
   Mit viel Milch.
6. SIBYLLE: _____ du auch Zucker in deinem Kaffee? (nehmen)
7. PETER: Nein, aber _____ mir trotzdem ein Päckchen, bitte. (geben)
   Ich _____ nämlich Zucker. (sammeln)
8. SIBYLLE: _____ schnell. (trinken)
   Dann _____ du wieder fit. (werden)
   Kaffee _____ bei Müdigkeit°. (helfen)   *tiredness*

B. Eine Anzeige.   Das Reisebüro Reeder hat in der Universitäts-
zeitung eine Anzeige° für Reisen nach Prag. Setzen Sie die richtigen   *advertisement*
Verbformen ein.

1. _____ ihr schon unser Angebot° nach Prag? (kennen)   *offer*
2. Unsere Busse _____ morgens in Berlin _____ und _____
   abends in Prag _____. (abfahren / ankommen)
3. Du _____ zum Beispiel Freitag morgens _____ und _____
   Sonntag abends _____. (losfahren / zurückkommen)
4. Wer _____ nicht gern mal _____? (wegfahren)
   Reisebüro Reeder _____, was Spaß macht! (wissen)
5. _____ uns doch _____! (***ihr***-*imperative:* anrufen)
   Unsere Mitarbeiter am Telefon _____ euch gern. (helfen)
6. _____ nicht unsere Telefonnummer: 0421/494776! Oder _____
   einfach _____! (***du***-*imperative:* vergessen / vorbeikommen)

C. Partnerarbeit.   Mit einer Partnerin/einem Partner machen
Sie Pläne fürs Wochenende. Sie erzählen, was Sie gern machen und
Ihre Partnerin/Ihr Partner erzählt, was sie/er gern macht.

D. Kurze Aufsätze°   *compositions*

1. Beschreiben Sie, was Sie gern in Ihrer Freizeit machen. Schreiben
   Sie im Präsens.

2. Monika hat ihren ersten Ferientag. Sie weiß nicht, was sie mit
   ihrer Freizeit machen soll. Ihre Mutter/Ihr Vater gibt ihr Tips° –   *advice*
   was sie zum Vergnügen° machen kann und wie sie im Haushalt   **zum Vergnügen:** *for fun*
   helfen kann. Sie sind Monikas Mutter/Vater. Gebrauchen Sie den
   du-Imperativ für die Tips.

3. Andrea fühlt sich schlecht. Sie ist immer nervös, aber trotzdem
   müde. Sie geht zum Arzt. Welche Fragen über ihre Lebensweise°   *way of life, habits*
   stellt ihr die Ärztin/der Arzt? Was rät sie/er ihr? Gebrauchen Sie
   den *Sie*-Imperativ.

4. Sie planen mit einem Freund/einer Freundin eine Radtour. Wohin
   fahren Sie? Was brauchen Sie? Was nehmen Sie mit? Schreiben
   Sie im Präsens.

KAPITEL

Modal Auxiliaries ■

Future Tense ■

1 Present tense of modal auxiliaries°

das Modalverb

	dürfen	können	mögen	müssen	sollen	wollen
ich	**darf**	**kann**	**mag**	**muß**	**soll**	**will**
du	**darfst**	**kannst**	**magst**	**mußt**	**sollst**	**willst**
er/es/sie	**darf**	**kann**	**mag**	**muß**	**soll**	**will**
wir	dürfen	können	mögen	müssen	sollen	wollen
ihr	dürft	könnt	mögt	müßt	sollt	wollt
sie	dürfen	können	mögen	müssen	sollen	wollen
Sie	dürfen	können	mögen	müssen	sollen	wollen

German modal auxiliaries are irregular in that they have no verb endings in the 1st person singular (**ich**-form) and 3rd person singular (**er/es/sie**-form); in addition, all modals except **sollen** show stem-vowel changes in the singular forms of the present tense.

2 Use of modal auxiliaries

Ich **kann** bis acht Uhr **bleiben**.	*I **can stay** until eight o'clock.*
Wir **wollen** die Musik **hören**.	*We **want to hear** the music.*
Peter **muß** jetzt **gehen**.	*Peter **has to leave** now.*

Modal auxiliaries in both German and English convey an attitude about an action, rather than expressing that action itself. For this reason, modals are generally used with dependent infinitives that express that action. The infinitive is in last position.

Ich **muß** nach Hause (**gehen**).	*I **have to go** home.*
Kannst du das (**machen**)?	*Can you **do** that?*
Du **darfst** das nicht (**machen**).	*You **must**n't **do** that.*

Modals may occur without a dependent infinitive. This happens most frequently if a verb of motion (**fahren, gehen**) or the idea of *to do* (**machen, tun**) is clearly understood from the context.

3 Meanings of the modal auxiliaries

dürfen	permission	Sie **darf** heute arbeiten.	*She's **allowed to** work today.*
können	ability	Sie **kann** heute arbeiten.	*She **can (is able to)** work today.*
mögen	liking, personal preference	**Magst** du Jazz?	***Do** you **like** jazz?*
müssen	compulsion	Sie **muß** heute arbeiten.	*She **has to (must)** work today.*
sollen	obligation	Sie **soll** heute arbeiten.	*She **is supposed to (is to)** work today.*
wollen	wanting, intention	Sie **will** heute arbeiten.	*She **wants (intends) to** work today.*

Note:

1. **Können** has the additional meaning of *to know a language* or *to know how to do something*:

   Können Sie Deutsch?   ***Do** you **know** German?*
   Stefan **kann** nicht tippen.   *Stefan **does**n't **know how** to type.*

2. **Mögen** usually expresses a fondness for or, when negated, a dislike for someone or something. With this meaning it appears most frequently in the interrogative and the negative and without a dependent infinitive:

   Magst du Dieter?   ***Do** you **like** Dieter?*
   —Nein, ich **mag** ihn nicht.   *—No, I **do**n't **like** him.*

3. **Wollen** is followed by an infinitive to express the idea that a person wants to do something himself or herself:

   Maria **will** den Teppich **saugen.**   *Maria **wants to vacuum** the carpet.*

   To express the idea that a person wants someone else to do something, the verb **wollen** is followed by a **daß**-clause that includes the new subject. In English an infinitive with a new subject is used:

   Maria **will, daß ich** Staub wische.   *Maria **wants me to** do the dusting.*

☐————————

A. Modalverben.   Restate with the cued modal.

▶ Ich gehe jetzt. (müssen)
  Ich muß jetzt gehen.

  1. Ich verstehe es nicht. (können)
  2. Hilfst du mir? (können)
  3. Arbeiten Sie bei uns? (wollen)

4. Ich höre heute abend Musik. (wollen)
5. Es regnet morgen. (sollen)
6. Wir arbeiten mehr. (sollen)
7. Gehst du schon? (müssen)
8. Er liest viel. (müssen)
9. Ich esse keinen Zucker. (dürfen)
10. Lars trinkt keinen Kaffee. (dürfen)

B. Vorbereitungen.   Yvonne and Andreas are preparing for a party. Give their conversation by using the cues.

1. ANDREAS: ich / sollen / einkaufen / im Supermarkt / ?
2. YVONNE: Ja, bitte, gute Idee. du / können / kaufen / auch / die Getränke° / ?   *beverages*
3. ANDREAS: ich / müssen / gehen / aber / vorher / zur Bank
4. YVONNE: was / Uwe / sollen / machen / ?
5. ANDREAS: er / sollen / decken / den Tisch
   er / können / vorbereiten / auch / die Salatsauce°   *salad dressing*
6. YVONNE: Uwe / können / das / ?
7. ANDREAS: Natürlich. Aber / er / wollen / schneiden / sicher / Obst für den Salat
8. YVONNE: du / mögen / Eis / ?
   wir / können / kaufen / zum Nachtisch / Eis
9. ANDREAS: wir / dürfen / ausgeben / nicht zuviel Geld
10. YVONNE: aber / du / wollen / haben / doch alles schön

C. Wim braucht ein Auto.   Wim needs to go to the airport and asks Veronika for her car. Complete their conversation with the modal that fits best (dürfen, können, mögen, müssen, sollen, wollen).

1. WIM: Brauchst du dein Auto heute nachmittag?
2. VERONIKA: Warum? _____ du es haben?
3. WIM: Ja, weißt du, ich _____ um vier am Flughafen sein. Ich _____ meinen Freund Gerd abholen. Ich _____ ihn damit überraschen. Und da _____ ich nicht zu spät kommen. Ich _____ nämlich erst um halb vier wegfahren. _____ ich dich um dein Auto bitten?
4. VERONIKA: Aber sicher. Oder _____ ich dich zum Flughafen bringen?
5. WIM: Ach, ich _____ gut allein fahren. Du _____ sicher arbeiten. In einer halben Stunde _____ ich es gut schaffen. Aber wenn du gern _____?
6. VERONIKA: Natürlich. Fahren wir doch zusammen. Ich _____ die Atmosphäre auf dem Flughafen. Da _____ man immer von der weiten Welt träumen. _____ wir uns dann um halb vier hier treffen?
7. WIM: Ja, das _____ wir machen.

——————————— □

4 The *möchte*-forms

ich **möchte**	wir **möchten**
du **möchtest**	ihr **möchtet**
er/es/sie **möchte**	sie **möchten**
Sie **möchten**	

Möchte and **mögen** are different forms of the same verb. The **möchte**-forms are subjunctive forms of **mögen** and are equivalent to *would like (to)* (see *Kapitel 12*).

OBER: **Möchten** Sie jetzt bestellen?   *Would* you *like to* order now?

JENS: Ja, ich **möchte** eine Tasse   *Yes, I'd like a cup of coffee,*
        Kaffee, bitte.   *please.*

☐ ――――――――――――

D. Kurze Gespräche.   Complete the minidialogues with the present tense of **mögen** or its subjunctive form **möchte,** as appropriate.

1. Wie findest du Harald? _____ du ihn?
   —Nein, ich _____ ihn nicht besonders. Er ist so unfreundlich.
2. Herr Ober, wir _____ zwei Tassen Tee und zwei Stück Apfelkuchen, bitte.
   —_____ Sie auch Sahne?
   —Nein, danke, ich _____ keine Sahne.
   —Aber ich _____ bitte gern eine Portion.
3. _____ du eine Tasse Kaffee?
   —Nein, danke, ich _____ keinen Kaffee. Ich trinke lieber Tee.
4. Karin ist immer so nett. Ich _____ sie wirklich gern.
   —Ja, ich _____ sie auch. Ich _____ sie gern näher kennenlernen.

―――――――――――― ☐

5 Negative of *müssen* and *dürfen*

	Compulsion	
Positive:	Ich **muß** heute arbeiten.	*I **must** work today* *I **have to** work today.*
Negative:	Ich **muß** heute **nicht** arbeiten.	*I **don't have to** work today.*

	Permission	
Positive:	Ich **darf** wieder arbeiten.	*I **may** work again.* *I'm **allowed to** work again.*
Negative:	Ich **darf** noch **nicht** arbeiten.	*I **mustn't** work yet.* *I'm **not allowed to** work yet.*

English *must* and *have to* have the same meaning in positive sentences. They have different meanings in negative sentences and hence different German equivalents.

Ich **muß** heute **nicht** arbeiten.
 Ich **brauche** heute **nicht zu** arbeiten. } *I **don't have to** work today.*

Brauchen nicht is often used instead of **müssen nicht. Brauchen** takes a dependent infinitive preceded by **zu.**

□ ——————————

E. Urlaubspläne.   The Mahler family wants to go to Italy for vacation. Now the parents and the children are thinking about whether they would rather stay in a hotel or rent an apartment there. Fill in the correct forms of the verbs **nicht dürfen** and **nicht müssen/nicht brauchen.**

1. FRAU MAHLER: Im Hotel _____ ich _____ zu kochen. Das gefällt mir.
2. HERR MAHLER: Und ich _____ das Geschirr _____ zu spülen, und die Kinder _____ _____ abzutrocknen.
3. SANDRA: Aber wir _____ unseren Hund _____ mitnehmen. Ich will lieber in ein Ferienhaus!
4. MARKUS: Ich auch! Da _____ wir _____ immer so leise zu sein. Außerdem _____ ich im Hotel _____ in der Badehose essen.
5. SANDRA: Genau! Und ihr _____ für ein Ferienhaus _____ so viel zu bezahlen.
6. FRAU MAHLER: Das _____ wir _____ heute zu entscheiden. _____ du _____ erst deinen Chef fragen, wann du Urlaub nehmen kannst?
7. HERR MAHLER: Stimmt! Ich _____ das _____ einfach selbst bestimmen.

—————————— □

6   *Hören, sehen, and lassen*

Ich **muß** jetzt **frühstücken.**

*I **have to eat breakfast** now.*

Ich **höre** die Kinder in der Küche **reden.**

*I **hear** the children **talking** in the kitchen.*

Ich **sehe** sie jeden Morgen **wegfahren.**

*I **see** them **drive off** every morning.*

Sie **läßt** uns das allein **machen.**

*She **lets** us **do** that alone.*

Like modal auxiliaries (e.g., **muß**), the verbs **hören, sehen,** and **lassen** can take a dependent infinitive without **zu.**

7   Meanings of *lassen*

Laß die Schlüssel nicht zu Hause.   *Don't **leave** the keys at home.*

Laß deine Sachen nicht hier **liegen.**   *Don't **leave** your things **lying** here.*

Like the modals, the verb **lassen** can stand alone or take a dependent infinitive (e.g., **liegen**) without **zu.**

     Lassen is one of the most commonly used verbs in German. Some basic meanings follow.

a. to leave (something or someone somewhere)

Laß die Teller im Schrank.   *Leave the plates in the cupboard.*

Heute **lasse** ich meinen Schirm zu Hause.   *I'm **leaving** my umbrella at home today.*

b. to permit

Laß mich den Brief lesen.   *Let me read the letter.*

Ich **lasse** dich fahren.   *I'll let you drive.*

Lassen Sie mich Ihnen helfen.   *Let me help you.*

c. let's

Gerd, **laß uns** jetzt arbeiten!   *Gerd, **let's** work now.*

Kinder, **laßt uns** gehen!   *Children, **let's** go.*

Frau Meier, **lassen Sie uns** anfangen!   *Mrs. Meier, **let's** begin.*

The imperative form of **lassen** plus the pronoun **uns** is often used in place of the 1st person plural imperative: **Arbeiten wir! Gehen wir! Fangen wir an!** (see *Kapitel 1*, Section 8).

d. to have something done or cause something to be done

Er **läßt sich** die Haare schneiden.	He's *having* his hair cut.
Sie **lassen sich** ein Haus bauen.	They're *having* a house built.
Wir **lassen** morgen den Elektriker kommen.	We're *having* the electrician come tomorrow.

☐ ——————————

F. Der Nachbar hat's gut.   Mr. Kleinmann is jealous of his neighbor, who apparently has an easy life. Give the English equivalents.

1. Ich sehe meinen Nachbarn oft im Garten sitzen.
2. Abends sehe ich ihn fröhlich von der Arbeit nach Hause kommen.
3. Oft höre ich ihn etwas im Hause reparieren.
4. Bei der Arbeit höre ich ihn singen.
5. Im teuersten Geschäft läßt er sich die Anzüge machen.
6. Manchmal höre ich ihn Klavier spielen.
7. Ich lasse mir jetzt auch ein schönes Haus bauen.

G. Wir ziehen um.   Tanja, Peter, and Alexander are moving into a new apartment. What do they have to do? Give the German equivalent of the following sentences.

1. Leave the table there!
2. Let me do that.
3. He has me do his work.
4. Are you leaving this bed in the basement?
5. Are we having the walls painted°?
6. Let me hold that.
7. Let's have something to drink.

to paint = *streichen*

—————————— ☐

8 future time: present tense

Ich **komme morgen** bestimmt.	*I'm going to come tomorrow* for sure.
Siehst du **heute abend fern?**	*Are you going to watch TV tonight?*

German generally uses the present tense (e.g., **ich komme, siehst du fern?**) to express future time when an adverb of time or the context makes the future meaning clear. English often uses a form of *go* in the present (*I'm going to, are you going to?*) to express future time.

9 | Future time: future tense°

das Futur

Pia **wird** alles selber **machen.**   Pia **will do** everything herself.

Detlev **wird** ihr nicht **helfen.**   Detlev **will** not **help** her.

German, like English, does have a future tense, although in German it is not used as often as the present tense to express future time. Future tense is used if it would otherwise not be clear from the context that the events will take place in the future. Future tense is also used to express the speaker's determination that the event will indeed take place.

In both English and German, the future tense is a compound tense. In English, the future tense is a verb phrase consisting of *will* or *shall* plus the main verb (e.g., *Pia will do, Detlev will help*). In German, the future tense is also a verb phrase and consists of a form of **werden** plus an infinitive in final position.

ich **werde** es **sehen**	*wir* **werden** es **sehen**
du **wirst** es **sehen**	*ihr* **werdet** es **sehen**
er/es/sie **wird** es **sehen**	*sie* **werden** es **sehen**
Sie **werden** es **sehen**	

10 | Future tense of modals

Du **wirst** bestimmt nicht   *You'll* surely not **be able to**
  schlafen können.   **sleep.**

Ich **werde** das Buch **lesen müssen.**   *I'll* **have to read** that book.

In the future tense a modal is in the infinitive form and is in final position. The modal follows the dependent infinitive.

The future tense of modals is used infrequently; present tense is more common. Although you will probably not use the future tense of modals in your own speech, you may come across this construction in your reading. For this reason, you should be able to recognize the structure.

11 Other uses of the future tense

Assumption: Er **wird** uns sicher **glauben.**   *He'll surely **believe** us.*

Determination: Ich **werde** es **machen.**   *I **shall do** it.*

The future tense is regularly used to express an assumption or a determination to do something.

Present probability: Er **wird** sicher müde **sein.**   *He's surely tired.*

Das **wird** wohl **stimmen.**   *That's probably **correct.***

Das **wird** schon in Ordnung **sein.**   *That's probably O.K.*

The future tense can express the probability of something taking place in the present time. Adverbs such as **sicher, wohl,** and **schon** are often used.

☐ ——————————

H. Sommerferien.   You and Silvia are discussing summer vacation plans. Restate your conversation, using the future tense.

▶ Fährst du mit deiner Familie nach Frankreich?
Wirst du mit deiner Familie nach Frankreich fahren?

1. Nein, dieses Jahr fahre ich nicht mit meinen Eltern.
2. Du bleibst doch nicht die ganze Zeit zu Hause, oder?
3. Nein, ich besuche meine Freundin in Florenz.
4. Sie studiert an der Akademie, und ich wohne dann bei ihr.
5. Sie zeigt mir Florenz und die Toskana°.   *Tuscany*
6. Das ist bestimmt schön!

I. Keiner hat Zeit.   You feel like going out tonight and have tried to call a few friends. But either they were not at home or they didn't have time. Finally you reach Sibylle and together you speculate about the others. Use the future tense + **wohl** to express what they are probably doing.

▶ Wo ist Rainer im Moment? (beim Sport)
Er wird im Moment wohl beim Sport sein.

1. Für wen arbeitet Gabi diese Woche? (für ihre Eltern)
2. Zu wem geht Maria heute? (zu Daniela)
3. An wen schreibt Meike? (an ihren Freund)

4. Wo sind Kurt und Karla? (im Schwimmbad)
5. Wie lange bleibt Claudias Besuch? (das ganze Wochenende)
6. Wo spielt Jan heute abend? (im Jazz-Club)
7. Rufst du noch jemand anders an? (nein, niemand mehr)
8. Wohin gehst du nun? (ins Kino)

J. Besuch aus Boston.   Gabi and Martin are having visitors—
Bill and Jeremy, two exchange students from Boston. Now they are
making plans for things to do together. Form complete sentences. When
you find an adverbial phrase referring to future time, use present tense;
otherwise set the sentence in future tense.

1. GABI: ihr Flugzeug / ankommen / morgen mittag
2. MARTIN: sie / müde sein / sicher
3. GABI: ich / abholen / Bill und Jeremy
4. MARTIN: hoffentlich / du / erkennen / die beiden
5. GABI: ich / mitnehmen / das Foto / zum Flughafen
6. MARTIN: Bill und Jeremy / besuchen / wohl / München
7. GABI: und / nächste Woche / sie / fahren / nach Italien
8. MARTIN: wir / Englisch sprechen / wohl / immer / ?
9. GABI: ich / reden / mit ihnen / sicher / Deutsch

————————————————— □

Zusammenfassung

A. Eine Pizza, bitte!   Mathias und Johannes lernen für ihre
Biologieklausur. Plötzlich ist es elf Uhr abends, und sie haben großen
Hunger. Ergänzen Sie den Dialog mit der richtigen Form der Verben in
Klammern°.

parentheses

1. MATHIAS: Ich _____ sofort etwas _____. (müssen / essen)
2. JOHANNES: Wirklich? Wir _____ vielleicht Pizza _____.
             (können / essen)
             _____ du auch etwas _____? (möchten / trinken)
3. MATHIAS: Natürlich. Aber wo _____ wir jetzt Pizza _____?
             (sollen / bekommen)
             _____ du nicht mehr für die Klausur _____?
             (wollen / lernen)
             Wir _____ keine Zeit _____. (dürfen / verlieren)
4. JOHANNES: Du _____ endlich die Pizzeria um die Ecke _____.
             (müssen / kennenlernen)
             Ich _____ zwei Pizzas _____, ja? (lassen / kommen)°
5. MATHIAS: Aber die Klingel° ist kaputt. Und in diesem Zimmer
             _____ wir den Boten° nicht _____. (hören / kommen)

etwas kommen lassen:
 to order
bell
delivery person

6. JOHANNES: Ich _____ hier am Fenster _____. (können / sitzen)

Dann _____ ich ihn _____. (sehen / kommen)

B. Nach der Vorlesung.   Nadine und Daniel unterhalten sich nach der Vorlesung. Übertragen° Sie das folgende Gespräch ins Deutsche.

translate

1. NADINE: I'd like a cup of coffee. You too? Should we go to a café?
2. DANIEL: I'd like to° but I can't. I have to go to a seminar°. History, you know.

Use schon. / *ins Seminar*

3. NADINE: Oh, is Professor Lange good?
4. DANIEL: Yes. He's excellent. I like him. We have to work hard, but we can also learn a lot.
5. NADINE: Do you have to write many papers°?

die Seminararbeit, pl. Seminararbeiten man / man ein Referat halten

6. DANIEL: We are supposed to write two. But if you° want, you° may also give an oral report°.

C. Partnerarbeit.   Mit einer Partnerin/einem Partner planen Sie zusammen einen Urlaub. Welche Art von Urlaub wollen Sie machen? Wohin werden Sie fahren? Gebrauchen Sie Modalverben.

D. Kurze Aufsätze

1. Sie schreiben Ihrer Brieffreundin/Ihrem Brieffreund in Österreich einen Brief. Beschreiben Sie, wie bei Ihnen ein typischer Tages- ablauf° aussieht. Schreiben Sie im Präsens und gebrauchen Sie Modalverben.

daily routine

2. Was werden Sie wohl in zehn Jahren tun? Beschreiben Sie Ihre berufliche und Ihre familiäre Situation (Beruf, Wohnort, Familie, Kinder usw.). Schreiben Sie im Präsens oder im Futur.

3. Wie sieht die Welt wohl in 50 Jahren aus? Beschreiben Sie, wie die Menschen leben werden. Schreiben Sie im Präsens oder im Futur. Gebrauchen Sie auch Wörter, die Wahrscheinlichkeit° ausdrücken (wohl, sicher usw.).

probability

KAPITEL

Simple Past Tense ■

Present Perfect Tense ■

Past Perfect Tense ■

1 | The simple past tense°

das Präteritum

Letzte Woche **arbeitete** Inge nur vormittags. Nachmittags **spielte**
  sie Tennis oder **besuchte** Freunde. Abends **blieb** sie zu Hause
  und **sah fern.**
*Last week Inge **worked** mornings only. In the afternoon she
  played tennis or **visited** friends. Evenings she **stayed** home
  and **watched** TV.*

The simple past tense, often called the narrative past, is used to narrate a series of connected events that took place in the past. It is used more frequently in formal writing such as literature and expository prose than in conversation.

2 | Regular weak verbs° in the simple past

das schwache Verb

Infinitive	Stem	Tense marker	Simple past
lernen	lern-	**-te**	lernte
arbeiten	arbeit-	**-ete**	arbeitete
öffnen	öffn-	**-ete**	öffnete

A regular weak verb is a verb whose infinitive stem remains unchanged in the past-tense forms. In the simple past a weak verb adds the past-tense marker **-te** to the infinitive stem. In some verbs the **-te** past-tense marker expands to **-ete** to ensure that the **-t,** as signal of the past, is audible. The **-te** past-tense marker becomes **-ete** if:

a. the verb stem ends in **-d** or **-t: arbei**t**en** → **arbei**t**ete.**
b. the verb stem ends in **-m** or **-n** preceded by a consonant: **öffnen** →
   öffnete. Exception: If the verb stem ends in **-m** or **-n** preceded by **-l**
   or **-r**, the **-te** past-tense marker does not expand: **lernen** → **lernte.**

ich spiel**te**		*wir* spiel**ten**	
du spiel**test**		*ihr* spiel**tet**	
er/es/sie spiel**te**		*sie* spiel**ten**	
	Sie spiel**ten**		

All forms except the 1st and 3rd person singular add endings to the **-te** tense marker.

Karin **machte** die Tür **auf.**   *Karin **opened** the door.*

Der Tourist **packte** den Koffer **aus.** *The tourist **unpacked** his suitcase.*

In the simple past, as in the present of independent clauses, the separable prefix is separated from the base form of the verb and is in final position.

☐ ————————————

A. Ein Film.   Philipp is describing a scene from the movie he saw last night. Complete his account by using the simple past tense of the cued verbs.

1. Die Männer _____ sich an den Tisch und _____ Karten. (setzen / spielen)
2. Erik _____ die Spielregeln°. (erklären)   *the rules of the game*
3. Da _____ er Julia. (bemerken)
4. Sie _____ die Gläser auf den Tisch und _____ nichts. (stellen / sagen)
5. Niels _____ eine verrückte Geschichte, und die Männer _____. (erzählen / lachen)
6. Dann _____ er seine Karten, und alle _____ ein ziemlich dummes Gesicht. (zeigen / machen)

———————————— ☐

3   Modals in the simple past

Infinitive	Simple past stem + tense marker	Examples
dürfen	**durf** + **te**	Ich **durfte** ihr helfen.
können	**konn** + **te**	Du **konntest** nicht mitkommen.
mögen	**moch** + **te**	Er **mochte** unsere Suppe nicht.
müssen	**muß** + **te**	Wir **mußten** Inge helfen.
sollen	**soll** + **te**	Ihr **solltet** es gestern machen.
wollen	**woll** + **te**	Sie **wollten** früher fahren.

The simple past stem of the modals is the infinitive stem. The modals **dürfen, können, mögen,** and **müssen** lose the umlaut in the simple past tense. In addition, **mögen** exhibits a consonant change. The past-tense marker -**te** is added to the simple past stem.

English equivalents of the simple past of modals are as follows.

Simple past	English equivalent
durfte	*was allowed to*
konnte	*was able to (could)*
mochte	*liked (to)*
mußte	*had to*
sollte	*was supposed to*
wollte	*wanted to*

B. Was will er denn?   Tell about your attempts to help a friend.
Use the simple past tense of the modal auxiliary.

▶   Mein Freund kann seine Arbeit nicht allein machen.
   Mein Freund konnte seine Arbeit nicht allein machen.

1. Ich soll ihm helfen.
2. Ich will es also versuchen.
3. Gut. Ich muß ihm alles genau erklären.
4. Und er kann es nicht verstehen.
5. Er muß die Arbeit bis Freitag fertig haben.
6. Bald mag er mich nicht mehr sehen.
7. Eigentlich will er gar keine Hilfe.
8. Schließlich darf ich gar nichts mehr sagen.

4   Irregular weak verbs° and *haben* in the simple past

*das unregelmäßige
schwache Verb*

Infinitive	Simple past stem + tense marker	Examples
brennen	**brann** + te	Das Holz **brannte** nicht.
kennen	**kann** + te	Sie **kannte** die Stadt gut.
nennen	**nann** + te	Sie **nannte** das Kind nach dem Vater.
rennen	**rann** + te	Er **rannte** jede Woche zum Arzt.
bringen	**brach** + te	Ich **brachte** ihr Blumen.
denken	**dach** + te	Du **dachtest** an uns.
haben	**hat** + te	Ihr **hattet** nicht viel Zeit.
wissen	**wuß** + te	Wir **wußten** die Antwort nicht.

A few weak verbs are irregular in the simple past. They add the past-tense marker **-te** of weak verbs but have a stem-vowel change. **Haben** has a consonant change; the verbs **bringen** and **denken** also have a consonant change.

5 | Strong verbs° in the simple past

das starke Verb

Infinitive	Simple past stem	Examples
sprechen	spr**a**ch	Im März **sprach** Alex mit seinen Kollegen in Berlin.
schreiben	schr**ie**b	Im April **schrieb** er ihnen Briefe.
fahren	f**u**hr	Im Mai **fuhr** er zu ihnen.
ziehen	z**o**g	Im Juni **zog** er nach Berlin.
gehen	g**i**ng	Das **ging** alles ziemlich schnell.

A strong verb is a verb that has a stem-vowel change in the simple past: **sprechen → sprach.** A few verbs have a consonant change as well: **ziehen → zog.** The tense marker **-te** is not added to strong verbs in the simple past. You must memorize the simple past forms of strong verbs because the stem change cannot always be predicted. (See Appendix A: 24 for a list of strong verbs in the simple past.)

ich sprach		*wir* sprach**en**	
du sprach**st**		*ihr* sprach**t**	
er/es/sie sprach		*sie* sprach**en**	
	Sie sprach**en**		

In the simple past the 1st and 3rd person singular have no endings.

6 | *Sein* and *werden* in the simple past

Infinitive	Simple past	Examples
sein	**war**	Gestern **war** es schön.
werden	**wurde**	Über Nacht **wurde** das Wetter schlechter.

Two common verbs in German are **sein** and **werden.** Note their simple past tense forms.

	sein	**werden**
ich	war	wurde
du	warst	wurdest
er/es/sie	war	wurde
wir	waren	wurden
ihr	wart	wurdet
sie	waren	wurden
Sie	waren	wurden

C. Verben.   Give the simple past of the following verbs. Use the **sie**-singular form as in the model.

▶   beginnen
     sie begann

1. nennen, denken, bringen, wissen, haben
2. essen, geben, helfen, bitten, finden, sitzen, kommen, tun, sein
3. fliegen, schließen, umziehen
4. gefallen, halten, schlafen, laufen, bleiben, scheinen, rufen
5. fahren, tragen, waschen, werden
6. leiden, schneiden, gehen

D. Ein komischer Mensch.   You meet a strange person in the park. Tell a friend about it. Use the simple past tense.

1. Heute fahre ich mit dem Rad durch den Park.
2. Da sehe ich einen Mann.
3. Er sitzt auf einer Bank.
4. Er trägt lustige Kleidung.
5. Sein Hut ist viel zu klein.
6. Die Hosen sind zu eng.
7. Das Hemd paßt nicht.
8. Er hat ganz große Schuhe an.
9. Er liest eine alte, schmutzige Zeitung.
10. Ich spreche ihn an, aber ich bekomme keine Antwort.
11. Vielleicht versteht er kein Deutsch.
12. Später steht er auf und geht weg.

7 | The present perfect tense°   *das Perfekt*

Ist Laura schon **gegangen?**   *Has Laura gone already?*

Ja, sie **hat** mir auf Wiedersehen   *Yes, she said goodbye to me.*
   gesagt.

Weißt du, wann sie **gegangen ist?**   *Do you know when she left?*

The present perfect tense consists of the present tense of either the auxiliary **haben** or **sein** plus the past participle of the verb. In compound
tenses such as the present perfect tense, it is the auxiliary **haben** or
sein that takes person and number endings, while the past participle
remains unchanged. The past participle is in last position, except in a
dependent clause (see *Kapitel 4*).

8 | Present perfect versus simple past

Was **habt** ihr gestern **gemacht?**   *What did you do yesterday?*

Wir **sind** zu Hause **geblieben.**   *We stayed home.*

The present perfect tense is often called the conversational past because
it is used most frequently in conversation to refer to events in past time.
Present perfect is also used in informal writing such as letters or notes,
which are basically written conversation.

Jan **war** gestern sehr müde. Er **schlief** bis zehn, **frühstückte** und
   ging dann wieder ins Bett.

*Jan was very tired yesterday. He slept until ten, ate breakfast, and
   then went back to bed.*

The simple past tense (narrative past) is used to narrate a series of
connected events in past time. The simple past is used especially in
formal writing such as literature and expository prose—for example,
newspaper and magazine articles.

DIETER: Wie **war** die Radtour übers Wochenende?
NADINE: Ich **konnte** leider nicht mitfahren.
DIETER: Schade. Das Wetter **war** sehr schön.
NADINE: Ja, aber ich **hatte** keine Zeit.

The simple past tense forms of **sein** (**war**), **haben** (**hatte**), and the
modals (e.g., **konnte**) are used more frequently than the perfect tense
forms, even in conversation.

9 | Past participles° of regular weak verbs

das Partizip Perfekt

Infinitive	Past participle	Present perfect tense
spielen	**ge** + spiel + **t**	Jörg **hat** Tennis **gespielt.**
arbeiten	**ge** + arbeit + **et**	Ilse **hat** lange **gearbeitet.**
öffnen	**ge** + öffn + **et**	Ich **habe** das Fenster **geöffnet**.
lernen	**ge** + lern + **t**	Wo **hast** du kochen **gelernt?**

The past participle of a weak verb is formed by adding **-t** to the unchanged stem. The **-t** expands to **-et** if the verb stem ends in **-d** or **-t**: **arbeiten → gearbeitet.** The **-t** also expands to **-et** if the verb stem ends in **-m** or **-n** preceded by another consonant: **öffnen → geöffnet**. If, however, the verb stem ends in **-m** or **-n** preceded by **-l** or **-r**, the **-t** does not expand: **lernen → gelernt**. The past participles of weak verbs have the prefix **ge-**, with the exception of those verbs with inseparable prefixes and those ending in **-ieren** (see Section 13).

10 | Past participles of irregular weak verbs and *haben*

Infinitive	Past participle	Present perfect tense
brennen	**ge** + **brann** + **t**	Das Holz **hat** nicht **gebrannt.**
kennen	**ge** + **kann** + **t**	Sie **hat** die Familie gut **gekannt.**
nennen	**ge** + **nann** + **t**	Sie **haben** das Kind nach dem Vater **genannt.**
rennen	**ge** + **rann** + **t**	Er **ist** jede Woche zum Arzt **gerannt.**
bringen	**ge** + **brach** + **t**	Ich **habe** dir Blumen **gebracht.**
denken	**ge** + **dach** + **t**	**Hast** du an uns **gedacht?**
wissen	**ge** + **wuß** + **t**	Wir **haben** es nicht **gewußt.**
haben	**ge** + **hab** + **t**	Ihr **habt** nicht viel Zeit **gehabt.**

The past participle of an irregular weak verb has the **ge-** prefix and the ending **-t**. Irregular weak verbs have a stem-vowel change; the verbs **bringen** and **denken** also have a consonant change.

11 Past participles of strong verbs

Infinitive	Past participle	Present perfect tense
sprechen	**ge + sproch + en**	**Hast** du mit Anna **gesprochen**?
schreiben	**ge + schrieb + en**	Ich **habe** das **geschrieben**.
fahren	**ge + fahr + en**	Jan **ist** allein **gefahren**.
ziehen	**ge + zog + en**	Sie **haben** das Boot an Land **gezogen**.
gehen	**ge + gang + en**	Wann **bist** du nach Hause **gegangen**?

The past participle of a strong verb is formed by adding **-en** to the participle stem. Many strong verbs have a change in the stem vowel of the past participle, and some verbs also have a change in the consonants. The past participles of strong verbs have the prefix **ge-,** with the exception of those verbs with inseparable prefixes (see Section 13). You must memorize the past participles of strong verbs because the stem change cannot always be predicted. (See Appendix A: 24 for a list of strong verbs.)

12 Past participles of separable-prefix verbs

Infinitive	Past participle	Present perfect tense
abholen	**ab + ge + holt**	**Hast** du Sabrina **abgeholt?**
mitnehmen	**mit + ge + nommen**	Erik **hat** den Schlüssel **mitgenommen**.

The **ge-** prefix of the past participle comes between the separable prefix and the stem of the participle. Both weak and strong verbs can have separable prefixes. In spoken German the separable prefix receives stress: **ab´geholt**.

13 Past participles without ge- prefix

Present tense	Present perfect tense
Nadine bezahlt das Essen.	Nadine **hat** das Essen **bezahlt**.
Ich verstehe die Frage nicht.	Ich **habe** die Frage nicht **verstanden**.

Some prefixes are never separated from the verb stem. Common inseparable prefixes° are **be-, emp-, ent-, er-, ge-, ver-,** and **zer-.** Inseparable-
prefix verbs° do not add the **ge-** prefix.

das untrennbare Präfix
das untrennbare Verb

Inseparable: Ich habe einen Brief von meinem Freund **bekom´men.**
  Separable: Ist dein Freund **mit´gekommen?**

Inseparable: Warum hast du dein Fahrrad **verkauft´?**
  Separable: Wir haben unsere Lebensmittel im Supermarkt
         ein´gekauft.

In spoken German an inseparable prefix does not receive stress
(e.g., **bekom´men, verkauft´**); a separable prefix does receive stress
(e.g., **mit´gekommen, ein´gekauft**) (see *Kapitel 1*).

Present tense	Present perfect tense
Wann passiert das?	Wann **ist** das **passiert?**
Benno studiert in Bonn.	Benno **hat** in Bonn **studiert.**

Verbs ending in **-ieren** do not add the **ge-** prefix to form the past participle. They are all weak verbs whose participle ends in **-t.** These verbs
are generally based on words borrowed from French and Latin; they are
often similar to English verbs.
  A few common **-ieren** verbs are:

diskutieren	interessieren	rasieren
gratulieren	komplimentieren	studieren

14 Use of the auxiliary° *haben*

das Hilfsverb

Ich **habe** den Brief selber **geschrieben.**   *I **wrote** the letter myself.*
Hast du **ferngesehen?**   ***Did** you **watch** TV?*

The auxiliary **haben** is used to form the present perfect tense of most
verbs.

15 Use of the auxiliary *sein*

Lisa **ist** gerade **weggegangen.**   *Lisa **has** just **left.***
Denis **ist** auf dem Sofa **eingeschlafen.**   *Denis **fell asleep** on the sofa.*

Some verbs use **sein** instead of **haben** as an auxiliary in the present perfect tense. Verbs that require **sein** meet two conditions. They must:
a. be intransitive verbs (i.e., verbs without a direct object).
b. indicate a change in location (e.g., **weggehen**) or condition (e.g., **einschlafen**).

Note: Some verbs that indicate change of location take **haben** if they are used transitively (i.e., have a direct object):

> Ich **habe** meine Freundin in die Stadt **gefahren.**

Compare: Ich **bin** nicht allein in die Stadt **gefahren.**

Wie lange **bist** du dort **geblieben?**   *How long **did** you **stay** there?*

Wo **bist** du die ganze Zeit **gewesen?**   *Where **were** you all this time?*

The verbs **bleiben** and **sein** also require the auxiliary **sein**, even though they do not indicate a change of location or condition.

Wie **war** das Wetter?   *How **was** the weather?*

Wir **waren** gestern nicht zu Hause.   *We **were**n't home yesterday.*

The simple past of **sein** (see Section 6) is used more commonly than the present perfect tense of **sein (ist gewesen).**

☐ ——————————

E. Verben.   Give the present perfect of the following verbs. Use the **ich**-form as in the models.

▶   essen   fahren
  ich habe gegessen   *ich bin gefahren*

  1. spielen, zeigen, machen, kaufen
  2. kennen, denken, wissen, haben, bringen, rennen
  3. sehen, geben, lesen
  4. helfen, nehmen, schließen
  5. schlafen, tragen
  6. schneiden, leiden, reiten
  7. rufen, finden
  8. schreiben, bleiben
  9. fliegen, kommen, gehen
 10. abholen, einkaufen, einladen, vorschlagen, aufstehen, anfangen
 11. bekommen, beginnen, erfahren, gewinnen, verbieten, verlieren
 12. sein, werden

F. Kurze Gespräche.   Restate the following conversational exchanges in the present perfect.

▶ —Was machst du am Wochenende?
—Ich lese und gehe spazieren.
—Was hast du am Wochenende gemacht?
—Ich habe gelesen und bin spazierengegangen.

1. —Lädst du Erik zu deinem Fest ein?
—Ja, ich rufe ihn an.

2. —Wie lange bleibst du in der Schweiz?
—Ich fahre gar nicht hin.

3. —Wieviel kostet das Bild?
—Zuviel. Ich kaufe es nicht.

4. —Spielst du heute morgen Tennis?
—Ja, ich fange um zehn an.

5. —Warum fliegst du nach Berlin?
—Ich gebe dort ein Konzert.

6. —Warum lachst du?
—Oh, ich denke gerade an einen guten Witz.

G. Stell dir vor°, was mir passiert ist.   Ingrid tells her room-   *imagine*
mate what happened to her during the afternoon. Complete her account
with the cued verbs, using the tense indicated.

1. Stell dir vor, was mir heute nachmittag _____ _____. (passieren; *present perfect*)
2. Ich _____ die Mozartstraße entlang, und da _____ plötzlich ein Auto ganz langsam neben mir her. (gehen, fahren; *simple past*)
3. Na, was will der denn, _____ ich mich. (fragen; *simple past*)
4. Weißt du, wer es _____? (sein; *simple past*)
5. Michael! Wir _____ zusammen in Hamburg _____. (studieren; *present perfect*)
6. Er _____ _____, und wir _____ beide herzlich _____. (aussteigen, lachen; *present perfect*)
7. Wir _____ uns natürlich sehr! (freuen; *simple past*)
8. Wir _____ uns seit zwei Jahren nicht mehr _____. (sehen; *present perfect*)
9. Im Café Mozart _____ wir eine Tasse Kaffee _____ und lange _____. (trinken, erzählen; *present perfect*)

H. Spielverderber°.   Daniel is being asked by his friends why he   *spoilsport*
was in such a strange mood last night at the party. Take his part, using
the simple past tense of the modal.

▶   Warum bist du nicht früher gekommen? (können)
      Ich konnte nicht.

1. Warum bist du nicht mit dem Auto gekommen? (dürfen)
2. Warum hat dir dein Vater sein Auto nicht gegeben? (wollen)
3. Warum hast du den ganzen Abend nicht getanzt? (mögen)
4. Warum ist deine Freundin nicht mitgekommen? (können)
5. Warum hast du Bernd nicht die Hand gegeben? (mögen)
6. Warum bist du nicht bis zum Ende geblieben? (wollen)

———————————————— □

16 The past perfect tense°   *das Plusquamperfekt*

Ich **hatte** schon zwei Tage   *I **had** already **waited** for two
   gewartet.   days.*
Sie **war** am Montag **angekommen**. *She **had arrived** on Monday.*

The past perfect tense consists of the simple past of **haben** (**hatte**) or
sein (**war**) plus the past participle of the main verb. Verbs that use a
form of **haben** in the present perfect tense (see Section 14) use a form
of **hatte** in the past perfect. Those that use a form of **sein** in the present perfect (see Section 15) use a form of **war** in the past perfect.

Ich wollte am Mittwoch ins Kino   *I wanted to go to the movies on
   gehen. Leider **hatte** mein   Wednesday. Unfortunately my
   Freund den Film am Montag   friend **had** already **seen** the film
   schon **gesehen.**   on Monday.*

The past perfect tense is used to report an event or action that took
place before another event or action in the past. In the example above,
when I wanted to go to the movies, my friend had seen the film two days
before.

    A time-tense line illustrates the relationship clearly:

second point further in the past	*first point in past time*	*present time*
Past perfect	Present perfect or simple past	Present

Note that the past perfect is generally used in conjunction with either
the simple past or present perfect.

□ ——————————

I. Schwierigkeiten.   Tell about the problems you had last night when you were going to the theater. Use the past perfect tense of the cued verbs.

▶   Wir sind zu spät ins Theater gekommen. Das Stück / anfangen / schon
     Das Stück hatte schon angefangen.

1. Wir wollten mit der Straßenbahn fahren. Aber / sie / wegfahren / gerade
2. Wir gingen in eine Telefonzelle°, um ein Taxi anzurufen. Aber / da / man / stehlen / Telefonbuch   *telephone booth*
3. Nach zwanzig Minuten kam die nächste Bahn. Inzwischen / es / beginnen / zu regnen
4. Genau um acht waren wir im Theater. Doch wo waren die Eintrittskarten? Ich / vergessen / sie / zu Hause
5. Ich mußte neue Karten kaufen. Für die alten / ich / ausgeben / viel Geld

—————————— □

| 17 | ## Double infinitive° construction with modals, *hören, sehen, lassen* | *der Doppelinfinitiv* |

Regular participle:	**Hast** du das **gewollt**?	***Did** you **want** that?*
Double infinitive:	Ich **habe** es nicht **schreiben wollen**.	*I **did**n't **want to write** it.*
Regular participle:	Ich **habe** die Nachbarn **gehört**.	*I **heard** the neighbors.*
Double infinitive:	Ich **habe** die Nachbarn **wegfahren hören**.	*I **heard** the neighbors **drive off**.*
Regular participle:	Ich **hatte** das Auto nicht **gesehen**.	*I **had**n't **seen** the car.*
Double infinitive:	Ich **hatte** das Auto nicht **kommen sehen**.	*I **had**n't **seen** the car **coming**.*
Regular participle:	Sie **hat** uns allein **gelassen**.	*She **left** us alone.*
Double infinitive:	Sie **hat** uns das allein **machen lassen**.	*She **let** us **do** that alone.*

In the present perfect and past perfect tenses, modals and the verbs **sehen, hören,** and **lassen** have two forms of the participle: a regular form with the prefix **ge-** (**gewollt, gehört, gesehen, gelassen**) and a form identical to the infinitive (**wollen, hören, sehen, lassen**).

The regular form is used when the modals and **sehen, hören,** and **lassen** are used without a dependent infinitive.

The alternate form, identical to the infinitive, is used when these verbs have a dependent infinitive. Therefore, this construction is often called the *double infinitive construction.* The double infinitive always comes at the end of the clause, with the modal or **sehen, hören,** or **lassen** the very last element. All double infinitives use the auxiliary verb **haben** because modals and **sehen, hören,** and **lassen** use **haben** as an auxiliary (e.g., **habe** die Nachbarn **wegfahren sehen**).

> *Simple past:*   Ich **wollte** den Brief nicht **schreiben.**
> *Present perfect:*   Ich **habe** den Brief nicht **schreiben wollen.**
>
> *I didn't want to write the letter.*

The simple past tense of modals is used more frequently than the perfect tense forms, even in conversation. The meaning is the same in both tenses.

☐ ————————————

J. Sommerabend.   Last night was a beautiful summer evening. Richard tells what he saw and heard and wonders if you did, too. Say that you did.

▶   Die Kinder spielten im Garten, nicht wahr? (sehen)
   Ja, ich sah sie im Garten spielen.

1. Peter übte gestern abend Cello, nicht wahr? (hören)
2. Er saß am offenen Fenster. (sehen)
3. Er zählte manchmal ganz laut. (hören)
4. Er spielte eine Menge Brahms. (hören)
5. Später packte er das Cello weg. (sehen)
6. Dann spazierte er im Garten herum. (sehen)
7. Dabei sang er leise Lieder. (hören)

K. Wir haben uns neu eingerichtet°.   Mrs. Haller has gone   *decorated* over to the house of a friend who has recently redecorated. The friend tells her how and why things happened. Give the English equivalents.

1. Die Vorhänge habe ich von meiner Mutter nähen lassen.
2. Die Spülmaschine habe ich billig von meiner Schwester kaufen können.
3. Den Spiegel habe ich mir aus Italien mitbringen lassen.
4. Den alten Tisch habe ich einfach nicht wegwerfen mögen.

5. Um die Stühle zu bekommen, habe ich lange telefonieren müssen.
6. Einen neuen Fernseher hatte ich eigentlich gar nicht kaufen wollen, aber mein Mann wollte absolut einen haben.
7. Die Gartenmöbel sind gar nicht neu; wir haben die alten einfach neu streichen lassen.

———————————— □

Zusammenfassung

A. Ein schöner Abend.   Gerd erzählt Ihnen, wie er Annette überrascht hat. Schreiben/Sprechen Sie im Präteritum.

1. In the evening I wanted to invite Annette to dinner.
2. But I didn't call her up.
3. I simply picked her up.
4. She opened the door and looked at me curiously.
5. I told her my plan.
6. She didn't think about it very long.
7. She shut her books.
8. She put on her coat, and we left.

B. Nicht in Hamburg, in Berlin.   Jan dachte, daß Rita ihre Ferien in Hamburg verbracht hatte, und hört gerade, daß sie in Berlin gewesen ist. Übertragen Sie das Gespräch ins Deutsche.

1. JAN: How did you get from Hamburg to Berlin?
2. RITA: I flew.
3. JAN: When did you buy the ticket?
4. RITA: I didn't buy it (at all). My mother sent it.
5. JAN: How nice! How long did you stay there?
6. RITA: Two weeks. I came back yesterday.
7. JAN: Did you visit friends?
8. RITA: Oh yes, and I went to the museum frequently.

C. Ein Brief.   Judiths Freundin ist umgezogen und hat ihr einen Brief geschrieben. Machen Sie aus den Stichwörtern° einen richtigen Text.   *cues*

1. Liebe Judith, ich / ankommen / vor zwei Wochen (Perfekt)
2. die Reise / gehen / gut (Präteritum)
3. ich / finden / ein schönes Zimmer (Perfekt)
4. ich / müssen / suchen / gar nicht lange (Präteritum)
5. leider / ich / können / nicht besuchen / meine Freunde (Präteritum)
6. ich / verlieren / ihre Adresse (Plusquamperfekt)

7. aber / ich / kennenlernen / schon / viele neue Leute (Perfekt)
8. an der Uni / ich / treffen / zwei nette Studentinnen (Präteritum)
9. wir / reden / lange (Präteritum)
10. sie / einladen / mich / zu einem Fest (Perfekt)
11. du / hören / schon etwas von Lisa? (Perfekt)
   Herzliche Grüße, Stefanie.

D. Partnerarbeit.   Erzählen Sie Ihrer Freundin/Ihrem Freund von einer Schwierigkeit, die Sie hatten, und wie Sie sie überwunden° *overcome*

haben. Ihre Freundin/Ihr Freund stellt viele Fragen. Sie können das folgende Beispiel gebrauchen oder sich selbst etwas ausdenken°: Sie essen **sich etwas ausdenken:** *make something up* in einem Restaurant und haben Ihr Geld vergessen.

E. Kurze Aufsätze

1. Schreiben Sie einen Brief, in dem Sie von einer Schwierigkeit erzählen, z.B., Sie haben vor der Deutschprüfung Ihr Buch verloren. Was haben Sie gedacht? Was haben Sie getan?
2. Führen Sie eine Woche lang Tagebuch°. Gebrauchen Sie das *diary* Präteritum.

KAPITEL

4

Word Order ■

Conjunctions ■

Infinitive Phrases ■

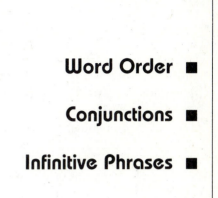

1 | Position of the finite verb° in statements°

das finite Verb / der Aussagesatz

	1	2	3	4
Normal:	Wir	**trinken**	um vier	Kaffee.
Inverted:	Um vier	**trinken**	wir	Kaffee.
	Kaffee	**trinken**	wir	um vier.
	Hoffentlich	**trinken**	wir	um vier Kaffee.

In a German statement or independent clause, the finite verb (the verb form that agrees with the subject) is always in second position.

In so-called normal word order, the subject is in first position. In so-called inverted word order, an element other than the subject is in first position, and the subject follows the verb. For stylistic variety or for emphasis of a particular element, a German statement can begin with a prepositional phrase (e.g., **um vier**), an object (e.g., **Kaffee**), or an adverb (e.g., **hoffentlich**). "Inverted" word order is just as normal and common in a German statement as "normal" word order.

□ ————————————

A. Ein neues Auto.   Since Sabine now has her own car, she visits her grandmother more often. Take the part of Sabine and tell about her visit.

▶ ich / haben / ein neues Auto
  Ich habe ein neues Auto.

1. am Sonntag / ich / fahren / aufs Land
2. dort / ich / besuchen / meine Großmutter
3. sie / wohnen / in einem alten Bauernhaus
4. hinter dem Haus / ein großer, schöner Garten / liegen
5. in dem Garten / viele Apfelbäume / stehen
6. wir / gehen / oft / in den Garten
7. wir / setzen uns / in den Schatten
8. da / es / sein / schön kühl
9. meine Großmutter / erzählen / immer / verrückte Geschichten
10. wir / lachen / immer sehr viel

———————————— □

2 Position of the finite verb in questions

a. specific questions°

die Ergänzungsfrage

Warum **findet** Christina den Film langweilig?	*Why **does** Christina **find** the film boring?*
Wann **hat** sie ihn gesehen?	*When **did** she **see** it?*

A specific question asks for a particular piece of information. It begins with an interrogative such as **wie, wieviel, warum, wann,** or **wer.** In German the interrogative is followed by the finite verb, then the subject. English often has to use a form of the auxiliary verb *to do* or *to be* plus the main verb *(does . . . find).*

b. general questions°

die Entscheidungsfrage

Hat Barbara einen festen Freund? —Ja.	*Does Barbara **have** a steady boyfriend?* —*Yes.*
Ist er gestern angekommen? —Nein.	*Did he **arrive** yesterday?* —*No.*
Kommt er gar nicht? —Doch.	*Isn't he **coming** at all?* —*Of course (he is).*

A general question can be answered with **ja, nein,** or **doch.** In German it begins with the finite verb. English often requires a form of the auxiliary verb *to do* or *to be* plus the main verb (e.g., *does . . . have, did . . . arrive, is . . . coming*).

☐———————————

B. Wie wohnen Studenten?   Susanne and Johannes are talking about Susanne's housing situation. Using the cues given, form specific or general questions to which the following statements are answers.

1. du / wohnen / im Studentenheim / ?
   —Nein, ich wohne in einer Wohngemeinschaft°.

   co-op
2. wo / die Wohnung / liegen / ?
   —Die Wohnung liegt sehr gut – direkt im Zentrum°.

   center of town
3. wie viele / Leute / wohnen / in deiner Wohngemeinschaft / ?
   —In meiner Wohngemeinschaft wohnen nur drei Leute. Doch das ist genug.

4. wieviel / die Wohnung / kosten / ?
—Die Wohnung kostet 1100 Mark. Das ist für Freiburg billig.
5. ihr / haben / einen Garten / ?
—Ja, wir haben sogar einen großen Garten mit Apfelbäumen.
6. wie / deine Mitbewohner / sein / ?
—Meine Mitbewohner sind sehr nett. Besonders Stefan – leider geht er bald von Freiburg weg.
7. wann / Stefan / ausziehen / ?
—Stefan zieht im August aus.
8. warum / du / fragen / ?
—Ich frage, weil ich ein Zimmer in einer Wohngemeinschaft suche.
9. ich / können / sehen / das Zimmer / ?
—Ja, natürlich kannst du das Zimmer sehen! Das ist sogar eine prima Idee.

──────────── □

3   Independent clauses° and coordinating conjunctions°

der Hauptsatz

die koordinierende Konjunktion

Juliane hat ein neues Buch gekauft, **aber** sie liest es nicht, **denn** sie hat keine Zeit.

An independent, or main, clause can stand alone as a complete sentence. Two or more independent clauses may be connected by *coordinating conjunctions* (e.g., **aber, denn**). Because coordinating conjunctions are merely connectors and not part of either clause, they do not affect the order of subject and verb. Five common coordinating conjunctions are listed below.

aber	*but*
denn	*because (for)*
sondern	*but, on the contrary*
und	*and*
oder	*or*

Lore geht ins Café, **und** ihre Freundin lädt sie zu einem Kaffee ein.
Lore geht ins Café **und** trinkt einen Kaffee.

In written German coordinating conjunctions are generally preceded by a comma. However, **oder** and **und** are not preceded by a comma when either the subject or the verb in the second clause is identical to the subject or verb in the first clause and is omitted in the second clause.

4 | The conjunctions *aber* and *sondern*

Maria geht ins Café, **aber** sie bestellt nichts.
*Maria goes into the café, **but** she doesn't order anything.*

Der Kuchen ist nicht teuer, **aber** Sabine kauft ihn trotzdem nicht.
*The cake is not expensive, **but** Sabine still doesn't buy it.*

Jürgen geht nicht ins Café, **sondern** in den Park.
*Jürgen doesn't go to the café **but** to the park.*

Aber as a coordinating conjunction is equivalent to *but, however, nevertheless*; it may be used after either a positive or negative clause.

Sondern is a coordinating conjunction that expresses a contrast or contradiction. It connects two ideas that are mutually exclusive. It is used only after a negative clause and is equivalent to *but, on the contrary, instead, rather.*

Sylvia ist **nicht nur** intelligent, **sondern auch** fleißig.
*Sylvia is **not only** intelligent **but also** industrious.*

The German construction **nicht nur...sondern auch** is equivalent to *not only . . . but also.*

C. Freunde.   Give some information about Elly and Frank. Combine each pair of sentences, using the coordinating conjunction indicated.

▶ Frank arbeitet bei Siemens. Elly studiert. (und)
  Frank arbeitet bei Siemens, und Elly studiert.

1. Frank hat seine Arbeit nicht sehr gern. Elly ist gern an der Uni. (aber)
2. Sie fahren jeden Tag mit der Straßenbahn. Sie haben kein Auto. (denn)
3. Frank ißt nicht im Restaurant. Er bringt sein Essen von zu Hause mit. Sie wollen sparen. (sondern / denn)
4. Im Sommer fahren sie nach Italien. Sie fliegen nach Amerika. (oder)
5. Dann muß er weiter bei Siemens arbeiten. Elly studiert weiter. (und)

D. Peters Hauptfach.   Your friend Peter has changed majors. Tell about the change, linking the clauses with **aber** and **sondern** as appropriate.

1. Peter studiert jetzt nicht mehr Mathematik, <u>sodern</u> er hat mit Geschichte angefangen.

2. Mit Geschichte verdient er vielleicht weniger Geld, _aber_ das Fach interessiert ihn mehr.

3. Das ist eine verrückte Idee, _aber_ er hat schon immer davon geträumt.

4. Seine Freunde verstehen ihn nicht, _aber_ das ist ihm egal.

5. Er hört nicht auf ihren Rat, _sodern_ macht das, was er für gut hält.

6. Er muß jetzt viel Neues lernen, _aber_ das macht ihm auch großen Spaß.

7. Er arbeitet nicht nur viel, _sodern_ auch gern.

─────────────────── □

5 | Dependent clauses° and subordinating conjunctions°

der Nebensatz

die subordinierende Konjunktion

Main clause	Dependent clause
Glaubst du,	**daß Karin morgen kommt?**
Sie kommt bestimmt,	**wenn sie Zeit hat.**

A dependent clause is a clause that cannot stand alone; it must be combined with a main clause to express a complete idea. A dependent clause is introduced by a *subordinating conjunction* (e.g., **daß, wenn;** see Section 7). In writing, a dependent clause is separated from the main clause by a comma.

Er möchte wissen, ob du heute Volleyball **spielst.**
ob du heute **mitspielst.**
ob du vielleicht Tennis **spielen willst.**
ob du gestern **gespielt hast.**

Unlike coordinating conjunctions, subordinating conjunctions affect word order. In dependent clauses:

1. The finite (conjugated) verb is in final position (e.g., **spielst**).
2. A separable prefix is attached to the base form of the verb, which is in final position (e.g., **mitspielst**).
3. A modal auxiliary follows the dependent infinitive and is in final position (e.g., **willst**).
4. In perfect tenses the auxiliary **haben** or **sein** follows the past participle and is in final position (e.g., **hast**).

Da ich zuviel gegessen hatte, **habe** ich schlecht geschlafen.

Obwohl ich müde war, **mußte** ich früh aufstehen.

When a dependent clause begins a sentence, it is followed directly by the finite verb of the independent clause (e.g., **habe, mußte**).

6 | Dependent clauses: indirect statements and questions

a. conjunction introducing indirect statements: *daß*

Direct statement: Ich fahre morgen weg.

Indirect statement: Erika weiß, **daß** du morgen wegfährst.

Indirect statements are introduced by the subordinating conjunction **daß.**

b. conjunction introducing indirect general questions: *ob*

General question: Habt ihr gewonnen?

Indirect question: Ich weiß nicht, **ob** wir gewonnen haben.

Indirect general questions are introduced by the subordinating conjunction **ob. Ob** can always be translated as *whether* and is used with main clauses such as **sie fragt, ob…** and **ich weiß nicht, ob… .**

c. conjunction introducing indirect specific questions

Specific question: Warum erzählt Rita immer diese Geschichte?

Indirect question: Ich weiß nicht, **warum** sie immer diese
                        Geschichte erzählt.

Indirect specific questions are introduced by the same question words, or interrogatives, that are used in direct specific questions, for example, **wann, warum,** and **wie.** The question word functions as a subordinating conjunction.

□——————————

E. Wie war es in Italien?   Stefan is picking up his Italian friend Maria from the train station. She has spent a couple of weeks with her family in Italy. Report on their conversation by using indirect statements and questions. Use **daß** or **ob** when appropriate.

▶   Stefan fragt Maria: „Wie war es in Italien?"
     Stefan fragt Maria, wie es in Italien war.

1. Sie antwortet: „Es war herrlich."
2. Natürlich will er wissen: „Was hast du gemacht? Wo warst du?
   Wen hast du besucht?"
3. Er fragt auch: „War das Wetter schön?"
4. Sie sagt: „Es war sonnig und warm."
5. Er fragt sie: „Was gibt es sonst Neues?"
6. Sie erzählt: „Meine Eltern haben ein neues Haus. Es ist sehr groß
   und sehr schön."
7. Stefan fragt: „Bist du nach der langen Reise sehr müde?"
8. Maria antwortet: „Ich bin sehr müde und möchte am liebsten
   zwölf Stunden schlafen."

───────────────────── ☐

7   Common subordinating conjunctions

Common subordinating conjunctions are listed below.

als	*when*	**ob**	*if, whether*
als ob	} *as if*	**obgleich**	
als wenn		**obschon**	} *although, even though*
bevor	} *before*	**obwohl**	
ehe		**seit**	} *since (temporal)*
bis	*until*	**seitdem**	
da	*because, since* (causal)	**sobald**	*as soon as*
damit	*so that*	**solange**	*as long as*
daß	*that*	**sooft**	*as often as*
falls	*in case, if*	**während**	*while; whereas*
indem	*by (doing something)*	**weil**	*because*
nachdem	*after*	**wenn**	*if; when, whenever*

8   Uses of *als, wenn,* and *wann*

Als wir letztes Jahr in Berlin
waren, haben wir das Museum
in Dahlem besucht.

When *we were in Berlin last year,
we visited the museum in
Dahlem.*

Als ich jung war, sind wir oft in
Berlin gewesen.

When *I was young, we were often
in Berlin.*

Wenn wir nach Berlin gefahren
sind, haben wir immer das
Museum in Dahlem besucht.

Whenever *we went to Berlin, we
always went to the museum in
Dahlem.*

Ich weiß nicht, **wann** wir wieder nach Berlin fahren.   *I don't know **when** we're going to Berlin again.*

Als, wenn, and **wann** are all equivalent to the English *when*, but they are not interchangeable.

Als is used to introduce a clause concerned with a single event in the past (e.g., **als wir letztes Jahr in Berlin waren**) or to refer to a single block of time in the past (e.g., **als ich jung war**).

Wenn is used to introduce a clause concerned with repeated events (*whenever*) in past time or with single or repeated events in present or future time.

Wann is used to introduce direct and indirect questions. Always use **wann** whenever you can substitute *at what time* for the word *when*.

9 | Uses of the conjunctions *da, weil, seitdem (seit), indem*

a. *da*

Da es heute regnet, machen wir kein Picknick.
***Since** it's raining today, we're not having a picnic.*

Da indicates a reason that is assumed to be known or understood. The sentence above implies that you know it is raining; therefore the picnic is canceled. **Da**-clauses usually begin the sentence. **Da** is more common in written than spoken German.

b. *weil*

Wir haben kein Picknick gemacht, **weil** es geregnet hat.
*We didn't have a picnic **because** it rained.*

Weil states a reason that is assumed not to be known and in this sense it contrasts with **da.** In the sentence above, you do not know why the picnic was canceled so I am informing you—it rained.

c. *seitdem (seit)*

Seitdem (Seit) Stefan in München **wohnt,** sehe ich ihn kaum mehr.
***Since** Stefan **has been living** in Munich, I hardly see him anymore.*

The conjunctions **seitdem** and **seit** are equivalent to English *since* when it refers to time. The German equivalent of *since* referring to cause is **da.**

Seitdem (seit) plus the present tense is used to express an action or condition that started in the past but is still continuing in the present (Stefan moved to Munich and still lives there). Note that English uses the present perfect tense (*has been living*) with *since* to express the same idea.

Stefan wohnt **seit** einem Jahr in München.
*Stefan has been living in Munich **for** a year.*

Seit (but not **seitdem**) can be used as a preposition (see *Kapitel 6*, Section 11).

d. *indem*

Jennifer hat Geld gespart, **indem**   *Jennifer saved money **by** doing the*
  sie die Gartenarbeit selbst   *yardwork herself.*

The conjunction **indem** + a clause is expressed in English by the preposition *by* + a gerund (e.g., *doing*). **Indem** expresses the means by which a result is obtained.

The conjunctions *nachdem* and *bevor* vs. prepositions *nach* and *vor*

Du kannst erst gehen, **nachdem**   *You can only go after you have*
  du die Arbeit gemacht hast.   *finished the work.*
  (conjunction)

Du kannst erst **nach** der Arbeit   *You can only go after work.*
  gehen. (preposition)

Nachdem and **nach** are equivalent to English *after* but are not interchangeable. **Nachdem** is a conjunction and introduces a clause. **Nach** is a preposition and is followed by a pronoun or a noun (e.g., **Arbeit**).

Er **geht** erst nach Hause, **nachdem** er die Arbeit **gemacht hat.**
He goes home only after he has finished the work.

Er **ging** nach Hause, **nachdem** er die Arbeit **gemacht hatte.**
He went home after he had finished the work.

The action in the clause introduced by **nachdem** precedes the action expressed in the main clause. If the verb in the main clause is in the present (e.g., **geht**) or future, the verb in the **nachdem** clause is in the simple past or present perfect (e.g., **gemacht hat**). If the verb in the main clause is in the simple past (e.g., **ging**) or present perfect, the verb in the **nachdem** clause is in the past perfect (e.g., **gemacht hatte**).

Willst du essen, **bevor** wir ins Konzert gehen?
Do you want to eat before we go to the concert?

Willst du **vor** dem Konzert essen?
Do you want to eat before the concert?

Bevor and **vor** are equivalent to English *before* but are not interchangeable. **Bevor** is a conjunction and introduces a clause. **Vor** is a preposition and is followed by a pronoun or noun (e.g., **Konzert**).

□——————————

F. Als, wenn oder wann?   Lore is expecting a visit from her cousin. Complete her account by supplying **als, wenn,** or **wann,** as appropriate.

1. _____ ich gestern nach Hause kam, lag ein dicker Brief da.
2. Ich freue mich immer, _____ ich Post bekomme.
3. Ich war sehr überrascht, _____ ich ihn öffnete. Er war von meiner Kusine.
4. _____ sie kann, kommt sie mich besuchen.
5. Aber sie schreibt nicht, _____ sie kommen will.
6. Ich weiß gar nicht mehr, _____ ich das letzte Mal von ihr gehört habe.
7. Es wird bestimmt ganz toll, _____ sie herkommt.
8. _____ sie mit dem Auto kommt, können wir schöne Ausflüge machen.
9. _____ sie mich das letzte Mal besucht hat, hatten wir viel Spaß miteinander.

G. Mit dem Fahrrad im Regen.   Tell about your experience bicycling in the rain. Choose the appropriate conjunction and combine each pair of sentences.

1. Es regnete fürchterlich. Ich fuhr von der Arbeit nach Hause. (als, damit)
2. Ich fuhr mit dem Fahrrad. Das Wetter war so schlecht. (indem, obwohl)
3. Ich fahre immer mit dem Fahrrad. Ich habe kein Auto. (weil, bis)
4. Ich war schon ganz naß. Ich war zwei Straßen gefahren. (ehe, seit)
5. Ich hoffe (es) sehr. Ich habe mich nicht erkältet. (ob, daß)
6. Ich fahre nicht mehr mit dem Fahrrad. Es regnet wieder so. (wenn, als)
7. Ich kaufe mir ein Auto. Ich habe genug Geld. (wann, sobald)

H. Noch einmal.   Restate the sentences in *Übung G*, beginning each sentence with the dependent clause.

I. Übers Wetter.   In Germany, as elsewhere, people often talk about the weather. Complete the sentences with **nachdem, seitdem, bevor, nach, seit,** or **vor,** as appropriate.

1. —_____ drei Wochen hat es nicht geregnet!
2. —Ja, der letzte Regen fiel, _____ das Sommersemester begann.

3. —_____ etwa zehn Jahren schneit es immer erst _____
   Weihnachten.
4. —Und _____ es dann geschneit hat, wünschen wir uns wieder
   wärmere Temperaturen.
5. —So ist es eben! Besonders _____ dem Winter freue ich mich
   wieder auf den Frühling.
6. —_____ es das Ozonloch° gibt, haben wir ein anderes Klima.   *hole in the ozone layer*
7. —_____ 100 Jahren waren die Winter viel kälter.

J. Gesund leben.   Jörg has decided to lead a healthier life. Here
he explains why. Fill in the conjunctions **da, weil, seitdem, indem,
nachdem,** or **bevor.**

1. Ich mußte endlich gesünder leben, _____ ich mich immer so
   schlecht gefühlt habe.
2. _____ Vitamine besonders wichtig sind, esse ich jetzt viel Obst.
3. _____ ich laufe, geht es mir viel besser!
4. _____ ich Sport treibe, trinke ich zwei Glas Wasser.
5. _____ ich dann gelaufen bin, trinke ich ein Glas Orangensaft.
6. Viele Leute halten sich fit, _____ sie jeden Tag schwimmen
   gehen.
7. _____ es hier kein Schwimmbad gibt, schwimme ich nicht oft.
8. Ich schwimme auch nicht gern, _____ das Wasser immer so kalt
   ist.
9. _____ ich Sport getrieben habe, esse ich oft eine große Portion
   Eis.
10. Ich bleibe gesund, _____ ich Obst und Gemüse esse, Sport treibe
    und auch genug schlafe.

——————————— □

11 │ Two-part conjunctions°

*die zweiteilige
Konjunktion*

Entweder hilfst du mir, ⎫
Entweder du hilfst mir, ⎬ **oder** ich mache es nicht.
                              ⎭
*Either you help me **or** I won't do it.*

Entweder...oder is a two-part conjunction equivalent to *either . . . or.*
Entweder can be followed by normal or inverted word order.

Er kann **weder** dir **noch** mir helfen.   *He can help **neither** you **nor** me.*

Weder...noch is the negative form of **entweder...oder** and is equivalent to *neither . . . nor.*

Je mehr Silke schreibt, **desto** besser wird ihr Stil.
The more Silke writes, the better her style becomes.

Je and **desto** are both followed by a comparative (e.g., **mehr, besser**). **Je** introduces a subordinate clause with the verb in final position, followed by the **desto** clause with inverted word order.

Uwe joggt **sowohl** abends **als auch** morgens.
*Uwe jogs in the evening **as well as** in the morning.*

The conjunction **sowohl...als auch** connects two possibilities in a sentence.

☐ ————————

K. Ein Ausflug.   Stefanie and Martin are talking about a trip they want to take. Although they have different ideas, they come to a compromise. Fill in **weder...noch, entweder...oder, sowohl...als auch,** or **je...desto.**

1. STEFANIE: Ich möchte einen Ausflug machen. Wir können _____ im Gebirge wandern _____ auf einem See surfen. Was meinst du, Martin?

2. MARTIN: Ich habe auch Lust auf Urlaub. Aber ich will _____ wandern _____ surfen gehen. Ich möchte _____ im Straßencafé sitzen _____ faul am Strand° liegen. _____ weniger ich machen muß, _____ erholsamer° ist so ein Urlaub für mich.   *beach / more relaxing*

3. STEFANIE: Wie wäre es dann zum Beispiel mit Korsika? Dort kann man _____ im Gebirge wandern _____ auch an den Strand gehen. Ich wandere, du liegst am Strand. Es gibt also keine Probleme zwischen uns. Und _____ weniger wir streiten°, _____ erholsamer ist der Urlaub für uns.   *to fight*

4. MARTIN: Ja, auch ich will _____ Streß _____ Streit. Und wenn ich weiß, daß ich _____ faul _____ aktiv sein darf, dann reise ich mit dir nach Korsika.

———————— ☐

12 Infinitives with *zu*

Nicole versuchte **zu arbeiten.**   *Nicole tried **to work.***
Es fängt an **zu regnen.**   *It's beginning **to rain.***
Ich bat ihn, hier **zu bleiben.**   *I asked him **to stay** here.*

Dependent infinitives used with most verbs are preceded by **zu** and are in last position. For infinitives used without **zu,** see *Kapitel 2:* modals, **sehen, hören, lassen,** and the future tense.

Haben Sie Lust, den Film **zu sehen?**	***Do you feel like seeing*** *the film?*
Es ist Zeit, nach Hause **zu gehen.**	***It's time to go*** *home.*

A number of expressions using the verb **haben** (e.g., **Lust haben**) or **sein** (e.g., **es ist Zeit**) are followed by the infinitive with **zu.**

An infinitive construction that contains other sentence elements, such as adverbs, objects, or prepositional phrases, is called an *infinitive phrase°* (e.g., **hier zu bleiben, den Film zu sehen, nach Hause zu gehen**). In writing, an infinitive phrase is set off by commas. *der Infinitivsatz*

Es wäre schön, wieder schlafen **zu** können.
It would be nice to be able to sleep again.

Note that when the infinitive phrase following an expression like **es wäre schön** contains a modal and a dependent infinitive (e.g., **schlafen können**), **zu** precedes the modal (e.g., **können**), not the dependent infinitive (e.g., **schlafen**).

Ich habe vor, alle meine Freunde ein**zu**laden.	*I plan **to** invite all my friends.*
Es ist Zeit an**zu**fangen.	*It's time **to** begin.*

When a separable-prefix verb is in the infinitive form, the **zu** comes between the prefix and the base form of the verb, and the construction is written as one word.

Some common expressions requiring infinitives with **zu** are:

Es macht Spaß,...
Es ist schwer (leicht),...
Es ist schön/Es wäre schön,...
Es ist Zeit,...
Es ist gut (nett)/Es wäre gut,...
Es ist langweilig,...
Hast du Lust (Zeit, Geld),...
Ich bin gewohnt,...

☐ ——————————

L. Griechenland.   Wolfgang is planning a trip and discusses it with Manuela. Complete the sentences using the cued words. Some of the expressions require the addition of **zu.**

▶ Es ist schon lange mein Wunsch (in den Süden fahren).
Es ist schon lange mein Wunsch, in den Süden zu fahren.

1. WOLFGANG: Jetzt habe ich endlich Zeit (eine Reise machen).
2. MANUELA: Und wohin?
3. WOLFGANG: Ich habe große Lust (nach Griechenland fahren).
   Athen muß (sehr interessant sein).
4. MANUELA: Aber es soll auch (furchtbar viel Verkehr geben).
5. WOLFGANG: Vielleicht sollte ich (lieber ans Meer fahren).
6. MANUELA: Es wäre ganz gut (die Sprache ein bißchen lernen).
   Meinst du nicht?
7. WOLFGANG: Ja, es wäre schön (mit den Leuten reden können).
8. MANUELA: Hast du vor (lange bleiben)?
9. WOLFGANG: Ich möchte schon (zwei Monate bleiben).
10. MANUELA: Glaubst du (genug Geld haben)?
11. WOLFGANG: Hm, das Leben dort scheint (nicht sehr teuer sein).
12. MANUELA: Na denn, gute Reise!

──────────────── □

13 | The expressions *um…zu*, *(an)statt…zu*, *ohne…zu*

Sie fuhr nach Bonn, **um** das Beethovenhaus **zu sehen.**
*She went to Bonn **in order to see** Beethoven's house.*

Wir werden sie anrufen, **(an)statt** einen Brief **zu schreiben.**
*We'll call her **instead of writing** a letter.*

Er ist weggegangen, **ohne** ein Wort **zu sagen.**
*He left **without saying** a word.*

The prepositions **um, (an)statt,** and **ohne** may combine with **zu** to introduce infinitive phrases. These phrases are set off by a comma.

The constructions **(an)statt…zu** and **ohne…zu** are used with infinitives (e.g., **schreiben, sagen**). The equivalent English expression has a verb ending in *-ing* (e.g., *writing, saying*).

Bist du gekommen, **um** mir   *Did you come **(in order) to** help*
  zu helfen?   *me?*

Hast du Lust, mir **zu** helfen?   ***Do you feel like** helping me?*

The construction **um…zu** is used to express purpose. It is equivalent to English *in order to* (often simply expressed by *to*). Do not confuse this structure with the expressions requiring the infinitive with **zu,** in Section 12 of this chapter (e.g., **Hast du Lust, ...**).

☐ ─────────────────────

M. Wien. Your cousin is definitely a different kind of tourist than you would be. Tell what he did in Vienna. Restate the sentences using **um ... zu, ohne ... zu,** and **(an)statt ... zu.**

▶ Er fuhr mit seinem alten Auto. Er fuhr nicht mit dem Zug.
   Er fuhr mit seinem alten Auto, statt mit dem Zug zu fahren.

▶ Er fuhr nach Wien. Er reservierte kein Hotelzimmer.
   Er fuhr nach Wien, ohne ein Hotelzimmer zu reservieren.

1. Er mußte lange suchen. Er fand ein hübsches Zimmer in einer kleinen Pension°.   *small hotel*
2. Er war eine Woche in Wien. Er besuchte kein einziges Mal den Stephansdom.
3. Er saß jeden Tag im Café. Er ging nicht in ein Museum.
4. Er verbrachte eine Woche in Wien. Er sah kein einziges Bild.
5. Er ging dauernd ins Kino. Er ging überhaupt nicht ins Theater.
6. Er ist wohl nach Wien gefahren. Er wollte nur im Café sitzen und die herrlichen Torten essen.

───────────── ☐

14 Word order°: time°, manner°, place°

die Wortstellung / die Zeit / die Art und Weise / der Ort

	Time			
	General	Specific	Manner	Place
Wir fahren	heute		mit dem Auto	nach Spanien.
Wir fahren	heute	um acht Uhr	mit dem Auto	nach Spanien.

When adverbs and adverbial prepositional phrases occur in a sentence, they occur in the following sequence: time (when?), manner (how?), place (where?). When a sentence contains two adverbial expressions of time, the general expression (e.g., **heute**) usually precedes the specific (e.g., **um acht Uhr**).

□ ——————————

N. In Paris.   Mr. Bader often goes to Paris. Using the cued words, tell what he usually does when he first arrives there.

▶   Herr Bader fährt (nach Frankreich / oft).
    Herr Bader fährt oft nach Frankreich.

1. Er fährt (nach Paris / immer / mit dem Zug).
2. Der Zug fährt (vom Hauptbahnhof / um 8.30 Uhr) ab.
3. Herr Bader sitzt (in der Eisenbahn / gern).
4. Er kommt (in Paris / um vier Uhr / am Nachmittag) an.
5. Dort geht er (in ein Café / zuerst / jedesmal).
6. Er setzt sich (an einen Tisch / gleich) und trinkt (schnell / immer) einen Kaffee.
7. Er geht (an den Taxistand / dann).
8. Er fährt (in sein Hotel / meistens / mit dem Taxi).

—————————— □

15   Position of *nicht*

Ruth **arbeitet nicht**.	*Ruth doesn't work.*
Sie macht ihre **Arbeit nicht**.	*She's not doing her work.*
Ich glaube **es nicht**.	*I don't believe it.*
Warum arbeitet sie **heute nicht?**	*Why isn't she working today?*

The position of **nicht** is determined by various elements in the sentence. **Nicht** always follows:

1. the finite verb (e.g., **arbeitet**)
2. nouns used as direct and indirect objects (e.g., **Arbeit**)
3. pronouns used as direct and indirect objects (e.g., **es**)
4. specific adverbs of time (e.g., **heute**)

Gerd ist **nicht mein Freund**.	*Gerd is not my friend.*
Er ist **nicht nett**.	*He's not nice.*
Ich arbeite **nicht gern** mit ihm zusammen.	*I don't like to work with him.*
Ich sehe ihn **nicht oft**.	*I don't see him often.*
Ich fahre **nicht zu ihm**.	*I'm not going to his place.*
Er kommt auch **nicht vorbei**.	*He doesn't come around either.*
Ich kann ihn **nicht verstehen**.	*I can't understand him.*
Warum hat er **nicht angerufen?**	*Why hasn't he called?*

Nicht precedes most other kinds of elements:

1. predicate nouns (e.g., **mein Freund**)
2. predicate adjectives (e.g., **nett**)
3. adverbs (e.g., **gern**)
4. general time adverbs (e.g., **oft**)
5. prepositional phrases (e.g., **zu ihm**)
6. separable prefixes (e.g., **vorbei**)
7. infinitives (e.g., **verstehen**)
8. past participles (e.g., **angerufen**)

Du solltest **nicht ihn** bitten, sondern seine Schwester.
You shouldn't ask him but rather his sister.

Nicht may also precede any word that is given special negative emphasis (e.g., **ihn**). This use of **nicht** is found mainly in contrasts.

Ich gehe **nicht oft** ins Theater.   *I don't often go to the theater.*

If several of the above elements occur in a sentence, **nicht** usually precedes the first one.

□ ————————————

O. Willst du sonst noch etwas wissen?   Because Rainer is in a bad mood today, he answers all his friend's questions in the negative. Take the part of Rainer.

▶   Gehst du heute in die Bibliothek?
    Nein, ich gehe heute nicht in die Bibliothek.

1. Machst du dein Referat diese Woche fertig?
2. Hast du die Bücher für das Kafka-Seminar gelesen?
3. Arbeitest du für Professor Groß?
4. Findest du Professor Groß nett?
5. Gehst du mit mir Kaffee trinken?
6. Rufst du mich heute abend an?
7. Bist du heute schlecht gelaunt°?

schlecht gelaunt: in a bad mood

———————————— □

Zusammenfassung

A. Das Geld ist weg.   Kürzlich hatte Frau Huber, Ihre Nachbarin, ein unangenehmes° Erlebnis°. Erzählen Sie es auf deutsch.

unpleasant / experience

1. When Mrs. Huber came out of the store, she noticed° that she had forgotten her purse.

Use **merken.**

2. She had neither her purse nor her money.
3. Although she went back immediately, she couldn't find the purse.
4. She had taken along a lot of money, because she wanted to buy a jacket.
5. Now Mrs. Huber could buy nothing more but had to go home.
6. It annoyed her, but she couldn't change it.

B. Die Amerikanerin.

Paul ist schüchtern°. In Köln hat er im Café eine Frau getroffen, die er nett findet. Erzählen Sie, wie er versucht hat, mit ihr ins Gespräch zu kommen. Gebrauchen Sie die angegebene Zeitform°.

shy

angegebene Zeitform:
specified tense
Use **von der Arbeit.**
ins Café

1. When I come home from work° in the evening, I sometimes go to a café°. (present)
2. Yesterday I saw a woman in the café. (simple past)
3. I don't know whether she sits there every day, but I saw her there° last week. (present perfect)

Use **schon dort.**

4. When she ordered ice water°, I realized° that she was [an] American. (simple past)

Eiswasser / Use **bemerken.**

5. Her German was very good. (simple past)
6. Suddenly she looked at me and smiled. (simple past)
7. Although I am very shy, I spoke to her then. (present perfect)

C. Als ich klein war!

Laura fragt ihre Mutter, wie es war, als sie jung war. Vervollständigen° Sie die folgenden Sätze mit **als, wenn** oder **wann.**

complete

1. LAURA: _____ mußtest du immer ins Bett gehen, _____ du klein warst?
2. MUTTER: Ich weiß nicht mehr genau, _____ ich abends ins Bett mußte, aber ich glaube, es war ziemlich früh. Nur _____ wir Besuch hatten, durften wir länger aufbleiben.
3. LAURA: _____ haben Oma und Opa einen Fernseher gekauft?
4. MUTTER: Wir bekamen erst einen Fernseher, _____ ich 14 war.
5. LAURA: Durftest du fernsehen, _____ Oma und Opa zu Hause waren?
6. MUTTER: Ja, aber _____ Oma und Opa da waren, haben sie immer das Programm ausgewählt. Und _____ ich dann älter wurde, war Fernsehen gar nicht mehr so interessant.
7. LAURA: Ja, ich weiß. Ich schalte auch immer ab°, _____ die Sendungen° langweilig sind.

abschalten: *to switch off*
programs

D. Ein Wochenende in Tübingen.   Christine besucht ihre Freundin Sandra in Tübingen. Sie überlegen sich°, was sie machen können. Bilden Sie Sätze mit einem Infinitiv oder mit einem Infinitivsatz.

sich überlegen: to think about

1. du / Lust haben // die Stiftskirche sehen / ?
2. wir / leider keine Zeit haben // ins Theater gehen
3. es / Spaß machen // auf dem Marktplatz Kaffee trinken
4. es / schwer sein // in der Stadt einen Parkplatz finden
5. was / wir / können / machen // anstatt / in die Stadt fahren / ?
6. es / schön sein // im Wald spazierengehen
7. ich / tragen / nicht die richtigen Schuhe // um / einen Spaziergang machen
8. du / genug Geld haben // eine Stadtrundfahrt° machen / ?
9. die / wir / machen // ohne / weiter darüber diskutieren

sightseeing tour

E. Partnerarbeit.   Sie wollen mit Ihrer Partnerin/Ihrem Partner zusammen etwas unternehmen. Sie/Er findet Ihre Pläne nicht gut. Versuchen Sie herauszufinden, warum nicht. Gebrauchen Sie einen der folgenden Vorschläge oder eine eigene Idee:

- Sie wollen Ihr Zimmer/Ihre Wohnung in Ordnung bringen.
- Sie wollen Ihr Auto waschen.
- Sie wollen eine Party machen.

F. Kurze Aufsätze.   Beschreiben Sie, wie Sie etwas tun. Gebrauchen Sie einen der folgenden Vorschläge oder eine eigene Idee. Verbinden Sie die Sätze mit Adverbien wie **daher, dann, erst, später** und **zuerst** und mit Konjunktionen wie **aber, als, bevor, da, damit, daß, denn, nachdem, obgleich, sobald, während, weil** und **wenn**.

- Was machen Sie jeden Morgen?
- Wie kommen Sie zur Arbeit/zur Uni?
- Wie bereiten Sie sich auf einen Test vor?
- Sie wollen eine Party machen. Wie bereiten Sie die vor?
- Ein Rezept: Wie macht man Spaghetti mit Tomatensauce?

KAPITEL

Nominative Case ■

Accusative Case ■

1 The definite article°, nominative° and accusative°

*der bestimmte Artikel /
der Nominativ
der Akkusativ*

	Masculine	Neuter	Feminine	Plural
Nominative:	der	das	die	die
Accusative:	den	das	die	die

2 *Der*-words, nominative and accusative

	Masculine	Neuter	Feminine	Plural
Nominative:	dieser	dieses	diese	diese
Accusative:	diesen	dieses	diese	diese

3 Meanings and uses of *der*-words

dieser	*this, these* (pl.)
jeder	*each, every* (used in singular only)
jener	*that, the one that, the one who*
mancher	*many a, several* (used mainly in the plural)
solcher	*such* (used mainly in the plural)
welcher	*which*

Ich denke an **jene,** die nicht hier sein können.
*I'm thinking of **those (the ones)** who can't be here.*

Jener points to something or someone known or previously mentioned.

Der Stuhl
Dieser Stuhl $\Big\}$ **da** ist neu.   ***That** chair is new.*

Note that the equivalent of *that one* (pl. *those*) is usually expressed by **der** (**das, die**) + **da** or by **dies**(**-er, -es, -e**) (not **jener**) in colloquial German.

Singular: Ich habe **manch ein** Buch darüber gelesen.
*I've read **many** a book on that.*

So einen Hut würde ich nicht tragen.
*I wouldn't wear **such a** hat.*

Plural: **Manche** Leute sind nie zufrieden.
Some people are never satisfied.

Solche Hüte würdest du auch nicht tragen.
You wouldn't wear such hats either.

Mancher and **solcher** are used mainly in the plural and replaced by a form of **manch ein** or **so ein** in the singular.

□—————————

A. Mark braucht einen Koffer.   Mark is going on a trip and is shopping for a new suitcase with his friend Susi. Complete their conversation by supplying the correct forms of the cued words.

1. MARK: _____ Koffer hier ist schön, nicht wahr? (jeder)
2. SUSI: Nö. _____ Koffer gefallen mir, _____ nicht. Schau mal, wie gefällt dir _____ Tasche? (mancher / mancher / so ein)
3. MARK: Ach nein, _____ Art und _____ Farbe mag ich überhaupt nicht. (dieser / so ein)
4. SUSI: Also, mußt du unbedingt° heute _____ Koffer kaufen, hm? (so ein)   *absolutely*
5. MARK: Ja, sei nicht ungeduldig. Du weißt, wie ich _____ Sachen hasse. (solcher)
6. SUSI: _____ Koffer nimmst du jetzt, _____ großen oder _____ kleinen _____ ? (welcher / dieser / der...da)
7. MARK: Ich nehme _____ Tasche hier. Die mag ich. (dieser)
8. SUSI: Also, _____ Leute haben schon einen merkwürdigen Geschmack°! (mancher)   *taste*

—————————— □

4   The indefinite article° *ein* and *kein*, nominative and accusative   *der unbestimmte Artikel*

	Masculine	Neuter	Feminine	Plural
Nominative:	ein	ein	eine	—
	kein	kein	keine	keine
Accusative:	einen	ein	eine	—
	keinen	kein	keine	keine

The German indefinite article **ein** corresponds to English *a, an.* It has no plural form.

The negative form of **ein** is **kein**. It is equivalent to English *not a, not any*, or *no*. **Kein** negates a noun that in the positive would be preceded by a form of **ein** or by no article at all:

Wo ist hier **ein** Telefon? —Es gibt hier **kein** Telefon.

Hast du jetzt Zeit? —Nein, ich habe im Moment **keine** Zeit.

5   Possessive adjectives°

das Possessiv-pronomen

Subject pronouns	Possessive adjectives	English equivalents
ich	**mein**	*my*
du	**dein**	*your* (fam. sg.)
er	**sein**	*his, its*
es	**sein**	*its, his, her*
sie	**ihr**	*her, its*
wir	**unser**	*our*
ihr	**euer**	*your* (fam. pl.)
sie	**ihr**	*their*
Sie	**Ihr**	*your* (formal, sg. & pl.)

Hast du **meinen** Kuli gesehen? —**Deinen** Kuli? Nein.

Possessive adjectives take the same endings as the indefinite article **ein**. They are therefore often called **ein**-words.

Ist Gerd **euer** Bruder und Ilse **eure** Schwester? —Nein, Kurt ist **unser** Bruder, und Martha ist **uns(e)re** Schwester.

Note that when **euer** has endings, the **e** before the **r** is dropped (**eure**). In colloquial German, when an ending is added to **unser,** the **e** is often dropped (**unsre**).

☐ ───────

B. Reisevorbereitungen.   You are going on a trip with friends. Check to see whether everyone has packed his or her things.

▶   du/Kamm
      Hast du deinen Kamm eingepackt?

1. Peter / Fotoapparat
2. Christa / Blusen
3. du / Seife
4. Gerd / Kassettenrecorder
5. Jürgen / Hemden
6. ihr / Zahnbürsten
7. du / Schuhe
8. Eva / Haartrockner
9. Gerd und Eva / Bücher

C. Kurze Gespräche.   Complete the minidialogues by using the correct form of the cued **ein**-word.

1. _____ Mann will Sie sprechen. (ein)
   —Ich kenne _____ Mann hier. Wie ist _____ Name? (kein / sein)
2. Wo sind _____ Bücher? (mein)
   —Ich habe sie auf _____ Schreibtisch gelegt. (dein)
   —Ich sehe _____ Bücher. (kein)
3. Ich möchte mir so gern _____ Paar neue Sommerschuhe kaufen, aber ich habe _____ Geld. (ein/kein)
   —Warum? Hast du _____ Job nicht mehr? (dein)
   —Doch, aber _____ Miete ist teurer geworden, und ich muß auch _____ Telefon bezahlen. (unser / unser)
4. Wie ist _____ Professorin für Geschichte? (euer)
   —Ich finde sie gut. _____ Kurs ist sehr interessant. _____ Noten sind auch besser geworden. Ich kenne _____ bessere Professorin. (unser / mein / kein)

——————————————— ☐

6 Nouns° indicating nationalities and professions

das Substantiv

Kathrin ist **Deutsche.**   *Kathrin is (a) German.*

Sie ist **Studentin.**   *She's a student.*

Sie wird **Ingenieurin.**   *She's going to be an engineer.*

Im Sommer arbeitet sie als   *In the summer she works as a*
 Informatikerin.   *computer specialist.*

To state a person's nationality, profession, or membership in a group, German uses the noun directly after a form of the verbs **sein** or **werden** or after **als** (*as*). The indefinite article **ein** is not used. English precedes such nouns with the indefinite article *a* or *an*.

Florian ist **kein Ingenieur.** ⎫   *Florian is not an engineer.*
Florian ist **nicht Ingenieur.** ⎭

Either **kein** or **nicht** is used to negate a sentence about someone's nationality, profession, or membership in a group.

Frau Dr. Braun ist **eine**   *Dr. Braun is a well-known German.*
 bekannte Deutsche.

Sie ist **eine gute Ärztin.**   *She's a good doctor.*

Ein is used with nouns designating professions, nationalities, and membership in groups when the nouns are preceded by an adjective.

□ ————————————

D. Eine internationale Familie.   Give the German equivalent of the English sentences.

1. My sister is German. She is a teacher.
2. Her husband is English. He was a pharmacist. Now he works as a photographer.
3. Oh, I thought he was° a doctor.   Use **ist.**
4. But your husband is American?
5. No, he's German.
6. And what does he do?
7. He's a professor.

———————————— □

7   Masculine *n*-nouns in the accusative case

Nominative	Accusative
Ist das Herr Biermann?	Ich kenne keinen **Herrn** Biermann.
Wo ist hier ein Polizist?	Warum suchst du einen **Polizisten?**

A number of masculine nouns add **-n** or **-en** in the singular accusative, the dative (see *Kapitel 6*), and the genitive (see *Kapitel 8*). These nouns are often called masculine **n**-nouns, or weak nouns.

The accusative forms of common masculine **n**-nouns are:

den Bauern	den Juristen	den Patienten
den Gedanken	den Kollegen	den Polizisten
den Glauben	den Menschen	den Präsidenten
den Herrn	den Nachbarn	den Soldaten
den Journalisten	den Namen	den Studenten
den Jungen	den Neffen	den Touristen

For a summary of the forms of masculine **n**-nouns, see Appendix A: 9.

□ ————————————

E. Auf Jobsuche.   Anja and Joachim are looking for jobs during their semester break. They ask one another about the connections they have. Complete their conversation by supplying the correct forms of the cued words.

1. MICHAEL: Ich suche einen Job bei der Zeitung. Kennst du vielleicht _____ (ein Journalist) beim „Tageblatt"°?   name of newspaper

2. ANJA: Nein, leider nicht. Aber das bringt mich auf _____ (ein Gedanke). Mein Vater hat _____ (ein Kollege), und der hat _____ (ein Neffe), der _____ (der Präsident) des Journalistenvereins kennt.

3. MICHAEL: Weißt du zufällig _____ (sein Name)?

4. ANJA: Nein, aber ich kann _____ (Herr Schumann), _____, (unser Nachbar), fragen. Er weiß immer alles.

5. MICHAEL: Au ja, bitte frag _____ (euer Nachbar)! Wo arbeitest du in den Ferien?

6. ANJA: Ich möchte _____ (der Jurist) in unserem Seminar fragen, ob ich für ihn arbeiten kann. Aber nach drei Semestern Jura° habe ich noch _____ (kein Glaube) an meine juristischen Fähigkeiten°.

law

capability, skills

7. MICHAEL: Versuche es doch einfach. Warum soll ein Jurist _____ (kein Student) anstellen°? Meine Mutter hat _____ (ein Patient), der Jurist ist. Ich frage ihn!

to hire

_____ □

8 Demonstrative pronouns°, nominative and accusative

das Demonstrativpronomen

	Masculine	Neuter	Feminine	Plural
Nominative:	**der** *he, it*	**das** *it*	**die** *she, it*	**die** *they*
Accusative:	**den** *him, it*	**das** *it*	**die** *her, it*	**die** *them*

Demonstrative pronouns are identical to the definite articles in the nominative and accusative.

Kaufst du den **Mantel** da?	*Are you going to buy that **coat?***
Nein, **der** ist zu teuer.	*No, **it** is too expensive.*

A demonstrative pronoun often replaces a personal pronoun if the pronoun is to be emphasized. Demonstrative pronouns usually occur at or near the beginning of a sentence. The English equivalent is usually a personal pronoun.

Kommt **Monika** mit?	*Is **Monika** coming along?*
Nein, **die** bekommt heute Besuch.	*No, **she**'s having company today.*

Demonstrative pronouns are also used in colloquial German to indicate familiarity with people or things.

□ —————————————

F. Kurze Gespräche.   Complete the minidialogues by supplying the correct form of the demonstrative pronoun.

▶   —Der Pulli ist schön, nicht?
     —Meinst du? *Den* finde ich häßlich.

1. —Der neue Herzog-Film läuft im Thalia. _____ interessiert mich.
   Sollen wir uns _____ ansehen?
   —Nein, _____ kenne ich schon.
2. —Wo ist denn Monika?
   —_____ ist in Amerika.
   —_____ hab' ich doch gestern noch gesehen.
   —Nein. _____ ist vorgestern abgeflogen.
3. —Wem gehört das Auto da?
   —_____ gehört meinem Bruder.
   —Wann hat er _____ gekauft?
   —Er hat es gar nicht gekauft. _____ hat ihm mein Vater
   geschenkt.
4. —Wer sind die Leute da drüben?
   —_____warten auf Professor Schwarz.
   —Was wollen _____?
   —_____ wollen mit ihm sprechen.
   —Wo ist denn _____?
   —_____ habe ich vor einer Stunde noch gesehen.

————————————— □

9   Personal pronouns°, nominative and accusative

das Personalpronomen

Nominative		Accusative	
German	English	German	English
ich	*I*	**mich**	*me*
du *(fam. sg.)*	*you*	**dich** *(fam. sg.)*	*you*
er	*he, it*	**ihn**	*him, it*
es	*it, he, she*	**es**	*it, him, her*
sie	*she, it*	**sie**	*her, it*
wir	*we*	**uns**	*us*
ihr *(fam. pl.)*	*you*	**euch** *(fam. pl.)*	*you*
sie	*they*	**sie**	*them*
Sie *(formal, sg. & pl.)*	*you*	**Sie** *(formal, sg. & pl.)*	*you*

Kennst du **den Herrn** da? —Ja, **er** ist mein Onkel.

Der Wagen ist schon wieder kaputt. —Wirklich? Wir haben **ihn** doch letzte Woche gerade erst repariert.

The personal pronouns **er, es, sie** agree in gender and number with the noun to which they refer. Personal pronouns refer to both persons and things.

□————————————

G. Alles über Oliver.   Kirsten and Sabine are having a glass of wine together. Kirsten hasn't seen Sabine for a while and asks a lot of questions about Sabine's friend Oliver. Take the role of Sabine and answer the questions with **ja** or **nein.** Use the personal pronoun in your answer.

▶   —Ist dieser Wein teuer?
     —*Ja (Nein), er ist (nicht) teuer.*

▶   —Magst du den Wein?
     —*Ja (Nein), ich mag ihn (nicht).*

1. Studiert Oliver in Marburg?
2. Kennst du seinen Bruder?
3. Hast du seine Eltern kennengelernt?
4. Ist seine Familie nett?
5. Hat er sein altes Auto verkauft?
6. Siehst du seine Freunde oft?
7. Laden sie euch oft ein?
8. Mag dein Vater Oliver?
9. Liebst du Oliver?
10. Liebt er dich?
11. Willst du Oliver heiraten?

————————————— □

---

10 The indefinite pronoun° man   *das Indefinitpronomen*

Wie sagt **man** das?
*How does **one** (do **you**) say that?*

Wann hat **man** die Kirche wiederaufgebaut?
*When did **they** rebuild the church?*

Wenn **man** nicht aufpaßt, kann **man** bei einer Party zuviel essen.
*If **you** don't watch out, **you** can eat too much at a party.*

The indefinite pronoun **man** has various equivalents in English: *one, you, they,* or *people.*

Das kann **einen** wirklich krank machen.   *That can make **one** really ill.*

Man is nominative and can only be used as a subject. In the accusative, the pronoun **einen** is used.

11   The interrogative pronouns° *wer* and *was*

das Interrogativ-pronomen

> Nominative: **wer** *who*   **was** *what*
> Accusative: **wen** *whom*   **was** *what*

Wer ist die Frau da? —**Wen** meinst du? Die Frau im blauen Rock?

Was war das? —**Was** hast du eben gehört? —Ach, nur die Tür.

The accusative form of **wer** is **wen**. The accusative of **was** is identical to the nominative form.

☐ —————————————

H. Wollen wir ins Kino?   Silvina and her friends are trying to decide whether to see a new film that has received mixed reviews. Complete their sentences with an interrogative pronoun or the indefinite pronoun **man**. (Remember to use **einen** in the accusative, not **man**.)

1. Weißt du, _____ den Film schon gesehen hat?
2. _____ steht in der Zeitung darüber?
3. _____ sagt, daß er sehr lustig sein soll.
4. Kann _____ das glauben?
5. Klar! Es kann _____ schon überzeugen°, _____ in der Zeitung steht.   *convince*
6. Manchmal kann _____ aber nicht wissen, was anderen Leuten gefallen wird.
7. _____ können wir noch fragen?

I. Aus den Augen, aus dem Sinn!   Ute and her friends are talking about Thomas, a student friend who moved to another university town. None of them is in touch with him. Complete their sentences with an interrogative pronoun or the indefinite pronoun **man**.

1. —_____ von euch hat etwas von Thomas gehört?

2. —_____ meinst du? Thomas Trautmann? Nein, er hat mir nie geschrieben. Das ist schon traurig. Da verspricht _____, daß _____ sich Briefe schreibt, und nie kommt auch nur eine Postkarte.

3. —_____ findest du daran komisch? So ist es doch immer: Jemand geht in eine andere Stadt, und dann verliert _____ einfach den Kontakt.

4. —Nicht jeder ist so! _____ kann auch weggehen und trotzdem seinen alten Freunden schreiben.

5. —Hat _____ dazu denn Zeit? Als Student hat _____ doch so viel zu tun.

6. —Das finde ich auch. Der Studienalltag streßt _____ doch ziemlich.

—————————————— □

12 Uses of the nominative case

Subject°: **Meine Tochter** studiert Mathematik.

das Subjekt

The subject designates a person, concept, or thing on which the sentence focuses; it is the starting point of the action or statement. The subject of a sentence is in the nominative case°.

der Fall

Predicate noun°: Der junge Mann heißt **Jürgen.** Jürgen ist **ein netter junger Mann.** Er wird **Arzt.**

das Prädikatsnomen

A predicate noun designates a person, concept, or thing that restates the subject or identifies with it. A predicate noun completes the meaning of linking verbs such as **heißen, sein,** and **werden.**

13 Uses of the accusative case

Direct object:	Kennst du **meinen Bruder?**
Object of a preposition:	Er arbeitet für **unseren Onkel.**
Time:	Wir bleiben nur **einen Tag** in Hamburg.
Measure:	Morgens laufen wir **einen Kilometer.**
*With **es gibt:***	Gibt es hier **einen guten Arzt?**

14   Direct object°

das direkte Objekt

Subject	Direct object
Wer ist **der Junge?**	Kennst du **den Jungen?**
Der rote Mantel ist schön.	Aber Julia kauft **den blauen Mantel.**
Wo ist **dein Freund?**	Ich habe **ihn** nicht gesehen.

The direct object receives or is affected by the direct action of the verb. The direct object answers the questions *whom* (**wen?**) for persons and *what* (**was?**) for things and concepts. A noun or pronoun used as the direct object of a verb is in the accusative case.

Do not confuse:

Das ist **der Junge.** (predicate noun)

Kennst du **den Jungen?** (direct object)

15   Prepositions with the accusative case°

die Präposition mit dem Akkusativ

Preposition	Meaning	Examples
bis	*until*	Ich bleibe **bis** nächsten Samstag. *I'm staying until next Saturday.*
	as far as	Ich fahre nur **bis** Nürnberg. *I'm going only as far as Nuremberg.*
	by (temporal)	Kannst du **bis** morgen fertig sein? *Can you be finished by tomorrow?*
durch	*through*	Sie fährt **durch** die Stadt. *She's driving through town.*
entlang	*along*	Wir gehen den Fluß **entlang.** *We're walking along the river.*
für	*for*	**Für** wen kaufst du das? *For whom are you buying that?*
gegen	*against*	Was hast du **gegen** ihn? *What do you have against him?*
	about, around (temporal)	Wir kommen **gegen** acht Uhr. *We're coming around eight o'clock.*
ohne	*without*	Er geht **ohne** seinen Freund. *He's going without his friend.*
um	*around*	Da kommt Inge **um** die Ecke. *There comes Inge around the corner.*
	at (temporal)	Jörg fährt **um** zehn Uhr nach Hause. *Jörg is going home at ten o'clock.*

The prepositions **bis, durch, entlang, für, gegen, ohne,** and **um** take the accusative case.

Usually **bis** is followed by other prepositions. The second preposition determines the case of the noun: **Er** geht **bis an** die Tür. Der Bus fährt nur **bis zum** Bahnhof.

Note that **entlang** follows the noun or pronoun in the accusative (e.g., **den Fluß entlang**).

durch das → durchs	Sabine geht **durchs** Zimmer.
für das → fürs	Frau Lange kauft das **fürs** Geschäft.
um das → ums	Der Hund läuft **ums** Haus.

Some prepositions contract with the definite article **das.** They are common in colloquial German but are not required.

Für **das** (häßliche) Bild zahle ich keine 500 Mark.
*I won't pay 500 marks for **that** (ugly) picture.*

Contractions are not used when the noun is emphasized or modified.

☐ ————————————

J. Nominativ oder Akkusativ?   Indicate whether each noun and pronoun is in the nominative or accusative case and state its use in the sentence (subject, predicate noun, direct object, or object of a preposition).

1. Petra hat einen neuen Freund.
2. Er ist Student.
3. Er studiert Sprachen an der Universität.
4. Er heißt Kai.
5. Kai ist ein sehr fleißiger Student.
6. Manchmal arbeitet Kai für seinen Professor.
7. Petra trifft ihren Freund am Nachmittag.
8. Gestern hat sie für ihn eine neue CD gekauft.
9. Die CD hat sie schon lange gesucht.
10. Sie lädt ihn zum Essen ein.

K. Viele Fragen.   Answer the questions in the negative using the cued words.

▶ Machst du es für deine Mutter? (mein Vater)
  Nein, für meinen Vater.

1. Seid ihr durch die Stadt gefahren? (die Felder und Wiesen)
2. Hast du Hans durch deine Arbeit kennengelernt? (ein Freund)
3. Machst du dir Sorgen um das Geld? (mein Job)

4. Mußt du das bis morgen fertig haben? (nächster Montag)
5. Bist du die Hauptstraße entlang gekommen? (der Fußweg)
6. Hast du etwas gegen Lisa? (mein Bruder)
7. Interessierst du dich für die Geschichte von Wien? (der Film über Wien)

L. Ein Wochenende allein!   Dagmar is under stress and plans to spend the following weekend all by herself. She tells what she wants to do. Complete the text with an appropriate preposition with the accusative case.

1. Das nächste Wochenende möchte ich allein _____ meine Freunde verbringen.
2. Am Samstag stehe ich _____ neun Uhr oder vielleicht auch erst _____ zehn Uhr auf.
3. Nach dem Frühstück bummle ich dann _____ die Fußgängerzone° und schaue die Geschäfte an.   *pedestrian zone*
4. Ich brauche _____ nächste Woche ein Geburtstagsgeschenk _____ meine Mutter.
5. Doch ich gehe nur _____ zum Rathaus. Dahinter sind die Geschäfte nicht so interessant.
6. Ich bleibe etwa _____ zwei Uhr nachmittags in der Stadt. Danach brauche ich ein bißchen Bewegung°.   *exercise*
7. Ich habe nichts _____ Sport, aber es darf kein Streß sein.
8. Ich jogge vielleicht den Fluß _____, oder ich laufe _____ den See herum.
9. Am Sonntag bleibe ich auch _____ Mittag im Bett.

———————————————— □

16 Time expressions° with the accusative case   *die Zeitangabe*

Definite point:	Sie kommen **nächsten Monat.**	*They're coming **next month.***
Duration:	Sie bleiben **den ganzen Sommer.**	*They're staying the **whole summer.***

When used without prepositions, noun phrases expressing a definite point in time (answering such questions as **wann? wie oft?**) or a duration of time (answering the question **wie lange?**) are in the accusative case. Examples for common expressions of time are given below.

Wann?/Wie oft?	Wie lange?
nächsten Winter	den ganzen Tag
jedes Jahr	das ganze Jahr
diese Woche	einen Monat

☐ ————————————

M. Wie lange?   Tell how long various activities lasted, using the nouns provided in expressions of time.

▶   Ausflug / Tag
    Der Ausflug hat einen Tag gedauert.

1. Fest / Woche
2. Kurs / Sommer
3. Ausflug / Nachmittag
4. Gespräch / Stunde
5. Reise / Monat

———————————— ☐

17 Accusative of measure°   *die Maßangabe*

Die Straße ist **einen Kilometer** lang. *The street is **one kilometer** long.*
Die Äpfel wiegen **ein halbes Kilo.**   *The apples weigh **one-half kilo.***
Das Kind ist erst **einen Monat** alt.   *The child is only **one month** old.*

Nouns expressing units of measure, weight, or age are in the accusative case.

18 Units of measure and quantity

Ich möchte **zwei Glas** Milch.   *I'd like **two glasses** of milk.*
Sie kauft **fünf Pfund** Kartoffeln. *She's buying **five pounds** of potatoes.*

In German, masculine and neuter nouns expressing measure, weight, or number are in the singular.

Sie bestellt **zwei Tassen** Kaffee. *She orders **two cups** of coffee.*
Er kauft **zwei Flaschen** Cola.   *He's buying **two bottles** of Coke.*

Feminine nouns ending in **-e** form plurals when they express measure.

☐——————————————

N. Essen, trinken, einkaufen.   Answer the questions using the German equivalents of the English expressions of quantity.

▶   Was trinkst du morgens? *(two glasses of juice)*
    Ich trinke zwei Glas Saft.

1. Was ißt du morgens? *(two pieces of bread)*
2. Was trinkst du mittags? *(three glasses of milk)*
3. Was trinkst du nachmittags? *(three cups of tea)*
4. Was trinkt Werner auf seiner Fahrradtour? *(two liters of water)*
5. Was trinkst du mit deinen Gästen? *(two bottles of wine)*
6. Was kaufst du für das Abendessen? *(500 grams of cheese)*
7. Wieviel Kartoffeln kaufst du im Supermarkt? *(five kilos)*
8. Wieviel Orangen kaufst du auf dem Markt? *(four pounds)*

——————————————— ☐

19   The expression *es gibt*

Es gibt hier **keine guten Restaurants.**	*There are no good restaurants here.*
Gibt es einen guten Grund dafür?	*Is there a good reason for that?*

The accusative case always follows the expression **es gibt**. Either singular or plural nouns may follow. The English equivalents are *there is* and *there are*.

Gibt's noch Kaffee?	*Is there any coffee left?*

In questions, the contraction **gibt's** may be used.

☐——————————————

O. Was gibt's noch?   Mr. Kurz wants to reserve a hotel room by telephone for a one-week vacation. He would like to know what things there are at the hotel or in the vicinity.

▶   Blumenladen
    Gibt's da einen Blumenladen?

▶   Telefon im Zimmer
    Gibt's ein Telefon im Zimmer?

1. Post
2. Garage im Hotel
3. Friseur
4. Apotheke

5. Kühlschrank im Zimmer
6. Arzt
7. Disco im Hotel
8. Lebensmittelgeschäft
9. Kino

———————————————— ☐

Zusammenfassung

A. Ein Märchen.   Sie kennen sicherlich eine Version dieses Märchens. Ergänzen Sie die Geschichte, indem Sie jeweils° die richtige Form des bestimmten oder unbestimmten Artikels, des Possessivpronomens oder des Pronomens einsetzen°.

in each instance

fill in

Ein Mädchen will _____ Großmutter besuchen. _____ Mutter packt _____ Korb mit Essen (Eier, Kuchen, Wein, Butter, Wurst) für _____ und schickt _____ auf den Weg. Im Wald trifft das Mädchen _____ Wolf. Er fragt, wohin _____ geht. „Zu Oma", bekommt er zur Antwort.

Bei der Großmutter macht das Mädchen _____ Tür auf, geht ins Schlafzimmer und schaut _____ Großmutter an.

„Großmutter", sagt das Mädchen, „was für große Augen du hast."

„Damit ich _____ besser sehen kann."

„Großmutter, was für große Ohren du hast."

„Damit ich _____ besser hören kann."

„Aber Großmutter, was für _____ großen Mund du hast."

„Damit ich _____ besser fressen kann." _____ Wolf springt aus dem Bett und will das Mädchen fressen. Das Mädchen, es heißt übrigens Rotkäppchen, nimmt _____ Korb und wirft _____ dem Wolf an _____ Kopf. Der Wolf fällt um, und Rotkäppchen bringt _____ hinaus und macht _____ Tür zu.

„Hilfe, Hilfe", hört Rotkäppchen.

„Oma, bist du's? Ich höre _____, aber ich sehe _____ nicht. Wo bist _____ denn?"

„Im Schrank."

Rotkäppchen macht _____ Schrank auf. Sie küßt _____ Großmutter und gibt ihr _____ Korb. Die Großmutter freut sich auf das Essen, macht _____ Korb auf und schreit: „Aber Kindchen, was ist denn passiert? Die Eier sind alle kaputt. Das nächste Mal paß bitte besser auf!"

Die Moral: Einigen Menschen kann man nichts recht machen.

B. Beim Umzug.   Brigitte ist erstaunt, daß Astrid nach einem Monat in der neuen Wohnung schon wieder umziehen will. Natürlich will sie wissen, warum. Übertragen Sie das Gespräch ins Deutsche.

1. BRIGITTE:	Hey, where's your furniture?	
2. ASTRID:	I'm moving.	
3. BRIGITTE:	Why? This apartment is° very practical—only one kilometer from the park.	*liegt*
4. ASTRID:	I know, but I've found an apartment with a° garden. I can't live without a° garden.	Omit in German. Omit in German.
5. BRIGITTE:	How did you find the apartment?	
6. ASTRID:	Through a colleague. I called him and he knew of° something for me.	Omit in German.
7. BRIGITTE:	Not bad. Some people have to look for a long time°.	for a long time = *lange*
8. ASTRID:	By Sunday everything is supposed to be done°. I'm having a party for our friends. We'll celebrate the whole evening. Of course you're invited too.	*fertig*
9. BRIGITTE:	Great! I'll be glad to come.	

C. Partnerarbeit.   Sie planen mit einer Freundin/einem Freund zusammen ein Fest. Sie diskutieren, was Sie für diese Party brauchen und wer (Familienmitglieder, Verwandte, Freunde) was mitbringt.

D. Kurze Aufsätze

1. Sie führen einen Freund, der bei Ihnen zu Besuch ist, in Ihrer Stadt herum. Beschreiben Sie, was Sie sehen, so daß Ihr Freund es interessant findet.

2. Sprechen Sie mit einer Freundin über die Geschenke, die Sie Ihren Familien zum Geburtstag schenken. Was kauft man für wen? Wer mag was? Schreiben Sie dieses Gespräch auf.

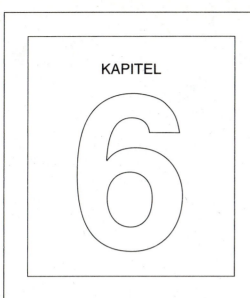

KAPITEL

6

Dative Case ■

1 | Forms of the dative° case

der Dativ

	Masculine	Neuter	Feminine	Plural
Definite article:	dem Mann	dem Kind	der Frau	den Freunden
der-words:	diesem Mann	diesem Kind	dieser Frau	diesen Freunden
Indefinite article:	einem Mann	einem Kind	einer Frau	—
Negative kein:	keinem Mann	keinem Kind	keiner Frau	keinen Freunden
Possessive adjectives:	ihrem Mann	unserem Kind	seiner Frau	meinen Freunden

The chart above shows the dative forms of the definite article, **der**-words, the indefinite article, the negative **kein**, and the possessive adjectives.

2 | Nouns in the dative plural

Nominative:	die Freunde	die Eltern	die Radios
Dative:	den Freunden	den Eltern	den Radios

Nouns in the dative plural add -**n** unless the plural form already ends in -**n** or -**s**.

3 | Masculine *n*-nouns in the dative

Nominative:	der Herr	der Student
Accusative:	den Herrn	den Studenten
Dative:	dem Herrn	dem Studenten

Masculine **n**-nouns add -**n** or -**en** in the dative as well as the accusative case.

A. Geben.   One can give all sorts of things—gifts, answers, even a kiss. Tell what the following people gave and to whom. Use the present perfect tense.

▶ Gerda / ihre Schwester Cornelia / eine interessante Kassette
   Gerda hat ihrer Schwester Cornelia eine interessante Kassette
   gegeben.

1. Karin / der Professor / ihr fertiges Referat
2. Paul / sein Bruder / der Kassettenrecorder
3. Dieter / der Lehrer / eine freche° Antwort   *impudent*
4. ich / die Schülerin / Privatunterricht°   *private lessons*
5. Susanne / ihre Mutter / viele schöne Blumen
6. der Bäcker / der Junge / die frischen Brötchen
7. Jürgen / seine Freundin / ein Kuß
8. der Clown / die Kinder / Ballons
9. der Ober / die Gäste / die Speisekarte°   *menu*

───────────────── □

4 Demonstrative pronouns in the dative

	Singular			Plural
	Masculine	Neuter	Feminine	
Nominative:	der	das	die	die
Accusative:	den	das	die	die
Dative:	dem	dem	der	**denen**

The forms of the demonstrative pronouns are the same as the forms of
the definite article except in the dative plural, which is **denen**.

□ ─────────────

B. Fragen über Fragen.   Mr. Haupt asks his wife a number of
questions about other people. Complete their dialogues with the appropriate demonstrative pronouns in the dative case.

▶ —Hilft Ulrike ihren Eltern?
   —*Nein,* **denen** *hilft sie nie!*

1. —Gehört das Klavier Herrn Herter?
   —Nein, _____ gehört das doch nicht. Der ist doch so
   unmusikalisch. Es gehört seiner neuen Mieterin°.   *tenant*
   —Ach so, _____!
2. —Ist das Frau Reiners Kind? Mit _____ geht sie immer spazieren!
3. —Sagt ihr eurem Chef nicht „Auf Wiedersehen"?
   —Nein, _____ nicht! Aber seiner Sekretärin. Mit _____ verstehen   **sich sehr gut verstehen:**
   wir uns nämlich sehr gut°.   *to get along well*

4. —Fanden deine Brüder das Familienfest langweilig?
   —Ja, aber _____ gefällt es sowieso nie zu Hause.
5. —Geht Monika noch mit ihrem Freund Dieter?
   —Nein, mit _____ geht sie zum Glück° nicht mehr.   **zum Glück:** *fortunately*

———————————————— □

5 | Personal pronouns in the dative

	Singular					Sg. & Pl.	Plural		
Nominative:	ich	du	er	es	sie	Sie	wir	ihr	sie
Accusative:	mich	dich	ihn	es	sie	Sie	uns	euch	sie
Dative:	mir	dir	ihm	ihm	ihr	Ihnen	uns	euch	ihnen

The chart above shows the personal pronouns in the nominative, accusative, and dative cases.

Note the regularity of endings between definite articles and 3rd-person pronouns:

Nominative: der/er, das/es, die/sie

Accusative: den/ihn

Dative: dem/ihm, der/ihr, den/ihnen

6 | The interrogative pronoun *wer* in the dative

Nominative: **Wer** ist das?

Accusative: **Wen** meinen Sie?

Dative: **Wem** geben Sie das Geschenk?

The dative form of the interrogative pronoun **wer** is **wem**.

□ ————————————————

C. Unsinn°.   Gerd has lots of suggestions, all of which sound crazy   *nonsense*
to you. Use personal pronouns as the indirect object in your responses.

▶ Kauf deiner Großmutter ein Fahrrad.
  Unsinn, ich kauf' ihr doch kein Fahrrad.

▶ Schenk deinem Freund deine Bilder.
  Unsinn, ich schenk' ihm doch nicht meine Bilder.

1. Schenk deinen Eltern ein Klavier.
2. Schreib deiner Freundin eine Karte.
3. Kauf mir ein Telefon.
4. Kauf uns ein Auto.
5. Erzähl dem Professor einen Witz°.   *joke*
6. Gib dem Mechaniker deinen Führerschein.
7. Erklär deiner Chefin die Arbeit.
8. Gib mir die Schlüssel.
9. Wünsch dem Polizisten frohe Ostern.

———————————————— □

7 | Uses of the dative case

Indirect object:	Sie schreibt **ihrer Mutter** einen Brief.
Object of certain verbs:	Ich danke **dir**.
Object of prepositions:	Er wohnt bei **seinem Onkel**.
Adjectives with the dative:	Das ist **mir** recht.

8 | Indirect object°   ***das indirekte Objekt***

Sie gibt **ihrem Freund** ein Radio. { *She's giving **her friend** a radio.*
{ *She's giving a radio **to her friend.***

The indirect object (e.g., **Freund**) is usually a person and answers the question *to whom* or *for whom* something is done. In German the indirect object is in the dative case. This distinguishes it from the direct object (e.g., **Radio**), which is always in the accusative case. To determine in English whether a noun or pronoun is an indirect object, add *to* or *for* before it: *She's giving a radio to her friend.* Unlike English, German never uses a preposition to signal the indirect object.

9 | Word order of direct and indirect objects

	Indirect object	Direct object
Inge gibt	ihrem Bruder	ein **Radio.**
Inge gibt	ihm	ein **Radio.**

The form of the direct object determines the order of objects. When the direct object (accusative) is a noun, it usually follows the indirect object (dative).

	Direct object	Indirect object
Inge gibt	**es**	ihrem Bruder.
Inge gibt	**es**	ihm.

When the direct object (accusative) is a personal pronoun, it always precedes the indirect object (dative). Note that a pronoun, whether accusative or dative, always precedes a noun.

☐ ————————————

D. Im Preisausschreiben° gewonnen.   Corinna has won   *contest*
DM 10,000 in a contest. Now she wants to give presents to friends and family. She has written a list of what she wants to give to whom. Indicate the direct and indirect object in each sentence, as in the model.

▶   Ich kaufe meinem Bruder neue Skier.
     indirect object: meinem Bruder
     direct object: neue Skier

1. Ich schenke den Großeltern einen Hund.
2. Der Tante bezahle ich eine Reise nach Italien.
3. Ich kaufe meiner Schwester und mir neue Rucksäcke.
4. Den alten Rucksack gebe ich Andreas.
5. Ich schenke Beatrix Ohrringe.
6. Meinen Freundinnen Cornelia und Edith kaufe ich neue CDs.
7. Meinem Freund Alex schenke ich ein Radio.
8. Eine Bootsfahrt spendiere° ich allen Freunden.   *treat*

E. Ja, das mache ich.   In Exercise C you turned down Gerd's crazy suggestions. This time Gerd has better suggestions, so you agree to follow them. Use a pronoun for the direct object in your answer. In saying these questions, stress the indirect object so that the response is logical.

▶   Schenkst du deinem Neffen diese Briefmarken?
     Ja, ich schenke sie meinem Neffen.

1. Kaufst du deiner Freundin diese Blumen?
2. Schreibst du deinen Eltern diese Karte?
3. Schenkst du deinem Freund dieses Radio?
4. Gibst du mir dein altes Fahrrad?
5. Erzählst du uns die Geschichte?
6. Beschreibst du uns deinen neuen Plan?
7. Schenkst du mir deinen alten Fernsehapparat?
8. Gibst du den Kindern den Kuchen?

———————————— ☐

10 Dative verbs

Ich möchte **Ihrem Freund helfen.**	*I'd like to **help your friend.***
Wir **danken Ihnen** für Ihre Hilfe.	*We **thank you** for your help.*
Die Kassette **gehört mir.**	*The cassette **belongs to me** (is mine).*
Das Bild **gefällt mir.**	*I **like** the picture.*

Most German verbs take objects in the accusative, but a few verbs—often called dative verbs—have objects in the dative. This dative object is usually a person. Some common dative verbs are:

antworten	gefallen	leid tun
befehlen	gehorchen	passen
begegnen	gehören	passieren
danken	gelingen	raten
dienen	glauben	schmecken
fehlen	gratulieren	verzeihen
folgen	helfen	weh tun

For a more complete list, see Appendix A: 17.

Dative		Accusative	
Er glaubt **ihm** nicht.	*He doesn't believe him.*	Er glaubt **es** nicht.	*He doesn't believe it.*
Ich kann **ihm** nicht verzeihen.	*I can't forgive him.*	So **etwas** kann ich nicht verzeihen.	*I can't forgive such a thing.*

Some of the dative verbs can take impersonal objects in the accusative case: **befehlen, danken, glauben, raten, verzeihen.**

□ ————————

F. Eine Reise nach Hamburg.   Angelika is telling about her friends, an American family, who visited Hamburg. Complete her account by using the cued words.

1. Hamburg hat _____ gut gefallen. (die Familie)
2. Die Leute in Hamburg waren so nett und haben _____ immer geholfen. (die Touristen)
3. Das deutsche Essen hat _____ recht gut geschmeckt. (die Amerikaner)
4. Viele tolle Sachen sind _____ dort passiert. (die Gäste)
5. Mitten in Hamburg begegneten sie _____. (ein Kollege aus New York)

6. Das konnte ich _____ kaum glauben. (meine Freunde)
7. Auf der ganzen Reise folgten sie _____ aus einem Reiseführer°.
   (ein Plan)   guidebook
8. Es tat _____ sehr leid, daß sie nicht länger bleiben konnten. (ich)
9. Ich habe _____ geraten, länger zu bleiben. (sie *pl.*)
10. Aber das hat _____ nicht gepaßt. (ihr Sohn Thomas)

G. Auf einem Spaziergang.   Cornelia is telling about what she saw while she was taking a walk. Give the German equivalent of her account. Use the simple past except in the first sentence (present perfect).

1. Yesterday I met° a girl in the park. She had a dog with her.°   Use **Perfekt.** / had with
2. The dog followed her very slowly.   her: Use **mithaben.**
3. She commanded the dog, "Come."
4. But the dog didn't obey her.
5. I asked the girl, "Does the dog belong to you?"
6. She said, "Yes. He has been sick for a week. His leg hurts. I feel so sorry for him."
7. Too bad. I liked the dog.

———————————— □

11   Prepositions with the dative case°

die *Präposition mit dem Dativ*

Preposition	Meaning	Examples
aus	*out of*	Anja kommt gerade **aus** der Bibliothek. *Anja is just coming out of the library.*
	from	Helene kommt **aus** der Schweiz. *Helene comes / is from Switzerland.*
	made of	Der Teller ist **aus** hellem Holz. *The plate is made (out) of light wood.*
außer	*besides, except*	**Außer** deinem Bruder kommt niemand zum Abendessen. *Except for your brother, no one is coming for dinner.*
	out of	Das Schiff ist **außer** Gefahr. *The ship is out of danger.*
bei	*at the home of*	Stefan wohnt nicht mehr **bei** seinen Eltern. *Stefan no longer lives with his parents.*
	near	Wo liegt der Ort? —**Bei** München. *Where is the town? —Near Munich.*
	at	Patrizia arbeitet **bei** der Post. *Patrizia works at the post office.*
	with	Hast du Geld **bei** dir? *Do you have any money with / on you?*

Preposition	Meaning	Examples
gegenüber	*opposite, across from*	Schmidts wohnen uns **gegenüber.** *The Schmidts live across from us.*
mit	*with*	Stefan geht **mit** seinen Eltern Ski laufen. *Stefan is going skiing with his parents.*
	by (vehicle)	Tobias fährt heute **mit** dem Bus. *Tobias is going by bus today.*
nach	*to* (cities and masc. or ntr. countries)	Fliegst du **nach** Österreich? *Are you flying to Austria?*
	after	**Nach** dem Frühstück spielen wir Tennis. *After breakfast we're playing tennis.*
	according to	Meiner Meinung **nach** tust du immer zuviel. *In my opinion you always do too much.*
		Dem Wetterbericht **nach** soll es morgen schön werden. *According to the weather report, it's supposed to be nice tomorrow.*
seit	*since* (time)	**Seit** jenem Abend esse ich keinen Fisch mehr. *Since that evening I no longer eat fish.*
	for (time)	Der junge Mann wartet **seit** einer Stunde im Büro. *The young man has been waiting in the office for an hour.*
von	*from*	Das Geschenk ist **von** meinen Eltern. *The present is from my parents.*
	by	Das Bild ist **von** Paul Klee. *The picture is by Paul Klee.*
	of, about	Die Touristen sprechen **von** ihrer Reise. *The tourists are talking about their trip.*
	of (relationship)	Jürgen ist ein Freund **von** mir. *Jürgen is a friend of mine.*
zu	*to* (buildings, institutions, businesses, persons, residences)	Wir gehen **zu** unseren Nachbarn. *We're going to our neighbors' (house).* Ich gehe **zur** Bank. *I'm going to the bank.*
	at	Bist du heute abend **zu** Hause? *Will you be at home this evening?*
	for	**Zum** Mittagessen gibt es heute Fisch. *There's fish today for lunch.*

The prepositions **aus, außer, bei, gegenüber, mit, nach, seit, von,** and **zu** are always followed by the dative case.

a. *bei*

In addition to the meanings given in the preceding list, **bei** has other uses. For example, it is used in a general way to indicate a situation: **beim Lesen** (*while reading*), **bei der Arbeit** (*at work*), **bei diesem Wetter** (*in weather like this*).

b. *bei* vs. *mit*

One meaning of both **bei** and **mit** is *with*. They are not interchangeable, however. **Bei** means *at the home of*: **Stefan wohnt nicht mehr bei seinen Eltern. Mit** expresses the idea of doing something together: **Stefan geht mit seinen Eltern Ski laufen.**

c. *gegenüber*

Gegenüber always follows a pronoun object: **uns gegenüber** (*across from us*). It generally follows a noun object: **dem Bahnhof gegenüber** (*opposite the train station*). It may also precede the noun object: **gegenüber dem Bahnhof.**

d. *nach*

Note that when **nach** means *according to*, it usually follows the noun: **meiner Meinung nach** (*in my opinion*).

e. *nach* vs. *zu*

One meaning of both **zu** and **nach** is *to*. **Zu** is used to show movement toward people (**zu unseren Nachbarn**) and toward a location (**zur Bank** *[to the bank]*). **Nach** is used with cities and masculine and neuter countries: **nach Österreich** (*to Austria*).

f. *seit*

Seit plus the present tense is used to express an action or condition that started in the past but is still continuing in the present: **Er wartet seit einer Stunde.** (*He has been waiting for an hour.*) Note that English uses the present perfect tense (*has been waiting*) with *since* or *for* to express the same idea.

Compare the use of **seit** as a conjunction (see *Kapitel 4*, Section 9).

12 Contractions of dative prepositions

bei dem → **beim**	Ich sehe Helga immer **beim** Frühstück.
von dem → **vom**	Wir sprechen nicht **vom** Wetter.

zu dem → **zum**   Was gibt's **zum** Mittagessen?

zu der → **zur**   Ich muß schnell noch **zur** Post.

The prepositions **bei, von,** and **zu** often contract with the definite article **dem,** and **zu** also contracts with the definite article **der.**

While contractions are generally optional, they are required

1. in certain common phrases:

beim Wort nehmen   zum Arzt gehen
vom Arzt kommen   zum Bäcker gehen
zum Beispiel   zur Post gehen
zum Geburtstag   zur Schule gehen

2. for infinitives used as nouns:

beim Essen   zum Essen

Contractions are not used when the noun is stressed or modified:

Gehen Sie immer noch **zu dem** Bäcker in der Lenzstraße?

Gehen Sie noch **zu dem** alten Arzt?

☐ ─────────────

H. Ein Paket aus der Schweiz.   Ruth tells about the package she has received from her parents, who are spending two years in Switzerland. Complete the sentences with the German equivalents of the English cues. Some statements require dative prepositions; others require accusative prepositions.

1. Ich kam nach Hause, und da war ein Paket _____. *(for me)*
2. Es war _____. *(from my parents)*
3. Es kam _____. *(from Switzerland)*
4. Meine Eltern wohnen _____ dort. *(for a year)*
5. Zu Weihnachten war ich _____. *(with them)*
6. Wir waren in einer kleinen Stadt im Hotel. Es war _____. *(across from the town hall)*
7. _____ sehe ich sie nicht mehr. *(until next summer)*
8. In dem Paket war eine neue Jacke. _____ habe ich doch schon eine Hose! *(made of this material)*
9. Da paßt die Jacke sehr gut _____. *(to the pants)*
10. _____ war noch eine Menge Schweizer Schokolade drin. *(besides the jacket)*
11. _____ kann ich nicht leben. Ich esse sie so gern! *(without this chocolate)*

I. Das ideale Zimmer.   Gregor praises his room for its perfect location: It is downtown Stuttgart, and everything is within walking distance. Use contractions of the dative prepositions **bei, von,** or **zu.**

1. Ich wohne direkt _____ (der Marktplatz).
2. _____ (der Marktplatz) sind es zu Fuß nur fünf Minuten _____ (die U-Bahn).
3. Wenn ich _____ (der Arzt) oder _____ (die Apotheke) muß, ist es auch nicht weit.
4. Mein Zimmer ist gleich _____ (das Theater), und _____ (das Theater) sind es dann nur ein paar Schritte° _____ (die Oper)   *steps* und _____ (der Park). Also Kultur und Natur sind gleich um die Ecke!
5. _____ (der Park) kommt man dann schnell _____ (die Königsstraße).
6. _____ (das Einkaufen) dort möchte ich gar nicht sprechen – ich habe leider nur wenig Geld.
7. Und das brauche ich _____ (das Wohnen)!

———————————————— ☐

13 Adjectives with the dative case

Paul sieht seinem Bruder sehr **ähnlich.**	*Paul looks very much like his brother.*
Ich bin dir für den guten Rat sehr **dankbar.**	*I'm very grateful to you for the good advice.*
Sei mir nicht **böse.**	*Don't be mad at me.*
Was bin ich Ihnen **schuldig?**	*What do I owe you?*

The dative case is used with many adjectives. Some common ones are:

ähnlich	dankbar	möglich	schuldig
angenehm	fremd	nahe	teuer
bekannt	gleich	nützlich	wert
böse	lieb	recht	willkommen

☐————————————————

J. Eine ehemalige° Freundin.   Two art students, Karin and   *former* Doris, had been renting a studio from their friend Angie. Last week she made them move, so they are angry. Complete the account with the appropriate form of the cued words.

1. Doris und Karin sind _____ sehr böse. (ihre Freundin Angie)
2. Denn es ist _____ nicht möglich, schnell etwas anderes nahe _____ zu finden. (die Studentinnen / die Universität)

3. Doris: „So eine arrogante Person! Das sieht _____ ähnlich! (sie)
4. Sie sollte _____ dankbar sein! (wir)
5. Wir waren _____ nie die Miete schuldig." (sie)
6. Karin: „Ja, wirklich, _____ ist das auch nicht recht. (ich)
7. _____ scheint ihre Freundin nicht viel wert zu sein. (manche Leute)
8. Aber _____ ist es jetzt auch gleich, was aus ihr wird." (ich)

———————————————— □

Zusammenfassung

A. Auf deutsch bitte.   Kims Freund Benno hat neue Pläne, die sie aber etwas komisch findet. Sagen Sie auf deutsch, was Kim Ihnen über Benno erzählt.

1. Since the concert, Benno has wanted to become a musician°.
2. That's just like° him.
3. In my opinion he should first° practice.
4. But he has already talked with his parents.
5. He says they like° this idea.
6. Well°, I don't quite° believe him.
7. For his birthday he got a piano.
8. His grandparents gave it to him.
9. Well, I'm curious.

Musiker
Use **ähnlich sehen.**
erst einmal

Use **gefallen.**
na / not quite = *nicht ganz*

B. Wie schmeckt's?   Laura backt einen Kuchen für ihren Freund Max. Leider sieht der Kuchen nicht so gut aus, obwohl er sonst ganz gut geworden ist. Ergänzen° Sie die Geschichte, indem Sie jeweils das richtige Personalpronomen einsetzen.

complete

▶ Laura sagt: „Na, der ist *mir* ja gar nicht gelungen!"

1. Lauras Schwester hat _____ beim Kuchenbacken geholfen.
2. Sie fragt: „Ist _____ so etwas schon oft passiert?"
3. Laura antwortet _____ traurig: „Nein, noch nie."
4. Da stehen sie beide und schauen den Kuchen an. Das tut _____ jetzt sehr leid.
5. Max hatte sich so auf den Schokoladenkuchen gefreut. Der schmeckt _____ gerade am besten.
6. Später geben sie _____ den Kuchen: „Kannst du _____ verzeihen, Max?"
7. Max antwortet _____ und lacht: „Ach, natürlich! Ich danke _____ trotzdem."
8. „Der Kuchen gefällt _____ ganz gut und schmeckt _____ bestimmt ausgezeichnet!"

C. Ein Sonntagnachmittag.   Petra erzählt ihrem Freund Torsten von ihrem Sonntag zu Hause in Regensburg. Ergänzen Sie die Sätze.

1. PETRA: Am Sonntag war ich _____ meinen Eltern.
   I was at my parents' (home) on Sunday.
   Ich hatte sie _____ zwei Monaten nicht mehr besucht.
   I hadn't visited them for two months.

2. TORSTEN: Bist du _____ dem Zug gefahren?
   Did you go by train?

3. PETRA: Nein, ich bin _____ dem Auto gefahren.
   No, I drove.
   Ich habe mir das Auto _____ Karin geliehen.
   I borrowed the car from Karin.

4. TORSTEN: Wann bist du denn _____ Regensburg gefahren?
   When did you drive to Regensburg?

5. PETRA: Sofort _____ dem Frühstück.
   Right after breakfast.
   Ich wollte _____ Mittagessen dort sein.
   I wanted to be there for lunch.

   TORSTEN: War deine Schwester auch in Regensburg?

6. PETRA: Nein, _____ meinem Bruder war niemand da.
   No, except for my brother there was no one there.
   Meine Schwester kommt erst nächste Woche _____ dem Urlaub zurück.
   My sister isn't coming back from her vacation until next week.

7. TORSTEN: Ich war auch schon lange nicht mehr _____ Hause.
   I haven't been home for a long time either.

8. PETRA: Das ist aber komisch. Deine Eltern wohnen doch dir _____, oder?
   That's strange. Your parents live across from you, don't they?

D. Partnerarbeit.   Sie brauchen Hilfe (im Garten, im Haushalt, bei den Hausaufgaben) und versuchen, Ihre Partnerin/Ihren Partner zu überreden°, Ihnen zu helfen.

persuade

E. Kurze Aufsätze

1. Erzählen Sie von einer Reise, die Sie letzten Sommer gemacht haben.

2. Inwiefern ähneln° Sie jemandem aus Ihrer Familie, oder inwiefern sind Sie anders?

   resemble

3. Was gefällt Ihnen? Was gefällt Ihnen nicht? Beschreiben Sie fünf Dinge oder Beschäftigungen°.

   activities

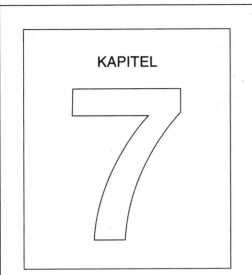

KAPITEL

7

Hin and *her* ■

Two-Way Prepositions ■

Da- and **wo-** **Compounds** ■

1 | *Hin* and *her*

Wohin fährst du?   } *Where are you going?*
Wo fährst du **hin?**   }

Woher kommen Sie?   } *Where do you come from?*
Wo kommen Sie **her?**   }

Komm mal **herunter**!   *Come on down.*

Er ist gestern **hingefallen**.   *He fell down yesterday.*

The adverbs **hin** and **her** are used to show direction. **Hin** indicates motion in a direction away from the speaker, and **her** shows motion toward the speaker. **Hin** and **her** function as separable prefixes and occupy the last position in a sentence. They may also be combined with various parts of speech such as adverbs (e.g., **wohin, woher**), prepositions (e.g., **herunter**), and verbs (e.g., **hinfallen**).

2 | Two-way prepositions°

die Präposition mit Dativ und Akkusativ

Teresa arbeitet **in der Stadt.**   *Teresa works in town.*

Alex fährt **in die Stadt.**   *Alex is going to town.*

German has nine prepositions, called two-way prepositions, that take either the dative or the accusative case. The dative case is used when the verb indicates position (place where), answering the question **wo?** (*where?*). The accusative case is used when the verb indicates a change of location (motion to a place), answering the question **wohin?** (*where to?*).

Accusative: motion to a place (**wohin?**)	Dative: motion in or at a place (**wo?**)
Alex fährt in die Stadt.	Alex fährt in der Stadt herum.
Alex is driving to town.	*Alex is driving around in town.*

Note that a two-way preposition after a verb of motion can take dative as well as accusative. Motion alone does not determine the case. When there is motion *to* a place (**wohin?**), the two-way preposition (e.g., **in**) takes the accusative. When there is motion *in* or *at* a place (**wo?**), the two-way preposition (e.g., **in**) takes dative.

Wo? Dative
Wohin? Acc.

Preposition	Meaning	Examples
an	*on* (vertical surfaces)	Das Bild hängt **an der Wand.** *The picture is hanging on the wall.*
	at (in respect to vertical surfaces or locations)	Sophie steht **an der Tür.** *Sophie is standing at the door.*
	to (vertical surfaces or locations)	Benno geht **an die Tür/an die Kasse/an den Strand.** *Benno is going to the door/to the cashier/to the beach.*
auf	*on (top of)* (horizontal surfaces)	Kurts Buch liegt **auf dem Tisch.** *Kurt's book is lying on the table.* Sabine legt ihr Buch **auf den Tisch.** *Sabine puts her book on the table.*
	at (functions and public buildings)	Ich war **auf einer Party.** *I was at a party.*
	to	Ich gehe **auf eine Party.** *I'm going to a party.* Ich gehe **auf die Post/auf die Bank/auf die Universität/auf die Burg/auf das Rathaus/ aufs Land.** *I'm going to the post office/to the bank/to the university/ to the castle/to the city hall/to the country.*
hinter	*behind*	Silke arbeitet **hinter dem Haus.** *Silke is working behind the house.* Benno geht **hinter das Haus.** *Benno goes behind the house.*
in	*in(side)*	Jürgen arbeitet **in der Küche.** *Jürgen is working in the kitchen.*
	into	Paula geht **in die Küche.** *Paula goes into the kitchen.*
	to (certain locations and countries with feminine or plural articles)	Geht sie **in die Schule/ins Kino/ins Geschäft/ ins Gasthaus?** *Is she going to school/to the movies/to the store/ to an inn?* Wir fahren jeden Sommer in **die Schweiz.** *We go to Switzerland every summer.*
neben	*beside, next to*	**Neben dem Sofa** steht eine Lampe. *Next to the sofa is a lamp.* Jan stellt eine zweite Lampe **neben das Sofa.** *Jan puts a second lamp next to the sofa.*
über	*over, above*	**Über dem Tisch** hängt eine Lampe. *Over the table is a lamp.* Andy hängt eine zweite Lampe **über den Tisch.** *Andy hangs a second lamp over the table.*
	across	Ich gehe **über die Straße.** *I'm going across the street.*

(continued)

Preposition	Meaning	Examples
unter	*under*	Kurts Schuhe stehen **unter dem Bett.** *Kurt's shoes are under the bed.*
		Er stellt sie jeden Abend **unter das Bett.** *He puts them under the bed every night.*
vor	*in front of*	**Vor dem Sofa** steht ein Couchtisch. *In front of the sofa is a coffee table.*
		Lilo stellt einen zweiten **vor das Sofa.** *Lilo puts a second one in front of the sofa.*
zwischen	*between*	**Zwischen den Büchern** liegt ein Stück Papier. *Between the books is a piece of paper.*
		Jens legt ein zweites Stück **zwischen die Bücher.** *Jens puts a second piece between the books.*

Note the general differences in uses of **an, auf,** and **in** to express English *to:*

an = *to* for vertical surfaces and edges
auf = *to* for horizontal surfaces, public buildings, and social events
in = *to* for locations one can enter

3 Contractions of two-way prepositions

Dative	Accusative
an dem → **am**	an das → **ans**
in dem → **im**	in das → **ins**
	auf das → **aufs**

The prepositions **an** and **in** may contract with **das** and **dem; auf** may contract with **das.** Other possible contractions are: **hinterm, hinters, unterm, unters, überm, übers, vorm,** and **vors.**

While contractions are generally optional, they are required

1. in idiomatic phrases such as:

   am Leben sein
   ans Telefon gehen
   aufs Land fahren
   im Kino/Theater sein
   ins Kino/Theater gehen

2. for days of the week, times of day, dates, months, and seasons:

am Mittwoch
am Morgen
am 5. Juli
im Juli
im Sommer

☐ ─────────────

A. Wo sind meine Sachen?　Mr. Stark, who is rather absent-minded, is ready to leave for work and asks his wife a lot of questions. Play her part and answer him, using the cues in parentheses.

▶　Wo sind meine Schuhe? (unter / Bett)
　　Unter dem Bett.

▶　Wohin hab' ich meine Handschuhe gesteckt? (in / Mantel)
　　In den Mantel.

1. Wo hab' ich meine Brille? (auf / Nase)
2. Wohin hast du meinen Mantel gehängt? (über / Stuhl)
3. Wo ist nun mein Portemonnaie? (unter / Brief)
4. Wo ist mein Hut? (in / Schrank)
5. Wo ist meine Tasche? (neben / Schreibtisch)
6. Wohin habe ich meine Schlüssel getan? (in / Tasche)
7. Wo hab' ich mein Auto geparkt? (hinter / Haus)
8. Wohin gehen wir heute Abend? (in / Kino)
9. Wann waren wir das letzte Mal im Kino? (in / Winter)
10. An welchem Tag sind die Kinokarten billiger? (an / Mittwoch)
11. Wo treffe ich dich? (vor / Kino)
12. Wohin gehen wir nach dem Film? (in / Gasthaus)
13. Wo ist das Gasthaus? (an / Marktplatz)
14. Wo kann man da parken? (in Parkhaus)

───────────── ☐

4 | The verbs *legen/liegen, setzen/sitzen, stellen/stehen, hängen, stecken*

Accusative	Dative
Erika **legt** das Buch **auf den Tisch.**	Es **liegt** jetzt **auf dem Tisch.**
Marta **setzt** das Kind **auf den Stuhl.**	Es **sitzt** jetzt **auf dem Stuhl.**
Paul **stellt** die Lampe **in die Ecke.**	Sie **steht** jetzt **in der Ecke.**
Dieter **hängt** die Uhr **an die Wand.**	Sie **hängt** jetzt **an der Wand.**
Monika **steckt** das Geld **in die Tasche.**	Ihr Geld **steckt in der Tasche.**

In English the all-purpose verb for moving something to a position is *to put: Erika puts the book on the table.* The all-purpose verb for the resulting position is *to be: It is on the table.* German uses several verbs to express the meanings *put* and *be.*

To express *put,* German uses:

legen (legte, gelegt)	*to lay*
stellen (stellte, gestellt)	*to stand upright*
setzen (setzte, gesetzt)	*to set*
hängen (hängte, gehängt)	*to hang*
stecken (steckte, gesteckt)	*to stick*

wohin?

These verbs all take direct objects and are weak. With these verbs the case after the two-way preposition is accusative: **Erika legt das Buch auf den Tisch.**

To express *be* as an indicator of position, German uses:

liegen (lag, gelegen)	*to be lying*
stehen (stand, gestanden)	*to be standing*
sitzen (saß, gesessen)	*to be sitting*
hängen (hing, gehangen)	*to be hanging*
stecken (steckte, gesteckt)	*to be inserted*

wo?

These verbs do not take direct objects and, except for **stecken,** are strong. With these verbs the case after the two-way preposition is dative: **Es liegt *auf dem Tisch.***

☐ ————————————

B. Ende gut, alles gut.   Bernd's room is in chaos. Tell how he straightens it up. Make complete sentences using the cues given.

1. die Bücher / liegen / auf / der Boden
2. er / stellen / sie / in / das Regal°   bookcase
3. die Lampe / stehen / auf / der Fernseher
4. er / stellen / sie / auf / der Tisch
5. die Hosen / liegen / auf / das Bett
6. er / hängen / sie / in / der Schrank
7. seine neuen Poster / hängen / hinter / die Tür
8. er / hängen / sie / an / die Wand
9. seine Papiere / liegen / unter / das Bett
10. er / legen / sie / auf / der Schreibtisch
11. seine kleine süße Katze / sitzen / auf / der Schrank
12. er / setzen / sie / auf / das Sofa
13. später / sitzen / er / dann auch / auf / das Sofa
14. er / legen / die Füße / auf / der Couchtisch / und betrachtet froh sein Werk

C. Noch einmal.   Retell the story using the simple past tense.

——————————— □

5   Special meanings of two-way prepositions

a. an

Pia **schreibt an** ihren Freund Tim.	*Pia is writing to her friend Tim.*
Sie **denkt** oft **an** ihn.	*She often thinks of him.*
Tim **studiert an der Universität.**	*Tim is studying at the university.*
Pia **geht** jetzt **an die Arbeit.**	*Pia is starting her work now.*
Wann **bist** du **an der Reihe?**	*When is it your turn?*

b. auf

Jürgen **antwortet** nicht **auf** meine Frage.	*Jürgen is not answering my question.*
Dieter **geht** jetzt nicht mehr **auf die Universität.**	*Dieter doesn't go to college anymore.*
Er **wohnt auf dem Land.**	*He lives in the country.*
Wir **fahren** morgen **aufs Land.**	*We're going to the country tomorrow.*
Warten Sie **auf** den Bus?	*Are you waiting for the bus?*
Sie **sagte** es **auf deutsch.**	*She said it in German.*

c. in

Gehst du heute **ins Theater?**	*Are you going to the theater today?*
Sonntags **fahren** wir gern **ins Grüne.**	*Sundays we like to drive out into nature.*
Morgen fahren wir **in die Schweiz.**	*Tomorrow we're going to Switzerland.*

d. über

Die Fahrkarte kostet **über 100 Mark.**	*The ticket costs over 100 marks.*
Lachst du **über** den Preis?	*Are you laughing about the price?*

e. unter

Was ich jetzt sage, bleibt **unter uns.**	*What I'm about to say must remain between us.*
Die Jacke bekommst du nicht **unter 200 Mark.**	*You won't get the jacket for less than 200 marks.*

f. *vor*

Das Kind **hat Angst vor** dem Hund.   *The child is afraid of the dog.*

In addition to their basic meanings, the two-way prepositions have special meanings when combined with specific verbs (e.g., **warten auf**) or in specific verb-noun combinations (e.g., **an der Reihe sein, an die Reihe kommen**). Since there is no way to predict the meaning and case, these expressions must be learned.

When **über** means *about, concerning,* it is always followed by the accusative case.

For additional verbs that combine with prepositions and have special meanings, see *Kapitel 10*, Section 8 and Appendix A: 15.

□ ————————

D. Peters alte Freundin.   Tell about Peter's former girlfriend by completing the sentences with an appropriate preposition.

1. Peter hat Nicole _an_ der Universität Heidelberg kennengelernt.
2. Peter geht nicht mehr _auf_ die Universität.
3. Er wohnt jetzt _auf_ dem Land.
4. Nicole ist _in_ die Schweiz gegangen und studiert in Genf°   *Geneva*
   _an_ der Uni.
5. Peter denkt noch oft _an_ seine Freundin.
6. Manchmal schreibt er noch _an_ sie.
7. Nicole ist Französin, und Peter schreibt ihr _auf_ französisch.
8. Aber sie antwortet nicht mehr _auf_ seine Briefe.
9. Er wartet nicht mehr _auf_ sie.
10. Manchmal muß er schon _über_ seinen Liebeskummer° lachen.   *lover's grief*

———————— □

6 │ Time expressions with the dative case

am Tag	*during the day*
am Montag, Dienstag usw.	*on Monday, Tuesday, etc.*
am Abend	*in the evening*
in der Nacht	*at night*
in einer Woche	*in a week*
im Januar, Februar usw.	*in January, February, etc.*
vor einer Woche	*a week ago*
vor dem Essen	*before dinner*

When used in expressions of time, the prepositions **an, in,** and **vor** are followed by the dative case.

☐ ——————————

E. Ingrid ist im Streß.   Ralf asks Ingrid whether she has time to go skiing with him. But she has no time, she is too busy. Complete their conversation using the cues in parentheses. Supply the missing prepositions and articles, or the contracted forms of the prepositions, as appropriate.

1. RALF: Sollen wir _____ (das Wochenende) Ski fahren gehen?
2. INGRID: Nein, ich habe leider zu viel zu tun. _____ (der Samstag) muß ich meine Hausarbeit für Professor Weber schreiben, und _____ (der Sonntag) muß ich für den Test in Geschichte lernen. _____ (der Abend) ist dann auch noch Katjas Geburtstagsparty.
3. RALF: Ach, ich wußte gar nicht, daß Katja _____ (der Dezember) Geburtstag hat. Wie wäre es dann mit dem Skifahren _____ (eine Woche)?
4. INGRID: Es tut mir leid, aber das ist auch unmöglich. Ich glaube, _____ (die Weihnachtsferien) können wir nicht mehr Ski fahren gehen. Bis dahin habe ich einen solchen Streß: _____ (der Tag) muß ich ins Seminar gehen, und _____ (der Abend) schreibe ich dann meine Hausarbeiten. Doch gleich nach den Ferien _____ (der Januar) komme ich gerne mit. Später _____ (der Winter) ist der Schnee sowieso besser.
5. RALF: Das ist ja dann erst _____ (ein Monat)! Aber du hast recht. _____ (eine Woche) hat es _____ (die Nacht) nur ein bißchen geschneit. _____ (das neue° Jahr) haben wir dann hoffentlich mehr Schnee.

In the dative, the adjective **neue** becomes **neuen.**

—————————— ☐

7 Da- compounds°

das da-*Kompositum*

Spricht er oft **von seinem Chef?**   Ja, er spricht oft **von ihm.**
Spricht er oft **von seiner Arbeit?** Ja, er spricht oft **davon.**
Freut er sich **auf die Ferien?**   Ja, er freut sich **darauf.**

In German, pronouns used after prepositions normally refer only to persons (e.g., **von ihm**). To refer to things and ideas, a **da-** compound consisting of **da** plus a preposition is generally used (e.g., **davon**). Da- expands to **dar-** when the preposition begins with a vowel: **darauf, darin, darüber.**

□ ————————————————

F. Die Arbeit im Reisebüro. Evelyn is curious about Steffi's work in the travel agency. Take Steffi's part and confirm Evelyn's assumptions. Use a **da-** compound or a preposition plus a pronoun, as appropriate.

▶ Bist du mit deiner Stelle zufrieden?
Ja, ich bin damit zufrieden.

▶ Bist du mit deiner Chefin auch zufrieden?
Ja, ich bin mit ihr auch zufrieden.

1. Mußt du viel über fremde Länder wissen?
2. Arbeitest du jeden Tag mit dem Computer?
3. Arbeitest du gern mit deinen Kollegen?
4. Interessieren sich deine Kollegen für dein Privatleben?
5. Sprichst du oft über deine Freunde?
6. Erzählst du viel von deinem Privatleben?
7. Möchtest du viel von deinen Kollegen wissen?
8. Arbeitest du gern für deine Chefin?

———————————————— □

8   Wo- compounds°

das wo-Kompositum

Von wem spricht sie?   Sie spricht **von ihrem Chef.**

Wovon spricht sie?   Sie spricht **von ihrer Arbeit.**

Worauf freut sie sich?   Sie freut sich **auf die Ferien.**

The interrogative pronouns **wen** (see *Kapitel 5,* Section 11) and **wem** (see *Kapitel 6,* Section 6) are used with a preposition to refer only to persons (e.g., **von wem**). The interrogative pronoun **was** (see *Kapitel 5,* Section 11) refers to things and ideas. As an object of a preposition, **was** and the preposition are generally replaced by a **wo-** compound consisting of **wo** plus the preposition (e.g., **wovon**). **Wo-** expands to **wor-** when the preposition begins with a vowel: **worauf, worin, worüber.**

□ ————————————————

G. Wie bitte? Susanne is talking to her grandfather about her boyfriend. Her grandfather is somewhat hard of hearing and never seems to get the end of the sentence. Take his part and ask Susanne to repeat what she said. Use a **wo-** compound or a preposition plus a pronoun, as appropriate.

▶ Ich interessiere mich nicht mehr für Heiner.
Für wen interessierst du dich nicht mehr?

1. Heute mußte ich eine halbe Stunde auf ihn warten.
2. Ich glaube, er denkt nicht mehr an mich.
3. Er interessiert sich nicht für meine Arbeit.
4. Er denkt nur noch an China.
5. Er schreibt über chinesische Literatur.
6. Ich glaube, er hat auch Angst vor den Prüfungen am Semesterende.
7. Er interessiert sich überhaupt nicht mehr für Spaß, Musik und Tanzen.
8. Ich bin mit Heiner nicht mehr zufrieden.

────────────── □

Zusammenfassung

A. Brigitte ist krank.   Brigitte ist seit zwei Wochen krank, und allmählich fällt ihr die Decke auf den Kopf°. Erzählen Sie auf deutsch, wie es ihr geht.

allmählich...Kopf: she's beginning to get cabin fever

1. Brigitte is standing at the window.
2. She is looking into the garden.
3. She has to stay in the house because she is ill.
4. Most of the time she has to stay° in bed.
5. Her friends come with flowers and put them beside her bed.
6. Brigitte is happy about this.
7. But she doesn't want to sit at home any more.
8. The doctor said that in a week she can get up again.
9. Then she's going to the country.
10. She wants to hike in the mountains.

liegen

B. Aufräumen°.   Familie Harms möchte ihr Haus verkaufen. In einer halben Stunde kommen Leute, die sich für das Haus interessieren. Vorher müssen die Harms aber noch aufräumen. Ergänzen Sie die Sätze mit **hängen, legen/liegen, setzen/sitzen, stecken, stellen/ stehen** und den Wörtern in Klammern.

to clear away

1. Herr Harms _hängt_ die Mäntel in _den_. (der Schrank)
2. Die Bücher _____ auf _dem_. (der Boden)
   Jürgen _____ sie in _das_. (das Regal)
3. Alexandra _____ die Blumenvase hinter _den_. (der Vorhang)
4. Das Fahrrad _steht_ in _dem_. (der Garten)
   Frau Harms _stellt_ es neben _das_. (das Tor)

5. Die Fotos _liegen_ unter _____. (der Schreibtisch)
   Alexandra _____ sie an _die_. (die Wand)
6. Die Katze _sitzt_ auf _dem_. (der Schrank)
   Alexandra _setzt_ sie vor _die_. (die Tür)
7. Jürgen _hängt_ den Spiegel über _das_. (das Waschbecken°)   *sink*
   Da _hängt_ er jetzt unter _der_. (die Lampe)
8. Herr Harms _stellt_ seinen Schreibtisch zwischen _das_ und
   dem. (das Bücherregal / der Sessel)
9. Ein Taschentuch _liegt_ auf _dem_. (der Küchentisch)
   Jürgen _steckt_ es schnell in _seinen_. (sein Rucksack)

C. Ein Psychologie-Test.   In einer Zeitschrift lesen Sie den Psychologie-Test „Sind Sie ein zufriedener Mensch?" Setzen Sie die fehlenden *wo*-Komposita ein. (Siehe Appendix A: 15 [verbs and prepositions] und Appendix A: 16 [nouns and prepositions].)

1. _____ lachen Sie gern?
2. _____ leiden Sie am meisten?
3. _____ freuen Sie sich dieses Jahr?
4. _____ interessieren Sie sich besonders?
5. _____ denken Sie, wenn Sie das Wort „Zukunft" hören?
6. _____ geben Sie das meiste Geld aus?
7. _____ beginnen Sie den Tag?
8. _____ träumen Sie?
9. _____ haben Sie nie Lust°?

Lust haben zu: *have desire for*

D. Wieder zurück.   Christine war zwei Semester als Austauschstudentin in den USA. Jetzt ist sie wieder in Deutschland, doch sie vermißt San Francisco und ihre Freunde dort sehr. Setzen Sie die fehlenden Präpositionen ein.

Christine hat ein Jahr _____ der Uni in San Francisco studiert, doch jetzt geht sie wieder _____ die Uni in Freiburg. Sie denkt oft _____ das Jahr in Kalifornien und vermißt das Land und ihre Freunde sehr. Dann schreibt sie schnell _____ ihre Freunde dort und wartet _____ ihre Antwort. Meistens schreibt sie _____ englisch, aber mit ihrem Freund Jonathan korrespondiert sie _____ deutsch, weil er sein Deutsch verbessern möchte. Er wird nämlich nächstes Jahr _____ der Uni Heidelberg studieren. Christine möchte bald wieder nach San Francisco zurück. Doch die Flüge kosten _____ 1.000 Mark. Ein bißchen hat sie auch Angst _____ dem Flug, weil der fast 13 Stunden dauert. Doch sie wird sicher fliegen, wenn die Flugpreise wieder _____ 1.000 Mark liegern. Und wenn sie dann in San Franzisko auf dem Flughafen steht, lacht sie bestimmt auch _____ ihre Flugangst.

E. Partnerarbeit.   Planen Sie mit Ihrer Partnerin/Ihrem Partner eine Reise. Besprechen Sie Ihr Reiseziel, die Kosten für die Reise, die Einkaufsmöglichkeiten dort und das, was Sie dort machen wollen (und warum).

F. Kurze Aufsätze

1. Beschreiben Sie, wie Ihr Zimmer jetzt eingerichtet° ist und wie Sie   *furnished* es gern anders einrichten würden. Sagen Sie auch, warum.

2. Beantworten Sie eine der folgenden Fragen in wenigen Sätzen:

   • Wovor haben Sie Angst?

   • Woran denken Sie oft?

   • Worüber lachen Sie gern?

Begründen° Sie Ihre Äußerungen°.   *support / statements*

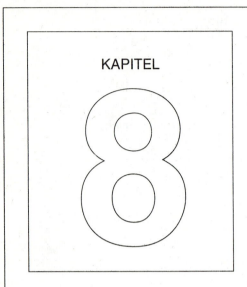

KAPITEL

8

Genitive Case ■

1 Forms of the genitive° case

der Genitiv

	Masculine	Neuter	Feminine	Plural
Definite article:	des Mann**es**	des Kind**es**	de**r** Frau	de**r** Freunde
der-words:	dies**es** Mann**es**	dies**es** Kind**es**	dies**er** Frau	dies**er** Freunde
Indefinite article:	ein**es** Mann**es**	ein**es** Kind**es**	ein**er** Frau	—
kein:	kein**es** Mann**es**	kein**es** Kind**es**	kein**er** Frau	kein**er** Freunde
ein-words:	ihr**es** Mann**es**	unser**es** Kind**es**	sein**er** Frau	mein**er** Freunde

The chart above shows the genitive forms of the definite article, **der**-words, indefinite article, **kein,** and **ein**-words. The masculine and neuter forms end in **-[e]s** in the genitive, and feminine and plural forms end in **-[e]r.**

2 Nouns in the genitive

	Masculine		Neuter			
	1 syllable	2 or more syllables	1 syllable	2 or more syllables	Feminine	Plural
Nominative:	der Mann	der Vater	das Kind	das Mädchen	die Frau	die Kinder
Genitive:	des Mann**es**	des Vater**s**	des Kind**es**	des Mädchen**s**	der Frau	der Kinder

Masculine and neuter nouns of one syllable generally add **-es** in the genitive; masculine and neuter nouns of two or more syllables add **-s.** Feminine and plural nouns do not add a genitive ending.

3 Masculine *n*-nouns in the genitive

Nominative:	der Herr	der Student
Accusative:	den Herr**n**	den Student**en**
Dative:	dem Herr**n**	dem Student**en**
Genitive:	**des Herrn**	**des Studenten**

Masculine **n**-nouns that add **-n** or **-en** in the accusative and dative singular also add **-n** or **-en** in the genitive. Some masculine **n**-nouns ending in **-e** add **-ns** in the genitive: e.g., **der Name** → **des Namens, der Gedanke** → **des Gedankens, der Glaube** → **des Glaubens.** (See Appendix A: 9 for a list of common masculine **n**-nouns.)

4 | Proper names in the genitive

Das ist **Ingrids** Buch.

Hans' Pullover gefällt mir.

Franz' Pullover gefällt mir nicht.

Vaters Krawatte ist interessant.

Mutters neue Jacke gefällt mir auch sehr gut.

The genitive of proper names is formed by adding **-s.** In writing, if the name already ends in an s-sound **(-s, -ß, -z, -tz),** no **-s** is added and an apostrophe is used instead.

☐ ─────────

A. Aber nein!   Answer the following questions in the negative, using the cues in parentheses.

▶   Ist das die Wohnung deiner Tochter? (mein Sohn)
     Nein, das ist die Wohnung meines Sohnes.

  1. Ist das die Telefonnummer deines Arztes? (das Krankenhaus)
  2. Hast du das Haus deines Onkels gekauft? (meine Großeltern)
  3. Schreibst du über die Geschichte eurer Familie? (diese Stadt)
  4. Ist das der Titel des Buches? (der Film)
  5. Ist das ein Bild deiner Freundin? (ihre Schwester)
  6. Ist das das Auto deines Vaters? (unser Nachbar)
  7. Ist das das Geschäft deiner Cousine? (ein Kollege)
  8. Hast du die Adresse deines Professors? (seine Sekretärin)
  9. Ist das der CD-Spieler deines Bruders? (Cornelia)
 10. Sind das die CDs deiner Schwester? (Hans)

───────── ☐

5 | The interrogative pronoun *wer* in the genitive

Wessen Buch ist das?   *Whose book is that?*

Wessen Jacke trägst du?   *Whose jacket are you wearing?*

Wessen is the genitive form of the interrogative **wer;** it is equivalent to *whose.*

□ ——————————————

B. Fragen über Gabi.   You and a friend are in Gabi's apartment. Your friend asks all kinds of questions about Gabi. Reply, but remain noncommittal.

▶   Sind das Gabis Bücher?
     Vielleicht. Ich weiß nicht, wessen Bücher das sind.

  1. Sind das Gabis Fotos?
  2. Ist das die Telefonnummer ihres neuen Freundes?
  3. Benutzt sie die Schreibmaschine ihrer Sekretärin?
  4. Fährt sie mit dem Fahrrad ihres Freundes?
  5. Liegt Gabis Bericht auf dem Schreibtisch?
  6. Ist das die Stereoanlage ihrer Schwester?

——————————————— □

6   Uses of the genitive case

Possession and other relationships:	Das Haus **meines Freundes** ist 100 Jahre alt. Der Titel **des Buches** ist viel zu lang.
Object of prepositions:	**Trotz des Wetters** gehen wir schwimmen.
Indefinite time expressions:	**Eines Tages** ist etwas Komisches passiert.

The genitive case is used to show possession and other close relationships. It is also used for objects of certain prepositions and for expressions of indefinite time.

7   Possession and other close relationships

der Koffer **der Frau**	the **woman's** suitcase
die Farbe **des Koffers**	the color **of the suitcase**

English shows possession or other close relationships by adding *'s* to a noun or by using a phrase with *of.* English generally uses the *'s*-form only for persons; for things and ideas, English uses an *of* construction. German uses the genitive case to show possession or other close relationships. The genitive is used for things and ideas as well as for persons. The genitive expression generally *follows* the noun it modifies.

Lauras Koffer   *Laura's suitcase*
Tobias' Freund   *Tobias's friend*

Proper names in the genitive generally *precede* the nouns they modify.

Katharina ist **die Freundin meines Bruders.**
*Katharina is **my brother's girlfriend.***

Possessive adjectives take the case of the noun they modify. Even though a possessive adjective already shows possession (**mein** = *my*), it must itself be in the genitive case when the noun it goes with is in the genitive (**meines Bruders** = *my brother's* or *of my brother*).

8 | Prepositions with the genitive case

Preposition	Meaning	Example
(an)statt	*instead of*	Kaufst du einen Stuhl **statt eines Tisches?**
trotz	*in spite of*	Kommst du **trotz des Wetters?**
während	*during*	**Während des Essens** sprach er kein Wort.
wegen	*on account of*	**Wegen der vielen Arbeit** blieb sie zu Hause.

The prepositions **(an)statt, trotz, während,** and **wegen** are the most commonly used prepositions that are followed by the genitive case. **Statt** is the shortened form of **anstatt**.

Special forms of the possessive pronouns (see *Kapitel 15*, Section 7) combine with **wegen: meinetwegen, deinetwegen, seinetwegen, unsertwegen/unsretwegen, euertwegen/euretwegen, ihretwegen, Ihretwegen.** Two examples of their uses are:

for my sake, because of me
Er macht das nur **meinetwegen.**   *He's doing that only for my sake.*

as far as I'm concerned
Meinetwegen kannst du es haben.   *As far as I'm concerned, you can have it.*

Some other genitive prepositions you should recognize are:

außerhalb	*outside of*	**unterhalb**	*under*
innerhalb	*inside of*	**diesseits**	*on this side of*
oberhalb	*above*	**jenseits**	*on that side of*

☐ ————————————

C. Der geschwollene Fuß.   Thomas wants to know all about your swollen foot. Answer using the cues in parentheses.

▶   Wann warst du in Österreich? (während / die Ferien)
Während der Ferien.

1. Fahrt ihr im April wieder in die Berge? (ja, trotz / das Wetter)
2. Warum kannst du nicht so schnell gehen? (wegen / mein Fuß)
3. Tut dein Fuß weh? (ja, trotz / die Wanderschuhe)
4. Wann bist du gestürzt°? (während / unsere Alpenwanderung)   *fall*
5. Warum bist du gestürzt? (wegen / die Steine auf dem Weg)
6. Wann ist dein Fuß angeschwollen? (während / diese Woche)
7. Ist dein Bruder mit dir gewandert? (ja, statt / mein Vetter)

D. Das Haus in Italien.   Tell about your stay in Italy. Complete the sentences using the German equivalent of the English cues.

1. Wo warst du _____ ? *(during the vacation)*
2. In Italien. Im Haus _____. *(of my friends)*
3. Das Haus steht am Ufer _____, und man kann weit sehen. *(of a river)*
4. _____ hat es einen großen Hof. *(instead of a garden)*
5. _____ ist es schön kühl dort _____, der da steht. *(during the summer / because of a tree)*
6. Die Fenster _____ sind klein, damit es _____ schön kühl bleibt im Haus. *(of the house / in spite of the sun)*
7. Alle Häuser _____ sind so gebaut. *(of this region)*
8. Die Farbe _____ ist meistens gelb. *(of the houses)*
9. Das sieht sehr schön aus zum Grün _____ . Ich bin sehr gern dort. *(of the trees)*

———————————— ☐

9 | Expressions of indefinite time

Eines Tages (Abends, Nachts) hatte Carmen eine Idee.
One day (evening, night) Carmen had an idea.

Letzten Endes können wir nichts dagegen machen.
In the final analysis, we can't do anything about it.

Note that, analogous to **eines Tages** and **eines Abends,** the phrase **eines Nachts** is used even though **Nacht** is feminine. Remember that definite time is expressed by the accusative: **Gehst du *jeden Tag* spazieren?** (See *Kapitel 5*, Section 16.)

10 Special expressions

The genitive is also used in a number of idiomatic expressions.

Ich fahre immer **erster Klasse.**	*I always go **first class.***
Einmal **zweiter Klasse** München.	*One **second-class** ticket to Munich.*
Er ist **guter Laune.**	*He's **in a good mood.***
Sie war **voller Freude.**	*She was **full of happiness.***
Sie verließ **schweren Herzens** ihre Familie.	*She left her family **with a heavy heart.***
Ich bin **ganz deiner Meinung.**	*I agree totally. (I am **of your opinion.**)*
Ich bin **anderer Meinung.**	*I am **of another opinion.***
Ich bin **anderer Ansicht.**	*I **don't agree with you.** (I **have a different view** of the matter).*
Er hat **meines Erachtens** den falschen Beruf.	***In my opinion,** he's in the wrong profession.*
Meines Wissens beginnt der Film um acht.	***As far as I know,** the film starts at eight.*

11 Dative as substitute for the genitive

a. possession

Genitive	Dative
die Freundin **meines Bruders**	die Freundin **von meinem Bruder**
zwei **ihrer Freunde**	zwei von **ihren Freunden**
Thomas' Freund	ein Freund **von Thomas**

In spoken German the genitive of possession is frequently replaced by **von** + dative.

die Ideen **von Studenten**

die Mutter **von vier Jungen**

Von + dative is normally used if the noun of possession is not preceded by a word that shows genitive case (i.e., definite article, **der**-word, etc.).

ein Freund **von mir**

ein Freund **von Nicole**

Von + dative is also used in phrases similar to the English *of mine, of yours,* etc.

b. prepositions

Genitive	Dative
wegen **des Wetters**	wegen **dem Wetter**
trotz **des Regens**	trotz **dem Regen**

In colloquial language many people use the prepositions **statt, trotz, wegen,** and sometimes **während** with the dative.

trotz **ihm**

wegen **dir**

In colloquial language, dative pronouns are frequently used with these prepositions: **statt ihr, trotz ihm, wegen mir** (compare **meinetwegen,** Section 8).

□ —————————

E. Anruf aus Amerika.   Gisela tells about a phone call from her American friend. Complete the sentences using the German equivalents of the English cues. Remember that time expressions may be in the accusative, dative, or genitive, depending on the meaning.

1. _____ klingelte° mein Telefon. Es war mein Freund aus Amerika.   *rang*
   (one night)
2. Er vergißt _____ , daß es hier sechs Stunden später ist. *(every time)*
3. Aber ich erinnere mich immer daran und rufe ihn nie _____ an. *(in the morning)*
4. Am Telefon erzählte ich ihm, daß ich _____ nach Amerika fliege. *(next month)*
5. _____ war ich schon einmal dort. *(many years ago)*
6. _____ beschloß ich einfach, eine große Reise zu machen. *(one day)*
7. _____ lernte ich viele Menschen kennen. *(in a week)*
8. _____ erlebte° ich etwas Neues. *(every day)*   *experienced*
9. Ich blieb insgesamt°_____ . *(two months)*   *all together*

F. Regen am Wochenende.   Tell about your rainy weekend—
in German, naturally.

1. On the weekend a girlfriend of mine came to see me°. (present perfect)
2. She always travels first-class.
3. I prefer to travel second-class.
4. In spite of the rain, we went for many walks°. (present perfect)
5. She put on° my sister's raincoat. (present perfect)
6. Many people find rain boring, but I am of a different opinion.
7. Because of the rain, only a few people were outside.
8. In the evening two of my friends came over° and we cooked together. (present perfect)

Use **zu Besuch kommen.**

Use **viel spazieren- gehen.**
put on: Use **anziehen.**

came over: Use **kommen.**

———————————— ☐

Zusammenfassung

A. Uwes Wochenende.   Martina fragt Uwe, was er am Wochenende gemacht hat. Beantworten Sie die Fragen mit den Wörtern in Klammern. Benutzen Sie den Genitiv.

1. Warum bist du denn nicht schwimmen gegangen? (wegen / das Wetter)
2. Wer hat dich am Samstag angerufen? (ein Freund / mein Bruder)
3. Ist er bei dir vorbeigekommen? (ja, während / das Essen)
4. Wen hast du am Sonntag besucht? (Ingrid / Schwester)
5. Wo wohnt sie? (außerhalb / die Stadt)
6. Habt ihr einen Spaziergang gemacht? (ja, statt / eine Wanderung)
7. Wo seid ihr spazierengegangen? (oberhalb / ein See)
8. Wo liegt dieser See? (innerhalb / der Stadtpark)
9. Wessen Idee war das? (das war / Ingrid / Idee)
10. War es schön? (ja, trotz / der Regen)

B. Sonja geht nach Stuttgart.   Kathrin und Ursula sprechen über Sonja, ihre Freundin. Sonja hat in Stuttgart einen Job gefunden und muß jetzt umziehen. Setzen Sie die passenden Ausdrücke a. bis i. in die Sätze ein.

a. ganz deiner Meinung
b. anderer Meinung
c. schweren Herzens
d. meines Erachtens
e. voller Freude

f. guter Laune
g. erster Klasse
h. meines Wissens
i. zweiter Klasse

1. —Sonja will nicht nach Stuttgart. Sie geht _____ von Hamburg weg.

2. —Komisch, sie ist doch sonst so eine Optimistin. Sie ist immer _____.

3. —Da bin ich _____. Ich kenne keine positivere Person als Sonja.

4. —Wir sollten jetzt zum Bahnhof gehen, um ihr auf Wiedersehen zu sagen. _____ fährt ihr Zug um 14 Uhr ab.

5. —Sie wollte eigentlich fliegen, aber die Flugpreise sind zu hoch, vor allem wenn man _____ fliegt.

6. —Sonja lebt aber im allgemeinen sehr sparsam°. Wenn sie mit dem Zug fährt, fährt sie immer _____. *frugally*

7. —Sie war _____, als sie den Job in Stuttgart bekam. Doch jetzt ist sie ein bißchen skeptisch.

8. —Stuttgart ist natürlich nicht so interessant wie Hamburg. _____ ist Hamburg sowieso die schönste Stadt in Deutschland.

9. —Findest du? Da bin ich aber _____ . Es regnet hier doch so oft.

C. Ein Tag in New York.   Sigrid und Ralf sind auf einer USA-Reise und verbringen ein paar Tage in New York. Setzen Sie die Wörter in Klammern in den Akkusativ, Dativ oder Genitiv. Gebrauchen Sie präpositionale Zusammenziehungen° (z.B. **zum, ins**), wenn sie passen. *contractions*

1. Während _____ (ihre USA-Reise) fahren Sigrid und Ralf auch nach New York.

2. Sie wohnen dort in _____ (ein Hotel) bei _____ (das Guggenheimmuseum).

3. Das Hotel liegt direkt an _____ (der Park).

4. Trotz _____ (die Hitze°) machen die beiden eine große Tour: Sie gehen _____ (der Park) entlang zu _____ (das Museum of Modern Art) und treffen sich dort mit _____ (ein Freund) zu _____ (das Kaffeetrinken). *heat*

5. Sigrid möchte die Warhol-Bilder sehen, aber wegen _____ (die Schlange°) an _____ (die Kasse) geht sie doch nicht in _____ (das Museum). *line, queue*

6. Doch wenigstens kauft sie in _____ (der Laden) neben _____ (das Museum) ein Poster für _____ (ihr Zimmer).

7. Nach _____ (der Besuch im Museum) gehen Sigrid und Ralf ohne _____ (ihr Freund) auf _____ (das Empire State Building).

8. Von _____ (dieses Gebäude) hat man einen phantastischen Blick über _____ (die Stadt), trotz _____ (der Smog).

9. Abends essen Ralf und Sigrid in _____ (ein Restaurant), und nach _____ (das Essen) gehen sie in _____ (ein Theater) an _____ (der Broadway).

10. Danach fallen sie dann todmüde in _____ (ihre Betten).

D. Partnerarbeit.   Ihr Freund/Ihre Freundin hat ein neues Zimmer. Sie möchten wissen, wie das Zimmer aussieht. Stellen Sie einige Fragen mit dem Genitiv.
(Beispiel: Wie ist die Farbe deiner Vorhänge?)

E. Kurze Aufsätze

1. Sie sprechen mit einem Freund/einer Freundin über Ihre Familien. Sie interessieren sich für alle Details: Alter, Beruf, Interessen, Hobbys, Freunde usw. Verwenden Sie den Genitiv.
(Beispiel: Der Mann meiner Tante heißt Karl. Der Bruder seiner Mutter war der Bürgermeister von Frankfurt.)

2. Sie sitzen in einem Straßencafé und klatschen° über andere   *gossip*
Leute. Verwenden Sie den Genitiv.
(Beispiel: Die Schwester ihres Freundes hat schon wieder einen neuen Freund. ...)

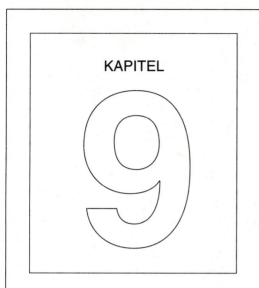

KAPITEL

9

Relative Pronouns ■

Relative Clauses ■

1   Relative clauses°

Wer ist der Gast, **der an dem Tisch sitzt?**
*Who's the guest (**who is**) sitting at the table?*

Das ist ihr Kind, **das ohne Schuhe herumläuft.**
*That's her child (**who**) is running around without shoes.*

Das ist dieselbe Frau, **die wir gestern in der Stadt gesehen haben.**
*That's the same woman (**whom**) we saw in town yesterday.*

A relative clause provides additional information about a previously mentioned noun. The clause is introduced by a relative pronoun (e.g., **der, das, die**) that refers back to the noun, which is the antecedent° (e.g., **Gast, Kind, Frau**). In English the relative pronouns are *who, whom, whose, that,* and *which,* but they are often not stated. In German the relative pronoun is always stated.

Ist das der Fernseher, den du kaufen **willst?**
*Is that the TV (that) you **want** to buy?*

Since a relative clause is a dependent clause, the finite verb is in final position. In writing, a comma separates the relative clause from the main clause.

2   Forms of relative pronouns°

	Masculine	Neuter	Feminine	Plural
Nominative:	der	das	die	die
Accusative:	den	das	die	die
Dative:	dem	dem	der	**denen**
Genitive:	**dessen**	**dessen**	**deren**	**deren**

The forms of the relative pronouns are the same as the definite article, except for the dative plural and all genitive forms.

Ist das die **Freundin, die** diese Karte geschrieben hat?
*Is that the **friend who** wrote this card?*

Die **Karte, die** du meinst, ist nicht von meiner Freundin.
*The **card (that)** you mean is not from my friend.*

In German, relative pronouns can refer to either persons (e.g., **Freundin**) or things (e.g., **Karte**).

Masculine: Wer ist der Mann, **der** an dem Tisch sitzt?

Neuter: Wer ist das Kind, **das** an dem Tisch sitzt?

Feminine: Wer ist die Frau, **die** an dem Tisch sitzt?

Plural: Wer sind die Leute, **die** an dem Tisch sitzen?

The *gender* (masculine, neuter, feminine) of a relative pronoun is determined by the gender of the antecedent. In the examples above, **der** is masculine because it refers to **der Mann** and **die** is feminine because it refers to **die Frau.** Whether a relative pronoun is singular or plural also depends on the noun to which it refers. The relative pronoun **die** that refers to **die Leute** is plural and therefore requires the plural verb **sitzen.**

Nominative: Ist das der Mann, **der** nebenan wohnt?
*Is that the man **who** lives next door?*

Accusative: Ist das der Mann, **den** wir gestern gesehen haben?
*Is that the man **whom** we saw yesterday?*

Dative: Ist das der Mann, **dem** Sie das Geld gegeben haben?
*Is that the man to **whom** you gave the money?*

Genitive: Ist das der Mann, **dessen** Frau Schweizerin ist?
*Is that the man **whose** wife is Swiss?*

The *case* of the relative pronoun depends on its function in the relative clause. In the examples above, **der** is nominative because it is the subject of its clause; **den** is accusative because it is the direct object of the verb **gesehen haben** in that clause; **dem** is dative because it is an indirect object in the clause; and **dessen** is genitive because it shows a close relationship in the clause.

Ist das die Frau, **für die** Sie arbeiten?
*Is that the woman **for whom** you work?*

Ist das die Firma, **bei der** Sie arbeiten?
*Is that the firm **(that)** you work **for**?*

A preposition followed by a relative pronoun may introduce a relative clause. The case of the relative pronoun then depends on what case the preposition takes. In **für die, die** is accusative because of **für;** in **bei der, der** is dative because of **bei.**

In German, whenever a relative pronoun is the object of a preposition, the preposition precedes the pronoun. In colloquial English the preposition is often in last position: *(that) you work **for**.*

☐ ——————————

A. Der falsche Koffer.
On their way to Salzburg, Karin and her friend change trains in Munich. Identify each relative clause in their conversation. Give the gender, case, and function of each relative pronoun and identify the antecedent.

▶ Die Tafel, auf der man die Abfahrtszeiten° lesen kann, hängt dort   *departure times*
drüben.
auf der man die Abfahrtszeiten lesen kann; feminine, dative; object
of a preposition; antecedent: *Tafel.*

1. GERTI: Wo ist der Zug, mit dem wir weiterfahren müssen?
2. KARIN: Keine Ahnung! Komm, wir schauen auf dem Plan nach,
der dort hängt.
3. GERTI: Mensch, Karin, das ist doch gar nicht dein Koffer, den du
da in der Hand hast.
4. KARIN: O je! Gehört er dem Herrn, dessen Kinder die ganze Zeit
so geschrien haben?
5. GERTI: Nein, ich glaube der Frau, die uns ihre Zeitung gegeben
hat. Schau, da drüben sitzt sie.
6. KARIN: Ach ja! Das ist mein Koffer, auf dem sie sitzt.

B. Verschiedene Interessen.
Read the statements about personal interests and think of your own friends and relatives. Say whether they are similar or different.

▶ Meine Tante kennt viele gute Geschichten.
Ich habe auch eine Tante, die viele gute Geschichten kennt.
Ich habe keine Tante, die…

1. Mein Freund schreibt ein Buch nach dem andern.
2. Mein Bruder spielt gern Computerspiele.
3. Meine Schwester ist im Fahrradclub.
4. Meine Cousine fährt immer nach Italien.
5. Mein Onkel malt wunderschöne Bilder.
6. Meine Freundin gibt ihr ganzes Geld für Kleidung aus.
7. Mein Nachbar interessiert sich für Musik aus fremden Ländern.
8. Meine Großeltern haben eine tolle Bibliothek.

C. Die gute alte Zeit.
John and Greg spent their junior year in Heidelberg. Some years later they return and the memories from the good old days come back. Complete the sentences with the appropriate relative pronouns.

1. JOHN: Ist das nicht das Hotel, in _____ wir die erste Nacht
verbracht haben?
2. GREG: Ja, und da ist die Marktfrau, bei _____ wir unser Obst
gekauft haben.

3. JOHN: Laß uns durch die Straße gehen, in _____ wir im Sommersemester gewohnt haben.

4. GREG: Das ist eine gute Idee! Und ich möchte wieder in dem Gasthaus einen Kaffee trinken, in _____ wir samstags immer gegangen sind.

5. JOHN: Sieh mal, dort! Das ist doch der, _____ wir im Hauptseminar° kennengelernt haben, nicht?   *advanced seminar*

6. GREG: Richtig. Ich möchte auch wieder den Spaziergang zum Schloß machen, auf _____ wir Barbara kennengelernt haben.

7. JOHN: Gut. Und was ist wohl aus dem kleinen Café geworden, _____ wir damals immer besucht haben?

D. Ein produktiver Mensch.   Complete the information about the journalist Peter Schreiber. Use the genitive form of the relative pronoun.

1. Wie heißt der Autor, _____ Bücher du so gern liest?
2. Er ist ein Journalist, _____ Namen jeder kennt: Peter Schreiber.
3. Er schreibt für eine Zeitschrift, _____ Berichte immer sehr interessant sind.
4. Er spielt auch in einer Rockband, _____ Musik recht gut ist.
5. Meine Schwester, _____ Freund auch in der Band spielt, kommt heute abend mit ihm zu mir.
6. Er spielt immer ein Lied für mich, _____ Melodie ich sehr gern mag.

E. Das Müller'sche Volksbad°.   Alice tells about her attempt   *public swimming pool*
to go swimming at the Müller'sche swimming pool in Munich. Combine the sentences using relative pronouns instead of the italicized words.

▶ In München gibt es ein Schwimmbad. *Sein* Baustil° ist wunder-   *style of architecture*
schön.
In München gibt es ein Schwimmbad, dessen Baustil wunderschön ist.

1. Ich wollte in ein Schwimmbad gehen. *Es* ist sehr alt.
2. Freunde hatten mir davon erzählt. *Ihnen* gefällt das Bad sehr.
3. Ich war schon neugierig auf das Bad. Ein bekannter Architekt hat *es* gebaut.
4. Meine Badetasche war sehr schwer. Ich hatte *sie* ganz vollgepackt.
5. An der Haltestelle traf ich einen Freund. *Sie* ist vor meinem Haus. Ich erzählte *ihm* davon.
6. Mein Freund ging mit. *Sein* liebster Sport ist Schwimmen.
7. Wir fuhren mit der Straßenbahn. *Sie* hält genau vor dem Schwimmbad.
8. Am Eingang° hing eine Tafel: Heute geschlossen. *Er* war zu.   *entrance*

F. Schön war's.   Louise and Eva have come back from a wonderful trip and are telling their friends about it. Complete the sentences with the appropriate prepositions and relative pronouns.

▶ Das war eine schöne Zeit, *an die* ich mich gern erinnern werde.

1. Das Leben in dem Land, _____ wir gefahren sind, ist ganz anders als hier.
2. Es war eine sehr interessante Reise, _____ ich am liebsten ein ganzes Buch schreiben würde.
3. Am schönsten war der große alte Baum, _____ wir immer gefrühstückt haben.
4. Das Zimmer, _____ wir geschlafen haben, war schön hell.
5. Wir haben uns auch die Schlösser angesehen, _____ ihr uns erzählt habt.
6. Bald hole ich die Fotos ab, _____ ich mich schon sehr freue°.   *freuen auf* + acc.

———————————— □

3 The indefinite relative pronouns *wer* and *was*

Wer zu spät kommt, bekommt nichts zu essen.
Whoever comes too late gets nothing to eat.

Wen du einlädst, ist mir gleich.
Whomever you invite makes no difference to me.

Was er von seinem Leben erzählte, war interessant.
What he told about his life was interesting.

The interrogative pronoun **wer** (**wen, wem, wessen**) can be used as a relative pronoun to refer to nonspecific persons. Similarly, **was** can be used to refer to nonspecific things or ideas.

Ich glaube nicht alles, **was** in der Zeitung steht.
*I don't believe everything **that**'s in the newspaper.*

Max will immer das machen, **was** seine Schwester macht.
*Max always wants to do **what** his sister does.*

Das war das Beste, **was** ich tun konnte.
*That was the best **(that)** I could do.*

Mark hat nicht die Wahrheit gesagt, **was** uns nicht überraschte.
*Mark didn't tell the truth, **which** didn't surprise us.*

The relative pronoun **was** is also used to refer to an antecedent that is an indefinite pronoun (**alles, etwas, nichts, viel[es], wenig[es]**), the demonstratives **das** and **dasselbe,** or a neuter superlative noun (e.g.,

das Beste, das Schönste). **Was** can also be used to refer to an entire clause (e.g., **er hat nicht die Wahrheit gesagt**). Note that some speakers use **das** to refer to **etwas:**

Ich habe etwas gehört, **was** (**das**) ich nicht glauben kann.

Tanja hat nicht die Wahrheit gesagt, **worüber** wir uns wundern.

Im Oktober fliegen wir nach Spanien, **worauf** wir uns freuen.

The adverb **wo(r)** is combined with a preposition (instead of **was** + preposition) to refer to an entire clause.

☐ ──────────────

G. Medizinstudium.   Tell about your friend Brigitte, who is studying medicine. Complete the sentences with a form of **wer, was,** or the compound **wo(r)- +** preposition.

▶ Meine Freundin Brigitte studiert Medizin, *worüber* sie sehr glücklich ist.

1. _____ ihr damals zur Medizin geraten hat, war ihre Mutter.
2. Das war das Beste, _____ Brigitte tun konnte.
3. Denn das Medizinstudium ist etwas, _____ sie sich schon immer gewünscht hatte.
4. _____ in diesem Studium nicht hart arbeitet, wird nie Ärztin.
5. Und _____ so viel Arbeit nicht gefällt, soll nicht Ärztin werden.
6. Zur Zeit muß Brigitte Anatomie lernen, _____ sie gar keine Lust° hat.   *Lust haben zu*
7. Im Sommer muß sie dann Examen machen, _____ sie ein bißchen Angst° hat.   *Angst haben vor*
8. Doch dann fährt sie für einen Monat nach Norwegen, _____ sie sich sehr freut°.   *sich freuen auf*
9. Ihre Eltern haben ihr nämlich einen Flug nach Oslo bezahlt, _____ sie sehr glücklich ist°.   *glücklich sein über*
10. Später möchte Brigitte vielleicht eine eigene Praxis° haben. Doch das ist etwas, _____ sie jetzt nur träumen° kann.   *practice* / *träumen von*

────────────── ☐

4   Extended modifiers°

das erweiterte Attribut

Relative clause: Sie wollte das Kind, das vor Müdigkeit eingeschlafen war, nicht stören.

Extended modifier: Sie wollte das **vor Müdigkeit eingeschlafene** Kind nicht stören.

Relative clause:	Er hat sich zu einem Menschen entwickelt, der mechanisch denkt.
Extended modifier:	Er hat sich zu einem **mechanisch denkenden** Menschen entwickelt.

In German, relative clauses, which follow nouns, can be replaced by special constructions that precede nouns. These constructions are called extended modifiers or extended participial modifiers. They function like relative clauses but without a relative pronoun and a main verb. Instead they have an adjective or a participle used as an adjective that immediately precedes the noun it modifies. The participle can be a past participle (e.g., **eingeschlafen**) or a present participle (e.g., **denkend**). Note that **mechanisch** is an adverb modifying **denkend**. It therefore has no ending.

Extended modifiers are found mainly in formal writing such as scholarly works, especially scientific articles.

Denken Sie an unser **schwer zu lösendes** Problem.
*Think of our problem **that is difficult to solve.***

Extended modifiers with a present participle preceded by **zu** indicate something that can(not) or should (not) be done. This construction is similar to a form of **sein** + **zu** + infinitive (see *Kapitel 13*, Section 9, "Alternatives to the passive voice").

☐────────────

H. Atomenergie.   Scientists and scholars are discussing nuclear energy. Give the English equivalents of their statements.

1. Eine oft gestellte Frage wurde hier diskutiert.
2. Nun ist also der größte anzunehmende Unfall° passiert.
3. Wir stehen vor einem schon lange bekannten Problem.
4. Wir befinden uns in einer oft diskutierten Situation.
5. Es stellen sich viele schwer zu beantwortende Fragen.
6. Viele nicht immer zu akzeptierende Antworten wurden angeboten.
7. Meine eigene, leider meistens mißverstandene Meinung ist:...
8. Die bis heute als umweltfreundlich geltende Atomenergie muß neu durchdacht werden.

der größte anzuneh-mende Unfall (der GAU): *worst-case scenario*

────────── ☐

Zusammenfassung

A. Das Rate-Quiz.   Sie haben Besuch von einer deutschen Familie. Den Kindern ist es schrecklich langweilig, und Sie müssen sie

unterhalten. Ergänzen Sie das Rate-Quiz mit passenden Relativpronomen. Die Antworten sind unten auf dieser Seite zu finden.

1. Wie heißt der amerikanische Staat, _____ Hauptstadt Hartford
   ist?
   What's the name of the American state whose capital is Hartford?
2. Kennst du die Autorin, _____ „Onkel Toms Hütte" geschrieben
   hat?
   Do you know the author who wrote Uncle Tom's Cabin?
3. Wie heißt der Feiertag, _____ man in den USA Ende November
   und in Kanada Mitte Oktober feiert?
   *What's the name of the holiday that is celebrated in the USA at the
   end of November and in Canada in the middle of October?*
4. Wie heißt die Insel, auf _____ die Freiheitsstatue steht?
   *What's the name of the island on which the Statue of Liberty
   stands?*
5. Wie heißt die Schauspielerin, _____ man aus dem Film
   „Casablanca" kennt?
   *What's the name of the actress whom lots of people know from the
   movie* Casablanca?
6. Wie nennt man die Menschen, _____ in Hamburg wohnen?
   What does one call the people who live in Hamburg?
7. Wie heißt der Regisseur, _____ Film „Himmel über Berlin" auch
   in den Vereinigten Staaten bekannt ist?
   *What's the name of the director whose film "Himmel über Berlin"
   [Wings of Desire] is also well known in the United States?*

B. Die Clique°.   Alice besucht ihre Kusine Cornelia und lernt ihre   *group of friends*
Freunde kennen. Alice hat schon viel über die Clique gehört, doch jetzt
trifft sie sie persönlich. Setzen Sie die fehlenden Relativpronomen (in
zwei Fällen mit Präpositionen) ein.

1. CORNELIA: Jetzt triffst du endlich meine Freunde, _____ ich so
               oft spreche. (+ Präposition)
2. ALICE: Und heute ist sogar noch euer großes Fest, _____ ihr
               jeden Sommer feiert. Ist auch Ulrike da, _____ du im
               Juli kennengelernt hast?
3. CORNELIA: Nein, sie ist die einzige von diesem Urlaub, _____
               heute abend nicht da ist. Doch Annette, _____
               Eltern uns ihr Auto gegeben haben, steht dort an der
               Bar.
4. ALICE: Und wo ist Carsten, _____ ihr immer warten
               mußtet? (+ Präposition)

Antworten: 5. Ingrid Bergman 6. Hamburger 7. Wim Wenders
1. Connecticut 2. Harriet Beecher Stowe 3. Thanksgiving 4. Bedloe's Island

5. CORNELIA: Er ist jemand, _____ mich immer ärgert. Er ist zu
               egoistisch. Annette und Dieter sind die einzigen,
               _____ Carsten mögen.

6. ALICE: Komisch, Carsten war doch der Freund, _____ dich
               immer besonders interessiert hat.

7. CORNELIA: Ja, doch dann habe ich gemerkt, daß Carsten ein
               Mensch ist, _____ man nicht vertrauen kann.

C. Sprichwörter.   Hier lesen Sie verschiedene deutsche Sprich-
wörter. Suchen Sie das englische Äquivalent.

1. Man ist, was man ißt.
2. Was Hänschen nicht lernt, lernt Hans nimmermehr.
3. Glücklich ist, wer vergißt, was nicht mehr zu ändern ist.
4. Wer zuletzt lacht, lacht am besten.
5. Was ich nicht weiß, macht mich nicht heiß°.   (here) *upset*
6. Wer einmal lügt, dem glaubt man nicht, und wenn er auch die
   Wahrheit spricht.
7. Wer anderen eine Grube° gräbt°, fällt selbst hinein.   *pit / digs*
8. Wer nicht hören will, muß fühlen.

a. Listen or you'll live to regret it.
b. Remember the boy who cried "wolf" once too often.
c. The one who laughs last, laughs best.
d. You can't teach an old dog new tricks.
e. One can easily fall into one's own trap.
f. What I don't know can't hurt me.
g. Don't worry about what you can't change.
h. You are what you eat.

D. Etwas, was Sie wollen.   Wählen Sie drei der folgenden
Ideen und ergänzen Sie.

• Ich möchte einen Beruf haben, …

• Ich möchte eine Freundin/einen Freund haben, …

• Ich stelle mir eine Zukunft vor, …

• Eine Politikerin/Ein Politiker, die/der mir gefällt, ist eine/einer, …

• Ich möchte ein Haus haben, …

• Ich möchte ein Leben führen, …

E. Partnerarbeit   Sie und Ihre Partnerin/Ihr Partner wollen ein
neues, ganz besonderes Haus. Sie diskutieren, wie Sie sich das Haus
vorstellen. Leider haben Sie unterschiedliche° Meinungen. Verwenden   *different*
Sie viele Relativsätze, wenn möglich auch mit den Relativpronomen **wer**
und **was.**

F. Kurze Aufsätze

1. Mit einem Autorenteam zusammen schreiben Sie ein Manuskript für eine Quizsendung°. Beschreiben Sie eine historische Persönlichkeit, die die Teilnehmer° erraten müssen. Verwenden Sie mindestens drei Relativpronomen.

   quiz show
   participants

2. Stefanie und Renate studieren ihr letztes Jahr an der Uni. Sie unterhalten sich über ihren idealen Beruf und wie sich jede ihr Berufsleben vorstellt. Schreiben Sie das Gespräch auf, und verwenden Sie dabei Relativsätze.

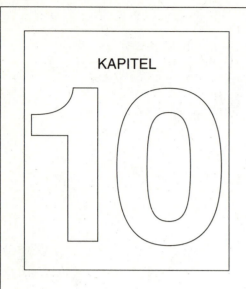

KAPITEL

10

Reflexive Verbs ■

1 Reflexive pronouns°

das Reflexivpronomen

Ich wasche **mich**.	*I wash (**myself**).*
Ich kaufe **mir** eine CD.	*I'm buying **myself** a CD.*

A reflexive pronoun is a pronoun that indicates the same person or thing as the subject. In this sense it "reflects back" on the subject. A reflexive pronoun may be either in the accusative or dative case, depending on its function in the sentence.

Personal (subject) pronoun:	ich	du	er/es/sie	wir	ihr	sie	Sie
Accusative reflexive:	mich	dich	sich	uns	euch	sich	sich
Dative reflexive:	mir	dir	sich	uns	euch	sich	sich

The 1st and 2nd person reflexive pronouns are identical to the accusative and dative forms of the personal pronouns. The pronoun **sich** is used for all 3rd person reflexives and for the **Sie**-form. In English, reflexive pronouns end in *-self/-selves* (e.g., *myself, himself, themselves*).

2 Accusative reflexive pronouns

Direct object:	Ich ziehe **mich** an.	*I'm getting dressed.*
Object of preposition:	Tobias redet immer über **sich.**	*Tobias always talks about himself.*

A reflexive pronoun is in the accusative case when it functions as direct object or as the object of a preposition that requires the accusative case.

3 Dative reflexive pronouns

Indirect object:	Ich kaufe **mir** eine Jacke.	*I'm buying **myself** a jacket.*
Dative verb:	Ich kann **mir** nicht helfen.	*I can't help **myself**.*
Object of preposition:	Sprichst du von **dir**?	*Are you speaking of **yourself**?*

A reflexive pronoun is in the dative case when it functions as an indirect object, the object of a dative verb, or the object of a preposition that requires the dative case.

4 | Verbs with either accusative or dative reflexive pronouns

Accusative:	Ich wasche **mich.**	*I wash (myself).*
Dative:	Ich wasche **mir** die Hände.	*I wash my hands.*

Some verbs can be used with either accusative or dative reflexive pronouns. The dative is used if there is also an accusative object.

5 | Reflexives with parts of the body and clothing

Ich muß **mir** die Zähne putzen.	*I have to brush my teeth.*
Zieh **dir** die Schuhe aus!	*Take off your shoes!*

German often uses a definite article and a dative reflexive pronoun in referring to parts of the body and articles of clothing. The dative reflexive pronoun (e.g., **mir, dir**) shows that the accusative object (e.g., **die Zähne, die Schuhe**) belongs to the subject of the sentence. English uses a possessive adjective (e.g., *my* teeth, *your* shoes).

6 | Position of reflexive pronouns

Kannst du **dir** das Auto **leisten?**

Kannst du es **dir leisten?**

The position of reflexive pronouns is the same as that of personal pronoun objects. The dative reflexive pronoun precedes noun objects (e.g., **das Auto**) but follows accusative pronouns (e.g., **es**).

Inverted word order:	Hoffentlich hat **sich Mark** nicht wieder erkältet.
Transposed word order:	Ich weiß nicht, ob **sich Mark** wieder erkältet hat.
	Ich glaube nicht, daß **er sich** wieder erkältet hat.

In inverted word order and in dependent clauses (transposed word order), the reflexive pronoun may and often does precede a noun sub-ject (e.g., **Mark**). It always follows a pronoun subject (e.g., **er**).

☐ ——————————

A. Der Filmkurs.
Some students in a film class are shooting a movie. Frank is the director, and he tells what the main character is supposed to do. Britta, who plays that role, repeats Frank's sentences in the **ich**-form. Take her part and change the sentences according to the model.

▶ Sie kommt heim und zieht sich den Mantel aus.
Ich komme heim und ziehe mir den Mantel aus.

1. Sie hat sich vorgestellt, daß sie sich an ihrem Geburtstag keine Arbeit macht.
2. Sie will sich ihr Geburtstagsessen nicht selbst kochen. Dazu hat sie keine Lust.
3. Also hat sie den Partyservice angerufen und hat sich viele gute Delikatessen° bestellt.   *special foods*
4. Von ihren Freunden hat sie sich nur Blumen und gute Laune gewünscht.
5. Sie will sich ein sehr elegantes Kleid anziehen.
6. Sie wünscht sich, daß es ein sehr lustiges Geburtstagsfest wird.

B. Duschen? Nö.
Erich is being questioned by his elder sister Birgit about his personal hygiene. Complete their conversation.

▶ Wie oft _____ du _____ die Haare? (sich kämmen)
Wie oft kämmst du dir die Haare?

1. ERICH: Ich _____ _____ nicht gern die Haare. (sich kämmen)
2. BIRGIT: Wie oft _____ du _____ die Zähne? (sich putzen)
   ERICH: Dreimal täglich, öfter als duschen.
3. BIRGIT: _____ du _____ nicht jeden Morgen? (sich duschen)
4. ERICH: Nö. Keine Zeit. Ich muß _____ ja schließlich auch _____ und _____ _____ _____. (sich rasieren / sich Kaffee kochen)
5. BIRGIT: Was soll ich da sagen? Ich mache das ja auch. Ich _____ _____ die Haare und dann _____ ich _____ ja noch. (sich waschen / sich schminken°)   *to put on make-up*
6. ERICH: Doch beim Rasieren geht das nicht so schnell. Sonst _____ ich _____. (sich schneiden)
7. BIRGIT: Du _____ auch manchmal, nicht? (baden)
8. ERICH: Ja, das hab' ich gern abends. Da muß ich _____ nicht so _____. (sich beeilen)
   Da kann ich _____ tolle Musik _____. (sich anhören)

——————————— ☐

7 | Verbs used reflexively and nonreflexively

Die Frau **erinnert** Marta an ihre Mutter.	*The woman **reminds** Marta of her mother.*
Marta **erinnert sich** an ihre Mutter.	*Marta **remembers** her mother.*
Was **ärgert** dich so?	*What is **making** you **angry**?*
Ich **ärgere mich** über alles.	*I'm **mad** about everything.*

Many German verbs are used both reflexively and nonreflexively. Some of these verbs change their meanings when used reflexively. Such verbs are noted in the end vocabulary as follows: **(sich) erinnern.**

8 | German verbs used reflexively vs. English equivalents

Ich habe **mich erkältet.**	*I **caught** a cold.*
Beeil dich!	***Hurry up!***
Sollen wir **uns** in die Sonne **setzen**?	*Should we **sit** in the sun?*

German has many verbs used reflexively that have English equivalents without a reflexive pronoun. Below is a list of common verbs used with an accusative reflexive pronoun. A number of them complete their meaning with prepositions.

sich amüsieren	*to have a good time*
sich anziehen	*to get dressed*
sich ärgern (über + *acc.*)	*to be annoyed (at)*
sich ausziehen	*to get undressed*
sich beeilen	*to hurry*
sich benehmen	*to behave*
sich entschuldigen	*to apologize*
sich entspannen	*to relax*
sich erholen	*to recover*
sich erinnern (an + *acc.*)	*to remember*
sich erkälten	*to catch a cold*
sich fragen	*to wonder*
sich freuen auf *(acc.)*	*to look forward to*
sich freuen über *(acc.)*	*to be happy about*
sich (wohl/schlecht) fühlen	*to feel (well/ill)*
sich fürchten (vor + *dat.*)	*to be afraid (of)*
sich gewöhnen an *(acc.)*	*to get used to*
sich interessieren für	*to be interested in*
sich irren	*to be mistaken*

sich langweilen	to be bored
sich legen *or* hinlegen	to lie down
sich rasieren	to shave
sich setzen *or* hinsetzen	to sit down
sich treffen	to meet
sich unterhalten (über + *acc.*)	to have a conversation (about)/to converse (about)
sich verfahren	to get lost (driving)
sich verirren	to get lost
sich verlaufen	to get lost (walking)
sich verspäten	to be late
sich versprechen	to misspeak
sich waschen	to wash (oneself)
sich wundern (über + *acc.*)	to be surprised (at)

Some verbs have dative reflexive pronouns:

sich etwas einbilden	*to imagine*	Das **bildest** du **dir** nur **ein.** *You're just **imagining** that.*
sich etwas leisten	*to afford*	Kannst du **dir** das **leisten?** *Can you **afford** that?*
sich etwas überlegen	*to think about*	**Überleg** es **dir** mal. ***Think about** it.*
sich etwas vorstellen	*to imagine*	Ich kann **mir** das nicht **vorstellen.** *I can't **imagine** it.*

□ ——————————

C. Alles ärgert mich.

Sonja is speaking with Jochen about her job. Complete their conversation with the German equivalent of the English cues. Notice that some verbs are reflexive and some are not.

1. JOCHEN: Was _____ _____ so? *(is making you angry)*
2. SONJA: Ich _____ _____, weil ich den Job nicht bekommen habe. *(am angry)*
3. JOCHEN: Ah, ich _____ _____, daß du davon gesprochen hast. *(remember)* Du hast mich angerufen, als ich gerade meine Wäsche gewaschen habe.
4. SONJA: Weißt du, meine alte Arbeit _____ _____ nicht mehr. *(interests me)*
5. JOCHEN: Wofür _____ du _____ denn? *(are you interested)*
6. SONJA: Ich weiß nicht. Ich _____ _____ in der Firma nicht wohl. *(feel)*
7. JOCHEN: Und dein Chef _____ _____ immer. *(annoys you)*
8. SONJA: Ach, _____ _____ nicht an ihn! *(remind me)*

D. Nichts als Schwierigkeiten.   Three men are having a brief conversation after class. Each is concerned with his own problems. Express their conversation in German.

1. BERND: I have to hurry up. I'm going to meet Julia at eight.
2. RAINER: I'm amazed at Dagmar. I think she didn't remember me.
3. DENNIS: I don't feel well. I think I've caught a cold. How stupid!
But I don't want to get upset°.   *sich ärgern*

E. Die Wanderung.   Jan is ill and in a bad mood. Silvia asks him how he got the flu. Form complete sentences with the correct word order of the reflexive pronouns.

1. SILVIA: warum / du / sich fühlen / schlecht / ?
2. JAN: ich / sich erkälten / gestern / auf unserer Wanderung
(present perfect)
3.   Ingrid und ich / sich verlaufen / im Wald *(present perfect)*
4. SILVIA: deshalb / Ingrid / sich verspäten / gestern abend / !
(present perfect)
5.   wo / ihr / sich verlaufen / ? *(present perfect)*
6. JAN: ich / können / sich erinnern / nicht *(present)*
7.   ich / sich setzen / ins Gras // als / ich / müde /
werden *(present perfect // simple past)*
8.   Ingrid / sich legen / sogar / auf den Boden *(present perfect)*
9.   doch / sie / sich erkälten / nicht *(present perfect)*
10. SILVIA: warum / ihr / sich beeilen /nicht / ? *(present perfect)*
11. JAN: wir / sich irren / in der Zeit *(present perfect)*
12. SILVIA: ich / sich wundern / über eure Naivität *(present)*
13. JAN: ja, und jetzt / ich / sich ärgern / ! *(present)*
14.   ich / sich freuen / sehr / auf die Party / heute abend
(past perfect)
15.   und / nun / ich / müssen / sich langweilen / zu Hause
(present)

—————————————— □

9 | The intensifiers *selbst* and *selber*

Das Kind kann sich schon   *The child can already dress*
  selbst (selber) anziehen.   ***himself/herself.***
Du hast es **selbst (selber)** gesagt.   *You said it* ***yourself.***

The intensifying pronouns **selbst** and **selber** emphasize that someone does something personally. **Selbst** and **selber** are interchangeable. They can be used with a reflexive (e.g., **sich selbst anziehen**) or alone (e.g., es **selbst gesagt**).

Selbst Helga kann es nicht verstehen.   *Even Helga can't understand it.*

When **selbst** precedes the word it qualifies, it is equivalent to English *even*. **Selber** cannot be used in this meaning.

10 Reciprocal use of reflexives and *einander*

Wann sehen sie **sich** wieder?   *When will they see **each other** again?*

The reflexive pronouns **uns, euch,** and **sich** may have a reciprocal meaning *(each other)*. The subject is in the plural.

Wir schreiben **uns** oft.
Wir schreiben **einander** oft. $\Big\}$ *We write (to) **each other** often.*

The pronoun **einander** may be used instead of the reflexive to express a reciprocal action.

Jochen und Marion sitzen **nebeneinander.**

Sie unterhalten sich **miteinander.**

A preposition and **einander** are written as one word. Note that **einander** never changes its form.
When **einander** plus a preposition is used with reflexive verbs (e.g., **sich unterhalten**), the reflexive pronoun is usually also stated.

☐————————————

F. Meine Freundin Sabrina.   Maria sees her friend Sabrina almost every day. But she doesn't know the latest about Sabrina's friend Thomas. Complete the sentences with **selbst/selber** or **einander.**

1. Ich sehe meine Freundin Sabrina oft. Wir besuchen _____ fast täglich.
2. Wir erzählen _____ viele lustige Geschichten.
3. Gestern wollte sie mir von einem Film erzählen. Sie sagte aber: „Du mußt ihn dir schon _____ ansehen.“
4. Ich fragte sie, was mit ihrem Freund Thomas los war. Sie antwortete nur: „Du mußt _____ mit ihm sprechen.“
5. Wir schauten _____ in die Augen und mußten plötzlich lachen.
6. Es scheint, daß Sabrina und Thomas _____ nicht mehr gut verstehen.

————————————— ☐

Zusammenfassung

A. Ein alter Freund.   Karin studiert in München. Sie trifft sich mit ihrer Freundin in Schwabing. Schwabing ist ein bei Künstlern und Studenten beliebter Stadtteil Münchens. Sie sind Karin. Erzählen Sie von gestern. Gebrauchen Sie jeweils die angegebene Zeitform°.   *tense*

▶   du / sich erinnern an / Frank? (Präsens)
  Erinnerst du dich an Frank?

1. wir / sich begegnen / gestern / in Schwabing (Perfekt)
2. wir / sich verstehen / immer / gut (Perfekt)
3. aber dann / wir / sich sehen / lange nicht (Perfekt)
4. ihr / sich kennenlernen / doch auch mal (Perfekt)
5. gestern im Café an der Uni / ich / sich wundern (Perfekt): „Mensch, das ist doch der Frank!"
6. ich / sich unterhalten / lange / mit ihm (Perfekt)
7. er / sich interessieren / sehr / für meine Arbeit (Präsens)
8. morgen abend / wir / wollen / sich treffen (Präsens)
9. ich / sich freuen / sehr darauf (Präsens)

B. Ein ideales Paar?   Götz und Florian sprechen über ihre Freundinnen und über Freundschaften ganz allgemein. Setzen Sie die richtigen Formen der reflexiven Verben in Klammern und die Wörter *selbst/selber* und *(-)einander* ein.

1. FLORIAN: Zuerst war es komisch, wieder eine Freundin zu haben. Doch inzwischen habe ich _____ daran _____. (sich gewöhnen) Wir _____ _____ jeden Abend, und ich kann es _____ gar nicht mehr _____ ohne Brigitte. (sich treffen / sich [etwas] vorstellen)

2. GÖTZ: _____ du _____ das nicht nur _____? (sich [etwas] einbilden) Tanja und ich _____ _____ höchstens zweimal pro Woche. (sich sehen) Aber wenn wir _____ dann _____, _____ wir _____ auch sehr _____. (sich treffen / sich aufeinander freuen)

3. FLORIAN: Früher habe ich _____ oft so _____. (sich langweilen) Ich mußte _____ auch immer _____ _____, wie ich _____ _____ kann. (sich selbst überlegen / sich amüsieren)

4. GÖTZ: Wirklich? Das wundert mich aber. Ich dachte immer, daß du _____ für so viele Dinge _____. (sich interessieren)

5. FLORIAN: Das war mal so! —Jetzt muß ich _____ aber _____, sonst _____ ich _____ noch. (sich beeilen / sich verspäten) Brigitte und ich gehen heute abend ins Ballett.

6. GÖTZ: Viel Spaß! ____ ____ gut. (sich amüsieren) Ich
kann ____ zur Zeit solche Vergnügungen° leider nicht   *entertainments*
____. (sich [etwas] leisten) Ich muß mein Studium ja
____ finanzieren. (selbst/selber)

C. Auf deutsch bitte.   Übersetzen Sie.

1. —We have to hurry.
   —Yes, I'll just brush my teeth quickly.
2. —What are you angry about?
   —You're wrong. I'm not angry.
3. —Do you remember Marta?
   —Yes. We write each other often.
4. —Why are you late?
   —I got lost.
5. —I've caught a cold.
   —I don't feel well myself.

D. Partnerarbeit.   Sie sind zu spät zu einer Verabredung° mit   *date*
Ihrer Freundin/Ihrem Freund gekommen. Sie/Er ist ärgerlich. Sie
versuchen zu erklären, warum Sie nicht früher kommen konnten.
Gebrauchen Sie so viele reflexive Verben wie möglich.

E. Kurze Aufsätze

1. Erklären Sie einer Freundin/einem Freund, wie Sie es schaffen,
   morgens länger zu schlafen. Beschreiben Sie Ihren morgendlichen
   Zeitplan. Gebrauchen Sie die folgenden reflexiven Verben: *sich
   anziehen, sich kämmen, sich die Zähne putzen* – und andere.

2. Stellen Sie sich vor, Sie sind Journalistin/Journalist bei einer
   Zeitschrift. Schreiben Sie für Ihre Leserinnen und Leser ein
   Erholungsprogramm für ein Wochenende. Verwenden Sie reflexive
   Verben, z.B. *sich erholen, sich entspannen, sich massieren
   (lassen), sich fit halten, sich hinlegen* usw.

3. Schreiben Sie ein Porträt über sich selbst oder eine
   Freundin/einen Freund: Welche Charaktereigenschaften Sie (oder
   sie/er) haben, worüber Sie sich amüsieren, freuen oder gern
   unterhalten, wofür Sie sich interessieren, wann Sie sich ärgern,
   wovor Sie sich fürchten usw. Verwenden Sie möglichst viele reflexive Verben und auch die Wörter *selbst/selber, einander.*

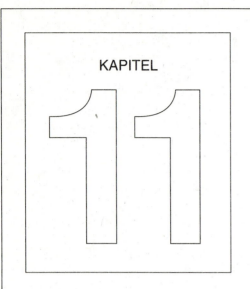

KAPITEL

11

Adjectives ■

1 | Predicate adjectives°

das prädikativ gebrauchte Adjektiv

Der Film ist **neu.**

Der Tag wird **lang.**

Das Wetter bleibt jetzt **schön.**

Predicate adjectives follow the verbs **sein, werden,** or **bleiben** and modify the subject of the sentence. They never add declensional endings.

2 | Attributive adjectives°

das attributive Adjektiv

Hast du den **neuen** Film gesehen?

Das wird ein **langer** Tag.

Wir haben endlich **schönes** Wetter, nicht?

Attributive adjectives precede the nouns they modify; they always add declensional endings. Their endings depend on the gender, number (singular or plural), and case of the nouns they modify and on whether the adjectives are preceded by (1) a definite article or **der**-word, (2) an indefinite article or **ein**-word, or (3) no article, **der**-word, or **ein**-word.

Das ist ein **guter alter** Wein.

Wir haben ein **schönes neues** Auto.

Adjectives in a series have the same ending.

3 | Adjectives° preceded by the definite article or *der*-words

das Adjektiv

	Masculine	Neuter	Feminine	Plural
Nominative:	der **neue** Hut	das **neue** Hemd	die **neue** Hose	die **neuen** Schuhe
Accusative:	den **neuen** Hut	das **neue** Hemd	die **neue** Hose	die **neuen** Schuhe
Dative:	dem **neuen** Hut	dem **neuen** Hemd	der **neuen** Hose	den **neuen** Schuhen
Genitive:	des **neuen** Hutes	des **neuen** Hemdes	der **neuen** Hose	der **neuen** Schuhe

	M	N	F	Pl
Nominative:	**e**	**e**	**e** °	en
Accusative:	en	**e**	**e**	en
Dative:	en	en	en	en
Genitive:	en	en	en	en

This is sometimes called the "Oklahoma chart" because it looks like that state.

Words preceding a noun indicate the gender (or number) and case of the noun. If the attributive adjective is preceded by a definite article or **der**-word (**dieser, jeder, jener, mancher, solcher, welcher**—see *Kapitel 5*), it does not need to give information about the gender and/or case because the definite article or **der**-word has already done so. Therefore, after the definite article or **der**-word, the adjective ending is noninformational. Noninformational adjective endings are **-e** or **-en**.

Dieser **blaue** Pulli ist schön.

Since **dieser** indicates that **Pulli** is masculine and in the nominative case, the ending on **blau** need not provide that information.

4 | Adjectives preceded by the indefinite article or *ein*-words

	Masculine	Neuter	Feminine	Plural
Nominative:	ein **neuer** Hut	ein **neues** Hemd	eine **neue** Hose	meine **neuen** Schuhe
Accusative:	einen **neuen** Hut	ein **neues** Hemd	eine **neue** Hose	meine **neuen** Schuhe
Dative:	einem **neuen** Hut	einem **neuen** Hemd	einer **neuen** Hose	meinen **neuen** Schuhen
Genitive:	eines **neuen** Hutes	eines **neuen** Hemdes	einer **neuen** Hose	meiner **neuen** Schuhe

	M	N	F	Pl
Nominative:	**er**	**es**	**e**	en
Accusative:	en	**es**	**e**	en
Dative:	en	en	en	en
Genitive:	en	en	en	en

Adjectives preceded by an indefinite article or an **ein**-word (**kein** and possessive adjectives, which are covered in *Kapitel 5*) have the same endings as those preceded by a **der**-word, except in the three instances when the **ein**-word itself has no ending: masculine nominative, and neuter nominative and accusative. Since, in these instances, **ein** does not indicate the gender and case of the noun, the adjective provides this information. Note that the adjective ending **-er** resembles the definite article **der** and the adjective ending **-es** resembles the definite article **das.**

Dein **blauer** Pulli ist schön.

Since **dein** does not indicate the gender and case of **Pulli,** the ending on the adjective **blau** must provide that information. The **-er** ending indicates that **Pulli** is masculine and in the nominative case.

5   Summary of preceded adjectives

	Masculine	Neuter	Feminine	Plural
Nominative:	der **neue** Hut	das **neue** Hemd	die **neue** Hose	die **neuen** Schuhe
	ein **neuer** Hut	ein **neues** Hemd	eine **neue** Hose	meine **neuen** Schuhe
Accusative:	den **neuen** Hut	das **neue** Hemd	die **neue** Hose	die **neuen** Schuhe
	einen **neuen** Hut	ein **neues** Hemd	eine **neue** Hose	meine **neuen** Schuhe
Dative:	dem **neuen** Hut	dem **neuen** Hemd	der **neuen** Hose	den **neuen** Schuhen
	einem **neuen** Hut	einem **neuen** Hemd	einer **neuen** Hose	meinen **neuen** Schuhen
Genitive:	des **neuen** Hutes	des **neuen** Hemdes	der **neuen** Hose	der **neuen** Schuhe
	eines **neuen** Hutes	eines **neuen** Hemdes	einer **neuen** Hose	meiner **neuen** Schuhe

	M	N	F	Pl
Nominative:	(der) **e**	(das) **e**	(die) **e**	en
	(ein) **er**	(ein) **es**	(eine) **e**	
Accusative:	en	(das) **e**	(die) **e**	en
		(ein) **es**	(eine) **e**	
Dative:	en	en	en	en
Genitive:	en	en	en	en

If the indication of gender, number, and case is given by the word preceding the adjective (that is, definite or indefinite articles, **der**-words, or **ein**-words) then no further information is required, and the adjective has the noninformational ending **-e** or **-en.**

If the indefinite article or **ein**-word does not give an indication about gender, number, and/or case, then the adjective requires the informational ending **-er** or **-es.**

A. Ferien.
Make the comments about vacation more descriptive by using the correct form of the cued adjectives before the italicized noun.

▶ Jeder *Lehrer* hat jetzt Ferien. (deutsch)
Jeder deutsche Lehrer hat jetzt Ferien.

1. Meine *Lehrerin* fährt in ihren Ferien nach Frankreich. (jung)
2. Welches *Auto* gehört ihr? (rot)
3. Sie unternimmt diese *Reise* in den Süden mit einer Kollegin. (schön)
4. Wer möchte nicht in jener *Landschaft* sein? (wunderbar)
5. Die *Städte* im Süden sind sehr interessant. (klein)
6. Sie besuchen so manchen *Markt*. (interessant)
7. Auch fahren sie nach Marseille und Paris. Solche *Städte* sind zu der Zeit voll von Touristen. (berühmt)

B. Der Ingenieur.
Ellen tells about Silvia's friend, who is an engineer. Make her account linguistically smoother by combining each pair of sentences as in the model.

▶ Ich erzähle euch eine Geschichte. Sie ist toll.
Ich erzähle euch eine tolle Geschichte.

1. Silvia hat einen Ingenieur kennengelernt. Er ist nett und reich.
2. Sein Beruf gefällt ihm. Er ist interessant.
3. Er wohnt in einem Haus. Es ist alt und schön.
4. Das Haus ist an einem See. Er ist groß.
5. Ihre Augen haben den Ingenieur fasziniert. Sie sind hübsch.
6. Er hat ein Boot. Es ist neu.
7. Mit dem Boot fahren sie auf den See hinaus. Er ist still.
8. In dem See ist eine Insel. Sie ist klein.
9. Dort machen sie ein Picknick. Es ist fein.

C. Weißt du wo?
A friend of yours is visiting you. Your friend has lots of questions about your city. Answer according to the model, using the cues.

▶ Weißt du, wo hier ein guter Zahnarzt ist? (Adresse)
Ja, ich kann dir die Adresse eines guten Zahnarztes geben.

1. Kennst du auch eine gute Ärztin? (Telefonnummer)
2. Weißt du, wo ein billiges Restaurant ist? (Adresse)
3. Kennst du eine große Buchhandlung hier? (Name)
4. Kennst du eine erstklassige Musiklehrerin? (Telefonnummer)
5. Weißt du, wo das nächste Reisebüro ist? (Adresse)
6. Kennst du ein billiges Hotel in Berlin? (Name)

——————————————— □

6 Unpreceded adjectives

	Masculine	Neuter	Feminine	Plural
Nominative:	**guter** Wein	**gutes** Brot	**gute** Wurst	**gute** Äpfel
Accusative:	**guten** Wein	**gutes** Brot	**gute** Wurst	**gute** Äpfel
Dative:	**gutem** Wein	**gutem** Brot	**guter** Wurst	**guten** Äpfeln
Genitive:	**gut<u>en</u>** Weines	**gut<u>en</u>** Brotes	**guter** Wurst	**guter** Äpfel

When adjectives are not preceded by a definite article, **der**-word, indefinite article, or **ein**-word, they must indicate gender (or number) and case. Unpreceded adjectives have the same endings as **der**-words (e.g., **dieser, jeder**), except for the masculine and neuter genitive, which have the ending **-en.**

□ ———————————————

D. Frühstück.   Monika and Kathrin are going to have breakfast together. Answer Monika's questions in the affirmative, using the cued adjectives as in the model.

▶ Trinkst du gern Kaffee? (stark)
   Ja, ich trinke gern starken Kaffee.

1. Trinkst du Tee? (schwarz)
2. Möchtest du ihn mit Zucker? (braun)
3. Hast du schon Zucker auf dem Tisch? (braun)
4. Ist noch Käse im Kühlschrank? (französisch)
5. Sind auch Brötchen da? (frisch)
6. Willst du zum Frühstück Musik hören? (schön)

——————————————— □

7 | Adjectives following indefinite adjectives°   *das unbestimmte Zahlwort*

a. *andere, einige, mehrere, viele, wenige*

Im Park gibt es **viele schöne** Blumen.

Hast du die **vielen schönen** Blumen gesehen?

The indefinite adjectives **andere, einige, mehrere, viele,** and **wenige** are in the plural and suggest indefinite quantities. When these indefinite adjectives are followed by attributive adjectives, they are the same as any other adjectives in a series, i.e., they both have the same endings. The endings depend on whether the adjectives are unpreceded (e.g., **viele schöne**) or preceded (e.g., **die vielen schönen**).

b. *alle, beide*

Paul kennt nicht **alle deutschen** Städte.

Die Mütter **beider jungen** Menschen sind Verwandte.

Alle and **beide** are plural **der**-words. Therefore an attributive adjective following **alle** or **beide** has the ending of a preceded adjective in the plural, which is **-en**.

☐ ──────────────

E. Wie war's?   Matthias has returned from a trip to several large cities. Take Matthias's part and answer his friend's questions about the trip, using the cues in parentheses.

▶ Hast du Studenten kennengelernt? (viele / amerikanisch)
  Ja, ich hab' viele amerikanische Studenten kennengelernt.

1. Warst du in Museen? (einige / berühmt)
2. Hast du auch Ausstellungen gesehen? (andere / ausgezeichnet)
3. Hast du Konzerte gehört? (einige / interessant)
4. Waren die Konzerte teuer? (alle / gut)
5. Warst du bei Freunden? (mehrere / alt)
6. Hast du Leute kennengelernt? (viele / nett)

────────────── ☐

8 | Adjectives used as nouns°   *das Nominaladjektiv*

Das ist ein **Bekannter.** (Mann)	*That's a **friend.** (male)*
Das ist eine **Bekannte.** (Frau)	*That's a **friend.** (female)*
Das sind meine guten **Bekannten.** (Leute)	*Those are my good **friends.** (people)*

Gute **Bekannte** haben wir gern zu Besuch.	*We like to have good **friends** over for a visit.*

Many adjectives can be used as nouns in German. They retain the adjective endings as though the noun were still there (e.g., **ein bekannter Mann**). In writing, adjectives used as nouns are capitalized.

Some common nouns declined like adjectives are: **der/die Angestellte, Erwachsene, Fremde, Jugendliche, Verwandte.**

Das Gute daran ist, daß es nicht so viel kostet.
The good thing about it is that it doesn't cost so much.

Wir haben **viel Schönes** gesehen.
*We saw **many beautiful things**.*

Alles Gute im Neuen Jahr.
Happy New Year.

Adjectives expressing abstractions (*the good, the beautiful*) are neuter nouns. They frequently follow words such as **etwas, nichts, viel,** and **wenig** and take the ending **-es (etwas Gutes)**. Note that adjectives following **alles** have an **-e (alles Gute)**. Neuter nouns are capitalized, except for **anderes: etwas anderes.**

9   *Hoch* and adjectives ending in *-el* or *-er*

Das ist ein **hoher** Turm.	*That's a **high** tower.*
Das ist eine **dunkle** Straße.	*That's a **dark** street.*
Das ist ein **teurer** Wagen.	*That's an **expensive** car.*

Hoch becomes **hoh-** when it takes an ending. Adjectives ending in **-el** or **-er** omit the **e** before the **l** or **r** when the adjective takes an ending: **dunkel → dunkl-; teuer → teur-.**

☐ ─────────

F. Bekannte und Verwandte.   Give the German equivalents.

1. FRANZ: Do you still have relatives in Switzerland?
2. ANNI: Yes, we have many relatives there.
3. FRANZ: My relatives live in Austria. But my father has a good friend° in Switzerland. He lives in a small village on a high mountain.   Use **Bekannter.**
4. ANNI: In Switzerland there are many high mountains.
5. FRANZ: Yes, I was there once and spent a few wonderful days with good friends.

───────── ☐

Ordinal numbers°   *die Ordinalzahl*

1.	erst-
2.	zweit-
3.	dritt-
6.	sechst-
7.	siebt- (*less common:* siebent-)
8.	acht-
15.	fünfzehnt-
16.	sechzehnt-
21.	einundzwanzigst-
32.	zweiunddreißigst-
100.	hundertst-
101.	hunderterst-
105.	hundertfünft-
1000.	tausendst-

Ordinal numbers are used as adjectives. They are formed by adding **-t** to numbers 1 through 19 and **-st** to numbers beyond. Note the special forms **erst-, dritt-,** and **siebt-,** and the spelling of **acht-.**

Heute ist der **achtzehnte** Juni.

Hast du dir ein **zweites** Stück Kuchen genommen?

Ordinals take adjective endings (e.g., der achtzehn**te**, ein zwei**tes**). When writing numbers, an ordinal is followed by a period: **den 1. Juni = den ersten Juni.** Dates in letterheads or news releases are in the accusative: **Hamburg, den 28.7.1994** (spoken as **den achtundzwanzigsten siebten, neunzehnhundertvierundneunzig**). Note that in German dates the day precedes the month: **den 3. Juli 1995.**

□ ————————————

G. Der wievielte?   Answer the questions about dates by using the cued words. First answer orally and then in writing. Write out the ordinals.

1. Wann feiert man den Tag der Arbeit? (am 1. Mai)
2. Wann öffnet man in Deutschland die Weihnachtsgeschenke? (am 24. Dezember)
3. Wann kommt der Nikolaus? (am 6. Dezember)
4. Welcher Tag im Dezember ist der Zweite Weihnachtstag? (der 26.)
5. Welcher Sonntag im Mai ist Muttertag? (der 2.)
6. Wann haben Sie Geburtstag? (am ?)
7. Den wievielten haben wir heute? (den ?)

———————————— □

11 │ Present participles° as adjectives

das Partizip Präsens

Infinitive + d	Present participle	English
schlafen + d	schlafen**d**	*sleeping*
lachen + d	lachen**d**	*laughing*

Present participles are formed by adding **-d** to the infinitive.

die **schlafende** Katze   *the **sleeping** cat*

ein **lachendes** Kind   *a **laughing** child*

Present participles used as attributive adjectives take adjective endings.

German does not use the present participle as a verb, as in English progressive forms: **sie lachte** *she was laughing.*

German often uses an infinitive where English uses a participle:

Ich hörte sie **lachen.**   *I heard her **laughing.***

12 │ Past participles as adjectives

Meine Eltern kauften eine **gebrauchte** Videokamera.   *My parents bought a **used** camcorder.*

Ich möchte ein weich**gekochtes** Ei.   *I would like a soft-**boiled** egg.*

Past participles used as attributive adjectives take adjective endings like other attributive adjectives.

☐ ─────────────

H. Eine verrückte Geschichte.   Complete the sentences with the German equivalent of the English cues.

1. Gestern hat mir Evelyn die _____ Geschichte erzählt: *(following)*
2. „Letzten Freitag habe ich einen viel_____ Wagen billig gekauft. *(driven)*
3. Später aß ich mit Kai und Uwe zu Abend. Wir aßen _____ Würstchen und frisch_____ Kartoffelsalat. *(grilled° / made)*   **grillen**
4. Kai schaute durch das _____ Fenster und rief: *(closed)*
5. ‚Schaut! Da ist eine _____ Untertasse° am Himmel!' *(flying)*   *saucer*
6. Wir schauten ihn mit _____ Gesichtern an und dachten, er ist verrückt. *(surprised)*
7. Es war nur das Spiegelbild° einer _____ Kerze°." *(burning)*   *reflection / candle*

───────────── ☐

13 Degrees of comparison°: adjectives and adverbs

die Komparation

Base form:	heiß	*hot*	schön	*beautiful*
Comparative:	heiß**er**	*hotter*	schön**er**	*more beautiful*
Superlative:	heiß**est-**	*hottest*	schön**st-**	*most beautiful*

Adjectives and adverbs have three forms of degrees: base form (positive°), comparative°, and superlative°. The comparative is formed by adding **-er** to the base form. The superlative is formed by adding **-st** to the base form. The ending -st is expanded to **-est** on words ending in **-d** (**wildest-**), **-t** (**ältest-**), or a sibilant° (**kürzest-**). The superlative of **groß** is **größt-**.

der Positiv / der Komparativ / der Superlativ

Sibilant endings are **-s, -ss, -ß, -tz, -z.**

Base form:	**a**lt	gro**ß**	j**u**ng
Comparative:	**ä**lter	gr**ö**ßer	j**ü**nger
Superlative:	**ä**ltest-	gr**ö**ßt-	j**ü**ngst-

Many one-syllable adjectives or adverbs with the stem vowel **a**, **o**, or **u** add an umlaut in the comparative and superlative. These adjectives and adverbs are noted in the end vocabulary as follows: **kalt (ä).** See Appendix A: 3a for other common adjectives and adverbs that add umlaut in the comparative and superlative forms.

Base form:	gern	gut	hoch	nah	viel
Comparative:	**lieber**	**besser**	**höher**	**näher**	**mehr**
Superlative:	**liebst-**	**best-**	**höchst-**	**nächst-**	**meist-**

Several adjectives and adverbs are irregular in the comparative and superlative.

Hörst du **lieber** Rock oder klassische Musik?
*Do you **prefer** listening to rock or classical music?*

To express preference about doing something, German uses the word **lieber** plus a verb.

14 | Expressing comparisons

Sigrid ist nicht **so** groß **wie** Ursula.   *Sigrid is not **as** tall **as** Ursula.*

Es ist heute **so** kalt **wie** gestern.   *Today it's **as** cold **as** yesterday.*

The construction **so...wie** is used to express the equality of a person, thing, or activity to another. It is equivalent to English *as . . . as*.

Ursula ist **größer als** Sigrid.   *Ursula is **taller than** Sigrid.*

Es ist heute **kälter als** gestern.   *Today it's **colder than** yesterday.*

The comparative form plus **als** is used to compare people, things, or activities. **Als** is equivalent to English *than*.

Im Herbst ist es hier **am schönsten**.   *In the fall it's **nicest** here.*

Ich esse **am liebsten** Fisch.   *I like fish **most of all**.*

The pattern **am** + superlative + **-en** (e.g., **am** + **schönst** + **-en**) is used to express the superlative degree of predicate adjectives and adverbs.

Von den sechzehn Ländern Deutschlands ist Bremen **das kleinste** [Land].

Von meinen drei Brüdern ist Uwe **der größte** [Bruder].

A second superlative pattern in the predicate is one that shows gender and number (**das kleinste** [Kind], **die jüngste** [Schwester], **die nettesten** [Leute]). This construction is used when the noun is understood.

Base form: Das ist kein **neues** Buch.

Comparative: Ich möchte ein **neueres** Buch lesen.

Superlative: Ist das dein **neu(e)stes** Buch?

Attributive adjectives in the comparative and superlative take the same adjective endings as those in the base form.

☐———————

I. Das neue Haus.   Herr Rüb has a new house and is being asked rather silly questions about it. He replies in kind. Answer for Herr Rüb according to the model.

▶   Ist das Arbeitszimmer so klein wie das Bad? *Ja, es ist sogar kleiner als das Bad.*

▶   Und die Küche? *Sie ist am kleinsten.*

1. Ist das Eßzimmer so warm wie das Schlafzimmer? Und das Wohnzimmer?

2. Ist der Keller so groß wie das Erdgeschoß? Und der Garten?

3. Sind die neuen Stühle so bequem wie die Sessel? Und das Sofa?

4. Ist die Küche so toll wie das Eßzimmer? Und das Badezimmer?

5. War der Kühlschrank so teuer wie die Spülmaschine? Und die Stereoanlage?

6. Ist der neue Briefträger so nett wie der alte? Und die neuen Nachbarn?

7. Finden Sie diese Fragen so dumm wie die Ihrer Nachbarn? Und diese Frage?

J. Freizeit.   Answer the questions on leisure time using the comparative and superlative as in the model.

▶ Flüsse und Wälder finde ich schön.
Und Berge? *Berge finde ich noch schöner.*
Und das Meer? *Das Meer finde ich am schönsten.*

1. Ich gehe gern ins Theater. Und ins Kino? Und in ein Rockkonzert?

2. Der Eintrittspreis° fürs Kino ist hoch. Und der fürs Theater? Und der für ein Rockkonzert?   *price of admission*

3. Der neue Film von Schlöndorff soll gut sein. Und der von Margarethe von Trotta? Und das neue Stück im Stadttheater?

4. Der Tennisplatz ist nah. Und das Schwimmbad? Und der Sportplatz?

5. Abends esse ich viel. Und mittags? Und zum Frühstück?

K. Fotos.   Herr Untermeier shows some photographs to his two friends who are very competitive and try to go him one better.

▶ Das ist mein schneller Wagen.
HERR MEIER: *Ich habe einen viel schnelleren Wagen.*
HERR OBERMEIER: *Ich habe den schnellsten Wagen.*

1. Das ist mein großes Haus.

2. Das ist mein schöner Garten.

3. Das ist mein teurer Swimmingpool.

4. Das ist mein gemütliches Wohnzimmer.

5. Das ist mein gutes Fahrrad.

6. Das ist mein hübscher Hund.

7. Das sind meine reichen Freunde.

——————————— ☐

Zusammenfassung

A. Einkaufsbummel°.   Antje und Bettina gehen einkaufen. Sie   *shopping spree*
brauchen Kleidung und ein paar Dinge für ihre Zimmer. Wählen Sie eins
der Adjektive in Klammern, und setzen Sie es in der richtigen Form ein.
Es kann auch ein Adjektiv im Komparativ oder Superlativ sein.

1. ANTJE: Ich möchte mir einen _____ Mantel kaufen. (warm, leicht)

2. BETTINA: Was ist denn mit deiner _____ Jacke vom letzten Jahr? (kurz, dunkel)

3. ANTJE: Ach, diese _____ Jacke. (alt, häßlich) Das war ein _____ Kauf°. (schlecht, dumm)

4. BETTINA: Ich probiere den _____ Rock hier an°. (lang, eng)

5. ANTJE: Das ist der _____ Rock, den es in diesem Laden gibt. (teuer, sportlich)

6. BETTINA: Die haben ziemlich _____ Preise hier. (hoch, niedrig)

7. ANTJE: Aber das ist einfach das _____ Geschäft (schick, gut) in dieser _____ Stadt. (langweilig, klein) Es gibt in Bernhausen einfach zu wenige _____ Läden. (schön, interessant)

8. BETTINA: So, jetzt brauche ich noch einige _____ Dinge (wichtig, praktisch) für mein _____ Zimmer. (neu, renoviert) Ich suche mehrere _____ Kissen° (blau, gemütlich) für mein _____ Sofa. (alt, gebraucht)

9. ANTJE: Die Kissen sind alle so _____. (teuer, häßlich) Wie wäre es denn mit einer _____ Decke? (bunt, groß)

10. BETTINA: Das ist eine _____ Idee. (ausgezeichnet, gut)

der Kauf: *purchase*
anprobieren: *to try on*

pillows

B. Die Reise.
Karoline ist nach einer langen Reise durch Europa wieder zu Hause. Sie vergleicht° die unten angegebenen Länder und Städte. Geben Sie ihren Bericht auf deutsch wieder.

compares

Länder	*Städte*
Deutschland	Köln
Frankreich	Prag
Italien	Warschau
Korsika	
Norwegen	
Österreich	
Schweden	
die Schweiz	
Spanien	

1. In France there was the best food, in Paris the most elegant clothes.
2. But in Italy it was warmer than in France.
3. In Germany the mountains are high, but in Switzerland there are higher mountains.
4. In the mountains it rained more; at the sea there was more sun.
5. In the cities people were not as friendly as in the country.
6. The hottest weather was in Spain.
7. In France we had less rain than in Germany.

8. The nicest° island° is Corsica, but there are also pretty islands in Sweden.   *nice = **schön / die Insel***

9. In Cologne, I visited the most interesting museums with many modern pictures.

10. In Prague I saw newer shops than in Warsaw.

11. But altogether°, I liked Austria best.   *insgesamt*

C. Persönliche Fragen.   Antworten Sie in ganzen Sätzen.

1. Welches Fach finden Sie am schwersten?
2. Was trinken Sie am liebsten?
3. Welche Musik ist am schönsten?
4. Was essen Sie am liebsten?
5. Welche Sprache sprechen Sie am besten?
6. Wer in dieser Klasse spricht am meisten?
7. Wer kommt immer am spätesten?
8. Welche Zeitung finden Sie am interessantesten?
9. Was für Fernsehsendungen gefallen Ihnen am besten?
10. Wie verbringen Sie Ihr Wochenende am liebsten?
11. Welchen amerikanischen (kanadischen) Politiker finden Sie am liberalsten?

D. Partnerarbeit.   Beschreiben Sie eine (berühmte) Person oder einen Gegenstand°. Verwenden Sie dabei möglichst viele attributive Adjektive und auch Adjektive im Komparativ oder Superlativ. Ihre Partnerin/Ihr Partner soll dann die Person oder den Gegenstand erraten°.

object

guess

▶ Diese Person ist seit einigen Jahren die berühmteste deutsche Tennisspielerin. (Steffi Graf)

▶ Wenn man die Bedeutung oder Definition eines Wortes nicht kennt, kann man die Definition in diesem Gegenstand finden. (ein Wörterbuch)

E. Kurze Aufsätze

1. Denken Sie an verschiedene Dinge oder Personen, die Sie miteinander vergleichen können. Vielleicht sind sie ziemlich ähnlich, vielleicht sind sie total verschieden. Schreiben Sie über den Vergleich.

2. Besprechen Sie Vor- und Nachteile° moderner Erfindungen° wie Auto, Fernsehen, Computer, Flugzeug, Telefon.

Vor- und Nachteile:
advantages and disadvantages / inventions

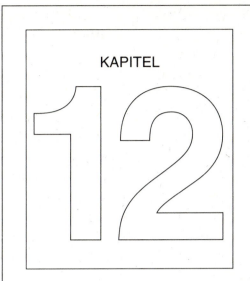

KAPITEL

12

General Subjunctive ■

1 Indicative° and subjunctive°

der Indikativ / der Konjunktiv

Indicative: Wenn das Wetter schön ist, gehe ich schwimmen.   *If the weather is nice, I'll go swimming.*

Subjunctive: Wenn das Wetter schön wäre, ginge ich schwimmen. würde ich schwimmen gehen. } *If the weather were nice, I would go swimming.*

In both English and German, the indicative mood is used to talk about real conditions or factual situations. It is a fact that the speaker will go swimming if the weather is nice.

The subjunctive mood indicates a speaker's attitude toward a situation, a feeling that the situation is hypothetical, uncertain, potential, unreal, or contrary to fact. When a speaker says that she/he would go swimming if the weather were nice, she/he is postulating a hypothetical situation since it is clear from the sentence that the weather is not nice.

Wishes: Ich **möchte** eine Tasse Kaffee. *I'd like a cup of coffee.*

Polite requests: **Würden** Sie mir bitte **helfen?** ***Would** you please **help** me?*

The subjunctive mood is also used to express wishes and polite requests.

German has two ways to express the subjunctive mood in present or future time. One way is to use the **würde**-construction (e.g., **Ich würde schwimmen gehen.**). The other way is to use the subjunctive form of the main verb (e.g., **Ich ginge schwimmen.**). The meaning of both sentences is the same (*I would go swimming.*). In colloquial German, the **würde**-construction is used much more frequently than the subjunctive form of main verbs, with the exception of a few verbs that are commonly used in the subjunctive (see Sections 5, 6, and 17).

Present time: Wenn Anna nur heute oder morgen **käme.** Wenn Anna nur heute oder morgen **kommen würde.** } *If Anna **would** only **come** today or tomorrow.*

Past time: Wenn Anna nur gestern **gekommen wäre.** *If Anna **had** only **come** yesterday.*

Subjunctive forms can express two time categories: present time, which also can refer to the future (if Anna would only come now or in the future), and past time (if Anna had only come in the past).

2 General subjunctive° (subjunctive II)

Konjunktiv II

German has two forms of the subjunctive, general subjunctive, also called subjunctive II, and special subjunctive, also called subjunctive I. Present-time general subjunctive is based on the simple past tense form: **er käme** (from **kam**). (The simple past stem is the second principal part of the verb, hence the designation subjunctive II.) Present-time special subjunctive is based on the infinitive stem: **er komme** (from **kommen**). (The infinitive is the first principal part of the verb, hence the designation subjunctive I.)

In this chapter you will work with the general subjunctive, which is the form used to talk about unreal and hypothetical events and to express wishes and polite requests. Both general and special subjunctive are used to express indirect discourse, that is, to report what someone has said. Indirect discourse is discussed in *Kapitel 14*.

3 │ Verb endings in present-time general subjunctive°

der Konjunktiv II der Gegenwart

ich käm**e**	*wir* käm**en**
du käm**est**	*ihr* käm**et**
er/es/sie käm**e**	*sie* käm**en**
Sie käm**en**	

The general subjunctive endings above are used for all verbs, strong and weak. In colloquial German, the endings **-est** and **-et** often contract to **-st** and **-t** if the form is clearly subjunctive, as indicated by the umlaut in strong verbs (**kämst, kämt;** see Section 7).

4 │ The *würde*-construction°

die **würde**-*Konstruktion*

Ich **würde** das nicht **sagen.**	*I would not* **say** *that.*
Würdest du ihm **helfen?**	*Would you* **help** *him?*

The **würde**-construction consists of a form of **würde** plus the infinitive of the main verb and is equivalent in meaning to the English construction *would* plus the infinitive of the main verb.

ich **würde** es machen	*wir* **würden** es machen
du **würdest** es machen	*ihr* **würdet** es machen
er/es/sie **würde** es machen	*sie* **würden** es machen
Sie **würden** es machen	

The verb **würde** is the general subjunctive form of **werden.** It is formed by adding an umlaut to **wurde,** the simple past of **werden.**

□————————————————

A. Ich nicht.   You don't approve at all of Teresa's lifestyle. Describe all the things she does that you definitely would not do. Use the **würde-**construction.

▶   Teresa schläft jeden Nachmittag.
    Ich würde nicht jeden Nachmittag schlafen.

1. Sie ißt nur Schokolade zum Frühstück.
2. Sie trinkt jeden Tag zehn Tassen Kaffee.
3. Sie duscht dreimal am Tag.
4. Sie telefoniert stundenlang mit ihrer Nachbarin.
5. Sie geht jede Woche zum Friseur.
6. Sie fährt so furchtbar Auto.
7. Sie sieht jeden Abend fern.
8. Sie geht immer nach Mitternacht ins Bett.
9. Sie redet dauernd über andere Leute.

————————————— □

5   Present-time general subjunctive of *sein* and *haben*

a. *sein*

ich wäre	*wir* wären	
du wärest	*ihr* wäret	
er/es/sie wäre	*sie* wären	
Sie wären		

b. *haben*

ich hätte	*wir* hätten	
du hättest	*ihr* hättet	
er/es/sie hätte	*sie* hätten	
Sie hätten		

The verbs **haben** and **sein** are more commonly used in their general subjunctive forms, **wäre** and **hätte,** than as part of the **würde-**construction. Notice that the general subjunctive of **sein** is the past tense **war** plus umlaut and subjunctive endings. The general subjunctive of **haben** is the past tense form **hatte** with an umlaut.

☐ ──────────

B. Wenn es nur schon Sommer wäre!   Beate and Christian are talking about summer vacation. Complete their conversation by filling in the missing subjunctive forms of **sein** and **haben.**

1. BEATE: Ich _____ so froh, wenn es schon Juli _____ und wir Semesterferien _____. Susanne und ich _____ schon in Italien im Urlaub.

2. CHRISTIAN: Du _____ doch sicher wieder kein Geld. Und Susanne _____ wahrscheinlich keine Zeit. Dann _____ du wieder so deprimiert wie letztes Jahr.

3. BEATE: Ach, Christian, was würde ich nur machen, wenn ich dich nicht als Freund _____. Alles _____ ja immer viel zu einfach. Natürlich _____ Susanne und ich dieses Jahr besser vorbereitet. _____ du denn Lust mitzukommen?

4. CHRISTIAN: Lust schon. Das _____ schön. Leider muß ich im Sommer Geld fürs nächste Semester verdienen.

────────────── ☐

6 │ Modals in present-time general subjunctive

Infinitive	Simple past indicative (**er/es/sie**-form)	Present-time general subjunctive (**er/es/sie**-form)
dürfen	durfte	**dürfte**
können	konnte	**könnte**
mögen	mochte	**möchte**
müssen	mußte	**müßte**
sollen	sollte	**sollte**
wollen	wollte	**wollte**

The present-time general subjunctive forms of modals are like the simple past-tense indicative forms except that the modals with an umlaut in the infinitive also have an umlaut in the subjunctive. Modals are some of the most commonly used verbs in the subjunctive.

Könntest du fahren?   *Could you drive?*

Like **sein** (**wäre**) and **haben** (**hätte**), the modals are generally used in their general subjunctive form rather than as infinitives with the **würde**-construction.

Dürfte ich Sie etwas fragen?	*Might I ask you something?*
Könntest du mir einen Gefallen tun?	*Could you do me a favor?*
Möchten Sie noch etwas Tee?	*Would you like some more tea?*
Sollten wir Andy nicht auch einladen?	*Shouldn't we also invite Andy?*
In diesem Fall **müßte** ich dir widersprechen.	*In this case I would have to contradict you.*

The subjunctive forms of the modals are frequently used to express polite requests or wishes or to soften the tone of a question or statement (e.g., **müßte widersprechen**).

Ich wollte, ich hätte Zeit.	*I wish I had time.*
Ich wollte, Klaus würde nicht soviel reden.	*I wish Klaus wouldn't talk so much.*

The expression **ich wollte** is often used to introduce wishes expressed in the subjunctive. Note that the verb **wollte** is also subjunctive.

□ —————————

C. Die Heimfahrt.

After an evening with acquaintances you are ready to leave. Soften the tone of your statements and make your requests seem more polite by restating the modals in present-time subjunctive.

▶ Ich muß jetzt eigentlich gehen.
  Ich müßte jetzt eigentlich gehen.

1. Ich soll um elf zu Hause sein.
2. Ich muß die Bahn um Viertel nach bekommen.
3. Das müssen unsere Freunde eigentlich verstehen.
4. Ich kann ja ein Taxi nehmen.
5. Darf ich mal telefonieren?
6. Oder darf ich Sie um etwas bitten?
7. Können Sie mich vielleicht nach Hause fahren?

D. Du bist unmöglich!

You are fed up with your roommate's habits. Discuss them with your roommate and tell him/her how you would like things changed. Use **nicht** before the italicized words. Use the **würde**-construction where appropriate.

▶ Du machst morgens *soviel* Lärm.
  Ich wollte, du würdest morgens nicht soviel Lärm machen.

▶ Deine Sachen liegen in der ganzen Wohnung herum.
  Ich wollte, deine Sachen würden nicht in der ganzen Wohnung herumliegen.

1. Dein schmutziges Geschirr steht *tagelang°* in der Küche. *for days*
2. Du spielst *immer* so fürchterliche CDs.
3. Du hast *jeden Tag* Besuch.
4. Du läßt *immer* die Haustür offen.
5. Du benutzt *immer* mein Handtuch.
6. Du bist morgens *so lange* im Bad.
7. Du telefonierst *dauernd*.
8. Ich höre *immer* dein Schnarchen° durch die Wand. *snoring*
9. Deine Freunde sind *immer* so unfreundlich zu mir.
10. Du hast *dauernd* schlechte Laune.

———————————— ☐

7 Present-time general subjunctive of strong verbs

Infinitive	Simple-past indicative stem	+ umlaut for **a, o, u**	+ subjunctive ending (**er/es/sie**-form)	Present-time general subjunctive (**er/es/sie**-form)
kommen	kam	käm	-e	**käme**
tun	tat	tät	-e	**täte**
fahren	fuhr	führ	-e	**führe**
fliegen	flog	flög	-e	**flöge**
bleiben	blieb	blieb	-e	**bliebe**
gehen	ging	ging	-e	**ginge**

The present-time general subjunctive of strong verbs is formed by adding general subjunctive endings to the simple past stem of the verb. An umlaut is added to the stem vowels **a, o,** or **u**.

Tätest du so etwas?
Würdest du so etwas **tun**? } ***Would*** *you* ***do*** *something like that?*

Although the general subjunctive form of the main verb and the **würde**-construction are equivalent in meaning, the **würde**-construction is more common in conversation. Only a few strong verbs (among them **bleiben, gehen, kommen, tun,** and **werden**) are used in their subjunctive form in colloquial German. In your reading of and listening to formal German (e.g., newspapers, newscasts, speeches, and lectures), however, you will need to recognize the subjunctive forms of additional strong verbs and understand their meaning. For a list of subjunctive forms of strong verbs, see Appendix A: 24.

8 Present-time general subjunctive of regular weak verbs

Infinitive	Simple past indicative (er/es/sie-form)	Present-time general subjunctive (er/es/sie-form)
sagen	sagte	**sagte**
kaufen	kaufte	**kaufte**
arbeiten	arbeitete	**arbeitete**
baden	badete	**badete**

The present-time general subjunctive and the simple past indicative forms of weak verbs are identical. For this reason, the **würde-**construction is normally used in place of the subjunctive form of weak verbs. In the following example, using **würde verdienen** in place of **verdiente** indicates that the second sentence is in the subjunctive and not indicative:

Indicative: Immer wenn Dieter **arbeitete, verdiente** er viel.
*Whenever Dieter **worked,** he **earned** a lot.*

General subjunctive: Wenn Dieter mehr **arbeitete, würde** er besser **verdienen.**
*If Dieter **worked** more, he **would earn** more.*

9 Present-time general subjunctive of irregular weak verbs

Infinitive	Simple past indicative (er/es/sie-form)	Present-time general subjunctive (er/es/sie-form)
bringen	brachte	**brächte**
denken	dachte	**dächte**
wissen	wußte	**wüßte**

The present-time general subjunctive forms of irregular weak verbs are like their simple-past indicative forms, but with the addition of an umlaut. The present-time general subjunctive forms of the irregular weak verbs **brennen, kennen, rennen,** and **nennen** are written with an **e** instead of **ä: brennte, kennte, rennte, nennte.**

With the exception of **wüßte,** the general subjunctive forms of irregular weak verbs are rarely used. The **würde**-construction is more common in colloquial German:

Ich **würde** ihn anrufen, wenn ich ihn besser **kennen würde.**

Ich **würde** das nicht so **nennen.**

☐ ────────────

E. Was wäre, wenn...?   The first list below contains sentences using the general subjunctive form of the main verb, followed by a list of English equivalents. Choose the appropriate meaning for each sentence.

1. Wir kämen gern.
2. Ich schliefe gern länger.
3. Sie ginge sicher mit.
4. So was gäb's bei mir nicht.
5. Wenn er nur länger bliebe.
6. Das wäre eine schöne Reise.
7. Und wenn sie krank würde?
8. Das ließe sie sich nicht gefallen.
9. Dann hieße sie ja auch Maier mit Nachnamen.
10. Ich ginge im Sommer gern in Urlaub.
11. Er behielte gerne seine alte Wohnung.
12. Auf dem Sofa säßen wir bequemer.
13. Wenn sie nur gesünder äßen.
14. Wenn ich das nur wüßte.
15. Das täte dir auch gut.
16. Hättest du Zeit für mich?
17. Wenn ich nur nicht immer an ihn dächte.

a. I would like to go on vacation in the summer.
b. We would sit more comfortably on the sofa.
c. She would not play along with that.
d. Such a thing would never happen with me.
e. We would be happy to come.
f. She would certainly go along.
g. If they would only eat healthier.
h. That would be good for you, too.
i. I would like to sleep longer.
j. And (what) if she got sick?
k. Then her last name would also be Maier.
l. He would like to keep his old apartment.
m. That would be a nice trip.
n. If he would only stay longer.
o. Would you have time for me?
p. If only I knew that.
q. If only I didn't think of him all the time.

F. Auf dem Fest.   Two people are gossiping at a party. They spend a lot of time saying how other people would behave differently. Restate their sentences in present-time general subjunctive, except where indicated that a **würde**-construction is preferable.

▶   Erika kommt nicht mit ihrem Freund.
    Erika käme nicht mit ihrem Freund.

1. Hans-Peter spricht nicht mit so vielen Leuten. (würde)
2. Ich ziehe so eine bunte Hose nicht an. (würde)
3. Ernst ißt auf einer Party nicht soviel. (würde)
4. Ich tue das nicht.
5. Mit kurzen Haaren sieht Lucie nicht besser aus.
6. Barbara unterhält sich nicht so laut über ihr Privatleben. (würde)
7. Meiers bleiben auch nicht länger.
8. Wir gehen nicht so spät.
9. Ich trinke nicht soviel Saft. (würde)
10. Du fährst nicht mit dem Wagen nach Hause. (würde)

G. Das Picknick.   You have planned a picnic with your friends, but all is not as it should be and you are a little worried. Say that the person in parentheses would do the right thing. Do each sentence twice, first using the present-time general subjunctive of the main verb and then using the **würde**-construction (except in 2 and 5.)

▶   Volker hat hoffentlich die Kamera dabei. (du)
    Du hättest natürlich die Kamera dabei.

1. Susi denkt hoffentlich an den Wein. (ich)
2. Peter hat hoffentlich Zeit. (ich)
3. Karla und Paula bringen hoffentlich die Gitarre mit. (wir)
4. Erwin bringt hoffentlich den Fußball mit. (du)
5. Müllers haben hoffentlich ihren Hund dabei. (wir)
6. Alle denken hoffentlich an einen Regenschirm. (ich)

———————————— □

10   Past-time general subjunctive°

der Konjunktiv II der Vergangenheit

ich **hätte** es **getan**	wir **hätten** es **getan**
du **hättest** es **getan**	ihr **hättet** es **getan**
er/es/sie **hätte** es **getan**	sie **hätten** es **getan**
Sie **hätten** es **getan**	

ich **wäre** nicht **gekommen**	*wir* **wären** nicht **gekommen**
du **wärest** nicht **gekommen**	*ihr* **wäret** nicht **gekommen**
er/es/sie **wäre** nicht **gekommen**	*sie* **wären** nicht **gekommen**
	Sie **wären** nicht **gekommen**

Past-time general subjunctive consists of the present-time general subjunctive forms of **haben (hätte)** or **sein (wäre)** and the past participle of the main verb.

Ich **hätte** dir gestern gern **geholfen**.
*I **would** gladly **have helped** you yesterday.*

Wenn ich nur genug Geld **gehabt hätte**!
*If only I **had had** enough money!*

Wenn Melanie das **gewußt hätte, wäre** sie **mitgekommen**.
*If Melanie **had known** that, she **would have come along**.*

The past-time subjunctive is used to express hypothetical situations, wishes, and contrary-to-fact conditions in past time. It corresponds to the English construction *would have* plus the past participle.

☐ ——————————

H. Am nächsten Tag.   The day after the party one of the people runs into a friend and relates all the comments made the night before. Restate the sentences in *Übung F* in past-time general subjunctive.

▶   Erika kommt nicht mit ihrem Freund.
    Erika wäre nicht mit ihrem Freund gekommen.

I. Wir hätten's anders gemacht.   Your picnic turned out to be a flop. Express the belief that things could have been very different. Restate the sentences in *Übung G* in past-time general subjunctive.

▶   Volker hat hoffentlich die Kamera dabei. (du)
    Du hättest natürlich die Kamera dabei gehabt.

—————————— ☐

11 | Modals in past-time general subjunctive

In past-time general subjunctive, modals have two forms of the participle: a regular form (**gekonnt**), and a form identical to the infinitive (**können**).

Du **hättest** es **gekonnt**.   *You **would have been able to** do it.*

Ich **hätte** das nicht **gedurft**.   *I **would** not **have been allowed** to do that.*

The regular form of the participle has the **ge**- prefix and the ending **-t (gedurft, gekonnt, gemocht, gemußt, gesollt,** and **gewollt).** The regular form is used when the modal is without a dependent infinitive because the meaning of the infinitive is clear from the context (see *Kapitel 2*, Section 2).

Lisa **hätte** dir **helfen müssen.**   Lisa *would have had to help* you.

Du **hättest** allein **fahren können.** *You could have driven* alone.

When a modal is used with a dependent infinitive, an alternative past participle that is identical with the modal infinitive is used **(dürfen, können, mögen, müssen, sollen,** and **wollen).** This construction is often called the *double infinitive construction* (see *Kapitel 3*, Section 17). The present-time general subjunctive form of the auxiliary **haben** is always used with modals in past-time general subjunctive.

□ ————————

J. Ein Unfall.   Chris has had a car accident. Torsten, with marvelous hindsight, tells him how he could have avoided it. Take Torsten's role and restate the sentences in past-time general subjunctive.

▶   Du mußt schneller reagieren.
    Du hättest schneller reagieren müssen.

1. Das darf nicht passieren.
2. Du mußt besser aufpassen.
3. Und es darf nicht regnen.
4. Du mußt vorsichtiger° sein.   *more careful*
5. Aber auch der andere soll langsamer fahren.
6. Die Straße darf eben nicht naß sein.
7. Na ja, es kann viel schlimmer ausgehen°.   *turn out*
8. Und ich will heute dein Auto benutzen.
    Aber das ist ja nun kaputt. *(Do not change.)*

———————— □

12 Contrary-to-fact conditions

Present time: **Wenn** ich Zeit **hätte, würde** ich **mitkommen.** }
          Wenn ich Zeit **hätte, käme** ich **mit.**
          *If I **had** time [but I don't], I **would come along.**

Past-time: **Wenn** ich Zeit **gehabt hätte, wäre** ich **mitgekommen.**
          *If I **had had** time [but I didn't], I **would have come along.***

Contrary-to-fact conditions describe a situation that does not exist or will not take place. The speaker only speculates on how something could or would be under certain conditions (for example, if the speaker had time). A contrary-to-fact condition contains two clauses: the condition (**wenn**-clause) and the conclusion.

To talk about the present, a speaker uses the present-time general subjunctive of the main verb (e.g., **hätte**) in the condition clause (**wenn**-clause) and generally uses a **würde**-construction (e.g., **würde mitkommen**) in the conclusion clause. In formal usage the conclusion may contain a general subjunctive form of the main verb instead (e.g., **käme ich mit**). Formal written German tends to avoid the **würde**-construction in the **wenn**-clause.

To talk about the past, a speaker uses past-time general subjunctive in both clauses. He/She speculates on how something might have been under certain conditions.

□ ─────────────────

K. Wenn ich nur...!   Holger has an important exam and is studying hard. While at his desk he dreams about how it would be if conditions were different. Finish his sentences using the **würde**-construction.

▶ Wenn ich mit der Arbeit fertig wäre, ... (ins Kino gehen)
   Wenn ich mit der Arbeit fertig wäre, würde ich ins Kino gehen.

1. Wenn das Examen nicht wäre, ... (ins Schwimmbad gehen)
2. Wenn ich nicht soviel arbeiten müßte, ... (die Zeitung lesen)
3. Wenn ich reich wäre, ... (nicht mehr arbeiten)
4. Wenn ich Zeit hätte, ... (in die Berge fahren)
5. Wenn wir auf dem Land wohnen könnten, ... (den ganzen Tag im Garten sitzen)
6. Wenn das Wetter besser wäre, ... (spazierengehen)
7. Wenn ich nicht studieren müßte, ... (ein herrliches Leben führen)

───────────────── □

13 Omission of *wenn* in conditional sentences

Hätte ich Zeit, würde ich mitkommen.	*If I had time, I would come along.*
Hätte ich Zeit, käme ich mit.	
Hätte ich Zeit gehabt, wäre ich mitgekommen.	*If I had had time, I would have come along.*

Wenn may be omitted at the beginning of the condition clause (**wenn**-clause); the verb then begins the sentence. The meaning of the sentence is the same as if **wenn** were stated: **Hätte ich Zeit = Wenn ich Zeit hätte.**

☐————————————

L. Wäre ich nur...!   Say again what Holger is dreaming about. This time omit **wenn.**

▶   Wenn ich mit der Arbeit fertig wäre,... (ins Kino gehen)
   Wäre ich mit der Arbeit fertig, würde ich ins Kino gehen.

————————————☐

14   Conclusions without stated conditions

Das **würde** ich nicht **machen.**	*I would**n't** **do** that.*
Würdest du das **glauben**?	*Would you **believe** that?*
Sowas **täte** Frank nie.	*Frank **would** never **do** such a thing.*
Hättest du sowas **getan**?	*Would you **have done** such a thing?*

General subjunctive is used to express hypothetical situations or conclusions without stated conditions. The unstated conditions are often implied. Saying "I wouldn't do that" may be implying "if I were you (or someone else)."

☐————————————

M. Das wäre schön.   Alexander describes how he would spend the summer if he could. Express his thoughts in German. Use the general subjunctive of the main verb or the **würde**-construction, as appropriate.

1. There would be no work.
2. I would sleep a lot.
3. My friends would always have time for me.
4. In the afternoons we would sit in the café and eat a lot of cake.
5. I would often go for a walk or go biking.
6. Sometimes I would watch TV or write a letter.
7. I would like such a life.
8. That would be nice.

————————————☐

15   Wishes and polite requests or questions

a. wishes

Wenn er nur leise **sprechen würde!**	*If only he **would speak** quietly!*
Wenn du nur **mitkommen könntest!**	*If only you **could come along!***

Wenn es nur **regnen würde!**	*If only it **would rain!***
Wenn es nur wärmer **wäre!**	*If only it **were** warmer!*
Ich **wünschte** (**wollte**), ich **hätte** das **gesehen.**	*I **wish** I **had seen** that.*

b. Polite requests or questions

Würden Sie einen Augenblick **warten?**	***Would** you **wait** a moment?*
Würdest du mir eine Zeitung **mitbringen?**	***Would** you **bring** me **back** a newspaper?*
Möchtet ihr jetzt Kaffee **trinken?**	***Would** you **like to have** coffee now?*
Könnten Sie das Fenster ein bißchen **aufmachen?**	***Could** you **open** the window a little?*

The general subjunctive is used to express wishes that cannot be realized and polite requests or questions.

☐ ───────────

N. Faule Ausreden°.   You are about to play a critical tennis   excuses
match. Express wishes that a number of things were different.

▶   Es ist furchtbar heiß.
    Wenn es nur nicht so furchtbar heiß wäre!

1. Die Sonne scheint so hell.
2. Der Wind ist so kalt.
3. Mein linker Fuß tut so weh.
4. Ich habe so einen Durst.
5. Die Bälle sind so weich.
6. Mein Partner kommt zum Match.
7. Ich habe so große Angst.
8. Wir fangen schon in fünf Minuten an.

─────────── ☐

16 | Suppositions and comparisons: clauses with *als ob* and *als wenn*

Present-time general subjunctive:	Er tut (tat), **als ob** (**als wenn**) er krank wäre.
	*He acts (acted) **as if** he were ill.*
Past-time general subjunctive:	Er tut (tat), **als ob** (**als wenn**) er krank gewesen wäre.
	*He acts (acted) **as if** he had been ill.*

Constructions with **als ob** and **als wenn** (*as if, as though*) express suppositions and comparisons. If the **als ob/als wenn**-clause refers to the same time as the main clause (e.g., **tut** or **tat**), the present-time general subjunctive is used. If the **als ob/als wenn**-clause refers to something that took place before the action of the main clause (e.g., **tut** or **tat**), the past-time general subjunctive is used.

Er sieht aus, **als** wäre er krank.   *He looks **as if** he were ill.*

Tun Sie, **als** wären Sie zu Hause!   *Act **as if** you were at home.*

The conjunction **als** can be used without **ob** or **wenn** to mean *as if*. In this usage the verb follows **als** directly.

□ —————————

O. Die Erkältung.   You don't feel well and your friend Marianne is asking about your symptoms. Describe what your symptoms feel like. Use **als ob** or **als wenn** with the cues in parentheses.

▶   Fühlst du dich so schlecht? (ich bin krank)
     Ja, ich fühle mich so schlecht, als ob (als wenn) ich krank wäre.

1. Läuft deine Nase? (ich habe eine Erkältung)
2. Tut dir der Kopf weh? (er will explodieren)
3. Brennt dein Hals? (ich habe Feuer gegessen)
4. Brummen° deine Ohren? (ein kaputtes Radio ist darin)   *ring*
5. Tun dir die Augen weh? (ich habe zuviel ferngesehen)
6. Bist du müde? (ich habe zwei Nächte nicht geschlafen)

————————— □

17   The *würde*-construction vs. the general subjunctive of the main verb

1. The meaning of the **würde**-construction and the general subjunctive of the main verb is identical:

Ich **käme** gern **mit**.   ⎫
                                 ⎬   *I **would** be glad to **come along.***
Ich **würde** gern **mitkommen**. ⎭

2. In colloquial German, the **würde**-construction is used in place of the general subjunctive of the main verb, with a few exceptions. The general subjunctive of **sein (wäre)**, **haben (hätte)**, **werden (würde)**, **wissen (wüßte)**, and the modals is preferred to the **würde**-construction. The subjunctive forms of **bleiben (bliebe)**, **gehen (ginge)**, **kommen (käme)**, and **tun (täte)** are also common in spoken German:

Wenn Christel nicht so fleißig **wäre, hätte** sie mehr Freizeit und **könnte** ein Hobby haben.	*If Christel **were** not so diligent she **would have** more free time and **could** have a hobby.*

3. Formal written German tends to avoid the **würde**-construction in the **wenn**-clause:

Auch wenn der Staat mehr Straßen **baute, gäbe** es trotzdem zu viel Verkehr.	*Even if the government **built** more roads, there **would** still **be** too much traffic.*

Note that in colloquial German, however, **würde** is often used in a **wenn**-clause, especially to avoid the subjunctive of weak verbs and many of the strong verbs:

Wenn es nur **regnen würde!**	*If only it **would rain**.*

Zusammenfassung

A. Schade!   Übertragen Sie das Folgende ins Deutsche.

1. ANDREA: Could you help me, please?
2. RUDI: I would like to° (do that). If I only had time. You look as   *Use **würde + gern**.*
   if you were ill.
3. ANDREA: I wish I felt better.
4. RUDI: Maybe you should go to bed.
5. ANDREA: I wish I hadn't eaten the fish.
6. RUDI: You should have asked me. Too bad. We could have
   gone to a nice restaurant tonight.

B. Die Umfrage°.   Tobias soll für seinen Psychologiekurs eine   *survey*
Umfrage unter seinen Bekannten machen: „Was wünschen Sie sich?"
Diese Frage stellt er mehreren Leuten. Verwenden Sie die Informationen, und bilden Sie ganze Sätze.

▶ Tobias: eine gute Note in Psychologie bekommen
   Tobias wünschte, er bekäme eine gute Note in Psychologie.

1. Frau Mauz: noch einmal studieren dürfen
2. Helmut: jeden Tag ins Schwimmbad gehen können
3. Herr Kaufmann: mehr Sport treiben
4. Frau Dr. Weiß: im Beruf interessante Bücher lesen müssen
5. Barbara: öfter ins Museum gehen
6. Margit: mehr Freizeit haben und Tennis spielen können
7. Oliver: den ganzen Tag am Computer sitzen und Computerspiele
   machen
8. Herr Ascher: Rentner sein° und nicht mehr arbeiten müssen   *Rentner sein: to be retired*
9. Nicole: Schauspielerin sein und in Hollywood leben
10. Holger: ein Segelboot haben und um die Welt segeln

C. Zu spät!   Es gibt immer Dinge, die man in der Vergangenheit hätte tun oder nicht tun sollen. Machen Sie aus den folgenden Satzteilen komplette Sätze, und verwenden Sie dabei den Konjunktiv II der Vergangenheit.

▶ ich / wünschen // letztes Semester / mehr lernen
   Ich wünschte, ich hätte letztes Semester mehr gelernt.

1. Frau Schneider / wünschen // nicht / Ärztin / werden
2. Michael / wünschen // im Gymnasium bleiben / und Abitur° machen
3. Familie Bauer / wünschen // nach Italien ziehen
4. Susanne / wünschen // als Kind / mehr spielen
5. die Kinder / wünschen // auf ihren Hund / besser aufpassen
6. Frau May / wünschen // das Haus ihrer Eltern / nicht verkaufen
7. Ursula / wünschen // in der Schule / fleißiger sein
8. Herr Burger / wünschen // seine Freundin Sabine / heiraten

final exams (in secondary school)

D. Was wäre, wenn...?   Was würden Sie machen, wenn sie in den folgenden Situationen wären? Wählen Sie *fünf* Situationen, und schreiben Sie ein bis zwei Sätze im Konjunktiv II. Verwenden Sie *würde* + *Infinitiv* oder die anderen Konjunktivformen.

▶ wenn Ihr Fahrrad kaputt wäre
   Wenn mein Fahrrad kaputt wäre, würde ich es reparieren.
   Wenn ich es nicht reparieren könnte, ginge ich eben zu Fuß.

1. wenn ich noch einmal 10 Jahre alt wäre
2. wenn ich ein Jahr Freizeit hätte
3. wenn ich noch einmal meine Universität wählen könnte
4. wenn ich ein Portemonnaie° auf der Straße fände
5. wenn ich in einem anderen Land, z.B. in _____ lebte
6. wenn ich in der Lotterie eine Million gewinnen würde
7. wenn ich 70 Jahre alt wäre
8. wenn ich _____ von Beruf wäre
9. wenn ich _____ hätte
10. wenn ich _____ müßte

billfold

E. Partnerarbeit.   Sie diskutieren mit einer Partnerin/einem Partner, wie Sie die Welt verbessern würden. Was müßte anders sein?

F. Kurze Aufsätze

1. Stellen Sie sich vor, Sie könnten so leben, wie Sie wollten. Wie würde so ein Leben aussehen?
2. Was wären Ihre wichtigsten Ziele° und Prioritäten, wenn Sie Präsidentin/Präsident oder Kanzlerin/Kanzler Ihres Landes oder Bürgermeisterin/Bürgermeister Ihrer Stadt wären? Was würden

goals

Sie verändern, was sollte anders werden? Denken Sie an Themen wie die Umwelt°, Arbeitswelt, medizinische und soziale Sicherheit°, Schulen usw.

environment / security

3. Schreiben Sie einen Brief an Ihren Freund/Ihre Freundin, in dem Sie ihn/sie einladen, ein Wochenende bei Ihnen zu verbringen. Schlagen Sie vor, was Sie alles tun und unternehmen könnten.

4. Stellen Sie sich vor, Sie wachten eines Morgens auf und wären in einem fremden Land. In welchem Land sind Sie? Beschreiben Sie, was sich in Ihrem Leben ändern würde.

KAPITEL

13

Passive Voice ■

1 The passive voice°

das Passiv

	Subject		Direct Object
Active voice:	**Die Firma Müller**	baut	unser Haus.
	The Müller company	*is building*	*our house.*
	Subject		Agent
Passive voice:	Unser Haus	wird	**von der Firma Müller** gebaut.
	Our house	*is being built*	*by the Müller company.*
	Subject		(No agent)
	Unser Haus	wird im Sommer	gebaut.
	Our house	*is being built in the summer.*	

German and English sentences are in either active voice or passive voice. In active voice, the subject is "active"; it is the agent that performs the action expressed by the verb. Active voice focuses attention on the agent, here, *the Müller company.*

In passive voice, the subject is "passive"; it performs no action. The subject is acted upon by an expressed or unexpressed agent. Passive voice focuses attention on the receiver of the action, here, *our house.*

The subject of an active sentence (e.g., **die Firma Müller**) corresponds to the agent in a passive sentence (e.g., **von der Firma Müller**). The direct object in an active sentence (e.g., **unser Haus**) corresponds to the subject in a passive sentence (e.g., **unser Haus**). The agent is often omitted in a passive sentence, as if the corresponding active sentence had no subject.

The passive is often used in technical and scientific writing, where an impersonal style is frequently preferred by the writer. In conversational German, the active voice is much more common. (See Section 9, "Alternatives to the passive voice.")

2 Tenses in the passive voice

Present:	Die Arbeit **wird gemacht.**
	*The work **is being done.***
Simple past:	Die Arbeit **wurde gemacht.**
	*The work **was done.***
Present perfect:	Die Arbeit **ist gemacht worden.**
	*The work **has been done.***

Past perfect: Die Arbeit **war gemacht worden.**
                  The work **had been done.**

Future: Die Arbeit **wird gemacht werden.**
            The work **will be done.**

In English a passive verb phrase consists of a form of the auxiliary verb *to be* and the past participle of the main verb (e.g., *done*). In German the passive verb phrase consists of a form of the auxiliary **werden** plus the past participle of the main verb (e.g., **gemacht**). Note that in the present perfect and past perfect tenses the participle **worden** is used instead of the form **geworden.**

   Passive voice can occur in any tense, but the future tense is rarely used.

Present-time general subjunctive: Die Arbeit **würde gemacht.**
                                      The work **would be done.**

Past-time general subjunctive: Die Arbeit **wäre gemacht worden.**
                                   The work **would have been done.**

The passive voice also occurs in the subjunctive.

3 Expressing agent° and means°   *das Agens / das Mittel*

von + *agent:*   Die Zeitung wird **von Studentinnen** geschrieben.
                     *The newspaper is being written **by students.***

durch + *means:*   Die Nachbarn wurden **durch die Musik** gestört.
                       *The neighbors were disturbed **by (as a result of) the music.***

A sentence in the passive voice often indicates by what agent or means an action is performed.

   The person(s) who causes an event to happen is known as the *agent* (e.g., **Studentinnen**). In the passive voice, the role of the agent is of secondary importance to the receiver of the action (the subject: e.g., **die Zeitung**). The agent is the object of the preposition **von** and thus in the dative case.

   The *means* (e.g., **Musik**) by which an event happens is usually impersonal; it is the object of the preposition **durch** and thus in the accusative case. **Durch** + *means* expresses the idea *as a result of* or *by the means of.*

□ —————————————

A. Wer macht die Hausarbeit?   Restate the following passive sentences in the tenses indicated.

▶ Der Haushaltsplan° wird von uns allen gemacht. *(simple past)*
  Der Haushaltsplan wurde von uns allen gemacht.   *housekeeping schedule*

1. Das Essen wird von meinem Vater gekocht. *(present perfect)*
2. Die Gartenarbeit wird von meinem Bruder gemacht. *(simple past)*
3. Die Wäsche wird von meiner Schwester gewaschen. *(simple past)*
4. Eingekauft wird von mir. *(simple past)*
5. Die Fenster werden von uns allen geputzt. *(future)*
6. Der Küchenplan wird von der ganzen Familie diskutiert. *(present perfect)*
7. Jeder wird von jedem kritisiert. *(future)*
8. Das Geld wird von meiner Mutter verdient. *(present perfect)*

B. Am Sonntag.   Helga describes a Sunday in her hometown. Change her statements from active to passive. Keep the same tense.

▶ Früher brachte der Bäcker die frischen Brötchen ins Haus.
  Früher wurden die frischen Brötchen vom Bäcker ins Haus gebracht.

1. Heute toasten wir die Brötchen vom Samstag. *(omit agent)*
2. Der Vater wäscht das Auto.
3. Mein Bruder kocht das Mittagessen.
4. Beim Spaziergang grüßen wir die Nachbarn freundlich. *(omit agent)*
5. Im Café bedient° uns ein italienischer Kellner.   *serves*
6. Das Abendessen essen wir zu Hause. *(omit agent)*
7. Am Abend sehen wir fern. *(omit agent)*

C. Ein Essen für die Gäste.   Tell in German about all the things you did last night to prepare for your guests.

1. The meat was put in wine°.   *to put in wine = **in Wein legen***
2. Then it was fried.
3. The rice was cooked (for) twenty minutes.
4. The salad was prepared too.
5. Apples were cut.
6. The sweet cream was beaten.
7. Flowers were put° on the table.   ***stellen***
8. And the guests were picked up at the station.

———————————— ☐

4 | Modals and the passive infinitive

Present: Der Wagen **muß repariert werden.**
             *The car **has to be repaired.***

Past: Der Wagen **mußte repariert werden.**
          *The car **had to be repaired.***

Present-time general
    subjunctive: Der Wagen **müßte** eigentlich **repariert werden.**
        *The car really **ought to be repaired.***

Modals are frequently used with passive infinitives. A passive infinitive (e.g., **repariert werden**) consists of a past participle plus **werden**. Note that only the modal changes in various tenses (e.g., **muß, mußte**). The passive infinitive remains the same. Although the modal construction can occur in all tenses, those listed above are the most common.

□———————————

D. Ein autofreier Sonntag.
For the protection of the environment, some cities are planning a day free of car traffic. The city planner says what can, must, and will be done. Restate using the cued modal and passive infinitive.

▶   Alle Leute werden informiert. (müssen)
    Alle Leute müssen informiert werden.

1. Autos werden nicht gefahren. (dürfen)
2. Fahrräder werden benutzt. (können)
3. Die Straßen werden vom Autoverkehr freigehalten. (sollen)
4. Auch Motorräder werden zu Hause gelassen. (müssen)
5. Energie wird gespart. (müssen)
6. Die Polizisten werden in Urlaub geschickt. (können)
7. Auf den Straßen wird an den Tankstellen Limonade verkauft. (sollen)

———————————□

5   Impersonal passive construction°

das unpersönliche Passiv

Active voice: Sonntags arbeitet man nicht.
          One doesn't work on Sundays.

Passive voice: Sonntags wird nicht gearbeitet.   } *(There is no work-*
          Es wird sonntags nicht gearbeitet. } *ing on Sundays.)*

A German active sentence without a direct object can have a corresponding passive sentence. Such a sentence does not have a subject and is called an impersonal passive construction. An English active sentence without a direct object does not have a corresponding passive sentence.

The pronoun **es** begins an impersonal passive construction if no other words precede the verb. **Es** is a *dummy* or *apparent* subject. An English equivalent of the German impersonal passive often uses an introductory phrase such as *there is* or *there are*.

Since you will not have occasion to use the impersonal passive construction very often, it is probably best simply to learn the meaning of any expression you come across, e.g., **Hier wird nicht geraucht** (*No smoking here*).

6 | Dative verbs in the passive voice

Active voice: Ich habe **ihm** nicht geholfen.   *I didn't help **him**.*

Passive voice: **Ihm** wurde nicht geholfen. ⎫ ***He** wasn't helped.*
                  Es wurde **ihm** nicht geholfen. ⎭

In German, only the accusative (direct) object in an active sentence may become the subject of a sentence in passive voice. The dative object in an active sentence (e.g., **ihm**) remains unchanged when used in a passive sentence. The resulting passive sentence has no subject, but **es** may be used as a dummy or apparent subject.

Since English makes no distinction between the dative and accusative, the object of the active sentence (e.g., *him*) corresponds to the subject of the passive sentence (e.g., *he*).

These constructions are infrequent in German, and you may not have occasion to use them. However, you should recognize them if you come across them.

E. Ein Unfall.   People are still talking about a recent accident. Restate the sentences using **es**, and give the English equivalents.

▶ Dem anderen Fahrer konnte nichts bewiesen werden.
  Es konnte dem anderen Fahrer nichts bewiesen werden.
  Nothing could be proved against the other driver.

1. Ihm wurde aber auch nicht geglaubt.
2. Nach dem Unfall ist viel diskutiert worden.
3. Uns wurde erklärt, daß wir zu schnell gefahren wären.
4. Beiden Fahrern wurde geraten, etwas vorsichtiger° zu fahren.   *more carefully*
5. Später ist beschlossen worden, die Polizei nicht zu rufen.
6. Schließlich ist nicht mehr über die Sache gesprochen worden.

7 | Past participle in passive vs. past participle as predicate adjective

Passive: Das Auto **wird** jetzt **repariert.**
              *The car **is being repaired** now.*

Predicate adjective: Das Auto **ist** schon **repariert.**
                          *The car **is** already **repaired.***

Passive voice expresses a process wherein something happens to the subject—e.g., **Auto**: *The car is being repaired.* Passive voice uses a form of **werden** and the past participle (e.g., **repariert**).

The past participle can also be used with the verb **sein** to express the state or condition of the subject that results from some action upon it: *The car is already repaired.* The past participle then functions like a predicate adjective. Because of its similarity to the passive, the construction **sein** + past participle is often referred to as an *apparent passive* or *statal passive.*

In English, the verb *to be* is used both for the passive (e.g., *is being repaired*) and for predicate adjectives (e.g., *is repaired*). For this reason, the difference between the passive and predicate adjective is sometimes not clear. In German, the difference between the passive (**werden** + past participle) that expresses a process and the predicate adjective (**sein** + past participle) that expresses a condition or state is distinct.

☐ ——————————

F. Abreise°.   Mr. and Mrs. Knoll are leaving on a trip. Mr. Knoll is   *departure*
a little bit nervous and checks to be sure everything has been taken care
of. Take the role of Mrs. Knoll and offer reassurances.

▶   Die Fahrkarten müssen noch abgeholt werden.
     Die Fahrkarten sind (doch/schon) abgeholt.

  1. Der Fotoapparat muß noch abgeholt werden.
  2. Die Koffer müssen noch gepackt werden.
  3. Das Geschirr muß noch gespült werden.
  4. Die Betten müssen noch gemacht werden.
  5. Die Fenster müssen geschlossen werden.
  6. Das Taxi muß bestellt werden.

—————————— ☐

8 | Summary of the uses of *werden*

a. Active voice: main verb°   *das Vollverb*

Herr Meier **wird** alt.   *Mr. Meier **is growing** old.*

Sophie **wurde** müde.   *Sophie **was getting** tired.*

Volker **ist** wieder krank **geworden**.   *Volker **has become** ill again.*

Werden as a main verb is equivalent to the English *to grow, get,* or *become.*

b. Active voice: auxiliary verb in future tense°

das Hilfsverb im Futur

Wir **werden** im Café **essen**.   *We'll eat in the café.*

Frau Lange **wird** wohl krank **sein**.   *Mrs. Lange **is** probably ill.*

Werden is used with a dependent infinitive to form the future tense. The future tense also expresses present probability.

c. Passive voice: auxiliary verb°

das Hilfsverb im Passiv

Bei Eberts **wird** jeden Samstag   ***There's a party** at the*
   gefeiert.   *Ebert's every Saturday.*

Letzten Samstag **wurde** viel **gelacht**.   *Last Saturday **there was** a lot*
                                               *of **laughing**.*

Wir **sind** auch **eingeladen worden**.   *We **were** also **invited**.*

A form of **werden** is used with a past participle to form the passive voice. Passive voice can occur in any tense.

□ ————————————

G. Beim Friseur.   Identify the way in which **werden** is used in each of the following sentences: (a) as main verb, (b) as auxiliary in the future tense, or (c) as auxiliary in passive voice. Then give the English equivalents of the sentences.

▶   Meine Haare werden gewaschen.
    auxiliary in passive voice; My hair is being washed.

  1. Sie werden kurz geschnitten.
  2. Ich werde so schön aussehen.
  3. Mich wird wohl keiner mehr erkennen.
  4. Durch die Sonne werden meine Haare immer sehr hell.
  5. Hinten werden sie wohl lang bleiben.
  6. Von der Friseuse wird mir eine Tasse Kaffee gebracht.
  7. Zum Schluß wird mein Haar mit dem Haartrockner in Form gebracht.

———————————— □

9 | Alternatives to the passive voice

In German, other constructions are frequently used instead of passive voice. Four possible alternatives follow:

a. *man* as subject

So etwas tut **man** nicht.
(*Passive*: So etwas wird nicht getan.)

One doesn't do that.
(*That's not done.*)

Von hier kann **man** den See sehen.
(*Passive*: Von hier kann der See gesehen werden.)

You can see the lake from here.
(*The lake can be seen from here.*)

The pronoun **man** as the subject of an active sentence is the most common alternative to the passive voice. English equivalents for the pronoun **man** are *one, you, we, they,* or *people.*

b. *sein...zu* + infinitive

Das **ist** leicht **zu lernen.**
(*Passive*: Das kann leicht gelernt werden.)

That **is** easy **to learn.**
(*That can be easily learned.*)

Diese Aufgabe **ist** noch **zu machen.**
(*Passive*: Diese Aufgabe muß noch gemacht werden.)

This assignment **is** still **to be done.**

(*This assignment still has to be done.*)

A form of **sein...zu** + infinitive is often used in German instead of a passive verb phrase. This construction expresses the possibility (e.g., **leicht zu lernen**) or necessity (e.g., **noch zu machen**) of doing something.

c. *sich lassen* + infinitive

Das **läßt sich machen.**
(*Passive*: Das kann gemacht werden.)

That **can be done.**
(*That can be done.*)

Das Radio **läßt sich** nicht **reparieren.**
(*Passive*: Das Radio kann nicht repariert werden.)

The radio **can't be fixed.**
(*The radio can't be fixed.*)

A form of **sich lassen** + infinitive can be used in place of a passive verb phrase. This construction expresses the possibility of something being done or not being done.

d. reflexive constructions

Solche Sachen **verkaufen sich** leicht.
(*Passive*: Solche Sachen können leicht verkauft werden.)

Such things **sell** easily.
(*Such things can be sold easily.*)

Die Tür **öffnete sich.**	*The door **opened.***
(*Passive:* Die Tür wurde geöffnet.)	(*The door was opened.*)

A reflexive construction is sometimes used as an alternative to passive voice.

The four active-voice alternatives to passive voice can be summarized as follows:

Passive voice:	Deutsch **kann** leicht **gelernt werden.**
	German can be learned easily.
(a) **man:**	Deutsch kann **man** leicht lernen.
	One can learn German easily.
(b) **sein…zu** + *infinitive:*	Deutsch **ist** leicht **zu lernen.**
	German is easy to learn.
(c) **sich lassen** + *infinitive:*	Deutsch **läßt sich** leicht **lernen.**
	German can be learned easily.
(d) *reflexive construction:*	Deutsch **lernt sich** leicht.
	German is easy to learn.

□————————————

H. In einem andern Land.   John is visiting Austria for the first time. Tell him how Sundays are often spent by restating the sentences using **man.**

▶   Sonntags wird nicht gearbeitet.
    Sonntags arbeitet man nicht.

1. Sonntags wird lange geschlafen.
2. Manchmal wird im Gasthaus zu Mittag gegessen.
3. Sonntag nachmittags wird ein Spaziergang gemacht.
4. Danach wird Kaffee getrunken.
5. Dazu werden viele Stücke Kuchen gegessen.
6. Bei schönem Wetter wird viel radgefahren°.   Note: *fährt…Rad*
7. Abends wird ferngesehen.

I. Reise nach Wien.   Mr. and Mrs. Münz are planning a trip to Vienna. They are at the travel agency asking many questions. You, the travel agent, respond according to the cues using **sein…zu** + infinitive.

▶   Können wir das Stadtzentrum vom Hotel aus leicht erreichen? (ja)
    Ja, das Stadtzentrum ist vom Hotel aus leicht zu erreichen.

1. Können wir den Wienerwald vom Hotel aus sehen? (nein)
2. Können wir die Oper leicht finden? (ja)
3. Müssen wir die Fahrkarten schon jetzt bezahlen? (ja)
4. Müssen wir die Plätze für die Donaufahrt° bei Ihnen reservieren? (ja)   *trip on the Danube*
5. Müssen wir morgen alle Papiere mitbringen? (ja)   *sightseeing tour /*
6. Können Sie die Stadtrundfahrt° in Wien empfehlen°? (nein)   *recommend*

J. Was ist es?   Jan has received a birthday gift, but he won't tell his friends what it is. So they ask him all sorts of questions in order to guess what the gift is. Answer for Jan using **sich lassen** + infinitive, and then make your own guess.

▶   Kann man das Ding gut gebrauchen? (ja)
    Ja, das Ding läßt sich gut gebrauchen.

1. Kann man das Ding essen? (nein)
2. Kann man das Ding draußen benutzen? (ja)
3. Kann man es auch im Haus benutzen? (ja)
4. Kann man Freunde damit unterhalten? (ja)
5. Kann man es leicht herumtragen? (ja)
6. Kann man Musik damit machen? (ja)
    Ist es ein _____?

K. Umzug° nach England.   The Schneiders are moving from   *move*
Germany to England. They discuss their move with friends. Restate their comments using reflexive constructions.

▶   Die alte Wohnung ist leicht zu verkaufen.
    Die alte Wohnung verkauft sich leicht.

1. Eine neue Wohnung ist sicher schnell zu finden.
2. Die britische Kultur ist aus ihrer Geschichte zu erklären.
3. Die englischen Zeitungen sind leicht zu lesen.
4. Denn die englische Sprache ist leicht zu lernen.
5. Gute Freunde sind aber nicht so leicht zu finden.
6. Geld verdient man auch nicht so leicht im Ausland.
7. Es ist fraglich, wie es der Familie gefallen wird.

─────────────── □

Zusammenfassung

A. Was wird dort gemacht?   Schreiben Sie, was an den folgenden Orten gemacht wird. Sie können als Hilfe die Verben in Klammern verwenden oder Ihre eigenen wählen (Sätze 7–10). Schreiben Sie ganze Sätze im Passiv.

▶   im Eßzimmer (essen)
    Es wird gegessen.

1. in der Bibliothek (lesen)
2. an der Uni (studieren)
3. im Kino (Filme zeigen)
4. im Stadion (Fußball spielen)
5. im Schwimmbad (schwimmen)
6. im Museum (Gemälde° und Skulpturen ausstellen°)   *pictures / to exhibit*

7. auf dem Tennisplatz
8. in der Garage
9. im Restaurant
10. im Café

B. Der perfekte Hausmann.   Herr Kleinmut denkt, daß Hausarbeit keine wirkliche Arbeit ist. Seine Frau ärgert sich sehr darüber und schlägt vor, daß er einmal alles allein macht. Was muß gemacht werden? Verwenden Sie die folgenden Informationen, und bilden Sie Sätze im Passiv Präsens.

▶   die Betten machen
     Die Betten müssen gemacht werden.

1. die Kinder wecken
2. das Baby baden
3. Eier kochen
4. Brötchen backen
5. das Frühstück machen
6. das Bad putzen
7. die Küche saubermachen
8. Teppich saugen°   **Teppich saugen:** to
9. den Hund spazierenführen   *vacuum*
10. das Auto aus der Garage holen
11. die Kinder zur Schule bringen
12. einkaufen gehen *(Use* **es**.)
13. das Mittagessen vorbereiten
14. oder soll er doch lieber eine Pizza bestellen? *(Omit agent.)*

C. Berühmte Leute und ihre Werke.   Lesen Sie, von wem die folgenden bekannten Werke, Erfindungen° und Taten sind. Schreiben   *inventions* Sie die Sätze ins Passiv Präteritum um.

▶   Mozart hat die „Zauberflöte" komponiert.
     Die „Zauberflöte" wurde von Mozart komponiert.

1. Michelangelo hat die David-Statue in Florenz geschaffen°.   *created*
2. Mutter Theresa hat vielen Kindern in der Dritten Welt geholfen.
3. Goethe hat den „Faust" geschrieben.
4. Edison hat die Glühbirne° erfunden°.   *light bulb / invented*
5. Madame Curie hat die chemische Substanz Polonium isoliert.
6. Frank Lloyd Wright hat das Guggenheimmuseum gebaut.
7. Harriet Beecher Stowe hat den Roman „Onkel Toms Hütte" geschrieben.
8. Gorbatschow hat die Perestroika* initiert.
9. Doris Dörrie hat den Film „Männer" gedreht°.   *shot, filmed*

*Attempt to *restructure* Soviet economy into a decentralized market-oriented economy (1985–1991)

D. Die Fahrradtour.   Dagmar und Ulrike wollen eine mehr-
tägige Radtour machen. Sie sind ein bißchen aufgeregt° und überprüfen   *excited*
noch einmal, ob alles fertig ist. Übersetzen Sie ins Deutsche.

1. The bicycles are well prepared.
2. The water bottle must not be forgotten.
3. It is already packed.°   *einpacken*
4. The sandwiches are already made.
5. But they still have to be packed.
6. The inn in Bad Tölz still has to be called.
7. The neighbors are already informed°.   *informieren*
8. Only the keys still have to be taken to the neighbors.

E. Im Büro.   Herr Kaiser wollte gerade nach Hause gehen, als Frau
Althaus ihn bittet, etwas länger zu bleiben. Geben Sie das Gespräch auf
deutsch wieder. Beachten Sie die Wörter in Klammern.

1. FRAU ALTHAUS: I was given this letter. (**man**)
2.   It must be written immediately. (Passiv)
3. HERR KAISER: I'm sorry, but such a letter isn't easy to write.
                    (**sein...zu** + Infinitiv)
4. FRAU ALTHAUS: It's understood of course° that you get an hour   *of course = **von selbst***
                    off tomorrow. (reflexives verb)
5.   That's easy to say, I know. (**sich lassen**)
6.   But the work must be done. (Passiv)

F. Partnerarbeit.   Diskutieren Sie mit Ihrer Partnerin/Ihrem
Partner über Ihre Universität. Sie wollen gewisse Verbesserungen°   *improvements*
vorschlagen°. Was muß geändert werden?   *suggest*

G. Kurze Aufsätze

1. Beschreiben Sie einen der folgenden Vorgänge. Was muß gemacht
   werden? Schreiben Sie fünf Sätze, in denen Sie das Passiv verwenden.

   a. Ihr Zimmer ist unordentlich. Sie wollen Ihr Zimmer aufräumen°.   *to straighten up*
      Was muß gemacht werden?

      Beispiel: *Das Bett muß gemacht werden.*

      - Zeitungen sortieren
      - Fenster putzen
      - Bücher ins Regal° stellen   *shelf*
      - Kleidung in den Schrank hängen
      - Teppich saugen°   *to vacuum*

   b. Sie geben eine Party und wollen die Party vorbereiten. Was
      muß gemacht werden?

      Beispiel: *Die Gäste müssen eingeladen werden.*

- Getränke kaufen
- Kassetten auswählen
- Obstsalat machen
- Haus dekorieren
- Nachbarn informieren

c. Sie wollen ein großes Essen kochen. Was muß gemacht werden?

Beispiel: *Die Lebensmittel müssen eingekauft werden.*

- Rezept lesen
- Salat waschen
- Gemüse schneiden
- Kartoffeln/Nudeln kochen
- Butter heiß machen
- Fleisch braten
- Sahne für den Pudding schlagen
- Tisch decken

d. Sie wollen…?

2. Wer hat bei Ihnen zu Hause welche Aufgaben? Was wird von wem gemacht? Sie können die folgenden Satzteile verwenden oder eigene Tätigkeiten° wählen. Bilden Sie ganze Sätze im Passiv.   *activities*

▶ Wäsche waschen
Die Wäsche wird von meinem Bruder und mir gewaschen.

- Lebensmittel einkaufen
- Geschirr abtrocknen
- Getränke aus dem Keller holen
- die Briefe schreiben
- Rechnungen° bezahlen   *bills*
- Wäsche bügeln°   *to iron*
- den Hund/die Katze/den Vogel füttern°   *to feed*
- Bilder aufhängen
- die Stereoanlage reparieren
- den Rasen mähen°   **den Rasen mähen:** *to mow the lawn*
- …?
- …?

3. Was sind Ihrer Meinung nach die fünf größten Errungenschaften°   *accomplishments* der Menschen? Sie können aus allen möglichen Gebieten sein (z.B. Kunst, Technik, Wissenschaft° usw.). Von wem wurden sie   *science* gemacht, entdeckt°, erfunden°, usw.? Schreiben Sie im Passiv.   *discovered / invented*

Beispiele: *Die Röntgenstrahlen wurden von Wilhelm Röntgen entdeckt.*
Die Mona Lisa wurde von Leonardo da Vinci gemalt.

KAPITEL

14

Indirect Discourse ■

Special Subjunctive ■

1 Indirect discourse°: statements   *die indirekte Rede*

Direct discourse:	Uwe sagte: „**Ich habe** keine Zeit.“	*Uwe said, "I don't have time."*
Indirect discourse:		
General subjunctive:	Uwe sagte, **er hätte** keine Zeit.	
Special subjunctive:	Uwe sagte, **er habe** keine Zeit.	*Uwe said he had* (coll.: *has*) *no time.*

Direct discourse or direct quotation is used to repeat the exact words of another person. In writing, the direct quotation is set off by quotation marks.

Indirect discourse is used to report what someone else has said. The pronouns change in indirect discourse to correspond to the perspective of the speaker. Uwe speaks of himself and says "**ich**." When you report his message, you refer to Uwe as "**er**."

Uwe sagte, er hätte keine Zeit. → Uwe sagte, **daß** er keine Zeit **hätte.**

The conjunction **daß** may or may not be stated in indirect discourse. Usually indirect quotations are not introduced by **daß.** When **daß** is stated, the finite verb (that is, the verb that agrees with the subject) is in last position; when **daß** is omitted, the finite verb is in second position. Note that a comma separates clauses in indirect discourse.

To report what someone else has said, German speakers may use one of two possible subjunctive forms: general subjunctive (e.g., **er hätte**) or special subjunctive (e.g., **er habe**). Some German speakers frequently use the indicative instead of the subjunctive: **Uwe sagte, er *hat* keine Zeit.**

2 General subjunctive (subjunctive II)

Present-time:	Karin sagte, sie **könnte** nicht mitkommen.
	Karin said she couldn't come along.
Past-time:	Cornelia sagte, sie **hätte** die Arbeit selbst **gemacht.**
	Cornelia said she had done the work herself.

In colloquial German, speakers often use the general subjunctive (also called subjunctive II) to report what someone else has said. The formation of general subjunctive is based upon the simple past tense indicative (see *Kapitel 12*).

Special subjunctive° (subjunctive I)   *Konjunktiv I*

Der Polizist behauptete, er **habe** es **gesehen.**
The policeman claimed he had seen (coll.: saw) *it.*

German also has a special subjunctive (called subjunctive I) that is used for indirect discourse. Special subjunctive usually occurs in formal German, which is used in newspapers, official statements, TV reporting, and literary works. The special subjunctive is also used in certain kinds of wishes and commands (see Section 8 of this chapter).

4   Present-time special subjunctive

ich geh**e**	*wir* geh**en**
du geh**est**	*ihr* geh**et**
er/es/sie geh**e**	*sie* geh**en**
Sie geh**en**	

The present-time special subjunctive is composed of the infinitive stem plus the above subjunctive endings. Note that the endings are the same for both special and general subjunctive.

Most of the forms of special subjunctive are the same as the indicative forms. Therefore, use of the special subjunctive is generally limited to the 3rd person singular, since that form is clearly distinct from the indicative.

Note that the 2nd person singular and plural are also distinct from the indicative, but these forms are considered stilted: **du gehest, ihr gehet; du gebest, ihr gebet.**

Infinitive	Special subjunctive (**er/es/sie**-form)	Indicative (**er/es/sie**-form)
dürfen	**dürfe**	darf
können	**könne**	kann
mögen	**möge**	mag
müssen	**müsse**	muß
sollen	**solle**	soll
wollen	**wolle**	will
haben	**habe**	hat
sein	**sei**	ist
werden	**werde**	wird

(continued)

Infinitive	Special Subjunctive (**er/es/sie**-form)	Indicative (**er/es/sie**-form)
geben	**gebe**	gibt
schlafen	**schlafe**	schläft
sehen	**sehe**	sieht

Modals and verbs that have stem-vowel or other changes in the 2nd and 3rd person singular forms of the indicative do not undergo vowel change in the special subjunctive.

Er sagte, er **habe** keine Zeit, aber seine Kollegen meinten, sie dagegen **hätten** sehr viel Zeit.

When the special subjunctive form is identical to the indicative (e.g., **haben**), general subjunctive (e.g., **hätten**) must be used.

5   Special subjunctive of *sein*

ich **sei**	*wir* **seien**
du **sei(e)st**	*ihr* **sei(e)t**
er/es/sie **sei**	*sie* **seien**
Sie **seien**	

Note that **sei** (the special subjunctive form of **sein**) does not have the **-e** ending characteristic of the **ich-** and **er/es/sie**-forms in the special subjunctive.

Meine Freunde sagten, sie **seien** zufrieden.
*My friends said they **were** (coll.: are) satisfied.*

Doris sagte, sie **sei** nicht zufrieden.
*Doris said she **was** (coll.: is) not satisfied.*

Sei occurs frequently in indirect discourse in both colloquial and formal German, since the forms are clearly different from the indicative.

6   Past-time special subjunctive

Ein Kritiker meinte, das Orchester **habe** endlich gut **gespielt.**
*A critic said the orchestra **had** finally **played** (coll.: played) well.*

Eine Polizistin sagte, die Demonstration **sei** friedlich **gewesen.**
*A policewoman said the demonstration **had been** (coll.: was) peaceful.*

Past-time special subjunctive consists of the special subjunctive forms
of the auxiliaries **haben (habe)** or **sein (sei)** plus the past participle of
the main verb.

ich **habe** es getan	*wir* **haben** es getan
du **habest** es getan	*ihr* **habet** es getan
er/es/sie **habe** es getan	*sie* **haben** es getan
Sie **haben** es getan	

ich **sei** nicht gegangen	*wir* **seien** nicht gegangen
du **seiest** nicht gegangen	*ihr* **seiet** nicht gegangen
er/es/sie **sei** nicht gegangen	*sie* **seien** nicht gegangen
Sie **seien** nicht gegangen	

The special subjunctive of the **ich, wir, sie** (pl.), and **Sie**-forms of **haben**
are identical to the indicative and therefore must be replaced by the
general subjunctive form **hätte** (e.g., **Sie hätten es getan.**) Because of
the mixture of special and general subjunctive forms of haven in indirect discourse, the actual paradigm is as follows:

ich **hätte** es getan *(gen. subj.)*	*wir* **hätten** es getan *(gen. subj.)*
du **habest** es getan *(sp. subj.)*	*ihr* **habet** es getan *(sp. subj.)*
er/es/sie **habe** es getan *(sp. subj.)*	*sie* **hätten** es getan *(gen. subj.)*
Sie **hätten** es getan *(gen. subj.)*	

7   Future-time special subjunctive

Die Präsidentin erklärte, man **werde** die politischen Probleme **lösen
  können.**
*The president declared one **would** (coll.: will) **be able to solve** the
  political problems.*

Der Beamte sagte, er **werde** die Frage morgen **beantworten.**
*The official said he **would** (coll.: will) **answer** the question tomorrow.*

Future-time special subjunctive consists of the special subjunctive
forms of the auxiliary **werden (werde)** plus a dependent infinitive.

---

ich **werde** es tun	wir **werden** es tun
du **werdest** es tun	ihr **werdet** es tun
er/es/sie **werde** es tun	sie **werden** es tun
Sie **werden** es tun	

The special subjunctive of the **ich, wir, sie** (pl.) and **Sie**-forms are identical to the indicative and must therefore be replaced by the general subjunctive form **würde** (e.g., **Sie würden es tun.**). Because of the mixture of special and general subjunctive forms of **werden** in indirect discourse, the actual paradigm is as follows.

---

ich **würde** es tun *(gen. subj.)*	wir **würden** es tun *(gen. subj.)*
du **werdest** es tun *(sp. subj.)*	ihr **werdet** es tun *(sp. subj.)*
er/es/sie **werde** es tun *(sp. subj.)*	sie **würden** es tun *(gen. subj.)*
Sie **würden** es tun *(gen. subj.)*	

---

8 Special subjunctive in wishes, commands, and requests

Certain wishes:	Gott **gebe** es!	*May God grant that.*
	Möge er noch lange leben!	*May he live long.*
	Gott **sei** Dank!	*Thank God.*
Certain commands and wishes:	**Nehmen** wir als Beispiel...	*Let's take as an example . . .*
	Essen wir!	*Let's eat!*
	So **sei** es!	*So be it!*
	Seien wir froh, daß alles vorbei ist.	*Let's be glad it's all over.*

The special subjunctive is used in certain standard wishes, commands, or requests.

□ ──────────────

A. Abgesagt°.   On the spur of the moment, Jens decides to have a party, but all his friends seem to have other plans. Jens, who doesn't quite believe them, now tells his friend Tobias what explanation each person gave him. Use special subjunctive.

invitation turned down

▶ Harald ist bei seiner Freundin in Köln.
   Harald sagte, er sei bei seiner Freundin in Köln.

1. Franziska hat Besuch von ihren Eltern.
2. Horst ist krank. Er hat eine schwere Erkältung.
3. Angelika fährt zu einem Sprachkurs nach Florenz.
4. Axel hilft seinem Vater im Garten.
5. Susanne muß in der Bibliothek arbeiten.
6. Natalie ist schon verabredet°.   *has something planned
7. Johannes repariert sein Motorrad.   (a date)*
8. Florian hat keine Lust auf eine Party.

B. Der Hypochonder.

Walter is known for being quite a hypochondriac. Once again, he thinks he's very ill. His friends are making fun of him and tell one another what Walter suspects this time. Use special subjunctive.

▶ Ich bin sehr krank.
   Walter sagte, er sei sehr krank.

1. Ich bin immer müde.
2. Ich schlafe jede Nacht zwölf Stunden.
3. Ich habe keinen Appetit.
4. Ich kann mich kaum bewegen.
5. Alles tut mir weh.
6. Ich muß zum Arzt gehen.
7. Ich habe Angst davor.
8. Der Arzt schickt mich sicher ins Krankenhaus.
9. Vielleicht gibt mir der Arzt auch starke Medikamente°.   *medication*
10. Dann werde ich sicher noch kränker.

C. Mehr Umweltschutz°.

As a reporter you attend a conference on the environment. Report the remarks of one of the speakers in your newspaper article. Use special subjunctive.

environmental protection

▶ Man muß mehr öffentliche Verkehrsmittel° benutzen.
   *Der Redner sagte, man müsse mehr öffentliche Verkehrsmittel
   benutzen.*

**offentliche Verkehrs-
mittel:** *public
transportation*

1. Die Luft soll reingehalten werden.
2. Es muß mehr Energie gespart werden.
3. Jeder soll weniger Auto fahren.
4. Jeder einzelne trägt Verantwortung° für die Zukunft°.   *responsibility / future*
5. Wir haben schon zuviel Zeit verloren. *(Use general subjunctive.)*
6. Unsere Seen sind schmutzig.
7. In den Flüssen sind schon viele Fische gestorben.
8. Es darf nicht länger gewartet werden.

——————————— □

9 | Summary: indirect discourse

a. forms

General subjective **(Konjunktiv II):**   Karla sagte, sie **hätte** keine Zeit.

Special subjective **(Konjunktiv I):**   Karla sagte, sie **habe** keine Zeit.

The subjunctive in indirect discourse may occur in two forms: general subjunctive and special subjunctive.

b. use of general subjunctive vs. special subjunctive

Karin sagte, sie **könnte** es nicht **verstehen.**

Max sagte, er **hätte** gestern schwer **gearbeitet.**

In colloquial German, general subjunctive is often used in indirect discourse. Some speakers frequently use indicative: **Karin sagte, sie *kann* es nicht verstehen.**

Der Fahrer behauptete, er **sei** nur 80 Stundenkilometer **gefahren.**

In formal German (typical of newspapers, TV, and literature), special subjunctive is generally used in indirect discourse.

General subjunctive: Der Redner sagte, die Leute **hätten** es nicht **verstanden.**

(Not *special subjunctive:*   Der Redner sagte, die Leute **haben** es nicht **verstanden.)**

The special subjunctive is always replaced by the general subjunctive when the special subjunctive forms are identical to the indicative forms.

Indirect discourse occurs in three time categories: present time, past time, and future time. The time used depends on the tense used in the direct quotation.

10 | Indirect discourse in present time

Direct discourse: Dieter sagte: „Ich **kann** morgen nicht arbeiten.“
Dieter said, "I can't work tomorrow."

Er sagte: „Ich **bin** krank.“
He said, "I'm ill."

Indirect discourse: Dieter sagte, er **könne/könnte** morgen nicht arbeiten.
Dieter said he couldn't (coll.: can't) work tomorrow.

Er sagte, er **sei/wäre** krank.
He said he was (coll.: is) ill.

In German, when the direct statement or quotation is in the present tense (e.g., **kann, bin**), the present-time subjunctive (e.g., **könne/könnte, sei/wäre**) is used in the corresponding indirect quotation. The present-time special or general subjunctive shows that the action or event was happening at the same time the speaker was telling about it. Dieter was ill when he commented on it. The verb in the introductory statement can be in any tense and does not affect the time category of the indirect quotation. In the sentences above, the verb **sagte** is simple past.

□ ————————————

D. Kein schlechter Job.   Tell a friend what Lore said about the conditions at a restaurant where she works. Use present-time special or general subjunctive.

▶ Mein Job gefällt mir ganz gut.
   Lore sagte, ihr Job gefalle/gefiele ihr ganz gut.

1. Die Musik ist immer ziemlich laut dort.
2. Man kann da ganz gut Geld verdienen.
3. Ich muß mich immer gut anziehen.
4. Die Kollegen sind alle jung und sehr nett.
5. Ich kann so lange dort arbeiten, wie ich will.
6. Freitag abends und samstags ist es immer knallvoll°.   *full to bursting*
7. Da muß ich ganz schön rennen.
8. Aber es macht auch Spaß.

———————————— □

11 Indirect discourse in past time

Direct discourse:

Simple past:	Lucy erklärte: „Ich **wußte** das nicht."
	Lucy explained, "I didn't know that."
Present perfect:	Lore sagte: „Ich **habe** gestern **angerufen**."
	Lore said, "I called yesterday."
Past perfect:	Michael sagte: „Ich **hatte** gerade **gegessen**."
	Michael said, "I had just eaten."

Indirect discourse: Lucy erklärte, sie **habe/hätte** das nicht **gewußt.**
Lucy explained she hadn't known (coll.: didn't know) that.

Lore sagte, sie **habe/hätte** gestern **angerufen.**
Lore said she had called (coll.: called) yesterday.

Michael sagte, er **habe/hätte** gerade **gegessen.**
Michael said he had just eaten.

In German, when a past tense (simple past, present perfect, past perfect) is used in the direct quotation, the past-time subjunctive (e.g., **habe/hätte gewußt, habe/hätte angerufen, habe/hätte gegessen**) is used in the indirect quotation. The past-time special or general subjunctive shows that the action or event happened at a time prior to the moment when the statement was made. For example, Lore called the day before she talked about it. The verb in the introductory statement can be in any tense and does not affect the time category of the indirect quotation.

☐————————————

E. Bei den Großeltern.   Five year old Karola has spent the weekend at her grandparents' place. When her father picks her up, Karola's grandparents tell him about the weekend. At home, he tells his wife what they said. Use past-time special or general subjunctive. Begin with the cued words.

▶   Karola war fröhlich. (Deine Eltern sagten,...)
Deine Eltern sagten, Karola sei/wäre fröhlich gewesen.

1. Karola hat mit dem Hund gespielt. (Dein Vater erzählte,...)
2. Morgens ist sie schon um sechs Uhr aufgewacht. (Deine Mutter sagte,...)
3. Abends war sie dann immer todmüde. (Dein Vater meinte,...)
4. Sie wollte nie frühstücken. (Deine Mutter erzählte,...)
5. Am Samstag ging sie mit uns spazieren. (Deine Eltern sagten,...)
6. Karola hat zuviel Eis gegessen. (Deine Mutter meinte,...)
7. Sie durfte nicht fernsehen. (Dein Vater sagte,...)
8. Heute hat sich Karola sehr auf euch gefreut. (Deine Mutter meinte,...)
9. Vielleicht hatte sie ein bißchen Heimweh°. (Dein Vater meinte,...)
10. Hoffentlich hat es Karola bei uns gefallen. (Deine Eltern sagten,...)

Heimweh haben: *to be homesick*

————————— ☐

12 Indirect discourse in future time

Direct discourse: Anton sagte: „Ich **werde** es später **machen.**"
Anton said, "I'll do it later."

Indirect discourse: Anton sagte, er **werde/würde** es später **machen.**
Anton said he would (coll.: *will*) *do it later.*

In German, when the future tense is used in the direct quotation, the future-time subjunctive is used in the indirect quotation. The future special or general subjunctive shows that the action or event was to happen at a time that had not yet occurred when the statement was made. In the example above, Anton said he hadn't done it yet but would do so later. The introductory statement can be in any tense and does not affect the time category of the indirect quotation.

□ ————————————

F. Vor dem Rennen.   Jürgen is going to participate in a track meet. Tell your friends what he said about his feelings and plans concerning the upcoming event. Use future-time special or general subjunctive.

▶   Ich werde bestimmt eine gute Zeit laufen.
     Jürgen sagte, er werde/würde bestimmt eine gute Zeit laufen.

1. Ich werde vorher viel trainieren müssen.
2. Ich werde jeden Tag zehn Kilometer laufen.
3. Meine Beine werden sehr stark werden.
4. Ich werde bald neue Sportschuhe brauchen.
5. Ich werde hoffentlich gewinnen.
6. Ich werde aber nicht traurig sein, wenn ich nicht gewinne.
7. Alle meine Freunde werden kommen.
8. Danach werden wir bestimmt zusammen feiern.

———————————— □

13 Time relationships between direct and indirect statements

Introductory statement	Direct statement	Indirect statement	Time relationship of indirect statement to introductory statement
Any tense	Present	Present-time subjunctive	Occurs at same time
Any tense	Simple past, Present perfect, Past perfect	Past-time subjunctive	Has already occurred
Any tense	Future	Future-time subjunctive	Has not yet occurred but will occur

14 | Indirect general questions in indirect discourse

Direct discourse: Werner fragte Antje: „**Hast** du den Schlüssel
                       gefunden?"
                       Werner asked Antje, "Did you find the key?"

Indirect discourse: Werner fragte Antje, **ob** sie den Schlüssel
                       gefunden habe/hätte.
                       *Werner asked Antje **if** (whether) she **had found**
                       (coll.: found) the key.*

In indirect discourse, a general indirect question (i.e., a question that requires a yes/no answer) is introduced by **ob** (*if, whether*) (see *Kapitel 4,* Section 6b). The verb is in the special or general subjunctive and is in last position. Indirect general questions in indirect discourse, like statements, may occur in present, past, or future time.

15 | Indirect specific questions in indirect discourse

Direct discourse: Werner fragte Antje: „Wo **hast** du den Schlüssel
                       gefunden?"
                       *Werner asked Antje, "Where **did** you **find** the key?"*

Indirect discourse: Werner fragte Antje, **wo** sie den Schlüssel
                       gefunden habe/hätte.
                       *Werner asked Antje **where** she **had found** (coll.:
                       found) the key.*

An indirect specific question (i.e., a question that elicits specific information) is introduced by an interrogative that functions like a subordinating conjunction (see *Kapitel 4,* Section 6c). The verb is in the special or general subjunctive and is in last position.

Indirect specific questions in indirect discourse, like statements, may occur in present, past, or future time.

□ ————————————————

G. Die Reise nach Österreich.   Report what you and your friends asked Stefanie about her trip to Austria. Use past-time special or general subjunctive.

▶ Bist du mit dem Zug gefahren?
   Wir fragten sie, ob sie mit dem Zug gefahren sei/wäre.

1. Bist du allein gefahren?

2. Wie war es in Österreich?
3. Welche Städte hast du besucht?
4. Warst du auch in Salzburg?
5. Bist du dort ins Mozarthaus gegangen?
6. Bist du auch im Gebirge gewandert?
7. Wo hat es dir am besten gefallen?
8. Warum bist du nicht länger geblieben?
9. Wie hat dir das österreichische Essen geschmeckt?
10. Hast du den Dialekt verstanden?

——————————————— □

16 Indirect commands in indirect discourse

Direct discourse: Kai sagte zu mir: „**Komm** doch **mit.**"
Kai said to me, "Come along."

Indirect discourse: Kai sagte zu mir, ich **solle/sollte** doch
mitkommen.
*Kai told me that I should come along./Kai told me
to come along.*

In German, an indirect command uses the special or general subjunctive form of the modal **sollen** + infinitive. The English equivalents can be expressed in two ways: with *should* plus the main verb (e.g., *should come along*), or with an infinitive (e.g., *to come along*).

□ ———————————————

H. Vor der Prüfung.   Stefan is very nervous about his exam tomorrow. Philipp has given him advice about being ready. Take Stefan's role as he tells his roommate about the advice. Use the special or general subjunctive.

▶   Geh früh ins Bett.
Philipp hat gesagt, ich solle/sollte früh ins Bett gehen.

1. Mach dir keine Sorgen.
2. Schlaf genug.
3. Steh nicht zu spät auf.
4. Iß ein gutes Frühstück.
5. Bleib ruhig.
6. Sei pünktlich.
7. Werd nicht nervös.
8. Denk an etwas Schönes.

——————————————— □

Zusammenfassung

A. Beim Arzt.   Lutz ist beim Arzt, weil er einen kleinen Unfall hatte. Geben Sie das Gespräch zwischen Lutz und dem Arzt wieder. Verwenden Sie den Konjunktiv I oder II.

▶ ARZT: Wie geht es Ihnen?
  Der Arzt fragte, wie es ihm gehe/ginge.
  LUTZ: Es geht mir schlecht.
  Lutz antwortete, es gehe/ginge ihm schlecht.

1. ARZT: Was ist los?
2. LUTZ: Ich habe mir am Fuß wehgetan.
3. ARZT: Wie ist das passiert?
4. LUTZ: Ich bin mit dem Fahrrad gestürzt.
5. ARZT: Oh, das sieht nicht gut aus. (Der Arzt sagte, ...)
6. LUTZ: Kann ich bald wieder richtig gehen?
7. ARZT: Na, das wird eine Zeit dauern.
8. LUTZ: Das ist doof°.   *stupid*
9. ARZT: Bewegen Sie den Fuß nicht! Er muß ruhig liegen.
10. LUTZ: Oh je! Das wird mir schwerfallen°. Ich tanze doch so gern.   *be difficult*

B. Der Streit°.   Gerhard, Dieter und Ralf wohnen zusammen in   *fight, argument*
einer Wohnung. Gerhard und Dieter hatten einen Streit und reden nun
nicht mehr miteinander. Die Atmosphäre in der Wohnung ist eisig. Ralf
möchte, daß sich die beiden wieder versöhnen°. Er unterhält sich mit   *to make up*
Dieter über die Situation. Übersetzen Sie das Gespräch.

1. RALF: Gerhard sagte, du wärst böse mit ihm, und er wüßte
            nicht warum.
2. DIETER: Ich habe ihm gesagt, er sollte auch manchmal das
            Geschirr spülen. Und dann schrie er, er hätte keine Zeit
            für so unwichtige Dinge.
3. RALF: Und dann sagtest du, er benähme sich wie ein Idiot?
4. DIETER: Nein, ich habe nie gesagt, er benähme sich wie ein Idiot,
            sondern er wäre ein sehr schwieriger Mitbewohner°.   *roommate*
5. RALF: Wir sollten nett zu Gerhard sein. Er erzählte mir, seine
            Prüfungen machten ihn sehr nervös. Er sagte auch, er
            würde wahrscheinlich durchfallen°.   *fail*
6. DIETER: Jetzt tut er mir leid. Bitte sag ihm, es täte mir leid.

C. Wohnungsnot° in Unistädten.   Der folgende Bericht ist   *housing shortage*
im Indikativ. Schreiben Sie die Sätze in den Konjunktiv I um. Beginnen
Sie mit *In dem Bericht steht,...* (Beachten Sie: Wenn der Konjunktiv I
mit dem Indikativ identisch ist, müssen Sie den Konjunktiv II verwenden.)

Studenten schlafen in Zelten.

Die Wohnungsnot ist in vielen Unistädten katastrophal. Es gibt kaum Zimmer für Studenten. Und die wenigen Zimmer, die vermietet werden, sind sehr teuer. Fast niemand kann sie bezahlen.

Die Studentin Antje B. aus München schläft sogar im Garten von Freunden in ihrem Zelt. Die wohnen zu zehnt° in einer 4-Zimmer-Wohnung. Jeder von ihnen bezahlt 300 DM Miete. So viel will Antje für so wenig Platz nicht ausgeben. Vielleicht ändert sie im Winter ihre Meinung.

zu zehnt: ten (people) to . . .

Die Städte müssen endlich etwas gegen die Wohnungsnot tun. Neue Studentenwohnheime sind nötig. Man kann nur hoffen, daß die Wohnungssituation bald besser wird. Viele Studenten sind permanent auf Zimmersuche und haben kaum Zeit für ihr Studium.

D. Partnerarbeit.   Fragen Sie Ihre Partnerin/Ihren Partner, was sie/er von Ihrer Universität hält. Geben Sie dann der Klasse einen Bericht. Gebrauchen Sie dabei die indirekte Rede.

▶   *Gisela glaubt,…*

E. Kurze Aufsätze

1. Diskutieren Sie mit Ihrer Partnerin/Ihrem Partner über ein Thema. Wählen Sie eine der folgenden Fragestellungen, oder überlegen Sie sich ein eigenes Thema, das Sie interessiert.

   • Was könnte man gegen die Arbeitslosigkeit° tun?
   • Sollte Alkohol schon unter 21 legal sein?
   • Sollte man auch in Privathaushalten Energie und Wasser sparen, und wie?

   unemployment

   Schreiben Sie auf, was Ihre Partnerin/Ihr Partner zu dem Thema gesagt hat. Gebrauchen Sie die indirekte Rede.

2. Sie hatten ein Interview mit einer bekannten Persönlichkeit. Berichten Sie in einem kurzen Zeitungsartikel, was diese Persönlichkeit gesagt hat. Gebrauchen Sie die indirekte Rede.

KAPITEL

Special Grammatical Points ■

In a dependent clause containing a double infinitive, the auxiliary **haben** (e.g., **hatte, hätte**) is not at the end, where it usually appears in a dependent clause. Rather, the auxiliary precedes the double infinitive (see *Kapitel 12*, Section 11). The double infinitive is always the last element in a clause.

Simone sagte, daß sie **hätte** froh sein sollen.
Simone said that she should have been happy.

If the clause contains a word that completes the meaning of the verb, such as a predicate adjective (e.g., **froh**), the auxiliary **haben** precedes that word directly rather than the infinitive itself.

☐ ————————

E. Vorwürfe°.   The Klinger family is finally on the road for their vacation. In the course of their conversation they discover all the things they didn't do before leaving and reproach each other. Various people say they know what they could or should have done. Translate their conversation.

reproaches

1. Ich weiß, daß ich die Kellertür hätte zumachen sollen.
2. Ich weiß, daß wir die Fahrräder in die Garage hätten stellen sollen.
3. Ich weiß, daß ich die Blumen hätte gießen° müssen.   *to water*
4. Ich weiß, daß Stefan die Koffer nicht hätte tragen dürfen.
5. Ich weiß, daß wir das Auto hätten reparieren sollen.
6. Ich weiß, daß wir Getränke hätten einkaufen können.
7. Ich weiß, daß Stefan sich die Reiseroute hätte überlegen sollen.
8. Ich weiß, daß wir noch den Wetterbericht hatten hören wollen.
9. Ich weiß, daß Claudia die Fenster hätte zumachen können.

———————— ☐

6   The future perfect tense°

das zweite Futur

a. formation

Future: Cornelia **wird** die Reparatur nächste Woche **machen.**
            *Cornelia **will make** the repair next week.*

Future perfect: Bis Freitag **wird** sie die Reparatur sicher **gemacht haben.**
            *By Friday she **will have made** the repair for sure.*

The future tense consists of a form of **werden** plus an infinitive (e.g., **machen**) in final position (see *Kapitel 2*, Section 9). The future perfect consists of a form of **werden** plus a perfect infinitive (e.g., **gemacht haben**). (For the formation of the perfect infinitive, see Section 3 of this chapter.)

b. usage

Erikas Freunde **werden wohl** das Museum **besucht haben.**
*Erika's friends **probably went** to the museum.*

Melanie wird das **schon** nicht vergessen haben.
*Melanie has **probably** not forgotten that.*

1. The most common use of future perfect is to express past probability, the idea that something has probably taken place. Adverbs such as **wohl, schon,** or **vielleicht** are often used to support the idea of probability. (Future tense is used in the same way to express present probability; see *Kapitel 2*, Section 11).

In einer Stunde **werde** ich das Fahrrad **repariert haben.**	*I'll **have repaired** the bicycle in an hour.*
Wenn du so weitermachst, wirst du das Buch in zwei Tagen **gelesen haben.**	*If you keep going like this, you **will have finished** the book in two days.*

2. The future perfect can also express the idea that something will have taken place by a certain time in the future. However, this use of future perfect does not occur frequently in German. To express the idea that something will have taken place by a certain time in the future, German generally uses the present tense or the future tense:

Wenn du so weitermachst, { **liest** du das Buch in zwei Tagen. *(present)*
{ **wirst** du das Buch in zwei Tagen lesen. *(future)*

☐ ————————

F. Gestern und morgen.   Tobias is in a pensive mood. He is meditating on what has happened lately and what will perhaps happen in the future. Give the English equivalents.

1. In zwei Jahren werde ich mein Studium beendet haben.
2. In ein paar Jahren werde ich hoffentlich meine Pläne realisiert haben und mit dem Fahrrad durch Europa gefahren sein.
3. Holger wird von seiner Fahrradtour wohl schon zurückgekommen sein.
4. Er wird sicher viel Spaß gehabt haben.
5. In zehn Jahren werde ich vielleicht schon über den Atlantik gesegelt sein.

6. Vielleicht werden Silke und ich dann schon geheiratet haben.
7. Sie wird unseren Streit° von gestern hoffentlich schon vergessen   *fight, argument*
   haben.

——————————————————— □

7 | *Ein-words as pronouns*

Ist das dein Buch?	*Is that your book?*
—Ja, ich glaube, das ist **ein(e)s** von meinen Büchern.	*—Yes, I think it's **one** of my books.*
Ich glaube, das war mein Fehler.	*I believe that was my mistake.*
—Nein, es war **meiner.**	*—No, it was **mine.***
Ich habe meinen Bleistift verloren. Kannst du mir **deinen** leihen?	*I lost my pencil. Can you lend me **yours**?*
—Nein, ich habe **keinen.**	*—No, I don't have **one.***
Wem gehört dieser Kuli? **Meiner** schreibt nicht mehr.	*Who (formal: Whom) does this pen belong to? **Mine** doesn't write anymore.*

Ein-words (**ein, kein,** and the possessive adjectives) are used most frequently as part of a noun phrase (e.g., **dein Buch, mein Fehler**). However, **ein**-words may stand alone as pronouns (e.g., **ein(e)s, meiner**). When used as pronouns, **ein**-words take the same endings as **der**-words (e.g., **diese̲r Kuli** → **Mein̲er;** see *Kapitel 5*, Section 2).

	Masculine	Neuter	Feminine	Plural
Nominative:	mein**er** (mein Kuli)	mein**(e)s** (mein Buch)	meine	meine
Accusative:	meinen	mein**(e)s** (mein Buch)	meine	meine
Dative:	meinem	meinem	meiner	meinen

Note that **ein**-words used as pronouns have the same endings as the article **ein, kein,** and possessive adjectives except in three instances. Unlike **ein**-words used before nouns, **ein**-words used as pronouns indicate gender, number, and case in masculine nominative (e.g., **meiner**) and neuter nominative and accusative (e.g., **mein(e)s**).

Genitive forms exist but are rarely used.

Wo mein Auto steht? Vor der Tür.   *Where's my car? At the door.*
Wo steht **deins**?   *Where is **yours**?*

In colloquial German, the shortened forms **eins, keins, meins, deins,** etc. are often used instead of **eines, keines, meines, deines,** etc.

□—————————

G. Kinderspiele.   Andreas is babysitting his sister's two children Karolin and Philipp. The kids have been fighting all afternoon, and Andreas tries to settle their arguments. Fill in the appropriate **ein**-words.

1. KAROLIN: Philipp hat einen grünen Fußball. Ich will auch _____ (ein).

2. ANDREAS: Karolin, du hast doch selbst _____ (ein). _____ (dein) lag doch gerade noch hier. Gib Philipp _____ (sein) sofort zurück.

3. KAROLIN: Mit _____ (mein) kann man aber gar nicht gut spielen. Er springt nicht mehr.

4. PHILIPP: Andreas, ich möchte ein Eis.
   ANDREAS: Du hast doch gerade _____ (ein) bekommen. Jetzt gibt es _____ (kein) mehr, Philipp.

5. PHILIPP: Aber Karolin hat _____ (mein) doch aufgegessen.

6. ANDREAS: Philipp, wo ist denn deine Puppe°?   *doll*
   KAROLIN: Er hat sie sicher verloren. Und mit _____ (mein) ist er gerade in die Badewanne gesprungen.

7. ANDREAS: Als ich kam, hatte ich wirklich Lust, mit euch zu spielen. Aber jetzt habe ich _____ (kein) mehr.

8. KAROLIN: Andreas, soll ich dir eine Geschichte erzählen – ich kenne _____ (ein), die ganz lustig ist!

H. Kurze Gespräche.   Some colleagues from work are sitting together and exchanging information about their families and their homes. Fill in the appropriate **ein**-words. Note that some of the colleagues say **Sie** to each other while some of the younger ones use **du.**

1. —Unser Haus hat vier Schlafzimmer.
   —_____ (unser) hat nur zwei.

2. —Wir haben einen Kamin°. Haben Sie auch _____ (ein)?   *fireplace*
   —Nein, wir haben _____ (kein).

3. —Mein Sohn beendet dieses Jahr sein Studium.
   —_____ (mein) kommt jetzt erst aufs Gymnasium.

4. —Für unser Schwimmbad mußten wir 2.000 Mark Reparatur bezahlen.
   —_____ (unser) war eigentlich noch nie kaputt.

5. —Wohnt Ihre Mutter bei Ihnen? _____ (unser) wohnt bei uns im Haus.

   —Nein, _____ (mein) ist letztes Jahr ins Altersheim° gezogen.   *retirement home*

6. —Ich sitze sonntags immer im Garten. Sitzt ihr oft in _____ (euer)?

   —Wir sitzen leider nie in _____ (unser).

7. —Mit unserer Tochter haben wir große Probleme. Hast du Probleme mit _____ (dein)?

   —Natürlich, _____ (unser) ist auch in einem schwierigen Alter.

8. —Unsere Nachbarn sind ziemlich unfreundlich. Wie sind _____ (Ihr)?

   —Mit _____ (unser) haben wir ein ausgezeichnetes Verhältnis°.   *relationship*

———————————————— □

8 Indefinite pronouns°   *das Indefinitpronomen*

jedermann	*everybody, everyone*
jemand	*someone, somebody, anyone, anybody*
niemand	*no one, nobody*

Jedermann weiß, wie die Geschichte weitergeht.	***Everyone*** *knows how the story continues.*
Kennst du **jemand,** der Russisch kann?	*Do you know* ***someone*** *who knows Russian?*
Nein, **niemand.**	*No,* ***no one.***

The indefinite pronouns **jedermann, jemand,** and **niemand** are used to refer to people. (For the indefinite pronouns referring to things and ideas—**etwas, nichts, alles**—see *Kapitel 9,* Section 3).

Hat **jemand** gesprochen? Was hat **er** gesagt?
Did ***someone*** *speak? What did* ***he/she*** *say?*

Kennst du **niemand, der** uns helfen kann?
Do you know ***no one*** *(Don't you know* ***anyone****) who can help us?*

Hat **jemand sein** Portemonnaie hier auf dem Tisch gelassen?
Did ***someone*** *leave* ***his/her*** *billfold here on the table?*

Like **man** (see *Kapitel 5,* Section 10), **jedermann, jemand,** and **niemand** can refer to persons of either gender, even though the form is masculine. The personal pronoun is **er,** the relative pronoun is **der,** and the possessive adjective is **sein.**

Jedermann (Jeder) weiß, wie schwierig das ist.

Everyone knows how hard that is.

Lilo ist höflich zu **jedermann (jedem).**

Lilo is polite to everyone.

The nominative, accusative, and dative forms of **jedermann** are the same. **Jedermann** may be used interchangeably with **jeder**. Unlike **jedermann, jeder** has a different form in the accusative (**jeden**) and dative (**jedem**). **Jeder** is actually more common than **jedermann**.

Jemand hat mir gesagt, daß Kathrin ihre Notizen verloren hat.
Someone told me that Kathrin has lost her notes.

Kennst du **jemand(en),** der ihr helfen kann?
Do you know someone who can help her?

Nein, ich kenne **niemand(en)/keinen.**
No, I don't know anyone.

Ich habe auch mit **niemand(em)/keinem** gesprochen.
I haven't spoken with anyone either.

The indefinite pronouns **jemand** and **niemand** may be used with or without endings in the accusative and dative. **Keiner** is often used in place of **niemand.**

☐ —————————————

I. Das Polizeiprotokoll.

I. Das Polizeiprotokoll.   The police were called to an apartment building, but it was a false alarm. An officer writes a short report about the incident. Fill in the appropriate indefinite pronouns **jemand, jedermann/jeder, niemand/keiner.**

Am Dienstag um 12.45 Uhr rief _____ aus der Kellerstr. 12 an. Der anonyme Anrufer sagte, wir sollten sofort kommen, weil _____ in großer Gefahr sei. Als wir dort ankamen, war _____ auf der Straße. _____ war wohl gerade beim Mittagessen. Wir klingelten° bei ein paar Leuten, doch von _____ bekamen wir irgendeine wichtige Information, und _____ wollte uns schnell wieder loswerden°. Wer der Anrufer sein könnte, wußte _____, und wir konnten auch nicht _____ fragen. Es kann _____ gewesen sein. Wahrscheinlich handelt es sich° um _____, dem es furchtbar langweilig war.

rang the doorbell

to get rid of

sich handeln um: *to concern*

————————————— ☐

9 Impersonal use of verbs and expressions

Es regnet.   *It's raining.*

Es klopft.   *There's a knock at the door.*

German verbs used impersonally have **es** as their subject. When used impersonally, verbs indicate activities without specifying who or what performs the activities. Some common verbs used impersonally are:

Es regnet.	*It's raining.*
Es schneit.	*It's snowing.*
Es blitzt.	*It's lightning.*
Es donnert.	*It's thundering.*
Es friert.	*It's freezing.*
Es klopft.	*There's a knock at the door.*
Es klingelt (läutet).	*The (door)bell is ringing.*
Es riecht (stinkt) nach…	*It smells (stinks) of . . .*
Es brennt.	*Something is burning.*

German also has a number of expressions in which **es** is the subject. Such expressions are referred to as "impersonal expressions." Note that the English equivalents have personal subjects, depending on the pronoun used in German (**mir, ihr, uns,** etc.). Some common impersonal expressions are:

Wie geht es?/Wie geht's?	*How are you?/How's it going?*
Es geht (mir/uns, etc.) gut/schlecht.	*I'm/We're fine/miserable.*
Es tut (mir/ihm, etc.) leid.	*I'm/He's sorry.*
Es gelingt (mir/ihr, etc.).	*I/She succeed/s.*
Es gefällt (mir/ihnen, etc.).	*I/They like it.*

□ —————————

J. Jahreszeiten°.   For Karin the weather is important because it strongly affects her mood. She recalls how the weather has been this year. Give the German equivalents, using impersonal verbs and expressions.   *seasons*

1. When it's raining, I'm always fine.
2. I like it when it smells of rain.
3. When a thunderstorm° comes and it's lightning and thundering, my dog is often miserable.   **das Gewitter**
4. But my sister and I like it when it's lightning.
5. This winter it hasn't snowed yet.
6. And last spring it rained constantly°. Sometimes it even froze. Of course, the plants didn't like that. *(Use present perfect.)*   *immer*

————————— □

Zusammenfassung

A. Die verregnete° Reise.   Beate und Dietmar sind auf einer Radtour nach Mailand°. Doch seit einer Woche regnet es, und sie sitzen   *rained out* *Milan* auf einem Zeltplatz in der Schweiz fest°. Sie überlegen sich, was sie machen sollen. Übersetzen Sie die Sätze ins Englische. Beachten Sie die Modalverben in ihrer subjektiven Bedeutung.

festsitzen: *to be stuck*

1. BEATE: Eigentlich müßten wir schon in Mailand sein.
2. DIETMAR: Ich weiß, und Mailand soll sehr schön und fast immer sonnig sein.
3. BEATE: Sollte das Wetter nicht besser sein heute?
4. DIETMAR: Ja, aber der Wetterbericht dürfte sich geirrt haben. Heute sollten es 30 Grad [degrees Celcius] werden.
5. BEATE: Aber wollen die Meteorologen nicht so zuverlässig° sein?

reliable

6. DIETMAR: Morgen kann es schon besser sein.
7. BEATE: Das mag wahr sein. Doch das Wetter in der Schweiz soll sich schnell ändern, wegen der Berge.

B. Kein gutes Semester.

Susanne war sehr unmotiviert in diesem Semester. In zwei Wochen ist es aber zum Glück° vorbei. Übersetzen Sie die Sätze ins Englische.

zum Glück: *fortunately*

1. Ich weiß, daß ich am Semesteranfang hätte fleißiger sein müssen.
2. Aber in zwei Wochen werde ich alle Hausarbeiten beendet haben.
3. Mein Englischprofessor wird meinen Test wohl schlecht benotet haben.
4. Ich werde in der Chemieprüfung vielleicht durchgefallen° sein.

failed

5. Ich denke, daß ich nicht immer hätte Tennis spielen sollen.
6. Ich weiß auch, daß ich nicht so oft auf Partys hätte gehen dürfen.
7. In zwei Monaten werde ich mit Rudi schon in die USA geflogen sein.
8. Anfang September werde ich schon mein Studienjahr in Amerika begonnen haben.

C. Gespräche.

Ein paar Freunde unterhalten sich über ihre Bekannte Sibylle, die besonders intelligent sein soll. Übersetzen Sie die folgenden Sätze ins Deutsche. Verwenden Sie die Modalverben in ihrer subjektiven Bedeutung.

1. Sibylle claims to be so smart°.

klug

2. She is supposed to know a lot.
3. It must be in° her family.

to be in = ***liegen in***

4. Her parents are supposed to be very well educated° as well.

gebildet

5. That can be a problem for the children.
6. But it is also probably an advantage°.

der Vorteil

7. You may be right°.

to be right = ***recht haben***

D. Die neue Stadt.

Tanja ist mit ihren Eltern von München nach Bremen gezogen. Nach ein paar Wochen schreibt sie ihrer alten Schulfreundin Ute einen Brief und erzählt ihr von der neuen Stadt.

Setzen Sie die fehlenden Pronomen ein. Verwenden Sie **es, jedermann/ jeder, jemand, niemand** oder die Possessivpronomen in Klammern. *(Use* **es, jedermann/jeder, jemand,** *or* **niemand** *unless the possessive pronoun in parentheses is required.)*

Liebe Ute!

Wie geht _____ Dir? _____ tut mir leid, daß ich jetzt erst schreibe. Am Anfang hat _____ uns hier in Bremen gar nicht gefallen. Alles war neu, und _____ regnete oft. Zuerst kannte ich auch _____, und _____ sagte, daß ich einen komischen Dialekt spräche. Fast _____ spricht hochdeutsch hier, und _____ hat mich verstanden.

Doch jetzt habe ich eine Freundin – sogar _____ (ein), die in unserer Straße wohnt. Sie heißt Gabi, und sie fährt auch gern Rollerblades. Gestern wollte ich mit _____ (mein) fahren, doch sie waren kaputt. Gabi hat mir dann _____ (ihr) gegeben. Ist das nicht nett? Sie hat auch einen Bruder. _____ (ihr) ist aber nicht so verrückt wie Jörg.

Wie geht es Deinen Eltern? _____ (mein) vermissen München noch sehr, denn sie kennen noch _____. Für Erwachsene ist es wohl noch schwieriger, _____ kennenzulernen.

So jetzt mache ich Schluß, denn _____ klingelt gerade. Das ist sicher Gabi. Schreib mir bald.

> Tschüs
> Deine Tanja

E. Partnerarbeit: Rollenspiel.

In Ihr Studentenwohnheim ist eine neue Studentin/ein neuer Student eingezogen, oder in Ihrer Firma wurde eine neue Kollegin/ein neuer Kollege angestellt. Sie oder er hat noch mit niemandem gesprochen und ist noch ziemlich zurückhaltend°. Sie und eine Freundin/ein Freund sprechen darüber, wie diese Person wohl ist, woher sie/er kommt usw. Verwenden Sie die Modalverben in ihrer subjektiven Bedeutung.

reserved

F. Kurze Aufsätze

1. Sie sind Programmleiterin/Programmleiter in einem Ferienheim° für Kinder. Ihr Haus ist das ganze Jahr über geöffnet. Überlegen Sie sich, was man mit den Kindern in den verschiedenen Jahreszeiten° unternehmen kann. Was machen Sie, wenn es regnet usw.? Verwenden Sie unpersönliche Verben und Ausdrücke.

   camp

   seasons

2. Sie waren für ein halbes Jahr in England, und Sie haben kaum Kontakt zu Ihren Freunden gehalten. Auf der Heimfahrt überlegen Sie sich, was zu Hause und bei Ihren Freunden wohl alles passiert ist, z.B. Franz und Anita werden sich wohl getrennt haben, usw. Verwenden Sie das zweite Futur.

Self-Tests

These self-tests give you an opportunity to see if you have understood the grammatical points introduced in each chapter and whether you can apply your understanding of the grammatical principles. An Answer Key, which begins on page 237, follows the Self-Tests. In addition to providing you with the correct answers, the Answer Key facilitates your review by directing you to the section in the chapter where a particular grammatical feature is discussed.

KAPITEL 1

A. Complete each sentence with the appropriate verb form.

1. Wann _____ du auf den Brief? (antworten)
2. Cornelia _____ oft im Park. (laufen, *sg.*)
3. _____ ihr jeden Tag die Zeitung? (lesen)
4. Du _____ aber viel Arbeit! (haben)
5. Ich _____ Briefmarken. (sammeln)
6. Sein Bruder _____ Bäcker. (werden)
7. Gisela _____ sehr gut. (tanzen, *sg.*)
8. Wie _____ ihr den Film „Das Boot"? (finden)
9. _____ Sie jeden Tag Vitamintabletten? (nehmen)
10. _____ jetzt endlich ruhig! (*ihr*-Imperativ: sein)
11. _____ endlich ein Eis! (*wir*-Imperativ: essen)
12. _____ bitte die erste Geschichte im Buch. (*du*-Imperativ: lesen)
13. _____ nicht mit dem Auto! (*ihr*-Imperativ: fahren)
14. _____ doch meinen Bleistift! (*Sie*-Imperativ: nehmen)
15. _____ zum Bäcker und _____ ein Brot! (*ihr*-Imperativ: laufen/kaufen)

B. Form complete sentences using the cues provided.

1. ich / zurückkommen / am Sonntag
2. anrufen / deine Familie (*du*-Imperativ)
3. ihr / wegfahren / am Wochenende / ?
4. er / ausgehen / jeden Freitag
5. der Film / anfangen / um acht Uhr / ?

C. Give the German equivalents of the following sentences.

1. I've been studying German for two years.
2. Do you know his mother?
3. She doesn't know that he's coming.
4. We're going to eat at nine o'clock.
5. They know Stuttgart very well.

KAPITEL 2

A. Complete each sentence with the appropriate verb form.

1. Ulrike fährt Auto. —_____ sie das denn? (dürfen)
2. Hilfst du mir? —Nein, ich _____ nicht! (wollen)
3. Sie _____ nicht schwimmen gehen. (möchte)
4. Wir _____ bis morgen die Wörter lernen. (sollen)
5. Warum _____ ihr den Hund nicht in den Garten? (lassen)
6. _____ du schon wieder krank? (werden)
7. Ich _____ heute mittag einkaufen. (müssen)
8. _____ ihr eure Katze? (mögen)
9. _____ er wirklich Ski laufen? (können)
10. Wir _____ uns das Frühstück ans Bett bringen. (lassen)

B. Form complete sentences using the cues provided.

1. er / dürfen / fahren / Auto
2. wir / sollen / spülen / das Geschirr / ?
3. ich / sehen / kommen / ihn / ins Haus
4. du / lassen / schneiden / deine Haare / ?
5. sie / hören / weinen / das Kind
6. er / müssen / putzen / die Wohnung
7. sie / werden / fahren / ans Meer
8. ihr / möchte / kaufen / einen Kuchen / im Café / ?
9. er / mögen / das Buch „Andorra" / nicht
10. sie / können / spielen / Klavier / ?

C. Give the German equivalents of the following sentences.

1. She doesn't have to work on Sunday.
2. We don't have to help Claudia.
3. Would you like to see a movie today? (Use **ihr.**)
4. Does Michael like rap°?
5. In the summer, I'm going to Hamburg. (Use **reisen.**)
6. Let me pay, please.
7. Are you leaving the children at home? (Use **du.**)
8. We're having the car repaired.

Rap-Musik

9. You mustn't be angry. (Use **du**.)
10. Do you know French°? (Use **Sie**.)   *Französisch*

KAPITEL 3

A. Complete the sentences using the verbs in parentheses in the simple past.

1. Andreas _____ nach dem Biologieseminar meistens auf Antje. (warten)
2. Britta _____ sich letztes Jahr beim Tennisspielen. (verletzen)
3. Unsere Großeltern _____ schon sehr früh. (heiraten)
4. Der Patient _____ unruhig. (atmen)
5. Die Studenten _____ oft die ganze Nacht. (tanzen)
6. Wir _____ nur sehr wenig in der Schule. (lernen)
7. Letzten Mai _____ er 23. (werden)
8. _____ ihr dieses Jahr schon im Urlaub? (sein)
9. Als Studentin _____ ich nie Geld. (haben)
10. Uwe _____ einen Apfelsaft. (bestellen)
11. Ich _____ schon 1990 mit dem Rauchen _____. (aufhören)
12. _____ ihr jeden Morgen das Frühstück machen? (müssen)
13. Ich _____ italienisches Essen noch nie. (mögen)
14. Am Wochenende _____ wir oft im Wald spazieren. (laufen)
15. Er _____ immer schrecklich viel. (essen)
16. Die Geschichte „Tod in Venedig" _____ mir in der Schule immer am besten. (gefallen)
17. Sie _____ oft in der Bibliothek _____, und Martin _____ sie dann wieder _____. (einschlafen, aufwecken)

B. Complete the sentences using the verbs in parentheses in the present perfect.

1. Sophie _____ heute morgen im Park ein Portemonnaie _____. (finden)
2. Oliver _____ gestern mit Lufthansa nach Deutschland _____. (fliegen)
3. Ich _____ ihm einen Stuhl in den Garten _____. (bringen)
4. Wo _____ ihr in Berlin _____? (wohnen)
5. _____ Sie mit ihrem Chef über das Projekt _____? (sprechen)
6. _____ du deinen Eltern aus dem Urlaub _____? (schreiben)
7. Warum _____ Stefanie am Samstag zu Hause _____? (bleiben)
8. Alle _____ den Konjunktiv _____! (verstehen)
9. Warum _____ sich Mark heute morgen nicht _____? (rasieren)
10. Ulrike _____ gestern ihren Freund nach Hause _____. (fahren)
11. Wo im Schwarzwald _____ ihr _____ ? (wandern)

12. Am Sonntag _____ wir ins Schwimmbad _____. (gehen)
13. Wie _____ der Unfall denn _____? (passieren)
14. Ich _____ meine Uhr _____. (verlieren)

C. Give the German equivalents of the following sentences.

1. I wasn't tired anymore. I had slept a little bit.
2. But my friends were not at home. They had just left.
3. I had not heard them leave.
4. They probably didn't go to the museum. They had been there on their last visit°.
5. We didn't want to visit our friend Karin. (2 translations: simple past and perfect tense)
6. Yesterday Karin had a tooth pulled°.

on . . . visit = **bei ihrem letzten Besuch**

to have a tooth pulled = **sich...ziehen lassen**

KAPITEL 4

A. Complete the sentences with the correct form: a, b, or c.

1. Wir wissen nicht, _____ Erikas Zug in München ankommt.
   a. als   b. wenn   c. wann
2. _____ sie heute nicht anruft, ist sicher etwas passiert.
   a. Wenn   b. Als   c. Wann
3. _____ ich früher Kaffee trank, wurde ich immer sehr nervös.
   a. Wann   b. Wenn   c. Als
4. _____ die Ferien am ersten Juli begannen, freuten sich meine Eltern sehr auf ihren Urlaub.
   a. Als   b. Wann   c. Wenn
5. Carolin geht ins Kino, _____ den Film „Metropolis" _____ sehen.
   a. ohne...zu   b. anstatt...zu   c. um...zu
6. _____ in der Bibliothek _____ lernen, ging sie im Park spazieren.
   a. Anstatt...zu   b. Ohne...zu   c. Um...zu
7. Erich aß eine Woche lang nur Obst, _____ ein Gramm _____.
   a. um...abzunehmen°   b. ohne...abzunehmen
   c. anstatt...abzunehmen
8. _____ das Kind ein Eis bekommen hatte, war es wieder guter Laune°.
   a. Bevor   b. Nach   c. Nachdem
9. Lernt ihr schon _____ vier Jahren Deutsch?
   a. vor   b. nach   c. seit
10. _____ Karin mehr schläft, ist sie nicht mehr so oft müde.
    a. Nach   b. Seitdem   c. Bevor

to lose weight

guter Laune: *in a good mood*

B. Complete the sentences with one of the following conjunctions: **aber, bis, da, damit, daß, denn, indem, oder, sondern, und,** or **weil.** (Look at the word order of the sentence before you choose a coordinating or a subordinating conjunction.)

1. Anna geht zum Arzt, _____ sie Fieber hat.
2. _____ es heute sehr heiß ist, sind viele Studenten am See.
3. Wir fahren nicht nach Hannover, _____ nach Hamburg.
4. Daniel und Christine waren in Paris, _____ sie haben den Eiffelturm nicht gesehen.
5. Er bleibt im Bett, _____ er hat eine Erkältung.
6. Wußtest du, _____ Sacramento die Hauptstadt von Kalifornien ist?
7. Kommt Vincent mit, _____ möchte er zu Hause bleiben?
8. Julia wartete, _____ der Zug abfuhr°.   *left*
9. _____ Dennis mich ansah, sagte er: „Ich mag dich."
10. Tobias fährt Ski, _____ er fährt auch Fahrrad.
11. Ich schließe die Tür, _____ ich die laute Musik nicht höre.

C. Form complete sentences in the present tense. Watch the word order.

1. ich / spazierengehen / im Park / mit meinem Freund / am Sonntag
2. du / sehen / nicht / das Auto / ?
3. warum / Erich / einladen / nicht / seinen Bruder / ?
4. meine Eltern / fahren / nach Wien / in den Ferien, // oder / sie / bleiben / in Salzburg
5. Andreas / können / gehen / nicht / ins Restaurant // weil / er / haben / kein Geld
6. seitdem / Petra / arbeiten // sie / sein / immer / müde
7. wir / spielen / heute / nicht / Tennis // sondern / Golf
8. du / wollen / Kaffee trinken / oder / Kuchen essen / ?
9. Elly und Martin / können / gehen / nicht / auf die Party / mit uns / am Samstag
10. Jens / Schach spielen / oft / mit seiner Freundin / nach der Arbeit

D. Give the German equivalent of the following sentences.

1. We're watching TV instead of doing our homework.
2. Either you (Use **du.**) write Klaus a letter, or you must call him soon.
3. I neither want to walk nor ride the bike.
4. It would be nice° to go to the movies tonight.   would be nice = ***wäre schön***
5. I have to go home in order to clean my room.
6. Irene doesn't have time to go shopping.

KAPITEL 5

A. Complete the sentences with the correct form: a, b, c, or d.

1. Beide Tische sind neu. Wie findest du _____ Tisch?
   a. dieser   b. diese   c. diesen   d. dieses
2. Nicht alle Leute liegen gern am Strand°. _____ wandern lieber.   *beach*
   a. Mancher   b. Manches   c. Manchen   d. Manche
3. _____ Bücher lese ich nicht. Sie sind mir zu trivial.
   a. So eine   b. Solche   c. Jede   d. Welche
4. Warum gefallen dir meine Ohrringe nicht? —Ich finde _____ zu groß.
   a. sie   b. es   c. ihr   d. ihn
5. Wann besuchst du deinen Großvater? —Ich besuche _____ nächsten Monat.
   a. es   b. ihn   c. sie   d. er
6. Kauft ihr Geschenke für das Fest? —Nein, wir kaufen _____ Geschenke.
   a. keines   b. kein   c. keine   d. keinen
7. Wo ist euer Auto? —_____ Auto ist in der Garage.
   a. Unser   b. Sein   c. Ihr   d. Dein
8. Gefällt dir ihr Kleid? —Ja, _____ Kleid möchte ich auch.
   a. welches   b. jedes   c. manches   d. so ein
9. Hat deine Schwester einen Freund? —Ja, aber _____ Freund lebt in Italien.
   a. euer   b. ihr   c. sein   d. Ihr
10. Kennst du diese Person? —_____ meinst du? Den Mann oder die Frau?
    a. Wer   b. Wen   c. Welchen   d. Was

B. Complete the sentences with the correct form of the cued words.

1. Der Polizist fragt _____ nach seinem Führerschein. (der Tourist)
2. Der Tourist sieht _____ böse an. (der Polizist)
3. Die Stürme beunruhigten° _____. (der Bauer)   *alarmed*
4. Wir wollen _____ durch Europa reisen. (ein Monat)
5. Ich kaufe ein Hemd für _____. (mein Bruder)

C. Give the German equivalents.

1. My friend Sabine is a teacher.
2. Andreas would like to become a lawyer.
3. Richard is not an American.
4. Don't go without your jacket. (**du**-imperative)
5. Come through the garden. (**du**-imperative)
6. We're visiting our friends next month.
7. Is there a park here?
8. Where can one park here?

9. Such a traffic jam° can annoy one.

10. The patient° must drink two glasses of water every morning.

traffic jam = *ein Stau*

der Patient

KAPITEL 6

A. Complete the sentences with the correct form: a, b, c, or d.

1. Warum hast du mit _____ Leuten gesprochen?
   a. diese   b. dieser   c. diesen   d. diesem

2. Können wir _____ Mädchen denn nicht helfen?
   a. dem   b. das   c. die   d. der

3. Andrea ist zu _____ Freunden oft unfreundlich.
   a. ihre   b. ihrem   c. ihrer   d. ihren

4. Die Katze hat Hunger. Gib _____ doch endlich etwas zu fressen.
   a. denen   b. dem   c. die   d. der

5. Ach, ihr wohnt jetzt in Münster? Wie gefällt _____ Münster?
   a. ihnen   b. euch   c. ihm   d. ihr

6. Michael ist Julias Freund. Sie schreibt _____ oft Postkarten.
   a. er   b. ihn   c. ihm   d. ihnen

7. _____ gehört diese Tasche?
   a. Wer   b. Wem   c. Wen   d. Wo

8. Wie soll ich wissen, mit _____ Dagmar in Urlaub fährt?
   a. wem   b. wo   c. wer   d. wen

9. Und dann hat Mario _____ einen Ring geschenkt?
   a. dich   b. du   c. dir   d. deinem

10. Judith hat _____ Menschen von ihrer Krankheit erzählt.
    a. keine   b. keinem   c. keiner   d. kein

11. Seit _____ Jahr haben wir nichts von unseren Freunden gehört.
    a. einem   b. ein   c. einen   d. eines

12. Was hat der Arzt _____ geraten?
    a. Sie   b. ihn   c. sie   d. Ihnen

B. Complete the sentences with the proper preposition governing the dative. Use contractions where appropriate.

1. Was schenkst du deinem Vater _____ Geburtstag?

2. Wo gehen Schmidts Kinder _____ Schule?

3. Wohnst du nicht mehr _____ deinen Eltern?

4. Können wir die Party in eurem Garten machen? Ich habe _____ mir keinen Platz.

5. Wer war auf Martas Party? —_____ ihrer Schwester waren alle da.

6. Wie fährst du im Sommer nach Österreich – _____ der Bahn oder _____ dem Auto?

7. Patrizia kommt _____ Österreich, nicht wahr?

8. Ich habe _____ einem Monat kein Deutsch gesprochen.

C. Complete the sentences using the proper form of the words in parentheses.

1. Gibt der Lehrer _____ eine gute Note? (der Student)
2. Du mußt _____ Kaffee anbieten. (dein Gast)
3. Mein Sohn geht mit _____ auf eine Radtour. (seine Freunde)
4. Was soll ich nur mit _____ machen? (meine vielen Bücher)
5. Haben Sie schon von _____ gehört? (die neuen Autos) Sie fahren ohne Benzin.
6. Ist es _____ recht, daß ich etwas früher gehe? (du)
7. Judith geht mit _____ spazieren. (ihre Hunde)
8. Ich glaube _____ nicht. (er)
9. Fisch schmeckt _____ nicht. (ich)

D. Give the German equivalents.

1. Help me please.
2. Show me the picture.
3. Give it [the picture] to me please.
4. What are you giving your mother for her birthday?
5. I'm giving her flowers and several CDs.

KAPITEL 7

A. Complete the sentences with the correct form: a, b, c, or d.

1. Thomas ist immer unpünktlich. Daher wartet Ute jetzt nicht mehr _____.
   a. darauf   b. auf ihn   c. worauf   d. für ihn
2. Bald ist mein Geburtstag. Ich freue mich sehr _____.
   a. darauf   b. auf es   c. worauf   d. auf ihm
3. Du bist nicht allein ins Kino gegangen? _____ warst du dort?
   a. Womit   b. Damit   c. Mit wem   d. Mit was
4. Andrea ist sehr kompliziert. _____ gehen wir nie wieder spazieren.
   a. Damit   b. Womit   c. Mit ihnen   d. Mit ihr
5. Laura soll sich bei uns amüsieren. _____ interessiert sie sich denn?
   a. Dafür   b. Wofür   c. Für es   d. Worin
6. Das ist ja ein tolles Geschenk. _____ hat sie es bekommen?
   a. Von wem   b. Wovon   c. Davon   d. Woraus

B. Complete the sentences using the following cues.

(a) **hin, her, wohin,** or **woher**

1. Komm mal _____! Du mußt mir helfen.
2. Sie sind so schick angezogen. _____ gehen sie?

3. Er spricht Dialekt. Wissen Sie, _____ er kommt?

4. Die Großeltern freuen sich immer über Besuch. Fahrt doch mal _____.

(b) the prepositions **an, auf, in, unter,** or **vor** (Use a definite or indefinite article or a contraction where appropriate.)

5. Nie geht sie _____ Telefon, dabei sind alle Anrufe° für sie.   *phone calls*

6. Wann habt ihr Zeit? —_____ Mittwoch.

7. _____ Juli fahren wir nach Spanien.

8. Sie gehen fast jeden Abend _____ Kino.

9. _____ Winter ist es mir in Neuengland viel zu kalt.

10. _____ Wochenende machen wir einen Ausflug. Wir fahren _____ Land.

11. Warum unterhaltet ihr euch nicht _____ englisch?

12. Denkst du noch oft _____ deinen Hund? Es tut mir leid, daß er nicht mehr _____ Leben ist.

13. Deutschland ist so teuer. Gute Schuhe gibt es kaum _____ hundert Mark.

14. _____ Woche sind Ulrikes Prüfungen. Doch sie hat schon _____ Monat mit dem Lernen begonnen.

15. _____ Abend kann ich mich oft nicht mehr konzentrieren.

(c) the correct form of **legen/liegen, setzen/sitzen, stellen/stehen, hängen,** or **stecken**

16. Deine Jacke _____ auf dem Boden. _____ sie doch in den Schrank.

17. Endlich _____ ein Teppich im Zimmer. So ist es viel gemütlicher.

18. Hast du das Geld ins Portemonnaie _____? Es _____ nicht mehr auf dem Tisch.

19. Gestern hat Patricks Vater nur im Bett _____, und heute hat er nur in seinem Lehnstuhl° _____.   *armchair*

20. Ich habe Corinna in ihren Kinderstuhl _____.

C. Form complete sentences using the cued words.

1. das Kind / liegen / unter / der Baum
2. die Autos / stehen / in / die Garage
3. warum / du / stellen / die Pflanze / nicht / auf / der Schreibtisch / ?
4. ich / hängen / die Lampe / über / der Spiegel
5. Markus / sitzen / zwischen / sein Freund / und / seine Mutter

D. Give the German equivalents of the following sentences.

1. I would like to go to the beach° on Sunday.   *to the beach = **an/der Strand***
2. Edith is studying at the University of Heidelberg.
3. Frank put the glass next to the plate. (simple past)

4. Did you look for° your watch behind the bed? (present perfect)   *look for = **suchen***
5. Are the children afraid of dogs?

KAPITEL 8

A. Complete the sentences with the correct forms of the cued words.

1. Die Brille _____ ist extravagant°. (das Mädchen)   *flashy*
2. Das Auto _____ ist zur Zeit in Reparatur°. (mein Mann)   **in Reparatur:** *being repaired*
3. Wie findest du den Hut _____ da drüben? (der Herr)
4. Franziska hat die Äpfel _____ gestohlen. (unser Nachbar)
5. Überall im Garten liegen die Spielsachen _____. (ihre Kinder)
6. _____ Heft ist das? (wer)
   —Das ist das Heft _____. (seine Freundin)
7. Die Koffer _____ würde der Gepäckträger nicht tragen. (dieser Tourist)
8. Die Bedeutung _____ ist mir nicht klar. (sein Name)
9. Wir wohnen jetzt im Haus _____. (unsere Eltern)
10. Wißt ihr, _____ Motorrad das ist? (wer)
    Es steht vor dem Eingang° _____. (unser Hof)   *entrance*
11. Die Phantasie _____ können sich Erwachsene nur schwer vorstellen. (ein Kind)
12. Der Humor _____ ist manchmal sehr makaber. (dieser Mensch)
13. Die Eltern _____ sind weggefahren. (mein Freund)
    Jetzt gibt es dort die größte Party _____. (das Jahr)
14. Die Klavierlehrerin _____ ist ziemlich streng. (unsere Tochter)
15. Die Farbe _____ kann man gar nicht definieren. (ihr Getränk)
16. Leider ist die Politik _____ nicht sehr demokratisch. (das Land)
17. Bei der Form _____ kann Werner keine Hüte tragen. (sein Kopf)
18. Statt _____ machen wir eben ein Abendessen. (eine Party)
19. Silke geht trotz _____ ins Schwimmbad. (ihre Erkältung)
20. Wir machen die Reise nur _____. (wegen / er)

B. Form complete sentences using the cues provided.

1. während / die Winterferien / wollen / Lilian / in die Karibik° reisen   *Caribbean*
2. die Wunde° / sein / oberhalb / das Knie   *wound*
3. Thomas / kommen / wegen / sein Neffe / nicht / auf das Fest / ?
4. Frankreich / liegen / von hier aus gesehen / jenseits / der Rhein
5. es / geben / viele Cafés und Restaurants / unterhalb / die Kirche

C. Give the German equivalents of the following sentences. Use the **du**- form in sentences 1, 3, and 5.

1. Do you like your brother's girlfriend? (two versions: gen. & dat.)

2. One day, he'll live in his grandparents' house. (two versions: gen. & dat.)
3. I totally agree with you. (I'm of your opinion.)
4. We can use my mother's car, as far as I am concerned.
5. After all, it is your sister's problem.

KAPITEL 9

A. Complete the sentences with the correct form: a, b, c, or d.

1. Für die Wanderung brauchst du Schuhe, _____ bequem° sind.   *comfortable*
   a. der   b. den   c. die   d. denen
2. Ich habe einen Mantel gekauft, _____ ich auch im Winter tragen kann.
   a. das   b. der   c. dem   d. den
3. Das sind die Kinder, _____ Eltern für zwei Monate in Indien sind.
   a. die   b. deren   c. dessen   d. denen
4. Ulrich gehört zu den Leuten, _____ gar nichts schmeckt.
   a. denen   b. dem   c. den   d. die
5. Karin sucht eine Wohnung, _____ groß, hell und billig ist.
   a. der   b. die   c. deren   d. das
6. Nadja und Andrea sind Studentinnen, _____ immer alle Hausaufgaben machen.
   a. dem   b. das   c. die   d. denen
7. Der Mann, _____ Sandra am Samstag kennengelernt hat, rief gleich am Sonntag an.
   a. dem   b. den   c. dessen   d. der
8. Ich kenne die Leute, _____ dieses schöne Haus gehört.
   a. deren   b. dessen   c. denen   d. die
9. Wie findest du das Kleid, _____ Isabelle heute trägt?
   a. dem   b. die   c. den   d. das
10. Mark ist ein Junge, _____ einziges Interesse Fußball ist.
    a. dessen   b. dem   c. den   d. deren
11. Zeig mir das Café, in _____ es den guten Kuchen gibt.
    a. das   b. dem   c. den   d. denen
12. Sind das die Leute, bei _____ Angelika übernachtet hat?
    a. deren   b. die   c. denen   d. dem
13. Wie heißt die Universität, an _____ Ben studiert?
    a. der   b. die   c. dem   d. den
14. Wir wollen uns ein Auto kaufen, mit _____ wir komfortabel reisen können.
    a. das   b. den   c. die   d. dem
15. Ist das die Lederjacke, für _____ du so lange gespart hast?
    a. das   b. die   c. der   d. den

B. Fill in the missing indefinite relative pronoun **wer** or **was**, or the relative adverb **wo(r)**-.

1. Ist das alles, _____ Jörg zum Geburtstag bekommen hat?
2. Es gibt nichts, _____ Hanna sich freut°.   *sich freuen über*
3. _____ man Kindern verspricht, muß man auch halten.
4. Ulla hat in ihrem Zimmer nichts, _____ sie sitzen° kann.   *sitzen auf*
5. _____ nie Vokabeln lernt, wird Probleme haben, eine Sprache zu lernen.
6. Mit _____ du ausgehst, ist mir egal.
7. Sibylle zu treffen war das Schönste, _____ Robert in diesem Jahr passiert ist.
8. Es gibt vieles, _____ Beate sich interessiert°.   *sich interessieren für*
9. _____ die Konzertkarte bis heute nicht abholt, bekommt keine.
10. Ich kenne nichts, _____ meine Tochter Angst° hat.   *Angst haben vor*

C. Give the German equivalents of the following sentences, using relative clauses. Remember to use a relative pronoun to begin the relative clause.

1. *Andreas is a colleague (whom) I met a year ago.*
   (Andreas / sein / ein Kollege // ich / kennenlernen / vor einem Jahr)
2. *Is he someone (who is) optimistic?*
   (er / sein / jemand // optimistisch sein / ?)
3. *That is something (that) only his girlfriend can answer.*
   (das / sein / etwas // nur / seine Freundin / können / beantworten)
4. *I like people who are always friendly.*
   (ich / mögen / Leute // immer / freundlich / sein)
5. *Claudia is a woman who rarely laughs.*
   (Claudia / sein / eine Frau // selten / lachen)
6. *That is something (that) I don't like.*
   (das / sein / etwas // ich / nicht / gut / finden)
7. *Andreas and Claudia are looking for an apartment that costs around 800 marks.*
   (Andreas und Claudia / suchen / eine Wohnung // etwa 800 Mark / kosten)
8. *They have a landlord (whom) they don't like.*
   (sie / haben / ein Vermieter // sie / nicht / mögen)
9. *Who are the people Andreas is speaking with?*
   (wer / sind / die Leute // Andreas / sprechen mit / ?)
10. *Show Claudia the room she can sleep in.* (Use **du**-imperative.)
    (zeigen / Claudia / das Zimmer // sie / können / schlafen)
11. *Is that the bed that is broken?*
    (das Bett / sein // kaputt / sein / ?)

KAPITEL 10

A. Complete each sentence with the appropriate reflexive pronoun.

1. Ihr wascht _____ doch vor dem Abendessen die Hände, nicht?
2. Ich erinnere _____ gern an den Sommerurlaub.
3. Putzt du _____ nach jedem Essen die Zähne?
4. Wir haben _____ für Peters Benehmen° entschuldigt.   *conduct*
5. Zum Geburtstag wünsche ich _____ eine neue Büchertasche.
6. Hat Sabine _____ schon wieder erkältet?
7. Kannst du _____ schon wieder neue CDs leisten?
8. Meine Eltern interessieren _____ für klassische Musik.
9. Amüsiert _____ gut auf der Party!
10. Warum hast du _____ die Haare nicht gekämmt?
11. Ihr habt _____ aber sehr verspätet.
12. Warum hast du _____ nicht beeilt?
13. Wir haben _____ schon gewundert, wo du bleibst.

B. Complete the sentences with the appropriate reflexive pronouns and/or **selbst/selber** or **(-)einander**.

1. Jetzt mußt du dir dein Essen _____ kochen.
2. Seit einem Jahr haben Andrea und Georg _____ nicht mehr geschrieben.
3. Georg hat es mir _____ erzählt.
4. Frau Peters und Herr Greiner reden nicht mehr mit _____. Sie haben immer noch Streit°.   *an argument*
5. Wenn Max und Anna neben _____ sitzen, lachen sie die ganze Zeit mit _____.
6. Petra hat sich dieses Kleid _____ genäht.
7. Ulrich hat sich über seine Fehler _____ am meisten geärgert.

C. Form complete sentences, using the cues provided.

1. warum / Martin / müssen / sich rasieren / jeden Tag /? *(present)*
2. ich / können / sich leisten / keine neue Stereoanlage *(present)*
3. du / sich überlegen /schon // ob / du / können / helfen / uns /? *(present perfect / present)*
4. leider / die zwei Hunde / sich gewöhnen an / einander / immer noch nicht *(present perfect)*
5. Stefan und Uwe / sich erkälten / am Wochenende / beim Skifahren *(present perfect)*

D. Give the German equivalents of the following short conversations.

1. PHILLIP: You're late°.   Use present perfect.
   JÖRG: I have to apologize. I got lost.

2. LISA: Did you have a good time at the party?
   BIRGIT: Yes. Daniel and I had a good conversation.

3. CHRISTINE: Are you ready?
   RITA: No, I have to shower, brush my teeth, comb my hair,
               and put on make-up.
   CHRISTINE: Well, please hurry.

KAPITEL 11

A. Fill in the correct form: a, b, c , or d.

1. Mein Geburtstag ist am _____ März.
   a. vierten   b. viertes   c. vierte   d. vierter

2. Ich brauche einen _____ Tag.
   a. freier   b. freien   c. freie   d. freiem

3. Mit dieser _____ Hose kannst du gut auf die Party gehen.
   a. elegantem   b. elegante   c. eleganten   d. eleganter

4. Das neue Gebäude ist sehr _____.
   a. hohes   b. höchsten   c. hohe   d. hoch

5. Robert hat nur wenige _____ Freunde.
   a. gute   b. guten   c. gutem   d. guter

6. Unserem Hund gefällt es am besten in _____ Zimmern.
   a. dunklem   b. dunkle   c. dunkles   d. dunklen

7. Sonja hat von Erich schon viele _____ Briefe bekommen.
   a. langen   b. langes   c. lange   d. langer

8. Das Eis ist gut. _____ Eis schmeckt mir am besten.
   a. Italienisches   b. Italienische   c. Italienischer   d. Italienischen

9. Gibt es in Mannheim kein _____ Museum?
   a. interessant   b. interessantes   c. interessante   d. interessanter

10. Ein BMW ist ein _____ Wagen.
    a. teure   b. teuersten   c. teurer   d. teuren

B. Complete the sentences with the correct basic, comparative, or superlative form of the adjective or participle in parentheses, as appropriate.

1. Der Februar ist der _____ Monat. (kurz)
2. Sandra hat _____ Haare als Ute. (lang)
3. Jörgs Auto fährt am _____. (schnell)
4. Wer soll die vielen _____ Kartoffeln essen? (gekocht)
5. Ulrike hat alle _____ Pralinen schon gegessen. (lecker°)   *delicious*
6. Viele _____ Studenten arbeiten in den Semesterferien. (deutsch)
7. Andere _____ Jacken habe ich nicht. (warm)
8. Welche Stadt in der Schweiz ist am _____? (groß)

9. Ich fahre _____ ans Meer als ins Gebirge. (gern)
10. Gehört dieser Rucksack dem _____ Touristen? (amerikanisch)
11. Mit manchen _____ Kindern kann man sich schon richtig unterhalten. (klein)
12. Welche _____ Leute gehen nicht gern auf Partys? (jung)
13. Ich kenne viele _____ Cafés hier. (nett)
14. Herr Ohlmann ist unser _____ Angestellter°. (gut)   *employee*
15. Es gibt eigentlich nichts _____ in unserer Familie. (neu)

C. Give the German equivalents.

1. The most expensive cars are often the best.
2. On the weekend, I would like to do something nice.
3. Do you know a cheaper restaurant here?
4. This restaurant has the highest prices.
5. I prefer to eat at home rather than in a restaurant.
6. What are you doing on the first of May?
7. Uncle Richard is my dearest° relative.   *liebst-*

KAPITEL 12

A. Complete the sentences with the present-time general subjunctive form of the verb in parentheses.

1. Wenn es doch nur _____. (regnen)
2. _____ Sie mir bitte den Zucker geben? (können)
3. Wenn es nach Ralf _____ (gehen), _____ wir immer zu Hause. (bleiben)
4. Sandra tut, als ob sie _____. (arbeiten)
5. _____ ihr Peter bitte helfen? (können)
6. Wenn ich nur _____ , wo meine Tasche ist. (wissen)
7. _____ wir nicht endlich die Meiers anrufen? (sollen)
8. Wenn Holger auch auf das Fest _____ (kommen), würde ich einen Kuchen mitbringen.
9. _____ du nicht mit uns fahren? (mögen)
10. Wenn es nicht so kalt _____ (sein), _____ ich größere Lust, schwimmen zu gehen. (haben)
11. _____ ich Sie kurz unterbrechen? (dürfen)
12. Wir _____ endlich anfangen, Sport zu treiben. (müssen)
13. Wann _____ ihr denn? (kommen)
14. Wenn mein Großvater nicht den ganzen Tag im Sessel _____ (sitzen), _____ er sicher nicht immer so müde. (sein)
15. Ich _____ (wünschen), du _____ dich mehr mit meinen Freunden. (unterhalten)

B. Make complete sentences in past-time general subjunctive.

1. meine Schwester und ich / haben / früher / gerne / einen Hund
2. Ulrich / werden / als Kind / am liebsten / Astronaut
3. du / essen wollen / noch ein Stück Kuchen / ?
4. ich / schreiben sollen / gestern / einen Brief an meine Freundin Anja
5. Ralf / bleiben / heute morgen / lieber / im Bett

C. Give the German equivalents.

1. I wouldn't call Alexander so often.
2. Almut acted as if she were angry.
3. Wouldn't you like to have more money?
4. That would be nice.
5. I should have helped Alex.
6. If Marion had more time, she would read more.
7. Couldn't we go to the supermarket now?
8. If I only knew that.

KAPITEL 13

A. Complete the following sentences, which are all in passive voice. Use the appropriate tense.

1. Der Fernseher _____ gestern repariert.
2. Nachdem Peter eine Anzeige° in die Zeitung gesetzt hatte, _____ die alten Möbel endlich verkauft.   *ad*
3. Ich verspreche es. Die Miete _____ in ein paar Tagen von meiner Firma bezahlt.
4. Wann _____ die Wäsche denn gebracht worden?
5. Die Handtücher _____ diese Woche jeden Tag gewaschen.

B. Change the following sentences from active voice into passive voice. Express the agent or means where indicated. Keep the same tense.

1. Der Lärm weckte die Kinder auf. *(means)*
2. Frau Gerber setzte den Hund in seinen Korb. *(agent)*
3. Die Universität hat Ulrich zum Wintersemester akzeptiert. *(no agent)*
4. Mein Vater hatte mich vor meinem Geburtstag angerufen. *(agent)*
5. Die Deutschen müssen mehr über die Probleme der Vereinigung° sprechen. *(impersonal passive)*   *unification*
6. Man müßte endlich die Garage aufräumen°. *(no agent)*   *straighten up*
7. Ihr solltet eure Tochter nicht immer kritisieren. *(agent)*
8. Jemand hat Angelikas Rucksack gestohlen. *(no agent)*
9. Die Polizei hatte die Tatwaffe° seit vielen Monaten gesucht. *(agent)*   *weapon used in the crime*
10. Ich habe das Haus selbst gestrichen. *(agent)*

C. Give the German equivalents. Use the words in parentheses.

1. *The apartment ought to be sold.*
   (die Wohnung / sollen / verkaufen) *(present-time general subjunctive)*
2. *Can the apartment be renovated?*
   (die Wohnung / können / renovieren / ?) *(present)*
3. *Yes, but then a lot would have to be done.*
   (ja / aber / dann / viel / müssen / machen) *(present-time general subjunctive)*
4. *New apartments are easy to find.*
   (neue Wohnungen / sein / finden / leicht) *(present)*
5. *Apartments are selling well this year.*
   (Wohnungen / sich verkaufen / gut / dieses Jahr) *(present)*
6. *The house was built in 1854.*
   (das Haus / bauen / 1854) *(simple past)*
7. *My old bike was thrown away.*
   (mein altes Fahrrad / wegwerfen) *(present perfect)*
8. *Why haven't I been asked?*
   (warum / ich / nicht / fragen / ?) *(present perfect)*
9. *The door was opened at eight o'clock.*
   (die Tür / aufmachen / um acht Uhr) *(simple past)*
10. *The politician was elected for the second time.*
    (die Politikerin / wählen / zum zweiten Mal) *(present perfect)*
11. *A thousand marks were collected by the organization.*
    (tausend Mark / sammeln / von der Organisation) *(simple past)*
12. *You aren't allowed to swim in this lake.*
    (in diesem See / man / dürfen / nicht schwimmen) *(present)*
13. *The problem can be easily solved.*
    (das Problem / sich lassen / lösen / leicht) *(present)*

KAPITEL 14

A. Complete the sentences with the appropriate form of the special subjunctive. Use general subjunctive when required.

1. Hat Stefan wirklich gesagt, ich _____ langweilig? (sein: *present time)*
2. Der Student behauptet, er _____ für den Test _____. (lernen: *past time)*
3. Die Kinder riefen, sie _____ die Vase nicht _____.
   (kaputtmachen: *past time)*
4. Die Managerin versprach, niemand _____ seinen Arbeitsplatz _____. (verlieren: *future time)*
5. Meinst du, du _____ klüger als ich? (sein: *present time)*

6. Mein Bruder erzählte, er _____ keinen Wein trinken. (dürfen: *present time*)
7. Der kleine Junge sagte, er _____ gern in den Kindergarten. (gehen: *present time*)
8. Er behauptete, er _____ schon lesen und schreiben. (können: *present time*)
9. Meine Tante sagte, sie _____ dieses Jahr ans Meer _____. (fahren: *past time*)
10. Unser Nachbar erzählte, er _____ im Urlaub jeden Tag _____. (joggen: *future time*)

B. Complete the sentences with the appropriate form of the general subjunctive.

1. Alex rief, wir _____ keine Zeit zu verlieren. (haben: *present time*)
2. Monika sagte, sie _____ sofort _____. (kommen: *future time*)
3. Die Eltern meinten, ihre Tochter _____ in Freiburg _____. (bleiben: *past time*)
4. Hat Peter wirklich geschrien, Ulla _____ besser nach Hause fahren? (sollen: *present time*)
5. Meine Freunde versprachen, sie _____ mich in Boston _____. (besuchen: *future time*)
6. Dagmar meinte, ihre Freundin _____ gern auf dem Sofa. (schlafen: *present time*)
7. Andrea sagte, ihre Eltern _____ das nicht _____. (bezahlen sollen: *past time*)
8. Alexandra dachte, Peter _____ noch nicht Auto fahren. (dürfen: *present time*)
9. Mein Bruder sagte, er _____ sein Zimmer heute mittag _____. (putzen: *future time*)
10. Mein Onkel erzählte, er _____ letzte Woche _____. (segeln: *past time*)

C. Change the following sentences from direct discourse into indirect discourse. Give both the general and special subjunctive forms for each sentence.

1. Monika sagte: „Ich gehe heute nicht zur Arbeit.“
2. Ihr Mann Georg fragte: „Warum kannst du denn nicht gehen? Bist du krank?“
3. Monika antwortete: „Nein, aber die Arbeit ist zur Zeit furchtbar. Ich habe den ganzen Tag Streß.“
4. Georg schlug vor: „Such dir doch einen anderen Job.“
5. Monika antwortete: „Das ist nicht so leicht. So viele gute Stellen gibt es nicht. Außerdem ist die Arbeit interessant.“
6. Georg meinte: „Vielleicht soll ich dir mehr im Haushalt° helfen?“   household
7. Monika sagte: „Das ist keine schlechte Idee.“

KAPITEL 15

A. Complete the sentences with **jemand, jedermann/jeder, niemand,** or **es**, as appropriate.

1. _____ weiß, daß heute Muttertag ist. Nur du hast es vergessen.
2. _____ tut mir leid, daß _____ Ihnen nicht gut geht.
3. Hallo, ist da _____? —Habt ihr auch etwas gehört?
4. _____ hat geklingelt. Würdest du bitte aufmachen?
5. Wenn _____ jetzt schneit und dann auch noch friert, wird _____ diesen Sommer nur wenig Obst geben.
6. Kann mir wieder _____ helfen? Muß ich schon wieder alles allein machen?

B.   Complete the sentences with the correct form of the cued **ein**-word or possessive pronoun.

1. Gefällt dir der Mantel? —Ist das wirklich _____? (dein)
2. Ulrike mußte sich ein neues Fahrrad kaufen. Ich habe _____ leider kaputtgefahren. (ihr)
3. Dieser Schlüssel lag unter dem Tisch. Ist das _____? (Ihr)
4. Wir haben auch einen Hund. _____ ist schon ziemlich alt. (unser)
5. Mark braucht neue Schuhe. _____ sind im Sommer zu warm. (sein)
6. Deine Stereoanlage ist phantastisch. Ich habe leider _____. (kein)
7. Wie ist denn dein Stuhl? _____ ist zu hart. (mein)
8. Warum putzt du jede Woche dein Auto? Wir putzen _____ fast nie. (unser)
9. Dieses Stück Kuchen schmeckt sehr gut. Geben Sie mir bitte noch _____. (ein)
10. Unser Großvater ist sehr krank. Geht es _____ auch so schlecht? (euer)

C. Give the English equivalents.

1. Cornelia durfte nie viel Geld ausgeben. Sie mußte alles sparen.
2. Rainer soll viele Freunde gehabt haben. Er war immer freundlich.
3. Sandra muß ein Architekturstudium gemacht haben. Sie plant jetzt das neue Haus für ihre Eltern.
4. Ulrich mußte Medizin studieren. Seine ganze Familie wollte es.
5. Meine Schwester hatte mein Zimmer putzen wollen, aber dann hat sie ihre Meinung geändert.
6. Meine Kusine Lisa will meinen Freund Gerd in einem Porsche gesehen haben. Aber das kann ich kaum glauben.
7. Rudi wird hoffentlich nicht die ganze Pizza gegessen haben. Wir haben nämlich auch Hunger.

8. Ich weiß nicht, wie lang der Film war. Er mag etwa zwei Stunden gedauert haben.
9. Sollte Mark den Brief wirklich nicht gelesen haben? Er lag doch auf seinem Schreibtisch.

D. Give the German equivalents.

1. Did it rain yesterday?
2. No, it snowed.
3. You may be right.
4. It's supposed to be nice tomorrow.
5. I can hardly believe it.
6. Do you have to go already?
7. I am sorry that the party doesn't please you.
8. And you claim to be my friend!

Answer Key to the Self-Tests

The number in parentheses following the answer refers to the number of the section of the chapter in which the grammatical points of the test item are discussed. For example, in *Kapitel 1*, exercise A, item 1, below, "see 2" refers you to Section 2: Basic Present-Tense Endings, which is found on page 2.

KAPITEL 1

A.
1. Wann **antwortest** du auf den Brief? (see 2)
2. Cornelia **läuft** oft im Park. (see 3)
3. **Lest** ihr jeden Tag die Zeitung? (see 3)
4. Du **hast** aber viel Arbeit! (see 4)
5. Ich **sammle** Briefmarken. (see 2)
6. Sein Bruder **wird** Bäcker. (see 4)
7. Gisela **tanzt** sehr gut. (see 2)
8. Wie **findet** ihr den Film „Das Boot"? (see 2)
9. **Nehmen** Sie jeden Tag Vitamintabletten? (see 3)
10. **Seid** jetzt endlich ruhig! (see 8)
11. **Essen wir** endlich ein Eis! (see 8)
12. **Lies** bitte die erste Geschichte im Buch. (see 8)
13. **Fahrt** nicht mit dem Auto! (see 8)
14. **Nehmen Sie** doch meinen Bleistift! (see 8)
15. **Lauft** zum Bäcker und **kauft** ein Brot! (see 8)

B.
1. Ich komme am Sonntag zurück. (see 7)
2. Ruf(e) deine Familie an! (see 8)
3. Fahrt ihr am Wochenende weg? (see 7)
4. Er geht jeden Freitag aus. (see 7)
5. Fängt der Film um acht Uhr an? (see 7)

C.

1. Ich studiere / lerne seit zwei Jahren Deutsch. (see 6)
2. Kennst du / Kennt ihr / Kennen Sie seine Mutter? (see 5)
3. Sie weiß nicht, daß er kommt. (see 5 and 6)
4. Wir essen um neun Uhr. (see 6)
5. Sie kennen Stuttgart sehr gut. (see 5)

KAPITEL 2

A.

1. Ulrike fährt Auto. —**Darf** sie das denn? (see 1)
2. Hilfst du mir? —Nein, ich **will** nicht! (see 1)
3. Sie **möchte/möchten** nicht schwimmen gehen. (see 4)
4. Wir **sollen** bis morgen die Wörter lernen. (see 1)
5. Warum **laßt** ihr den Hund nicht in den Garten? (see *Kapitel 1*, Section 3)
6. **Wirst** du schon wieder krank? (see *Kapitel 1*, Section 3)
7. Ich **muß** heute mittag einkaufen. (see 1)
8. **Mögt** ihr eure Katze? (see 1)
9. **Kann** er wirklich Ski laufen? (see 1)
10. Wir **lassen** uns das Frühstück ans Bett bringen. (see *Kapitel 1*, Section 3)

B.

1. Er darf Auto fahren. (see 2)
2. Sollen wir das Geschirr spülen? (see 2)
3. Ich sehe ihn ins Haus kommen. (see 6)
4. Läßt du deine Haare schneiden? (see 7)
5. Sie hören/hört das Kind weinen. (see 6)
6. Er muß die Wohnung putzen. (see 2)
7. Sie wird/werden ans Meer fahren. (see 9)
8. Möchtet ihr einen Kuchen im Café kaufen? (see 4)
9. Er mag das Buch „Andorra" nicht. (see 3)
10. Können sie/Kann sie/Können Sie Klavier spielen? (see 2)

C.

1. Sie braucht am Sonntag nicht zu arbeiten (muß...nicht arbeiten). (see 5)
2. Wir brauchen Claudia nicht zu helfen. (see 5)
3. Möchtet ihr heute einen Film sehen? (see 4)
4. Mag Michael Rap-Musik? (see 3)
5. Im Sommer reise ich nach Hamburg. (see 8)
6. Laß/Laßt/Lassen Sie mich bitte bezahlen! (see 7b)
7. Läßt du die Kinder zu Hause? (see 7a)
8. Wir lassen das Auto/den Wagen reparieren. (see 7b)

9. Du darfst nicht böse sein. (see 5)
10. Können Sie Französisch? (see 3)

KAPITEL 3

A.
1. Andreas **wartete** nach dem Biologieseminar meistens auf Antje. (see 2)
2. Britta **verletzte** sich letztes Jahr beim Tennisspielen. (see 2)
3. Unsere Großeltern **heirateten** schon sehr früh. (see 2)
4. Der Patient **atmete** unruhig. (see 2)
5. Die Studenten **tanzten** oft die ganze Nacht. (see 2)
6. Wir **lernten** nur sehr wenig in der Schule. (see 2)
7. Letzten Mai **wurde** er 23. (see 6)
8. **Wart** ihr dieses Jahr schon im Urlaub? (see 6)
9. Als Studentin **hatte** ich nie Geld. (see 4)
10. Uwe **bestellte** einen Apfelsaft. (see 2)
11. Ich **hörte** schon 1990 mit dem Rauchen **auf.** (see 2)
12. **Mußtet** ihr jeden Morgen das Frühstück machen? (see 3)
13. Ich **mochte** italienisches Essen noch nie. (see 3)
14. Am Wochenende **liefen** wir oft im Wald spazieren. (see 5)
15. Er **aß** immer schrecklich viel. (see 5)
16. Die Geschichte „Tod in Venedig" **gefiel** mir in der Schule immer am besten. (see 5)
17. Sie **schlief** oft in der Bibliothek **ein,** und Martin **weckte** sie dann wieder **auf.** (see 2 and 5)

B.
1. Sophie **hat** heute morgen im Park ein Portemonnaie **gefunden.** (see 11 and 14)
2. Oliver **ist** gestern mit Lufthansa nach Deutschland **geflogen.** (see 11 and 15)
3. Ich **habe** ihm einen Stuhl in den Garten **gebracht.** (see 10 and 14)
4. Wo **habt** ihr in Berlin **gewohnt?** (see 9 and 14)
5. **Haben** Sie mit ihrem Chef über das Projekt **gesprochen?** (see 11 and 14)
6. **Hast** du deinen Eltern aus dem Urlaub **geschrieben?** (see 11 and 14)
7. Warum **ist** Stefanie am Samstag zu Hause **geblieben?** (see 11 and 15)
8. Alle **haben** den Konjunktiv **verstanden!** (see 13 and 14)
9. Warum **hat** sich Mark heute morgen nicht **rasiert?** (see 13 and 14)
10. Ulrike **hat** gestern ihren Freund nach Hause **gefahren.** (see 11 and 14)
11. Wo im Schwarzwald **seid** ihr **gewandert?** (see 9 and 15)

12. Am Sonntag **sind** wir ins Schwimmbad **gegangen.** (see 11 and 15)
13. Wie **ist** der Unfall denn **passiert**? (see 13 and 15)
14. Ich **habe** meine Uhr **verloren.** (see 11 and 14)

C.

1. Ich war nicht mehr müde. Ich hatte ein bißchen geschlafen. (see 6, 11, and 16)
2. Aber meine Freunde waren nicht zu Hause. Sie waren gerade gegangen/weggegangen/weggefahren. (Sie hatten gerade das Haus verlassen.) (see 6, 11, and 16)
3. Ich hatte sie nicht gehen/weggehen/wegfahren hören. (see 16 and 17)
4. Sie sind wahrscheinlich nicht ins Museum gegangen. Sie waren bei ihrem letzten Besuch dort gewesen. (see 15 and 16)
5. Wir wollten unsere Freundin Karin nicht besuchen. (Wir haben unsere Freundin Karin nicht besuchen wollen.) (see 3 and 17)
6. Gestern hat Karin sich einen Zahn ziehen lassen. (Gestern ließ Karen sich einen Zahn ziehen.) (see 17)

KAPITEL 4

A.

1. (c) Wir wissen nicht, **wann** Erikas Zug in München ankommt. (see 8)
2. (a) **Wenn** sie heute nicht anruft, ist sicher etwas passiert. (see 8)
3. (b) **Wenn** ich früher Kaffee trank, wurde ich immer sehr nervös. (see 8)
4. (a) **Als** die Ferien am ersten Juli begannen, freuten sich meine Eltern sehr auf ihren Urlaub. (see 8)
5. (c) Carolin geht ins Kino, **um** den Film „Metropolis" **zu** sehen. (see 13)
6. (a) **Anstatt** in der Bibliothek **zu** lernen, ging sie im Park spazieren. (see 13)
7. (b) Erich aß eine Woche lang nur Obst, **ohne** ein Gramm **abzunehmen.** (see 13)
8. (c) **Nachdem** das Kind ein Eis bekommen hatte, war es wieder guter Laune. (see 10)
9. (c) Lernt ihr schon **seit** vier Jahren Deutsch? (see 9c)
10. (b) **Seitdem** Karin mehr schläft, ist sie nicht mehr so oft müde. (see 9c)

B.

1. Anna geht zum Arzt, **weil/da** sie Fieber hat. (see 7 and 9)
2. **Da/Weil** es heute sehr heiß ist, sind viele Studenten am See. (see 7 and 9)

3. Wir fahren nicht nach Hannover, **sondern** nach Hamburg. (see 3 and 4)
4. Daniel und Christine waren in Paris, **aber** sie haben den Eiffelturm nicht gesehen. (see 3 and 4)
5. Er bleibt im Bett, **denn** er hat eine Erkältung. (see 3)
6. Wußtest du, **daß** Sacramento die Hauptstadt von Kalifornien ist? (see 6 and 7)
7. Kommt Vincent mit, **oder** möchte er zu Hause bleiben? (see 3)
8. Julia wartete, **bis** der Zug abfuhr. (see 7)
9. **Indem** Dennis mich ansah, sagte er: „Ich mag dich." (see 7 and 9)
10. Tobias fährt Ski, **und/aber** er fährt auch Fahrrad. (see 3, p. 46)
11. Ich schließe die Tür, **damit/so daß** ich die laute Musik nicht höre. (see 7, p. 50)

C.

1. Ich gehe am Sonntag mit meinem Freund im Park spazieren. / Am Sonntag gehe ich mit meinem Freund im Park spazieren. (see 14)
2. Siehst du das Auto nicht? (see 15)
3. Warum lädt Erich seinen Bruder nicht ein? (see 2, 14, and 15)
4. Meine Eltern fahren in den Ferien nach Wien, oder sie bleiben in Salzburg. / In den Ferien fahren meine Eltern nach Wien, oder sie bleiben in Salzburg. (see 3 and 14)
5. Andreas kann nicht ins Restaurant gehen, weil er kein Geld hat. (see 7, 9, 14, and 15)
6. Seitdem Petra arbeitet, ist sie immer müde. (see 9 and 14)
7. Wir spielen heute nicht Tennis, sondern Golf. (see 4 and 15)
8. Willst du Kaffee trinken oder Kuchen essen? (see 2 and 3)
9. Elly und Martin können am Samstag nicht mit uns auf die Party gehen./Am Samstag können Elly und Martin nicht mit uns auf die Party gehen. (see 14 and 15)
10. Nach der Arbeit spielt Jens oft mit seiner Freundin Schach. / Jens spielt nach der Arbeit oft mit seiner Freundin Schach. / Jens spielt oft nach der Arbeit mit seiner Freundin Schach. (see 14)

D.

1. Wir sehen fern, (an)statt unsere Hausaufgaben zu machen. (see 13)
2. Entweder schreibst du Klaus einen Brief, oder du mußt ihn bald anrufen. / Entweder du schreibst Klaus einen Brief, oder du mußt ihn bald anrufen. (see 3 and 11)
3. Weder möchte ich (zu Fuß) gehen noch mit dem Fahrrad fahren (Rad fahren). / Ich möchte weder (zu Fuß) gehen noch mit dem Fahrrad fahren (Rad fahren). (see 11)
4. Es wäre schön, heute abend ins Kino zu gehen. (see 12 and 14)
5. Ich muß nach Hause (gehen), um mein Zimmer zu putzen. (see 13)
6. Irene hat keine Zeit, einkaufen zu gehen. (see 12)

KAPITEL 5

A.
1. (c) Beide Tische sind neu. Wie findest du **diesen** Tisch? (see 2)
2. (d) Nicht alle Leute liegen gern am Strand. **Manche** wandern lieber. (see 2)
3. (b) **Solche** Bücher lese ich nicht. Sie sind mir zu trivial. (see 2 and 3)
4. (a) Warum gefallen dir meine Ohrringe nicht? —Ich finde **sie** zu groß. (see 9)
5. (a) Wann besuchst du deinen Großvater? —Ich besuche **ihn** nächsten Monat. (see 9)
6. (c) Kauft ihr Geschenke für das Fest? —Nein, wir kaufen **keine** Geschenke. (see 4)
7. (a) Wo ist euer Auto? —**Unser** Auto ist in der Garage. (see 5)
8. (d) Gefällt dir ihr Kleid? —Ja, **so ein** Kleid möchte ich auch. (see 2 and 3)
9. (b) Hat deine Schwester einen Freund? —Ja, aber **ihr** Freund lebt in Italien. (see 5)
10. (b) Kennst du diese Person? —**Wen** meinst du? Den Mann oder die Frau? (see 11)

B.
1. Der Polizist fragt **den Touristen** nach seinem Führerschein. (see 7)
2. Der Tourist sieht **den Polizisten** böse an. (see 7)
3. Die Stürme beunruhigten **den Bauern.** (see 7)
4. Wir wollen **einen Monat** durch Europa reisen. (see 16)
5. Ich kaufe ein Hemd für **meinen Bruder.** (see 5 and 15)

C.
1. Meine Freundin Sabine ist Lehrerin. (see 6)
2. Andreas möchte Rechtsanwalt werden. (see 6)
3. Richard ist nicht (kein) Amerikaner. (see 6)
4. Geh(e) nicht ohne deine Jacke. (see 15)
5. Komm(e) durch den Garten. (see 15)
6. Wir besuchen nächsten Monat unsere Freunde. / Wir besuchen unsere Freunde nächsten Monat. / Nächsten Monat besuchen wir unsere Freunde. (see 16)
7. Gibt es hier einen Park? / Gibt es einen Park hier? (see 19)
8. Wo kann man hier parken? (see 10)
9. So ein Stau kann einen ärgern. (see 10)
10. Der Patient muß jeden Morgen zwei Glas Wasser trinken. / Jeden Morgen muß der Patient zwei Glas Wasser trinken. (see 16 and 18)

KAPITEL 6

A.

1. (c) Warum hast du mit **diesen** Leuten gesprochen? (see 1 and 11)
2. (a) Können wir **dem** Mädchen denn nicht helfen? (see 1 and 10)
3. (d) Andrea ist zu **ihren** Freunden oft unfreundlich. (see 1 and 11)
4. (d) Die Katze hat Hunger. Gib **der** doch endlich etwas zu fressen. (see 4 and 10)
5. (b) Ach, ihr wohnt jetzt in Münster? Wie gefällt **euch** Münster? (see 5 and 10)
6. (c) Michael ist Julias Freund. Sie schreibt **ihm** oft Postkarten. (see 5 and 10)
7. (b) **Wem** gehört diese Tasche? (see 6 and 10)
8. (a) Wie soll ich wissen, mit **wem** Dagmar in Urlaub fährt? (see 6 and 11)
9. (c) Und dann hat Mario **dir** einen Ring geschenkt? (see 5 and 10)
10. (b) Judith hat **keinem** Menschen von ihrer Krankheit erzählt. (see 1 and 8)
11. (a) Seit **einem** Jahr haben wir nichts von unseren Freunden gehört. (see 1 and 11)
12. (d) Was hat der Arzt **Ihnen** geraten? (see 5 and 10)

B.

1. Was schenkst du deinem Vater **zum** Geburtstag? (see 12)
2. Wo gehen Schmidts Kinder **zur** Schule? (see 12)
3. Wohnst du nicht mehr **bei** deinen Eltern? (see 11)
4. Können wir die Party in eurem Garten machen? Ich habe **bei** mir keinen Platz. (see 11)
5. Wer war auf Martas Party? —**Außer** ihrer Schwester waren alle da. (see 11)
6. Wie fährst du im Sommer nach Österreich – **mit** der Bahn oder **mit** dem Auto? (see 11)
7. Patrizia kommt **aus** Österreich, nicht wahr? (see 11)
8. Ich habe **seit** einem Monat kein Deutsch gesprochen. (see 11)

C.

1. Gibt der Lehrer **dem Studenten** eine gute Note? (see 3)
2. Du mußt **deinem Gast** Kaffee anbieten. (see 1)
3. Mein Sohn geht mit **seinen Freunden** auf eine Radtour. (see 2 and 11)
4. Was soll ich nur mit **meinen vielen Büchern** machen? (see 2 and 11)
5. Haben Sie schon von **den neuen Autos** gehört? Sie fahren ohne Benzin. (see 2 and 11)
6. Ist es **dir** recht, daß ich etwas früher gehe? (see 13)
7. Judith geht mit **ihren Hunden** spazieren. (see 2 and 11)

8. Ich glaube **ihm** nicht. (see 5 and 10)

9. Fisch schmeckt **mir** nicht. (see 5 and 10, pp. 84 and 87)

D.

1. Hilf/Helft/Helfen Sie mir bitte. (see 10)

2. Zeig(e)/Zeigt/Zeigen Sie mir das Bild/das Foto. (see 8 and 9)

3. Gib/Gebt/Geben Sie es mir bitte. (see 8 and 9)

4. Was schenkst du deiner Mutter zum Geburtstag? / Was schenkt ihr eurer Mutter zum Geburtstag? (see 8 and 12)

5. Ich schenke ihr Blumen und mehrere/einige/ein paar CDs. (see 5 and 9)

KAPITEL 7

A.

1. (b) Thomas ist immer unpünktlich. Daher wartet Ute jetzt nicht mehr **auf ihn.** (see 5 and 7)

2. (a) Bald ist mein Geburtstag. Ich freue mich sehr **darauf.** (see 7)

3. (c) Du bist nicht allein ins Kino gegangen? **Mit wem** warst du dort? (see 8)

4. (d) Andrea ist sehr kompliziert. **Mit ihr** gehen wir nie wieder spazieren. (see 7)

5. (b) Laura soll sich bei uns amüsieren. **Wofür** interessiert sie sich denn? (see 8)

6. (a) Das ist ja ein tolles Geschenk. **Von wem** hat sie es bekommen? (see 8)

B.

(a)

1. Komm mal **her**! Du mußt mir helfen. (see 1)

2. Sie sind so schick angezogen. **Wohin** gehen sie? (see 1)

3. Er spricht Dialekt. Wissen Sie, **woher** er kommt? (see 1)

4. Die Großeltern freuen sich immer über Besuch. Fahrt doch mal **hin.** (see 1)

(b)

5. Nie geht sie **ans** Telefon, dabei sind alle Anrufe für sie. (see 3)

6. Wann habt ihr Zeit? —**Am** Mittwoch. (see 3)

7. **Im** Juli fahren wir nach Spanien. (see 3)

8. Sie gehen fast jeden Abend **ins** Kino. (see 3)

9. **Im** Winter ist es mir in Neuengland viel zu kalt. (see 3)

10. **Am** Wochenende machen wir einen Ausflug. Wir fahren **aufs** Land. (see 3)

11. Warum unterhaltet ihr euch nicht **auf** englisch? (see 5)

12. Denkst du noch oft **an** deinen Hund? Es tut mir leid, daß er nicht mehr **am** Leben ist. (see 3 and 5)

13. Deutschland ist so teuer. Gute Schuhe gibt es kaum **unter** hundert Mark. (see 5)

14. **In einer** Woche sind Ulrikes Prüfungen. Doch sie hat schon **vor einem** Monat mit dem Lernen begonnen. (see 6)

15. **Am** Abend kann ich mich oft nicht mehr konzentrieren. (see 6)

(c)

16. Deine Jacke **liegt** auf dem Boden. **Häng(e)** sie doch in den Schrank. (see 4)

17. Endlich **liegt** ein Teppich im Zimmer. So ist es viel gemütlicher. (see 4)

18. Hast du das Geld ins Portemonnaie **gesteckt**? Es **liegt** nicht mehr auf dem Tisch. (see 4)

19. Gestern hat Patricks Vater nur im Bett **gelegen,** und heute hat er nur in seinem Lehnstuhl **gesessen.** (see 4)

20. Ich habe Corinna in ihren Kinderstuhl **gesetzt.** (see 4)

C.

1. Das Kind liegt unter dem Baum. (see 2, 3, and 4)
2. Die Autos stehen in der Garage. (see 2 and 4)
3. Warum stellst du die Pflanze nicht auf den Schreibtisch? (see 2 and 4)
4. Ich hänge die Lampe über den Spiegel. (see 2, 3, and 4)
5. Markus sitzt zwischen seinem Freund und seiner Mutter. (see 2 and 4)

D.

1. Ich möchte am Sonntag an den Strand gehen. (see 2 and 6)
2. Edith studiert an der Universität (in) Heidelberg. (see 5)
3. Frank stellte das Glas neben den Teller. (see 2 and 4)
4. Hast du deine Uhr (schon) hinter dem Bett gesucht? (see 2)
5. Haben die Kinder Angst vor Hunden? (see 5)

KAPITEL 8

A.

1. Die Brille **des Mädchens** ist extravagant. (see 1 and 2)
2. Das Auto **meines Mannes** ist zur Zeit in Reparatur. (see 1 and 2)
3. Wie findest du den Hut **des Herrn** da drüben? (see 1 and 3)
4. Franziska hat die Äpfel **unseres Nachbarn** gestohlen. (see 1 and 3)
5. Überall im Garten liegen die Spielsachen **ihrer Kinder.** (see 1 and 2)
6. **Wessen** Heft ist das?
   —Das ist das Heft **seiner Freundin**. (see 1, 2, and 5)
7. Die Koffer **dieses Touristen** würde der Gepäckträger nicht tragen. (see 1 and 3)

8. Die Bedeutung **seines Namens** ist mir nicht klar. (see 1 and 3)
9. Wir wohnen jetzt im Haus **unserer Eltern.** (see 1 and 2)
10. Wißt ihr, **wessen** Motorrad das ist?
    Es steht vor dem Eingang **unseres Hofes.** (see 1, 2, and 5)
11. Die Phantasie **eines Kindes** können sich Erwachsene nur schwer
    vorstellen. (see 1 and 2)
12. Der Humor **dieses Menschen** ist manchmal sehr makaber. (see
    1 and 3)
13. Die Eltern **meines Freundes** sind weggefahren. Jetzt gibt es dort
    die größte Party **des Jahres.** (see 1 and 2)
14. Die Klavierlehrerin **unserer Tochter** ist ziemlich streng. (see 1
    and 2)
15. Die Farbe **ihres Getränk(e)s** kann man gar nicht definieren. (see
    1 and 2)
16. Leider ist die Politik **des Landes** nicht sehr demokratisch. (see
    1 and 2)
17. Bei der Form **seines Kopfes** kann Werner keine Hüte tragen.
    (see 1 and 2)
18. Statt **einer Party** machen wir eben ein Abendessen. (see 1, 2,
    and 8)
19. Silke geht trotz **ihrer Erkältung** ins Schwimmbad. (see 1, 2,
    and 8)
20. Wir machen die Reise nur **seinetwegen (wegen ihm).** (see 8
    and 11)

B.
1. Während der Winterferien will Lilian in die Karibik reisen. (see 8)
2. Die Wunde ist oberhalb des Knies. (see 8)
3. Kommt Thomas wegen seines Neffen nicht auf das Fest? (see 3
   and 8)
4. Frankreich liegt von hier aus gesehen jenseits des Rheins.
   (see 8)
5. Es gibt viele Cafés und Restaurants unterhalb der Kirche. (see 8)

C.
1. Magst du die Freundin deines Bruders?
   Magst du die Freundin von deinem Bruder? (see 7 and 11)
2. Eines Tages wird er im Haus seiner Großeltern wohnen.
   Eines Tages wird er im Haus von seinen Großeltern wohnen. (see
   7, 9, and 11)
3. Ich bin ganz deiner Meinung/Ansicht. (see 10)
4. Meinetwegen können wir das Auto meiner Mutter benutzen. (von
   meiner Mutter) (see 7, 8, and 11)
5. Letzten Endes ist es das Problem deiner Schwester. (von deiner
   Schwester) (see 9 and 11)

KAPITEL 9

A.

1. (c) Für die Wanderung brauchst du Schuhe, **die** bequem sind. (see 2)
2. (d) Ich habe einen Mantel gekauft, **den** ich auch im Winter tragen kann. (see 2)
3. (b) Das sind die Kinder, **deren** Eltern für zwei Monate in Indien sind. (see 2)
4. (a) Ulrich gehört zu den Leuten, **denen** gar nichts schmeckt. (see 2)
5. (b) Karin sucht eine Wohnung, **die** groß, hell und billig ist. (see 2)
6. (c) Nadja und Andrea sind Studentinnen, **die** immer alle Hausaufgaben machen. (see 2)
7. (b) Der Mann, **den** Sandra am Samstag kennengelernt hat, rief gleich am Sonntag an. (see 2)
8. (c) Ich kenne die Leute, **denen** dieses schöne Haus gehört. (see 2)
9. (d) Wie findest du das Kleid, **das** Isabelle heute trägt? (see 2)
10. (a) Mark ist ein Junge, **dessen** einziges Interesse Fußball ist. (see 2)
11. (b) Zeig mir das Café, in **dem** es den guten Kuchen gibt. (see 2)
12. (c) Sind das die Leute, bei **denen** Angelika übernachtet hat? (see 2)
13. (a) Wie heißt die Universität, an **der** Ben studiert? (see 2)
14. (d) Wir wollen uns ein Auto kaufen, mit **dem** wir komfortabel reisen können. (see 2)
15. (b) Ist das die Lederjacke, für **die** du so lange gespart hast? (see 2)

B.

1. Ist das alles, **was** Jörg zum Geburtstag bekommen hat? (see 3)
2. Es gibt nichts, **worüber** Hanna sich freut. (see 3)
3. **Was** man Kindern verspricht, muß man auch halten. (see 3)
4. Ulla hat in ihrem Zimmer nichts, **worauf** sie sitzen kann. (see 3)
5. **Wer** nie Vokabeln lernt, wird Probleme haben, eine Sprache zu lernen. (see 3)
6. Mit **wem** du ausgehst, ist mir egal. (see 3)
7. Sibylle zu treffen war das Schönste, **was** Robert in diesem Jahr passiert ist. (see 3
8. Es gibt vieles, **wofür** Beate sich interessiert. (see 3)
9. **Wer** die Konzertkarte bis heute nicht abholt, bekommt keine. (see 3)
10. Ich kenne nichts, **wovor** meine Tochter Angst hat. (see 3)

C.

1. Andreas ist ein Kollege, den ich vor einem Jahr kennengelernt habe. / Andreas ist ein Kollege, den ich vor einem Jahr kennenlernte. (see 2)
2. Ist er jemand, der optimistisch ist? (see 2)

3. Das ist etwas, was nur seine Freundin beantworten kann. (see 3)
4. Ich mag Leute, die immer freundlich sind. (see 2)
5. Claudia ist eine Frau, die selten lacht. (see 2)
6. Das ist etwas, was ich nicht gut finde. (see 3)
7. Andreas und Claudia suchen eine Wohnung, die etwa 800 Mark kostet. (see 2)
8. Sie haben einen Vermieter, den sie nicht mögen. (see 2)
9. Wer sind die Leute, mit denen Andreas spricht? (see 2)
10. Zeig(e) Claudia das Zimmer, in dem sie schlafen kann. (see 2)
11. Ist das das Bett, das kaputt ist? (see 2)

KAPITEL 10

A.

1. Ihr wascht **euch** doch vor dem Abendessen die Hände, nicht? (see 2 and 5)
2. Ich erinnere **mich** gern an den Sommerurlaub. (see 2, 7, and 8)
3. Putzt du **dir** nach jedem Essen die Zähne? (see 3 and 5)
4. Wir haben **uns** für Peters Benehmen entschuldigt. (see 2 and 8)
5. Zum Geburtstag wünsche ich **mir** eine neue Büchertasche. (see 3)
6. Hat Sabine **sich** schon wieder erkältet? (see 2 and 8)
7. Kannst du **dir** schon wieder neue CDs leisten? (see 2 and 8)
8. Meine Eltern interessieren **sich** für klassische Musik. (see 2 and 8)
9. Amüsiert **euch** gut auf der Party! (see 2 and 8)
10. Warum hast du **dir** die Haare nicht gekämmt? (see 3 and 5)
11. Ihr habt **euch** aber sehr verspätet. (see 2 and 8)
12. Warum hast du **dich** nicht beeilt? (see 2 and 8)
13. Wir haben **uns** schon gewundert, wo du bleibst. (see 2 and 8)

B.

1. Jetzt mußt du dir dein Essen **selbst/selber** kochen. (see 9)
2. Seit einem Jahr haben Andrea und Georg **sich/einander** nicht mehr geschrieben. (see 10)
3. Georg hat es mir **selbst/selber** erzählt. (see 9)
4. Frau Peters und Herr Greiner reden nicht mehr **miteinander.** Sie haben immer noch Streit. (see 10)
5. Wenn Max und Anna **nebeneinander** sitzen, lachen sie die ganze Zeit **miteinander.** (see 10)
6. Petra hat sich dieses Kleid **selbst/selber** genäht. (see 9)
7. Ulrich hat sich über seine Fehler **selbst/selber** am meisten geärgert. (see 9)

C.

1. Warum muß sich Martin jeden Tag rasieren? / Warum muß Martin sich jeden Tag rasieren? (see 6)

2. Ich kann mir keine neue Stereoanlage leisten. (see 6 and 8)

3. Hast du dir schon überlegt, ob du uns helfen kannst? (see 6 and 8)

4. Leider haben sich die zwei Hunde immer noch nicht aneinander gewöhnt. / Leider haben die zwei Hunde sich immer noch nicht aneinander gewöhnt. (see 6, 8, and 10)

5. Stefan und Uwe haben sich am Wochenende beim Skifahren erkältet. / Am Wochenende haben sich Stefan und Uwe beim Skifahren erkältet. / Am Wochenende haben Stefan und Uwe sich beim Skifahren erkältet. (see 2, 6, and 8)

D.

1. PHILLIP: Du hast dich verspätet. (see 2 and 8)

   JÖRG: Ich muß mich entschldigen. Ich habe mich verirrt/ver-
               fahren/verlaufen. (see 2 and 8)

2. LISA: Hast du dich auf der Party (gut) amüsiert? (see 2
               and 8)

   BIRGIT: Ja. Daniel und ich haben uns gut unterhalten. (see
               2 and 8)

3. CHRISTINE: Bist du fertig?

   RITA: Nein, ich muß mich duschen, mir die Zähne putzen,
               mir die Haare kämmen und mich schminken. (see 2,
               3, and 5)

   CHRISTINE: Gut, bitte beeil(e) dich. (see 2 and 5)

KAPITEL 11

A.

1. (a) Mein Geburtstag ist am **vierten** März. (see 10)

2. (b) Ich brauche einen **freien** Tag. (see 4)

3. (c) Mit dieser **eleganten** Hose kannst du gut auf die Party gehen. (see 3)

4. (d) Das neue Gebäude ist sehr **hoch.** (see 1)

5. (a) Robert hat nur wenige **gute** Freunde. (see 7)

6. (d) Unserem Hund gefällt es am besten in **dunklen** Zimmern. (see 6 and 9)

7. (c) Sonja hat von Erich schon viele **lange** Briefe bekommen. (see 7)

8. (a) Das Eis ist gut. **Italienisches** Eis schmeckt mir am besten. (see 6)

9. (b) Gibt es in Mannheim kein **interessantes** Museum? (see 4)

10. (c) Ein BMW ist ein **teurer** Wagen. (see 9)

B.

1. Der Februar ist der **kürzeste** Monat. (see 3 and 13)

2. Sandra hat **längere** Haare als Ute. (see 6 and 13)

3. Jörgs Auto fährt am **schnellsten.** (see 14)

5. Über die Probleme der Vereinigung muß mehr gesprochen werden.
   / Es muß mehr über die Probleme der Vereinigung gesprochen
   werden. (see 4 and 5)
6. Die Garage müßte endlich aufgeräumt werden. / Es müßte
   endlich die Garage aufgeräumt werden. (see 4 and 5)
7. Eure Tochter sollte nicht immer von euch kritisiert werden. /
   Eure Tochter wollte von euch nicht immer kritisiert werden. (see 3
   and 4)
8. Angelikas Rucksack ist gestohlen worden. (see 2)
9. Die Tatwaffe war von der Polizei seit vielen Monaten gesucht
   worden. (see 2 and 3)
10. Das Haus ist von mir selbst gestrichen worden. (see 2 and 3)

C.

1. Die Wohnung sollte verkauft werden. (see 4)
2. Kann die Wohnung renoviert werden? (see 4)
3. Ja, aber dann müßte viel gemacht werden. (see 4)
4. Neue Wohnungen sind leicht zu finden. (see 9b)
5. Wohnungen verkaufen sich gut dieses Jahr. (see 9d)
6. Das Haus wurde 1854 gebaut. (see 2)
7. Mein altes Fahrrad ist weggeworfen worden. (see 2)
8. Warum bin ich nicht gefragt worden? (see 2)
9. Die Tür wurde um acht Uhr aufgemacht. (see 2)
10. Die Politikerin ist zum zweiten Mal gewählt worden. (see 2)
11. Tausend Mark wurden von der Organisation gesammelt. (see 2
    and 3)
12. In diesem See darf man nicht schwimmen. (see 9a)
13. Das Problem läßt sich leicht lösen. (see 9c)

KAPITEL 14

A.

1. Hat Stefan wirklich gesagt, ich **sei** langweilig? (see 5)
2. Der Student behauptet, er **habe** für den Test **gelernt.** (see 6)
3. Die Kinder riefen, sie **hätten** die Vase nicht **kaputtgemacht.**
   (see 6)
4. Die Managerin versprach, niemand **werde** seinen Arbeitsplatz
   verlieren. (see 7)
5. Meinst du, du **sei(e)st** klüger als ich? (see 5)
6. Mein Bruder erzählte, er **dürfe** keinen Wein trinken. (see 4 and 10)
7. Der kleine Junge sagte, er **gehe** gern in den Kindergarten. (see 4
   and 10)
8. Er behauptete, er **könne** schon lesen und schreiben. (see 4 and 10)

9. Meine Tante sagte, sie **sei** dieses Jahr ans Meer **gefahren.** (see 6 and 11)
10. Unser Nachbar erzählte, er **werde** im Urlaub jeden Tag **joggen.** (see 7 and 12)

B.
1. Alex rief, wir **hätten** keine Zeit zu verlieren. (see 10)
2. Monika sagte, sie **würde** sofort **kommen.** (see 12)
3. Die Eltern meinten, ihre Tochter **wäre** in Freiburg **geblieben.** (see 11)
4. Hat Peter wirklich geschrien, Ulla **sollte** besser nach Hause fahren? (see 10)
5. Meine Freunde versprachen, sie **würden** mich in Boston **besuchen.** (see 12)
6. Dagmar meinte, ihre Freundin **schliefe** gern auf dem Sofa. (see 10)
7. Andrea sagte, ihre Eltern **hätten** das nicht **bezahlen sollen.** (see 11 and 16)
8. Alexandra dachte, Peter **dürfte** noch nicht Auto fahren. (see 10)
9. Mein Bruder sagte, er **würde** sein Zimmer heute mittag **putzen.** (see 12)
10. Mein Onkel erzählte, er **wäre** letzte Woche **gesegelt.** (see 11)

C.
1. Monika sagte, daß sie heute nicht zur Arbeit ginge/gehe. / Monika sagte, sie ginge/gehe heute nicht zur Arbeit. (see 4 and 10)
2. Ihr Mann Georg fragte, warum sie denn nicht gehen könnte/könne. (Er fragte), ob sie krank wäre/sei. (see 4, 5, 14, and 15)
3. Monika antwortete, daß die Arbeit zur Zeit furchtbar wäre/sei. / Monika antwortete, die Arbeit wäre/sei zur Zeit furchtbar. (Sie antwortete), sie hätte/habe den ganzen Tag Streß. (see 4, 5, and 10)
4. Georg schlug vor, daß sie sich doch einen anderen Job suchen sollte/solle. / Georg schlug vor, sie sollte/solle sich doch einen anderen Job suchen. (see 4 and 16)
5. Monika antwortete, daß das nicht so leicht wäre/sei. / Monika antwortete, das wäre/sei nicht so leicht. (Sie antwortete), daß es nicht so viele gute Stellen gäbe/gebe/geben würde. / (Sie antwortete), es gäbe/gebe nicht so viele gute Stellen. / (Sie antwortete), es würde nicht so viele gute Stellen geben. Außerdem wäre/sei die Arbeit interessant. (see 4, 5, and 10)
6. Georg meinte, daß er ihr vielleicht mehr im Haushalt helfen sollte/solle. / Georg meinte, vielleicht sollte/solle er ihr mehr im Haushalt helfen. (see 4 and 10)
7. Monika sagte, daß das keine schlechte Idee wäre/sei. / Monika sagte, das wäre/sei keine schlechte Idee. (see 5 and 10)

KAPITEL 15

A.

1. **Jedermann/Jeder** weiß, daß heute Muttertag ist. Nur du hast es vergessen. (see 8)
2. **Es** tut mir leid, daß **es** Ihnen nicht gut geht. (see 9)
3. Hallo, ist da **jemand**? —Habt ihr auch etwas gehört? (see 8)
4. **Es/Jemand** hat geklingelt. Würdest du bitte aufmachen? (see 8 and 9)
5. Wenn **es** jetzt schneit und dann auch noch friert, wird **es** diesen Sommer nur wenig Obst geben. (see 9)
6. Kann mir wieder **niemand/keiner** helfen? Muß ich schon wieder alles allein machen? (see 8)

B.

1. Gefällt dir der Mantel? —Ist das wirklich **deiner**? (see 7)
2. Ulrike mußte sich ein neues Fahrrad kaufen. Ich habe **ihres** leider kaputtgefahren. (see 7)
3. Dieser Schlüssel lag unter dem Tisch. Ist das **Ihrer**? (see 7)
4. Wir haben auch einen Hund. **Uns(e)rer** ist schon ziemlich alt. (see 7)
5. Mark braucht neue Schuhe. **Seine** sind im Sommer zu warm. (see 7)
6. Deine Stereoanlage ist phantastisch. Ich habe leider **keine.** (see 7)
7. Wie ist denn dein Stuhl? **Meiner** ist zu hart. (see 7)
8. Warum putzt du jede Woche dein Auto? Wir putzen **uns(e)res** fast nie. (see 7)
9. Dieses Stück Kuchen schmeckt sehr gut. Geben Sie mir bitte noch **ein(e)s.** (see 7)
10. Unser Großvater ist sehr krank. Geht es **eurem** auch so schlecht? (see 7)

C.

1. Cornelia was never allowed to spend much money. She had to save all of it. (see 1 and 4)
2. Rainer is said to have had many friends. He was always friendly. (see 1, 3, and 4)
3. Sandra must have studied architecture. She is planning the new house for her parents now. (see 1, 3, and 4)
4. Ulrich had to study medicine. His whole family wanted it/wanted him to. (see 1 and 4)
5. My sister (had) wanted to clean my room, but then she changed her mind. (see 1 and 4)
6. My cousin Lisa claims to have seen my friend Gerd in a Porsche. But I can hardly believe that. (see 1, 3, and 4)

7. I hope Rudi hasn't eaten the whole pizza. We're hungry, too. (see 1, 3, 4, and 6)
8. I don't know how long the movie was. It may have lasted for about two hours. (see 1, 3, and 4)
9. Might/Could Mark really not have read the letter? It was lying on his desk. (see 1, 3, and 4, pp. 204 and 205)

D.
1. Hat es gestern geregnet? (see 9)
2. Nein, es hat geschneit. (see 9)
3. Du dürftest/magst / Sie dürften/mögen recht haben. (see 1 and 4)
4. Es soll morgen schön sein. (see 1 and 4)
5. Ich kann es kaum glauben. (see 1 and 4)
6. Mußt du/Müßt ihr/Müssen Sie schon gehen? (see 1 and 4)
7. Es tut mir leid, daß die Party dir/euch/Ihnen nicht gefällt. (see 9)
8. Und du willst mein Freund/meine Freundin sein? (see 1 and 4)

Appendix A: Grammatical Tables

1 Personal pronouns

Nominative:	ich	du	er	es	sie	wir	ihr	sie	Sie
Accusative:	mich	dich	ihn	es	sie	uns	euch	sie	Sie
Dative:	mir	dir	ihm	ihm	ihr	uns	euch	ihnen	Ihnen

2 Reflexive pronouns

	ich	du	er/es/sie	wir	ihr	sie	Sie
Accusative:	mich	dich	sich	uns	euch	sich	sich
Dative:	mir	dir	sich	uns	euch	sich	sich

3 Interrogative pronouns

Nominative:	wer	was
Accusative:	wen	was
Dative:	wem	
Genitive:	wessen	

4 Relative and demonstrative pronouns

	Masculine	Neuter	Feminine	Plural
Nominative:	der	das	die	die
Accusative:	den	das	die	die
Dative:	dem	dem	der	denen
Genitive:	dessen	dessen	deren	deren

5   Definite articles

	Masculine	Neuter	Feminine	Plural
Nominative:	der	das	die	die
Accusative:	den	das	die	die
Dative:	dem	dem	der	den
Genitive:	des	des	der	der

6   *Der*-words

	Masculine	Neuter	Feminine	Plural
Nominative:	dieser	dieses	diese	diese
Accusative:	diesen	dieses	diese	diese
Dative:	diesem	diesem	dieser	diesen
Genitive:	dieses	dieses	dieser	dieser

The **der**-words are **dieser, jeder, jener, mancher, solcher,** and **welcher.**

7   Indefinite articles and *ein*-words

	Masculine	Neuter	Feminine	Plural
Nominative:	ein	ein	eine	keine
Accusative:	einen	ein	eine	keine
Dative:	einem	einem	einer	keinen
Genitive:	eines	eines	einer	keiner

The **ein**-words include **kein** and the possessive adjectives: **mein, dein, sein, ihr, unser, euer, ihr,** and **Ihr.**

8   Plural of nouns

Type	Plural signal	Singular	Plural	Notes
1	Ø (no change)	das Zimmer	**die Zimmer**	masc. and neut. nouns ending in **-el**, -en, or -er
	¨ (umlaut)	der Mantel	**die Mäntel**	
2	**-e**	der Tisch	**die Tische**	
	¨e	der Stuhl	**die Stühle**	
3	**-er**	das Bild	**die Bilder**	Stem vowel **e** or **i** cannot take umlaut.
	¨er	das Buch	**die Bücher**	Stem vowel **a, o,** or **u** takes umlaut.
4	**-en**	die Uhr	**die Uhren**	
	-n	die Lampe	**die Lampen**	
	-nen	die Freundin	**die Freundinnen**	
5	**-s**	das Radio	**die Radios**	mostly foreign words

9   Masculine *n*-nouns

	Singular	Plural
Nominative:	der Herr	die Herren
Accusative:	den Herrn	die Herren
Dative:	dem Herrn	den Herren
Genitive:	des Herrn	der Herren

Some other masculine **n**-nouns are: **der Komponist, der Kunde, der Bauer, der Journalist, der Junge, der Jurist, der Kollege, der Mensch, der Nachbar, der Neffe, der Patient, der Pilot, der Polizist, der Präsident, der Soldat, der Student, der Tourist, der Zeuge.**

10   Preceded adjectives

	Masculine	Neuter	Feminine	Plural
Nominative:	der **alte** Tisch ein **alter** Tisch	das **alte** Buch ein **altes** Buch	die **alte** Uhr eine **alte** Uhr	die **alten** Bilder keine **alten** Bilder
Accusative:	den **alten** Tisch einen **alten** Tisch	das **alte** Buch ein **altes** Buch	die **alte** Uhr eine **alte** Uhr	die **alten** Bilder keine **alten** Bilder
Dative:	dem **alten** Tisch einem **alten** Tisch	dem **alten** Buch einem **alten** Buch	der **alten** Uhr einer **alten** Uhr	den **alten** Bildern keinen **alten** Bildern
Genitive:	des **alten** Tisches eines **alten** Tisches	des **alten** Buches eines **alten** Buches	der **alten** Uhr einer **alten** Uhr	der **alten** Bilder keiner **alten** Bilder

11   Unpreceded adjectives

	Masculine	Neuter	Feminine	Plural
Nominative:	kalter Wein	kaltes Bier	kalte Milch	alte Leute
Accusative:	kalten Wein	kaltes Bier	kalte Milch	alte Leute
Dative:	kaltem Wein	kaltem Bier	kalter Milch	alten Leuten
Genitive:	kalten Weines	kalten Bieres	kalter Milch	alter Leute

12   Nouns declined like adjectives

a. Nouns preceded by definite articles or *der*-words

	Masculine	Neuter	Feminine	Plural
Nominative:	der Deutsche	das Gute	die Deutsche	die Deutschen
Accusative:	den Deutschen	das Gute	die Deutsche	die Deutschen
Dative:	dem Deutschen	dem Guten	der Deutschen	den Deutschen
Genitive:	des Deutschen	des Guten	der Deutschen	der Deutschen

b. Nouns preceded by indefinite articles or *ein*-words

	Masculine	Neuter	Feminine	Plural
Nominative:	ein Deutscher	ein Gutes	eine Deutsche	keine Deutschen
Accusative:	einen Deutschen	ein Gutes	eine Deutsche	keine Deutschen
Dative:	einem Deutschen	einem Guten	einer Deutschen	keinen Deutschen
Genitive:	eines Deutschen	—	einer Deutschen	keiner Deutschen

Other nouns declined like adjectives are **der/die: Angestellte, Bekannte, Erwachsene, Fremde, Jugendliche, Reisende, Verwandte.** *Note:* **der Beamte/die Beamtin.**

13   Degrees of comparison

a. Adjectives and adverbs with umlaut

Base form:	alt	dumm	groß	kurz
Comparative:	älter	dümmer	größer	kürzer
Superlative:	ältest-	dümmst-	größt-	kürzest-

Other adjectives and adverbs that take an umlauted vowel in the comparative and superlative forms are: **arm, hart, jung, kalt, klug, krank, lang, oft, scharf, schwach, schwarz, stark,** and **warm.**

b. Irregular adjectives and adverbs

Base form:	bald	gern	gut	hoch	nah	viel
Comparative:	eher	lieber	besser	höher	näher	mehr
Superlative:	am ehesten	am liebsten	best-	höchst-	nächst-	meist-

14   Prepositions

With accusative	With dative	With either accusative or dative	With genitive
bis	aus	an	(an)statt
durch	außer	auf	trotz
entlang	bei	hinter	während
für	entgegen	in	wegen
gegen	gegenüber	neben	diesseits
ohne	mit	über	jenseits
um	nach	unter	außerhalb
wider	seit	vor	innerhalb
	von	zwischen	oberhalb
	zu		unterhalb

15   Verbs and prepositions with special meanings

Prüfung (handwritten, left margin)

abhängen von *depend on*
achten auf (+ *acc.*) *pay atten to*
anfangen mit *to start*
anrufen bei
antworten auf (+ *acc.*) *answer to*
arbeiten bei (*at a company*)
aufhören mit *stop doing s.th.*
beginnen mit
sich beschäftigen mit
bestehen aus *made of* *acc*
bitten um *to ask for*
blicken auf (+ *acc.*)
danken für
denken an (+ *acc.*) *to think of*
diskutieren über (+ *acc.*)
sich erinnern an (+ *acc.*)
erkennen an (+ *dat.*) *recognize by*
erzählen von; erzählen über (+ *acc.*) *to tell about*
fahren mit (*by a vehicle*)
fliehen vor (+ *dat.*)

fragen nach
sich freuen auf (+ *acc.*)
sich freuen über (+ *acc.*)
sich fürchten vor (+ *dat.*)
sich gewöhnen an (+ *acc.*)
glauben an (+ *acc.*)
halten für
halten von
helfen bei
hoffen auf (+ *acc.*)
sich interessieren für
klettern auf (+ *acc.*)
sich kümmern um
lachen über (+ *acc.*)
lächeln über (+ *acc.*)
leiden an (+ *dat.*)
mitmachen bei (*with a group*)
reden über (+ *acc.*); reden von
riechen nach
schicken nach

schimpfen über (+ *acc.*)
schreiben an (+ *acc.*)
schreiben über (+ *acc.*)
sorgen für
sprechen über (+ *acc.*); sprechen von
sterben an (+ *dat.*)
studieren an (+ *dat.*)
suchen nach
teilnehmen an (+ *dat.*)
vergleichen mit
sich vorbereiten auf (+ *acc.*)
warnen vor (+ *dat.*)
warten auf (+ *acc.*)
sich wenden an (+ *acc.*)
werden aus
wissen über (+ *acc.*); wissen von
wohnen bei
zeigen auf (+ *acc.*)
zweifeln an (+ *dat.*)

16   Idiomatic combinations of nouns and prepositions

Angst vor (+ *dat.*)   *fear of*
Freude über (+ *acc.*)   *joy over/in*
Interesse an (+ *dat.*); Interesse für   *interest in*
Lust an (+ *dat.*)   *pleasure in*
Mitleid mit   *sympathy with*
Schuld an (+ *dat.*)   *guilty of*
Sehnsucht nach   *longing for*

17   Dative verbs

antworten	erlauben	gelingen [ist]	leid tun	schmecken
befehlen	fehlen	genügen	nützen	trauen
begegnen [ist]	folgen [ist]	geschehen [ist]	passen	verzeihen
danken	gefallen	glauben	passieren [ist]	weh tun
dienen	gehorchen	gratulieren	raten	
einfallen [ist]	gehören	helfen	schaden	

The verbs **glauben, erlauben,** and **verzeihen** may take an impersonal accusative object: **ich glaube es; ich erlaube es.**

18   Adjectives with the dative case

ähnlich	bewußt	gleich	nahe	teuer
angenehm	böse	klar	nützlich	wert
bekannt	dankbar	lieb	recht	willkommen
bequem	fremd	möglich	schuldig	

19   Present tense

	lernen[1]	arbeiten[2]	tanzen[3]	geben[4]	lesen[5]	fahren[6]	laufen[7]	auf·stehen[8]
ich	lern**e**	arbeite	tanze	gebe	lese	fahre	laufe	stehe…auf
du	lern**st**	arbeit**est**	tan**zt**	g**i**bst	l**ie**st	f**ä**hrst	l**äu**fst	stehst…auf
er/es/sie	lern**t**	arbeit**et**	tan**zt**	g**i**bt	l**ie**st	f**ä**hrt	l**äu**ft	steht…auf
wir	lern**en**	arbeiten	tanzen	geben	lesen	fahren	laufen	stehen…auf
ihr	lern**t**	arbeit**et**	tanzt	gebt	lest	fahrt	lauft	steht…auf
sie	lern**en**	arbeiten	tanzen	geben	lesen	fahren	laufen	stehen…auf
Sie	lern**en**	arbeiten	tanzen	geben	lesen	fahren	laufen	stehen…auf
imper. sg.	lern(e)	arbeite	tanz(e)	g**i**b	**lies**	fahr(e)	lauf(e)	steh(e)…auf

1. The endings are used for all verbs except the modals and **wissen, werden,** and **sein.**
2. A verb with a stem ending in **-d** or **-t** has an **e** before the **-st** and **-t** endings. A verb with a stem ending in **-m** or **-n** preceded by another consonant has an **e** before the **-st** and **-t** endings, e.g., **regnen.** Exception: If the stem of the verb ends in **-m** or **-n** preceded by **-l** or **-r,** the **-st** and **-t** do not expand, e.g., **lernen** → **lernst, lernt.**

3. The **-st** ending of the 2nd person contracts to **-t** when the verb
   stem ends in a sibilant (**-s, -ss, -ß, -z,** or **-tz**). Thus, the 2nd and
   3rd person forms are identical.
4. Some strong verbs have a stem-vowel change **e** → **i** in the 2nd
   and 3rd person singular and the imperative singular.
5. Some strong verbs have a stem-vowel change **e** → **ie** in the 2nd
   and 3rd person singular and the imperative singular. The strong
   verbs **gehen, heben,** and **stehen** do not change their stem vowel.
6. Some strong verbs have a stem-vowel change **a** → **ä** in the 2nd
   and 3rd person singular.
7. Some strong verbs have a stem-vowel change **au** → **äu** in the 2nd
   and 3rd person singular.
8. In the present tense, separable prefixes are separated from the
   verb and are in last position.

20   Simple past tense

	Weak verbs		Strong verbs
	lernen[1]	arbeiten[2]	geben[3]
ich	lern**te**	arbeit**ete**	gab
du	lern**test**	arbeit**etest**	gab**st**
er/es/sie	lern**te**	arbeit**ete**	gab
wir	lern**ten**	arbeit**eten**	gab**en**
ihr	lern**tet**	arbeit**etet**	gab**t**
sie	lern**ten**	arbeit**eten**	gab**en**
Sie	lern**ten**	arbeit**eten**	gab**en**

1. Weak verbs have the past-tense marker **-te** plus endings.
2. A weak verb with a stem ending in **-d** or **-t** has a past-tense
   marker **-ete** plus endings. A weak verb with a stem ending in **-m**
   or **-n** preceded by another consonant has a past-tense marker
   -ete plus endings, e.g., **regnete.** Exception: If the verb stem ends
   in **-m** or **-n** preceded by **-l** or **-r,** the **-te** past-tense marker does
   not expand, e.g., **lernte.**
3. Strong verbs have a stem-vowel change plus endings.

21   Present tense of the auxiliaries *haben, sein, werden*

ich	habe	bin	werde
du	hast	bist	wirst
er/es/sie	hat	ist	wird
wir	haben	sind	werden
ihr	habt	seid	werdet
sie	haben	sind	werden
Sie	haben	sind	werden

Imperative of *sein*

	Imperative
Familiar singular:	sei
Familiar plural:	seid
Formal:	seien Sie

22   Modal auxiliaries: present, simple past, and past participle

	dürfen	können	mögen	(möchte)	müssen	sollen	wollen
ich	darf	kann	mag	(möchte)	muß	soll	will
du	darfst	kannst	magst	(möchtest)	mußt	sollst	willst
er/es/sie	darf	kann	mag	(möchte)	muß	soll	will
wir	dürfen	können	mögen	(möchten)	müssen	sollen	wollen
ihr	dürft	könnt	mögt	(möchtet)	müßt	sollt	wollt
sie	dürfen	können	mögen	(möchten)	müssen	sollen	wollen
Sie	dürfen	können	mögen	(möchten)	müssen	sollen	wollen
Simple past:	durfte	konnte	mochte		mußte	sollte	wollte
Past participle:	gedurft	gekonnt	gemocht		gemußt	gesollt	gewollt
Past participle with dependent infinitive:	dürfen	können	mögen		müssen	sollen	wollen

23   Verb conjugations: strong verbs *sehen* and *gehen*

a. Indicative

	Present		Simple past	
ich	sehe	gehe	sah	ging
du	siehst	gehst	sahst	gingst
er/es/sie	sieht	geht	sah	ging
wir	sehen	gehen	sahen	gingen
ihr	seht	geht	saht	gingt
sie	sehen	gehen	sahen	gingen
Sie	sehen	gehen	sahen	gingen

	Present perfect				Past perfect			
ich	habe		bin		hatte		war	
du	hast		bist		hattest		warst	
er/es/sie	hat		ist		hatte		war	
wir	haben	gesehen	sind	gegangen	hatten	gesehen	waren	gegangen
ihr	habt		seid		hattet		wart	
sie	haben		sind		hatten		waren	
Sie	haben		sind		hatten		waren	

	Future			
ich	werde		werde	
du	wirst		wirst	
er/es/sie	wird		wird	
wir	werden	sehen	werden	gehen
ihr	werdet		werdet	
sie	werden		werden	
Sie	werden		werden	

b. Imperative

	Imperative	
Familiar singular:	sieh	geh
Familiar plural:	seht	geht
Formal:	sehen Sie	gehen Sie

c. Subjunctive

Present-time subjunctive

	General subjunctive		Special subjunctive	
ich	sähe	ginge	sehe	gehe
du	sähest	gingest	sehest	gehest
er/es/sie	sähe	ginge	sehe	gehe
wir	sähen	gingen	sehen	gehen
ihr	sähet	ginget	sehet	gehet
sie	sähen	gingen	sehen	gehen
Sie	sähen	gingen	sehen	gehen

Past-time subjunctive

	General subjunctive				Special subjunctive			
ich	hätte		wäre		habe		sei	
du	hättest		wärest		habest		seiest	
er/es/sie	hätte		wäre		habe		sei	
wir	hätten	gesehen	wären	gegangen	haben	gesehen	seien	gegangen
ihr	hättet		wäret		habet		seiet	
sie	hätten		wären		haben		seien	
Sie	hätten		wären		haben		seien	

Future-time subjunctive

	General subjunctive				Special subjunctive			
ich	würde				werde			
du	würdest				werdest			
er/es/sie	würde				werde			
wir	würden	} sehen	würden	} gehen	werden	} sehen	werden	} gehen
ihr	würdet		würdet		werdet		werdet	
sie	würden		würden		werden		werden	
Sie	würden		würden		werden		werden	

d. Passive voice

	Present passive		Past passive	
ich	werde		wurde	
du	wirst		wurdest	
er/es/sie	wird		wurde	
wir	werden	} gesehen	wurden	} gesehen
ihr	werdet		wurdet	
sie	werden		wurden	
Sie	werden		wurden	

	Present perfect passive		Past perfect passive	
ich	bin		war	
du	bist		warst	
er/es/sie	ist		war	
wir	sind	} gesehen worden	waren	} gesehen worden
ihr	seid		wart	
sie	sind		waren	
Sie	sind		waren	

	Future passive	
ich	werde	
du	wirst	
er/es/sie	wird	
wir	werden	gesehen werden
ihr	werdet	
sie	werden	
Sie	werden	

24   Principal parts of strong and irregular weak verbs

The following list includes all the strong verbs and irregular weak verbs used in this book. Compound verbs like **hereinkommen** and **hinausgehen** are not included since the principal parts of those compound verbs are identical to the basic forms **kommen** and **gehen**. Inseparable prefix verbs like **beweisen** are included only when the basic verb (**weisen**) is not listed elsewhere in the table. Basic English equivalents are given for all verbs in this list. For additional meanings consult the German-English end vocabulary.

Infinitive	Present-tense vowel change	Simple past	Past participle	General subjunctive	Meaning
anfangen	fängt an	fing an	angefangen	finge an	*to begin*
backen		backte	gebacken	backte	*to bake*
befehlen	befiehlt	befahl	befohlen	beföhle (befähle)	*to command*
beginnen		begann	begonnen	begönne (begänne)	*to begin*
beißen		biß	gebissen	bisse	*to bite*
betrügen		betrog	betrogen	betröge	*to deceive*
beweisen		bewies	bewiesen	bewiese	*to prove*
sich bewerben	bewirbt	bewarb	beworben	bewürbe	*to apply for*
biegen		bog	gebogen	böge	*to bend*
bieten		bot	geboten	böte	*to offer*
binden		band	gebunden	bände	*to bind*
bitten		bat	gebeten	bäte	*to request*
bleiben		blieb	ist geblieben	bliebe	*to remain*
braten	brät	briet	gebraten	briete	*to roast*
brechen	bricht	brach	gebrochen	bräche	*to break*

Infinitive	Present-tense vowel change	Simple past	Past participle	General subjunctive	Meaning
brennen		brannte	gebrannt	brennte	*to burn*
bringen		brachte	gebracht	brächte	*to bring*
denken		dachte	gedacht	dächte	*to think*
einladen	lädt ein	lud ein	eingeladen	lüde ein	*to invite*
empfangen	empfängt	empfing	empfangen	empfinge	*to receive*
empfehlen	empfiehlt	empfahl	empfohlen	empföhle	*to recommend*
empfinden		empfand	empfunden	empfände	*to feel*
entscheiden		entschied	entschieden	entschiede	*to decide*
erschrecken	erschrickt	erschrak	erschrocken	erschräke	*to be frightened*
essen	ißt	aß	gegessen	äße	*to eat*
fahren	fährt	fuhr	ist gefahren	führe	*to drive; to travel*
fallen	fällt	fiel	ist gefallen	fiele	*to fall*
fangen	fängt	fing	gefangen	finge	*to catch*
finden		fand	gefunden	fände	*to find*
fliegen		flog	ist geflogen	flöge	*to fly*
fliehen		floh	ist geflohen	flöhe	*to flee*
fließen		floß	ist geflossen	flösse	*to flow*
fressen	frißt	fraß	gefressen	fräße	*to eat (of animals)*
frieren		fror	gefroren	fröre	*to freeze*
geben	gibt	gab	gegeben	gäbe	*to give*
gefallen	gefällt	gefiel	gefallen	gefiele	*to please*
gehen		ging	ist gegangen	ginge	*to go*
gelingen		gelang	ist gelungen	gelänge	*to succeed*
gelten	gilt	galt	gegolten	gälte	*to be worth*
genießen		genoß	genossen	genösse	*to enjoy*
geschehen	geschieht	geschah	ist geschehen	geschähe	*to happen*
gewinnen		gewann	gewonnen	gewönne (gewänne)	*to win*
gießen		goß	gegossen	gösse	*to pour*
gleichen		glich	geglichen	gliche	*to resemble*
gleiten		glitt	ist geglitten	glitte	*to glide, slide*
graben	gräbt	grub	gegraben	grübe	*to dig*
greifen		griff	gegriffen	griffe	*to grab*
haben	hat	hatte	gehabt	hätte	*to have*
halten	hält	hielt	gehalten	hielte	*to hold*
hängen		hing	gehangen	hinge	*to hang*
heben		hob	gehoben	höbe	*to lift*
heißen		hieß	geheißen	hieße	*to be called*
helfen	hilft	half	geholfen	hülfe	*to help*
kennen		kannte	gekannt	kennte	*to know*

Infinitive	Present-tense vowel change	Simple past	Past participle	General subjunctive	Meaning
klingen		klang	geklungen	klänge	*to sound*
kommen		kam	ist gekommen	käme	*to come*
kriechen		kroch	ist gekrochen	kröche	*to crawl*
laden	lädt	lud	geladen	lüde	*to load*
lassen	läßt	ließ	gelassen	ließe	*to let, permit*
laufen	läuft	lief	ist gelaufen	liefe	*to run*
leiden		litt	gelitten	litte	*to suffer*
leihen		lieh	geliehen	liehe	*to lend*
lesen	liest	las	gelesen	läse	*to read*
liegen		lag	gelegen	läge	*to lie*
lügen		log	gelogen	löge	*to tell a lie*
messen	mißt	maß	gemessen	mäße	*to measure*
nehmen	nimmt	nahm	genommen	nähme	*to take*
nennen		nannte	genannt	nennte	*to name*
pfeifen		pfiff	gepfiffen	pfiffe	*to whistle*
raten	rät	riet	geraten	riete	*to advise*
reiben		rieb	gerieben	riebe	*to rub*
reißen		riß	gerissen	risse	*to tear*
reiten		ritt	ist geritten	ritte	*to ride*
rennen		rannte	ist gerannt	rennte	*to run*
riechen		roch	gerochen	röche	*to smell*
rufen		rief	gerufen	riefe	*to call*
schaffen		schuf	geschaffen	schüfe	*to create*
scheinen		schien	geschienen	schiene	*to shine*
schieben		schob	geschoben	schöbe	*to push*
schießen		schoß	geschossen	schösse	*to shoot*
schlafen	schläft	schlief	geschlafen	schliefe	*to sleep*
schlagen	schlägt	schlug	geschlagen	schlüge	*to hit*
schließen		schloß	geschlossen	schlösse	*to shut*
schneiden		schnitt	geschnitten	schnitte	*to cut*
schreiben		schrieb	geschrieben	schriebe	*to write*
schreien		schrie	geschrie(e)n	schriee	*to cry out, scream*
schreiten		schritt	ist geschritten	schritte	*to step*
schweigen		schwieg	geschwiegen	schwiege	*to be silent*
schwimmen		schwamm	ist geschwommen	schwömme (schwämme)	*to swim*
sehen	sieht	sah	gesehen	sähe	*to see*
sein	ist	war	ist gewesen	wäre	*to be*
senden		sandte	gesandt	sendete	*to send*

Infinitive	Present-tense vowel change	Simple past	Past participle	General subjunctive	Meaning
singen		sang	gesungen	sänge	*to sing*
sinken		sank	ist gesunken	sänke	*to sink*
sitzen		saß	gesessen	säße	*to sit*
spinnen		spann	gesponnen	spönne	*to spin*
sprechen	spricht	sprach	gesprochen	spräche	*to speak*
springen		sprang	ist gesprungen	spränge	*to spring*
stechen	sticht	stach	gestochen	stäche	*to sting, stick*
stehen		stand	gestanden	stände (stünde)	*to stand*
stehlen	stiehlt	stahl	gestohlen	stähle	*to steal*
steigen		stieg	ist gestiegen	stiege	*to climb*
sterben	stirbt	starb	ist gestorben	stürbe	*to die*
stinken		stank	gestunken	stänke	*to stink*
stoßen	stößt	stieß	gestoßen	stieße	*to push*
streichen		strich	gestrichen	striche	*to paint*
streiten		stritt	gestritten	stritte	*to quarrel*
tragen	trägt	trug	getragen	trüge	*to carry, wear*
treffen	trifft	traf	getroffen	träfe	*to meet*
treiben		trieb	getrieben	triebe	*to drive*
treten	tritt	trat	ist getreten	träte	*to step; to kick*
trinken		trank	getrunken	tränke	*to drink*
tun	tut	tat	getan	täte	*to do*
unterscheiden		unterschied	unterschieden	unterschiede	*to distinguish*
verbergen	verbirgt	verbarg	verborgen	verbärge (verbürge)	*to hide*
verderben	verdirbt	verdarb	verdorben	verdürbe	*to spoil*
vergessen	vergißt	vergaß	vergessen	vergäße	*to forget*
verlieren		verlor	verloren	verlöre	*to lose*
verschwinden		verschwand	ist verschwunden	verschwände	*to disappear*
verzeihen		verzieh	verziehen	verziehe	*to pardon*
wachsen	wächst	wuchs	ist gewachsen	wüchse	*to grow*
waschen	wäscht	wusch	gewaschen	wüsche	*to wash*
wenden		wandte	gewandt	wendete	*to turn*
werden	wird	wurde	ist geworden	würde	*to become*
werfen	wirft	warf	geworfen	würfe	*to throw*
wiegen		wog	gewogen	wöge	*to weigh*
wissen	weiß	wußte	gewußt	wüßte	*to know*
ziehen		zog	gezogen	zöge	*to pull, move*
zwingen		zwang	gezwungen	zwänge	*to compel*

Appendix B: Grammatical Terms

The following is a list of German grammatical terms used in *Concise German Review Grammar*. Since the grammatical explanations in the book are in English, the list is organized alphabetically according to the English equivalents of the German terms. The German term does, however, immediately follow its English equivalent. A brief explanation of each term is provided along with an example in German. In the example the term being illustrated is italicized.

Plurals are provided only for the basic form of a word. Thus, there is a plural entry for **Pronomen, -,** but not for **Reflexivpronomen.** No plural entry is given if the plural is rarely used. A stress mark (´) follows the accented syllable. Only primary stress is indicated.

For convenience in looking up a German grammatical term, an alphabetical list of the German terms with their English equivalents is provided at the end of Appendix B.

ENGLISH–GERMAN

accusative (der Ak´kusativ)
The case used for the direct object. Accusative is also used for the object of certain prepositions and expressions of measure and definite time.
➢ Kennst du *meinen Freund Frank*? Er kommt *nächsten Montag* und bleibt *einen Monat.*

active voice (das Ak´tiv)
A verb form that indicates that the subject is performing the action of the verb.
➢ Frank *schreibt* in seiner Freizeit Kurzgeschichten.

adjective (das Ad´jektiv, -e)
A word used to modify (describe, limit, or qualify) a noun or pronoun.
➢ Frank wohnt in einer *kleinen* Wohnung, die aber sehr *gemütlich* ist.

adjective used as a noun (das Nominal´adjektiv)
An adjective that functions as a noun. It retains adjective endings and is capitalized in writing. It is also called a nominal adjective.
➢ Das **Schöne** an der Wohnung ist die Aussicht.

adverb (das Ad´verb, Adver´bien)
A word used to modify (describe or qualify) a verb, adjective, or another adverb. See *manner, place,* and *time.*
➢ Franks Freundin Anna schreibt auch **gut,** aber sie zeichnet noch **besser.**

agent (das A´gens)
A person or thing that causes the action to be performed. In a passive sentence it is the object of the preposition **von.**
➢ Franks Geschichten werden von **Anna** illustriert.

alternative to passive voice (see *passive voice, alternative to*)

alternative question (see *general question*)

antecedent (das Bezugs´wort, ¨er)
The word to which a pronoun refers.
➢ Die **Geschichten,** die sie illustriert, sind am beliebtesten.

apostrophe (der Apostroph´, -e)
A punctuation mark (') used to indicate that letters or syllables have been omitted.
➢ Eine Geschichte heißt „G'schichten zum Spiel'n".

apparent passive (see *statal passive*)

apparent subject (see *impersonal passive*)

article (der Arti´kel, -)
A word that indicates gender, number, and case of a noun. German has definite and indefinite articles in three genders (see Appendix A: 5 and 7). Articles may function as pronouns (see *demonstrative pronoun*).
➢ **Die** Geschichten von Frank und **die** Bilder von Anna sind **eine** gute Kombination.

attributive adjective (das attributi´ve Ad´jektiv)
An adjective that precedes the noun it modifies. In German attributive adjectives add declensional endings. (See Appendix A: 10 and 11.)
➢ Frank und Anna sind wirklich **gute** Freunde.

auxiliary verb (das Hilfs´verb)
A verb used to form tenses or passive voice. The main German auxiliaries are **haben, sein,** and **werden.**
➢ Frank und Anna **sind** zusammen nach Amerika gefahren und **haben** dort studiert.

cardinal number (die Kardinal´zahl)
The basic form of numbers used in counting (e.g., **eins, zwei**). They do not take endings. Exception: Before a noun **eins** is identical to the indefinite article **ein** (e.g., *Ich habe nur **einen** Hut.*).
➢ Frank und Anna haben schon *zwanzig* Geschichten verkauft.

case (der Ka´sus, -/der Fall, ¨e)
The signal used to indicate the grammatical function of nouns and pronouns in a sentence. German has four cases: nominative, accusative, dative, and genitive.
➢ Vor einer Woche hat Anna ihm, dem Frank, einen neuen Computer geschenkt.

colon (der Dop´pelpunkt)
A punctuation mark (:) used to introduce direct quotations or to direct attention to an explanation or a series of related items.
➢ Frank hat zu Anna gesagt: „Du, das ist aber nett von dir."

comma (das Kom´ma)
The punctuation mark (,) used to set off dependent clauses and infinitive phrases. A comma is also used to set off decimals (e.g., **1,5 = eins Komma fünf**). A comma does not set off the last word in a series before **und** (e.g., **naß, grau und kalt**).
➢ Anna weiß, daß Frank wirklich einen Computer braucht.

comparative (der Kom´parativ)
A form of an adjective or adverb that compares one person or thing to another.
➢ Anna meint, daß Franks *kürzere* Geschichten *besser* sind als seine *längeren.*

comparison (die Komparation´)
The change in the form of adjectives and adverbs to indicate degrees in quantity, quality, or manner. The degrees are positive, comparative, and superlative.
➢ Anna glaubt, daß Franks *kürzeste* Geschichten auch seine *besten* sind.

conclusion (der Fol´gesatz)
The clause in a conditional sentence that indicates what may happen as the result of some other event stated in the condition.
➢ Anna sagt zu Frank: „Wenn du willst, *schreiben wir zusammen Bildergeschichten."*

condition (wenn-clause) (der Konditional´satz)
The clause that states the condition under which some event mentioned in the conclusion may or may not take place. It usually begins with **wenn** or the finite verb.
➢ Frank sagt zu Anna: *„Wenn die Geschichten gut sind,* werden wir vielleicht berühmt."

conditional sentence (der **Konditional´satz**)
A sentence that states what may or may not happen as a result of some other event. A conditional sentence contains two clauses: the condition and the conclusion.
➢ **Wenn wir eines Tages berühmt sind, können wir uns ein großes Haus kaufen.**

condition contrary to fact (der **ir´reale Konditional´satz**)
A sentence that describes a condition, situation, or event that does not exist and will not take place. The speaker only speculates on how something would be under certain conditions. Subjunctive verb forms are used in conditions contrary to fact.
➢ **Wenn wir jetzt schon berühmt wären, könnten wir längere Ferien machen.**

condition of fact (der **rea´le Konditional´satz**)
A sentence that describes a condition, situation, or event that is capable of taking place. Indicative verb forms are used in conditions of fact.
➢ **Wenn du Lust hast, können wir heute abend ins Kino gehen.**

conjunction (die **Konjunktion´, -en**)
A word used to connect words, phrases, or clauses.
➢ **Anna zeichnet, *während* Frank schreibt.**

conversational past (see *present perfect*)

contraction (die **Zusam´menziehung**)
A word formed with parts of two other words. The contraction of certain prepositions with the definite article is common in colloquial German (e.g., **ans, zum**).
➢ **Frank geht nicht gern *ans* Telefon.**

coordinating conjunction (die **koordinie´rende/ne´benordnende Konjunktion´**)
A conjunction that connects words, phrases, and clauses of equal grammatical rank (e.g., two independent clauses).
➢ **Die beiden arbeiten zusammen, *und* sie gehen miteinander aus.**

da- compound (das **da´-Kompo´situm, Komposita**)
A compound consisting of **da-** plus a preposition that replaces a preposition plus a pronoun to refer to things and ideas (e.g., **darüber** = *about it*).
➢ **Frank kocht gern. *Darüber* freut sich Anna.**

dash (der **Gedan´kenstrich, -e**)
A punctuation mark (–) used to indicate a sudden break in thought or a change of speakers, or to set off an explanation or parenthetical thought.
➢ **Eines Tages – Frank kocht gerade ein gutes Essen – bekommen sie einen Anruf.**

dative (der Da′tiv)
The case used for indirect objects. Dative is also used for the object of certain prepositions, verbs, and adjectives. (See Appendix A: 14–17.)
➢ Ein Freund will **ihnen** ein Auto schenken.

declarative sentence (der Aus′sagesatz)
A sentence that presents a statement.
➢ Das Auto kostet 3 500 Mark.

declension (die Deklination′)
The changes in a noun, pronoun, article, or adjective to indicate gender, number, or case.
➢ Mit dem Auto können sie nicht nur eine Reise, sondern viele schöne Reisen machen.

definite article (der bestimm′te Arti′kel)
An article used to indicate a specific noun or nouns. The form of the definite article varies according to the gender, number, and case of the noun (e.g., **das Hemd, die Bluse**). (See Appendix A: 5.)
➢ **Die** beiden laden **den** Freund zu einer Reise in **die** Schweiz ein.

demonstrative pronoun (das Demonstrativ′prono′men)
A pronoun identical to the definite article (except in dative plural and genitive case) used in place of a personal pronoun for emphasis. Demonstrative pronouns occur at or near the beginning of a sentence. (See Appendix A: 4.)
➢ Sie kennen den Freund gut. **Dem** gefällt eine solche Reise bestimmt.

dependent clause (der Ne′bensatz)
A clause that cannot stand alone; it must be combined with a main clause to express a complete idea. It is usually introduced by a subordinating conjunction or a relative pronoun. In German the finite verb of a dependent clause is in final position. The clause is set off by a comma. This clause is also called a subordinate clause.
➢ **Obwohl die Schweiz ein teures Land ist,** wollen sie dort Ferien machen.

direct discourse (die direk′te Rede)
The reporting of what someone has said or written, repeating his/her exact words. Direct discourse is set in quotation marks.
➢ Sie haben zu ihrem Freund gesagt: **„Komm doch mit. Wir laden dich ein.“**

direct object (das direk′te Objekt′)
A word that receives or is affected by the action of the verb directly. The direct object is in the accusative case.
➢ Sie haben **ihren Freund** in die Schweiz eingeladen.

double infinitive (**der Dop´pelinfinitiv**)
The use of an alternate form of the past participle, identical to the infinitive of modals, **sehen, hören,** and **lassen,** when these verbs are used in the perfect tenses and have a dependent infinitive.
➤ Aber der Freund hat nicht *mitfahren wollen.*

dummy subject (see *impersonal passive*)

exclamation point (**das Aus´rufezeichen, -**)
A punctuation mark (!) used after a word, phrase, clause, or sentence to express surprise or strong emotion.
➤ Anna sagt: „Wie schade!" Frank sagt: „Wenn er doch nur mitfahren würde!"

extended modifier (**das erwei´terte Attribut´**)
An adjective that precedes a noun and is modified or extended by other words or phrases. Most frequently the adjective is formed from a present or past participle. For this reason, this grammatical element is also called an "extended participial modifier."
➤ Das wäre doch *eine für uns alle sehr schöne* Reise gewesen.

feminine (**fe´minin/weib´lich**)
A natural and grammatical gender for nouns, pronouns, and modifiers. The definite article in the nominative singular is **die.**
➤ *Die Reise* in *die Schweiz* – das war doch *die Idee.*

finite verb (**das fini´te Verb**)
The verb form that agrees with the subject in person and number and shows tense and mood.
➤ Vielleicht *hat* unser Freund Angst, daß wir zuviel Geld *ausgeben.*

flavoring particle (see *particle*)

future (tense) (**das Futur´/die Zu´kunft**)
Future time may be expressed by present tense or future tense. Future tense consists of a form of **werden** plus an infinitive in final position. Future tense is also used to express present probability.
➤ Das *wird* sicher der Grund *sein,* warum er nicht mitfahren will.

future perfect (**das zweite Futur´**)
A compound tense consisting of a form of **werden,** the past participle of the main verb, and the infinitive of **haben** or **sein.** Future perfect indicates that something will have taken place by a certain time in the future, but in this meaning it is rarely used in German. It is more commonly used to express past probability.
➤ Der Freund *wird* wohl *gedacht haben,* daß die Schweiz für die beiden zu teuer ist.

gender (**das Geschlecht´/das Ge´nus**)
The grammatical classification of nouns and pronouns as masculine, feminine, and neuter.

➢ **der Pullover:** The gender of **Pullover** is masculine.
die Bluse: The gender of **Bluse** is feminine.
das Hemd: The gender of **Hemd** is neuter.

general question (**die Entschei´dungsfrage**)
A question that can be answered by **ja, nein,** or **doch** or offers a choice
between alternatives (e.g., **Kommst du heute oder morgen?**). A general question begins with the finite verb. A general question is also
called an "alternative question."
➢ **Die beiden fragen den Freund: „*Kommst du nun mit oder nicht?*"**

general subjunctive (**der Kon´junktiv II**)
A form of the subjunctive based on the past tense of verbs. It is the form
used to talk about unreal and hypothetical events and to express wishes
and requests. The general subjunctive is frequently used in indirect discourse. It is also called "subjunctive II."
➢ **Anna: „Wenn er doch nur *mitkäme!*" Frank: „Zusammen *hätten*
wir viel mehr Spaß!"**

genitive (**der Ge´nitiv**)
The case used to show possession or other close relationships between
nouns. The objects of certain prepositions and indefinite time expressions (e.g., **eines Tages**) are in the genitive.
➢ ***Franks* Bruder hat keine Zeit mitzufahren. *Annas* Schwester hat
keine Lust.**

hyphen (**der Bin´destrich, -e**)
A punctuation mark (-) used to combine words to form a compound and
to divide words at the end of lines.
➢ **Der Frank wohnt übrigens in der Anton-Schneider-Straße.**

imperative (**der Im´perativ**)
A verb form used to express commands, requests, suggestions, and
instructions, directed to one or more persons.
➢ **Der Freund sagt zu Frank und Anna: „*Fahrt* allein. *Genießt* die
Ferien."**

impersonal passive (**das un´persönliche Pas´siv**)
A passive construction without a subject. The pronoun **es** often begins
an impersonal passive construction, but is only an apparent or
"dummy" subject.
➢ **Frank sagt zu Anna: „*Dem Mann kann nicht geholfen werden.*"**

impersonal pronoun (**das un´persönliche Prono´men**)
The pronoun **es** used as an impersonal subject.
➢ **Hoffentlich regnet *es* nicht, wenn sie in der Schweiz sind.**

impersonal verb (**das un´persönliche Verb**)
A verb used impersonally has **es** as its subject and indicates an activity without a specific doer.
➢ Es *regnet.*
   Es *klopft.*

indefinite adjective (**das un´bestimmte Zahl´wort**)
An adjective denoting unspecified or indefinite quantities (e.g., **einige, andere**).
➢ *Einige* Leute fahren gern in die Schweiz, *andere* fahren lieber an die See.

indefinite article (**der un´bestimmte Arti´kel**)
An article (**ein**) used to designate any one of a class of nouns (e.g., **ein Zimmer**). Endings are added to show gender and case. The indefinite article is used only with a singular noun. The negative form **kein** has plural endings.
➢ Die beiden mieten *ein* kleines Haus in *einer* kleinen Stadt in der Schweiz. *Ein* Problem: Es gibt *keine* Parkplätze.

indefinite pronoun (**das Indefinit´prono´men**)
A pronoun with no definite antecedent. It designates unspecified persons or things (e.g., **man, etwas, jemand**).
➢ Wenn *man* parken will, dauert es lange, bis *man etwas* findet.

independent clause (**der Haupt´satz**)
A clause that can stand alone as a complete sentence. It is also called a "main clause."
➢ *Die beiden gehen viel zu Fuß,* aber *ihre Freunde fahren lieber Rad.*

indicative (**der In´dikativ**)
A verb in the indicative mood is used to express or indicate facts or describe actual situations.
➢ Es *gibt* keine Parkplätze. Also *gehen* sie zu Fuß in die Stadt.

indirect discourse (**die in´direkte Rede**)
A way of reporting what someone has said or written without quoting his/her exact words. In German, indirect discourse is usually in the subjunctive.
➢ Frank sagt, *daß er das nächste Mal ohne Auto käme.*

indirect object (**das in´direkte Objekt´**)
A noun or pronoun indicating to whom or to what the action of the verb is directed or for whom or for what the action is performed. The indirect object is in the dative case.
➢ Anna will *ihrem Freund* das nächste Mal eine Fahrkarte für die Bahn schenken.

infinitive (der In´finitiv, -e)
The basic form of the verb; the form listed in dictionaries. It is used with modals, in future tense, and in infinitive clauses.
➤ **Beide hoffen, das nächste Mal zufriedener zu *sein.***

infinitive clause (der In´finitivsatz)
A phrase with an infinitive and other sentence elements such as objects or adverbs. The infinitive clause is set off by a comma. The infinitive clause corresponds to an infinitive phrase or participial phrase in English.
➤ **Beide hoffen, *die nächsten Ferien wieder in der Schweiz zu verbringen.***

infinitive phrase (see *infinitive clause*)

informational question (see *specific question*)

inseparable prefix (das un´trennbare Prä´fix)
A prefix that is never separated from the verb in any form or tense. An inseparable prefix does not receive stress in spoken German (e.g., **bekom´men, verges´sen**).
➤ **Es ist leicht, ein Ferienhaus zu *be*kommen.**

inseparable verb (das un´trennbare Verb)
A verb with an inseparable prefix. The past participle of an inseparable verb never adds the prefix **ge-.**
➤ **Sie haben ihr Ferienhaus durch ein Reisebüro *bekommen.***

interrogative (see *question*)

interrogative pronoun (das Interrogativ´prono´men)
A pronoun that introduces a specific question (e.g., **wer, was**). The form of **wer** varies depending on the case (see Appendix A: 3).
➤ ***Was* muß man für ein Ferienhaus bezahlen?**

intransitive verb (das in´transitive Verb)
A verb that does not require a direct object to complete its meaning. Some verbs may be intransitive in one sentence and transitive in another.
➤ **Die beiden *sind* mit dem Auto in die Schweiz *gefahren,* aber sie haben es dort wenig gefahren.**

irregular weak verb (das un´regelmäßige schwache Verb)
One of a very small number of verbs that adds **-te** in the simple past and **-t** to the past participle as weak verbs do but undergoes a stem-vowel change in the past tenses as strong verbs do. They are thus "irregular." **Bringen** and **denken** also undergo a consonant change.
➤ **Sie haben gar nicht *gewußt,* wie schön Ferien ohne Auto sein können.**

linking verb (**die Ko´pula**)
A verb (mainly **sein,** but also **werden, bleiben,** and **scheinen**) that links
the subject and the predicate nominative.
➤ Frank *ist* auch ohne Auto ein zufriedener Feriengast.

main clause (see *independent clause*)

main verb (**das Haupt´verb/das Voll´verb**)
The verb that expresses an action or describes an event or state of being,
not a helping verb.
➤ Die Ferien in der Schweiz *sind* erholsam. Die beiden *laufen* und
  schlafen viel.

manner (adverb of) (**das Adverb der Art und Weise**)
An adverb of manner answers the question **wie?** (how?, in what man-
ner?). It follows adverbs of time and precedes adverbs of place.
➤ Sie sind im August *mit dem Auto* in die Schweiz gefahren.

masculine (**männ´lich/mas´kulin**)
A natural and grammatical gender for nouns, pronouns, and modifiers.
The definite article in the nominative singular is **der.**
➤ *Ihr bester Freund* in der Schweiz ist *ihr Schirm.* Sie brauchen
  ihn fast täglich.

means (**das Mit´tel**)
A phrase that expresses the means by which an event happens. In pas-
sive voice the "means" is the object of the preposition **durch.**
➤ Ihre Ferien werden *durch den häufigen Regen* kaum gestört.

measure (**die Maß´angabe, -n/die Men´genangabe**)
In German, nouns expressing units of measurement (e.g., **einen
Kilometer**), weight (e.g., **ein Kilo**) and age (e.g., **einen Monat alt**) are
in the accusative. (See also *quantity.*)
➤ Sie bleiben *einen Monat* in der Schweiz.

modal auxiliary (**das Modal´verb**)
One of six verbs that convey an attitude about an action rather than
expressing that action itself. The attitude may be objective (e.g.,
expressing permission or ability) or subjective (e.g., expressing doubt or
supposition). Modals are usually combined with an infinitive that
expresses the action itself.
➤ Sie *können* nicht länger bleiben, weil sie wieder arbeiten *müssen.*

mood (**der Mo´dus**)
The form of a verb that indicates the attitude of the speaker toward what
he/she is saying or writing. The mood of a verb can be indicative, imperative, or subjunctive.
➤ Sie *bleiben* einen Monat in der Schweiz. Sie *möchten* gern länger
  bleiben. Am letzten Tag *sagt* Anna zu Frank: *„Komm, steig ein,*
  wir *fahren los."*

narrative past (see *simple past*)

neuter (**säch´lich/neutral´**)
A natural and grammatical gender for nouns, pronouns, and modifiers.
The definite article in the nominative singular is **das.**
➢ *Ein gutes Gewissen* ist *ein sanftes Ruhekissen.*

nominal adjective (see *adjective used as a noun*)

nominative (**der No´minativ**)
The case used for subjects and predicate nouns. Words in the dictionary
are listed in nominative singular (e.g., **der Pulli**).
➢ *Franks Freundin* fährt meistens ihren neuen Wagen. Aber *Frank*
ist auch *ein guter Fahrer.*

noun (**das No´men, -/das Sub´stantiv, -e**)
A word that names a person, place, thing, or idea. All German nouns
are capitalized (e.g., **das Haar**).
➢ Das *Auto* von ihrem *Freund* fährt sehr gut.

number (**die Zahl**)
The designation of a word as singular or plural (e.g., **die Bluse, die
Blusen; ich gehe, wir gehen**).
➢ Frank und Anna haben ein Jahr in Amerika studiert. Sie möchten
aber noch einmal mehrere Wochen dort Ferien machen.

numeral (**das Zahl´wort**)
A word that indicates the number or quantity. Numerals include cardi-
nal numbers (e.g., **zwei**) and ordinal numbers (e.g., **zweit**).
➢ Wenn *zwei* sich streiten, freut sich der *Dritte.*

object of the preposition (**das präpositiona´le Objekt´**)
The noun or pronoun that follows a preposition. The case of the object
depends on the preposition.
➢ Ein Spatz in der *Hand* ist besser als eine Taube auf dem *Dach.*

ordinal number (**die Ordinal´zahl**)
A number that indicates the order in a series (e.g., **erst, zweit**). Ordinal
numbers take adjective endings (e.g., **das zweite Auto**).
➢ Anna hat am *zweiten* Januar Geburtstag.

particle (**die Parti´kel, -n/die Modal´parti´kel**)
A word used to express a speaker's attitude about an utterance, such
as interest, surprise, impatience, or denial (e.g., **doch, ja, schon**).
Particles are very common in spoken German. They are often called
"flavoring particles."
➢ Ein Bekannter sagt: „Was wollt ihr *denn* in Amerika? Ihr könnt
doch schon Englisch." —„Wir werden *mal* was anderes sehen."

passive infinitive (der pas´sive In´finitiv)

A verb phrase that consists of the infinitive **werden** and the past participle of the main verb. The passive infinitive occurs frequently with modals.

➤ Bevor sie auf ihre Amerikareise gehen können, muß noch vieles *erledigt werden.*

passive voice (das Pas´siv)

The verb phrase that indicates that the subject is acted upon rather than performing the action. The passive verb phrase consists of a tense of the auxiliary **werden** plus the past participle of the main verb.

➤ Als erstes *werden* die Flugkarten *bestellt.*

passive voice, alternative to (die Pas´siversatz´form)

A construction used instead of passive voice: **man; sein...zu** + infinitive; **sich lassen** + infinitive; reflexive construction. (See Appendix A: 23d.)

➤ Vor der Reise *sind* noch viele Dinge *zu machen.* Einige Sachen *lassen sich* leicht *erledigen,* z.B. den Nachbarn einen Schlüssel geben. Aber was macht *man* mit einer jungen Katze? Ein guter Mieter *findet sich* nicht so leicht.

past (die Vergan´genheit)

A verb form used to indicate that an event or action occurred before the present. German has three past tenses: simple past, present perfect, and past perfect.

➤ Als sie zum Flughafen *kamen, war* ihre Maschine gerade *gelandet.*

past participle (das Partizip´ Per´fekt)

A verb form used to make compound tenses (e.g., present perfect) and passive voice. It indicates completed action. A past participle may also be used as an adjective or adverb. The past participle of weak verbs ends in **-t,** of strong verbs in **-en;** most have the prefix **ge-** (e.g., **gespielt, gesprochen**). It is also called the perfect participle.

➤ Nachdem sie ihre Bordkarte *bekommen* hatten, sind sie *eingestiegen.*

past perfect (das Plus´quamperfekt)

A compound tense that consists of the past participle of the verb and simple past tense of **haben (hatte)** or **sein (war).** The past perfect is used to report an event or action that took place before another event or action in the past. It is also called "pluperfect." (See Appendix A: 23a.)

➤ Nachdem sie *eingestiegen waren,* gab es in der ersten Klasse Sekt. Sie saßen in der zweiten.

past-time subjunctive (der Kon´junktiv der Vergan´genheit)

The subjunctive form used to express hypothetical conditions, wishes, or indirect discourse in the past. It consists of the past participle of the

verb and the general or special subjunctive form of **haben (hätte/habe)**
or **sein (wäre/sei)**. (See Appendix A: 23c.)
> ➤ Wenn sie in der ersten Klasse *gesessen hätten, hätten* sie auch
>   Sekt *bekommen.*

perfect participle (see *past participle*)

period **(der Punkt, -e)**
The punctuation mark (.) used at the end of declarative sentences, non-
emphatic imperative sentences, indirect questions, and after most
abbreviations. In German, periods are also used to indicate ordinal
numbers (e.g., **am 5. Mai**) and to separate numbers over a thousand
(e.g., **2.453**).
> > Die Leute in der 1. Klasse haben es gut. Frank und Anna fragen
> > sich, wieviel ein solches Ticket wohl kostet. Es kostet sicher
> > über 3.000,00 Mark.

person **(die Person´)**
A grammatical category indicating the person(s) speaking, the person(s)
spoken to, or the person(s) spoken of. First person indicates the speaker
(ich), or includes the speaker **(wir)**; second person indicates one or
more persons spoken to **(du, ihr, Sie)**; and third person indicates one
or more persons or things spoken of **(er, sie, es, sie** pl.).
> ➤ Frank sagt zu Anna: „ *Du, ich* habe noch eine Frage. Haben *wir*
>   *deine* Eltern angerufen? *Sie* haben *uns* Geld für die Reise
>   geschenkt.“

personal pronoun **(das Personal´prono´men)**
A pronoun referring to specified people or things. (See Appendix A: 1.)
> ➤ Anna antwortet: „Ja, *ich* habe mit meinem Vater gesprochen. *Er*
>   wünschte *uns* eine gute Reise.“

place (adverb of) **(das Adverb des Ortes)**
An adverb of place answers the question **wo?** (where?), **wohin?**
(where to?), or **woher?** (where from?) and follows adverbs of time and
manner.
> ➤ Die beiden sind am 5. Mai mit dem Flugzeug *in Boston*
>   angekommen.

pluperfect (see *past perfect*)

plural **(der Plu´ral/die Mehr´zahl)**
A grammatical category that refers to more than one person, thing, or
concept.
> ➤ *Ihre alten Freunde* James und Jessica *haben sie* vom Flughafen
>   abgeholt.

positive degree **(der Po´sitiv)**
The basic form or degree of an adjective or adverb showing no comparison. (See Appendix A: 13.)
> ➤ Die vier sind schon seit Jahren *gute* Freunde.

possessive adjective (das Possessiv´prono´men/das Possessiv´adjektiv)
An adjective that describes a noun by indicating a possessive relation-
ship (e.g., **mein Pulli**).
➤ Sie sind mit *ihren* Freunden nach Hause gefahren.

possessive pronoun (das substanti´visch gebrauch´te
Possessiv´prono´men)
A pronoun that shows a possessive relationship to the noun it replaces.
The possessive pronoun is the same word as the possessive adjective,
but with endings to indicate gender, number, and case throughout (e.g.,
mein Freund und *deiner*).
➤ Plötzlich sagt Frank: „Du, ich kann mein Ticket nicht finden. Ich
   habe nur *dein(e)s.*"

predicate adjective (das prädikativ´ gebrauch´te Ad´jektiv)
An adjective that follows a linking verb and modifies the subject.
Predicate adjectives never add declensional endings.
➤ Ihre Freunde in Boston sind *berufstätig.*

predicate nominative (der Prädikats´nominativ)
A noun, pronoun, or noun phrase that follows a linking verb and
explains or modifies the subject.
➤ James ist *ein guter Ingenieur.* Jessica ist *eine bekannte Ärztin.*

predicate noun (das Prädikats´nomen)
A noun that is equated with the subject and completes the meaning of
a linking verb.
➤ James ist *Ingenieur.* Jessica ist *Ärztin.*

prefix (das Prä´fix, -e/die Vor´silbe, -n)
A syllable or word added to the beginning of a word to change its meaning (e.g., **bekommen**).
➤ Am ersten Abend in Boston können Frank und Anna nicht *ein*-
   schlafen. Am nächsten Morgen ist es schwer für sie *auf*zustehen.

pre-noun insert (see *extended modifier*)

preposition (die Präposition´, -en)
A word that shows the relationship between a noun or pronoun (the
object of the preposition) and some other word in the sentence. The
preposition governs the case of the noun or pronoun that follows it.
➤ Am ersten Tag fahren sie *mit* der Bahn *in* die Stadt.

present participle (das Partizip´ Prä´sens)
A verb form that consists of the infinitive plus **-d** (e.g., **schlafend**). A
present participle may be used as an adjective or adverb.
➤ In der Stadt sehen sie, wie ein Kind vor ein *fahrendes* Auto läuft.

present perfect (das Perfekt´)
A compound tense that consists of the past participle of the verb and

the present tense of **haben** or **sein**. The present perfect is used most frequently in conversation to refer to events in past time. It is also called the conversational past. (See Appendix A: 23a.)

➤ Anna: *„Hast du das gesehen?* Das Auto *hat* das Kind Gott sei Dank nur *angefahren."*

present tense (das Prä´sens/die Ge´genwart)
A verb tense used to talk about an event taking place at the same time as it is being described. Present tense can also express an action intended or planned for the future or express an action begun in the past that continues in the present (often with the word **seit**). (See Appendix A: 19, 21–23.)

➤ Anna sagt: „Schau, schon wieder *scheint* die Sonne. Wir *haben* schon seit Montag schönes Wetter. Hoffentlich *ist* es morgen auch schön, wenn wir nach Cape Cod *fahren."*

present-time subjunctive (der Kon´junktiv der Ge´genwart)
The form of the subjunctive used to express hypothetical conditions, wishes, or indirect discourse in the present. Present-time general subjunctive is based on the simple past tense. Present-time special subjunctive is based on the infinitive. (See Appendix A: 23c and 24.)

➤ Frank: „Ja, wenn Kinder weniger Glück *hätten,* würde viel mehr passieren."

pronoun (das Prono´men, -)
A word used in place of a noun. It may stand for a person, place, thing, or idea.

➤ Um die Mittagszeit gehen *sie* in ein Fischrestaurant. *Das* gefällt *ihnen* sehr.

quantity (die Maß´angabe/die Men´genangabe)
A unit of measurement or weight. In German, masculine and neuter nouns expressing measure, weight, or number are in the singular (e.g., **zwei Pfund Äpfel**). Feminine nouns ending in **-e** form plurals even when they express units of measure (e.g., **zwei Dosen Cola**).

➤ Zum Essen trinkt Frank *zwei Glas Bier* und Anna *zwei Dosen Cola.*

question (die Fra´ge, -n/der Fra´gesatz)
A sentence asking for information (see *specific question*) or confirmation (see *general question*).

➤ Anna: *„Wieviel kostet das Bier hier?"* Frank: *„Haben wir genug Geld dabei?"*

question mark (das Fra´gezeichen, -)
The punctuation mark (?) used at the end of a question.

➤ Anna fragt: „Wie schmeckt dir das amerikanische Bier?"

quotation (das Zitat´, -e)
The repeating of someone's exact words.
➤ **An einem Kiosk lesen sie die Schlagzeile einer deutschen
  Zeitung: *„Kanzler fährt nach China."***

quotation marks (die An´führungszeichen/die Gän´sefüßchen)
Punctuation marks (") used to enclose direct quotations. The position
of quotation marks in German (" …") differs from English (" . . . ").
➤ **„Ja, ja", sagt Frank, „der asiatische Markt wird immer wichtiger."**

reciprocal pronoun (das Reziprok´prono´men)
A pronoun indicating that the action or relationship affects two or more
people mutually (e.g., **einander**). Reflexive pronouns may be used recip-
rocally (e.g., **Wir rufen uns jeden Tag an.**).
➤ **Anna: „Immer mehr Länder treiben *miteinander* Handel."**

reflexive pronoun (das Reflexiv´prono´men)
A personal pronoun in either dative or accusative that indicates the
same person or thing as the subject. The pronoun **sich** is used in place
of the third person personal pronouns.
➤ **Frank: „Die Deutschen müssen *sich* anstrengen, um *sich* auf
  dem Weltmarkt zu behaupten."**

reflexive verb (das reflexi´ve Verb)
A verb that has a reflexive pronoun as its object, either in accusative or
dative (e.g., **Erinnerst du dich?, Ich kann mir nicht helfen.**).
➤ **Anna: „Und wir müssen *uns beeilen,* daß wir den Zug nicht
  verpassen."**

relative clause (der Relativ´satz)
A clause that is introduced by a relative pronoun and supplies additional information about an antecedent (previously mentioned noun,
pronoun, or clause). All relative clauses are dependent clauses, with the
verb in final position and set off by commas.
➤ **Der Zug, *mit dem sie nach New York fahren,* ist sehr voll.**

relative pronoun (das Relativ´prono´men)
A pronoun that refers back to a noun, pronoun, or clause previously
mentioned (antecedent) and introduces a clause that supplies additional information about the antecedent. In German the relative pronoun may not be omitted as it often is in English.
➤ **Im Zug lernen sie einen Mann kennen, *dessen* Frau aus Hamburg
  stammt.**

result clause (see *conclusion*)

sentence (der Satz, ¨e)
A group of words expressing a complete thought. A sentence must have
a verb and a subject. In an imperative sentence the subject is understood.
➤ **Der Mann stammt aus Paris und spricht ausgezeichnet Englisch.**

separable prefix (**das trenn´bare Prä´fix**)
A prefix, usually an adverb or preposition and occasionally another verb, added to a verb. The prefix is separated from the verb under certain conditions and in certain forms of the verb. In spoken German stress falls on the prefix.
➢ **Der Mann *steigt* auch in New York *aus.***

separable verb (**das trenn´bare Verb**)
A verb with a separable prefix.
➢ **In New York *gehen* die beiden oft mit Freunden *aus.***

simple past (**das Im´perfekt/das Präte´ritum**)
A verb tense formed without an auxiliary verb, used to indicate an event or action that occurred before the present. It is used to narrate a series of past events and is common in narrative prose. The simple past is also called the "narrative past." (See Appendix A: 20, 22, and 24.)
➢ **In New York *besuchten* sie viele Museen und *gingen* in die Oper.**

singular (**der Sin´gular/die Ein´zahl**)
A grammatical term that refers to one person, thing, or concept.
➢ **Frank hört lieber klassische Musik, seine Freundin zieht Jazz vor.**

special subjunctive (**der Kon´junktiv I**)
A form of the subjunctive based on the infinitive, used primarily in indirect discourse and in certain wishes. It is also called "subjunctive I."
➢ **Frank erzählt seinen Freunden, daß er lieber klassische Musik *höre*, während Anna Jazz *vorziehe.***

specific question (**die Ergän´zungsfrage**)
A question that asks for a specific piece of information. It begins with an interrogative adverb (e.g., **wann?**) or interrogative pronoun (e.g., **wer?**), followed by the finite verb which precedes the subject. It is also called an "informational question."
➢ **Anna fragt die Freunde: *„Wie oft geht ihr ins Konzert?"***

statal passive (**das Zu´standspassiv**)
A term sometimes applied to a construction with **sein** and the past participle that is used to express the state or condition of the subject. Statal passive (also called apparent passive) is not really passive voice, which expresses a process (rather than a state) and consists of a form of **werden** and the past participle.
➢ **Frank fragt Anna: „Du, die Karten für die Oper, *sind* die schon *bestellt*?" Anna antwortet: „Ja, sie *sind bestellt,* aber noch nicht *bezahlt.“***

statement (**der Aus´sagesatz**)
A sentence that describes a situation.
➢ **Frank und Anna sind am Samstag in die Oper gegangen.**

strong verb (**das starke Verb**)

A verb that has a stem-vowel change (and sometimes a consonant change) in the simple past. Strong verbs do not add the suffix -**te** in the simple past. The participles of strong verbs end in -**en** and may show stem change. (See Appendix A: 24.)

➤ Während sie im Taxi *saßen,* haben sie mit dem Fahrer eine Unterhaltung *begonnen.*

subject (**das Subjekt´, -e**)

The sentence unit that designates the person, concept, or thing that acts or is described in a sentence in active voice or is acted upon in passive voice. The subject and the finite verb agree in person and number.

➤ *Der Taxifahrer* fuhr sehr schnell, so daß *Frank und Anna* große Angst hatten.

subjunctive (**der Kon´junktiv**)

A verb mood that expresses suppositions, uncertainty, hypothetical conditions, and wishes. It is also used in indirect discourse.

➤ Wenn der Taxifahrer nicht so schnell *gefahren wäre, hätten* Frank und Anna keine Angst *gehabt.*

subjunctive I (see *special subjunctive*)

subjunctive II (see *general subjunctive*)

subordinate clause (see *dependent clause*)

subordinating conjunction (**die subordinie´rende [un´terordnende] Konjunktion´**)

A conjunction that introduces a dependent (subordinate) clause.

➤ Frank und Anna hatten Angst, *weil* der Taxifahrer so schnell fuhr.

suffix (**das Suf´fix, -e**)

One or more syllables added to the end of a word that change or modify the meaning or function of the word (e.g., **gedankenlos**).

➤ Frank und Anna sind keine ängst*lichen* Menschen, aber die Rücksichts*losigkeit* des Fahrers störte sie wirklich.

superlative (**der Su´perlativ**)

A form of an adjective or adverb that indicates the highest degree of a quality (e.g., **das schönste Bild**). (See Appendix A: 13.)

➤ Das war der *rücksichtsloseste* Fahrer, dem sie je begegnet waren.

tense (**die Zeit/die Zeitform**)

The form of a verb that indicates the time of the action (e.g., present, past, future).

➤ Gestern *waren* sie im Museum, heute *gehen* sie in die Oper, und morgen *werden* sie bestimmt noch die Freiheitsstatue *besuchen.*

time (adverb of) (das Adverb der Zeit)
An adverb of time answers the question **wann?** (when?) or **wie lange?** (how long?) and precedes adverbs of manner and place. The general expression of time precedes the specific (e.g., **Er kommt heute um zehn Uhr.**).
➤ Sie sind *gestern um acht* mit dem Taxi in die Oper gefahren.

time expression (die Zeit´angabe/der Zeit´ausdruck)
An adverbial time expression that indicates a definite point in time (e.g., **nächsten Monat**), duration of time (e.g., **den ganzen Sommer**), or indefinite time (e.g., **eines Abends**). Some time expressions are prepositional phrases (e.g., **vor einer Woche**).
➤ *Nächsten Montag* fliegen Frank und Anna wieder nach Hause. Der Flug dauert *zehn Stunden.* Sie hoffen, *eines Tages* ihre Freunde in Boston wieder zu besuchen.

transitive verb (das tran´sitive Verb)
A verb that requires a direct object to complete its meaning. Some verbs may be transitive in one sentence and intransitive in another.
➤ Vom Flughafen sind sie mit dem Taxi nach Hause gefahren. Zu Hause wollte ihr Auto nicht anspringen, weil sie es mehrere Wochen nicht *gefahren hatten.*

two-part conjunction (die zwei´teilige Konjunktion´)
A conjunction consisting of two parts (words) that link words, phrases, and clauses of equal grammatical rank and provide additional emphasis (e.g., **entweder…oder**).
➤ *Entweder* können sie / *Entweder* sie können vom Flughafen ein Taxi nehmen, *oder* sie können mit dem Bus fahren.

two-way preposition (die Präposition´ mit Da´tiv oder Ak´kusativ)
A preposition whose object can be in either the accusative or dative case. Accusative is used when the verb indicates a change of location, dative when the verb indicates location.
➤ Sie kommen *in* die Wohnung und sehen, daß *im* Wohnzimmer der Fernseher fehlt.

verb (das Verb, -en)
A word that expresses an action or describes an event or state of being. Every sentence has a verb.
➤ Die Stereoanlage *steht* an ihrem Platz. Nur der Fernseher *ist* weg.

voice (die Hand´lungsrichtung/die Verhal´tensrichtung)
The form of the verb that indicates whether the subject performs the action (active voice) or is acted upon (passive voice).
➤ Sie *rufen* bei der Polizei an: „Unser Fernseher *ist gestohlen worden.* …Nein, wir *haben* keine Ahnung, wer ihn *gestohlen haben könnte.“*

weak verb (das schwache Verb)

A verb whose infinitive stem remains unchanged in the past tenses. A weak verb forms the simple past by adding **-te** to the infinitive stem. It forms the past participle by adding **-t** to the infinitive stem. The past participle of most weak verbs has the prefix **ge-**.

➤ Die Freunde *fragten* Frank und Anna, was sie alles *gemacht* hätten.

wo- compound (das wo´-Kompo´situm)

A compound consisting of **wo-** plus a preposition to refer to things and ideas. The **wo-** compound introduces a question and can replace a preposition plus the pronoun **was,** which is considered very colloquial (e.g., **Wovon? [Von was?]**).

➤ Stefan wollte wissen, *wofür* sie sich in Amerika besonders interessiert hätten.

word order (die Wort´stellung/die Wort´folge)

The sequence of words, phrases, and clauses in a sentence. Adverbs follow the order of time, manner, and place. The position of a verb depends on the type of sentence.

➤ Wie immer fahren sie am nächsten Morgen mit dem Fahrrad zur Arbeit.

würde-construction (die wür´de-Konstruktion´/die wür´de-Umschrei´bung)

A construction made up of **würde** (the general subjunctive of **werden**) and the infinitive of the main verb. In spoken German the **würde-**construction is used in place of the subjunctive of the main verb, with a few exceptions.

➤ Es *würde* Frank und Anna sehr *gefallen,* wenn ihre Freunde aus Boston sie nächstes Jahr in Bonn *besuchen würden.*

GERMAN–ENGLISH

das Ad´jektiv, -e *adjective*

das Ad´verb, Adver´bien *adverb*

das Adverb der Art und Wiese *adverb of manner*

das Adverb des Ortes *adverb of place*

das Adverb der Zeit *adverb of time*

das A´gens *agent*

der Ak´kusativ *accusative*

das Ak´tiv *active voice*

die An´führungszeichen *quotation marks*

der Apostroph´, -e *apostrophe*

die Art und Weise *manner (adverb)*

der Arti´kel, - *article*

das attributi´ve Ad´jektiv *attributive adjective*

das Aus´rufezeichen, - *exclamation point*

der Aus´sagesatz *declarative sentence, statement*

der bestimm´te Arti´kel *definite article*

das Bezugs´wort, ¨er *antecedent*

der Bin´destrich, -e *hyphen*

das da´-Kompo´situm, Komposita *da- compound*

der Da´tiv *dative*

die Deklination´ *declension*

das Demonstrativ´prono´men *demonstrative pronoun*

das direk´te Objekt´ *direct object*

die direk´te Rede *direct discourse*

der Dop´pelinfinitiv *double infinitive*

der Dop´pelpunkt *colon*

die Ein´zahl *singular*

die Entschei´dungsfrage *general question, alternative question*

die Ergän´zungsfrage *specific question, informational question*

das erwei´terte Attribut´ *extended modifier, extended participial modifier, pre-noun insert*

der Fall, ¨e *case*

fe´minin *feminine*

das fini´te Verb *finite verb*

der Fol´gesatz *conclusion, result clause*

die Fra´ge, -n *question, interrogative*

der Fra´gesatz *question*

das Fra´gezeichen, - *question mark*

das Futur´ *future (tense)*

die Gän´sefüßchen *quotation marks*

der Gedan´kenstrich, -e *dash*

die Ge´genwart *present (tense)*

der Ge´nitiv *genitive*

das Ge´nus *gender*

das Geschlecht´ *gender*

die Hand´lungsrichtung *voice*

der Haupt´satz *independent clause, main clause*

das Haupt´verb *main verb*

das Hilfs´verb *auxiliary verb*

der Im´perativ *imperative*

das Im´perfekt *simple past, narrative past*

das Indefinit´prono´men *indefinite pronoun*

der In´dikativ *indicative*

das in´direkte Objekt´ *indirect object*

die in´direkte Rede *indirect discourse*

der In´finitiv, -e *infinitive*

der In´finitivsatz *infinitive clause, infinitive phrase*

das Interrogativ´prono´men *interrogative pronoun*

das in´transitive Verb *intransitive verb*

der ir´reale Konditional´satz *condition contrary to fact*

die Kardinal´zahl   *cardinal number*

der Ka´sus, -   *case*

das Kom´ma, -s   *comma*

die Komparation´   *comparison*

der Kom´parativ   *comparative*

der Konditional´satz   *conditional sentence; condition (**wenn**-clause)*

die Konjunktion´, -en   *conjunction*

der Kon´junktiv   *subjunctive*

der Kon´junktiv I   *special subjunctive, subjunctive I*

der Kon´junktiv II   *general subjunctive, subjunctive II*

der Kon´junktiv der Ge´genwart   *present-time subjunctive*

der Kon´junktiv der Vergan´genheit   *past-time subjunctive*

die koordinie´rende Konjunktion´   *coordinating conjunction*

die Ko´pula, -s   *linking verb*

männ´lich   *masculine*

mas´kulin   *masculine*

die Maß´angabe, -n   *measure; quantity*

die Mehr´zahl   *plural*

die Men´genangabe, -n   *measure; quantity*

das Mit´tel   *means*

die Modal´parti´kel   *flavoring particle*

das Modal´verb   *modal auxiliary*

der Mo´dus   *mood*

die ne´benordnende Konjunktion´   *coordinating conjunction*

der Ne´bensatz   *dependent clause, subordinate clause*

neutral´   *neuter*

das No´men, Nomina   *noun*

das Nominal´adjektiv   *adjective used as a noun, nominal adjective*

der No´minativ   *nominative*

die Ordinal´zahl   *ordinal number*

der Ort   *place (adverb)*

die Parti´kel, -n   *particle, flavoring particle*

das Partizip´ Per´fekt   *past participle, perfect participle*

das Partizip´ Prä´sens   *present participle*

das Pas´siv   *passive voice*

der pas´sive In´finitiv   *passive infinitive*

die Pas´siversatz´form   *alternative to passive voice*

das Per´fekt   *present perfect, conversational past*

die Person´   *person*

das Personal´prono´men   *personal pronoun*

der Plu´ral   *plural*

das Plus´quamperfekt   *past perfect*

der Po´sitiv   *positive degree*

das Possessiv´adjektiv   *possessive adjective*

das Possessiv´prono´men   *possessive adjective*

das prädikativ´ gebrauch´te Ad´jektiv   *predicate adjective*

das Prädikats´nomen   *predicate noun*

der Prädikats´nominativ   *predicate nominative*

das Prä´fix, -e   *prefix*

die Präposition´, -en   *preposition*

das präpositiona´le Objekt´   *object of the preposition*

die Präposition´ mit Da´tiv oder Ak´kusativ   *two-way preposition*

das Prä´sens   *present tense*

das Präte´ritum   *simple past, narrative past*

das Prono´men, -   *pronoun*

der Punkt, -e   *period*

der rea´le Konditional´satz   *condition of fact*

das reflexi´ve Verb   *reflexive verb*

das Reflexiv´prono´men   *reflexive pronoun*

das Relativ´prono´men   *relative pronoun*

der Relativ´satz   *relative clause*

das Reziprok´prono´men   *reciprocal pronoun*

säch´lich   *neuter*

der Satz, ¨e   *sentence*

das schwache Verb   *weak verb*

der Sin´gular   *singular*

das starke Verb   *strong verb*

das Subjekt´, -e   *subject*

die subordinie´rende Konjunktion´   *subordinating conjunction*

das Sub´stantiv, -e   *noun*

das substanti´visch gebrauch´te Possessiv´prono´men   *possessive pronoun*

das Suf´fix, -e   *suffix*

der Su´perlativ   *superlative*

das tran´sitive Verb   *transitive verb*

das trenn´bare Prä´fix   *separable prefix*

das trenn´bare Verb   *separable verb*

der un´bestimmte Arti´kel   *indefinite article*

das un´bestimmte Zahl´wort   *indefinite adjective*

das un´persönliche Pas´siv   *impersonal passive*

das un´persönliche Prono´men   *impersonal pronoun*

das un´persönliche Verb   *impersonal verb*

das un´regelmäßige schwache Verb   *irregular weak verb*

die un´terordnende Konjunktion´   *subordinating conjunction*

das un´trennbare Prä´fix   *inseparable prefix*

das un´trennbare Verb   *inseparable verb*

das Verb, -en   *verb*

die Vergan´genheit   *past (tense)*

die Verhal´tensrichtung   *voice*

das Voll´verb   *main verb*

die Vor´silbe, -n   *prefix*

weib´lich   *feminine*

das wo´-Kompo´situm   **wo**- *compound*

die Wort´folge   *word order*

die Wort´stellung   *word order*

die wür´de-Konstruktion´   **würde**-*construction*

die wür´de-Umschrei´bung   **würde**-*construction*

die Zahl   *number*

das Zahl´wort   *numeral*

die Zeit´angabe   *time expression*

der Zeit´ausdruck   *time expression*

die Zeit´form   *tense*

das Zitat´, -e   *quotation*

die Zu´kunft   *future (tense)*

die Zusam´menziehung   *contraction*

das Zu´standspassiv   *statal passive*

das zweite Futur´   *future perfect*

die zwei´teilige Konjunktion´   *two-part conjunction*

German-English Vocabulary

The German-English end vocabulary includes all words used in *Concise German Review Grammar* except common function words such as articles, pronouns, and possessive adjectives; days of the week; names of the months; numbers; obvious cognates; and low-frequency words that are glossed in the margins.

Words included in the basic list of 1,200 are marked with an asterisk (*). These words occur in the three standard frequency lists; *Das Zertifikat Deutsch als Fremdsprache* (Deutscher Volkshochschul-Verband and Goethe-Institut), *Grundwortschatz Deutsch* (Heinz Oehler), and *Grunddeutsch; Basic (Spoken) German Word List* (J. Alan Pfeffer).

Nouns are listed in this vocabulary with their plural forms: **die Aufgabe, -n.** No plural entry is given if the plural is rarely used or nonexistent. If two entries follow a noun, the first one indicates the genitive and the second one the plural: **der Vorname, -ns, -n.** For strong and irregular weak verbs, the vowel changes of the principal parts are given in parentheses. The present-tense vowel change is followed by a semicolon and the stem vowels in the simple past and past participle. Forms with consonant changes are written out in the their entirety. All verbs take **haben** in the perfect tenses except those marked with [**ist**]: **fahren (ä; u, [ist] a).** Separable prefix verbs are indicated with a raised dot: **auf·stehen.** Adjectives and adverbs that take umlaut in the comparative and superlative forms are noted as follows: **warm (ä).**

The symbol - indicates repetition of a key word or phrase. Where appropriate, noun compounds or adjectives derived from nouns or verbs follow the main entries.

The following abbreviations are used in this vocabulary:

acc. accusative	*conj.* conjunction	*inf.* infinitive
adj. adjective	*dat.* dative	*pl.* plural
adv. adverb	*decl.* declined	
coll. colloquial	*gen.* genitive	

*ab off, down, away

ab·biegen (o, [ist] o) to turn off; to diverge

*der Abend, -e evening; **am ~** in the evening; **heute abend** this evening; **zu ~ essen** to eat supper

*das Abendessen, - supper; **zum ~** for supper

*abends in the evening, evenings

*aber (*conj.*) but, however; (*flavoring particle*) really, certainly

*ab·fahren (ä; u, [ist] a) to depart; to drive off

die Abfahrt, -en departure

*ab·fahren (ä; u, [ist] a) to drive off, leave

ab·fliegen (o, [ist] o) to fly off, take off (*of an airplane*)

ab·hängen von (i, a) to depend on

*ab·holen to fetch; to pick up

das Abitur final comprehensive examination at **Gymnasium**

ab·nehmen (nimmt ab; a, abgenommen) to remove; to lose weight

die Abreise departure

ab·reisen [ist] to leave, to depart

ab·sagen to turn down, cancel

der Absatz, ⸚e paragraph

ab·schaffen to get rid of, to abolish

ab·schalten to switch off

absolut absolute

ab·stauben to dust

*ab·trocknen to dry off; to dry dishes

ab·waschen (ä; u, a) to wash dishes

*ach oh

achten to esteem, respect; **~ auf** + *acc.* to pay attention to

das Adjektiv, -e adjective; **das prädikativ gebrauchte ~** predicate adjective

*die Adresse, -en address

das Adverb, -ien adverb

das Agens agent

*aggressiv aggressive

ähneln to resemble

ähnlich (+ *dat.*) similar; **das sieht ihm ~** that's just like him

die Ähnlichkeit, -en similarity

die Ahnung, -en presentiment, idea; **keine ~** no idea

die Akademie, -n academy, school

der Akkusativ accusative case

*aktiv active

die Aktivität, -en activity

*akzeptieren to accept

der Alkohol alcohol

*alle all, everybody

*allein(e) alone

*alles everything

*allgemein general; **im allgemeinen** in general

allmählich gradual

der Alltag, -e daily life

alltäglich commonplace; daily

die Alpen Alps

*als when; than; ***als ob** as if; **als wenn** as if

*also thus, therefore

*alt (ä) old

das Alter age, old age

das Altersheim, -e nursing home

*(das) Amerika America, USA

*der Amerikaner, -/die Amerikanerin, -nen American

*amerikanisch American

die Ampel, -n traffic light

sich amüsieren to have a good time

*an (+ *dat./acc.*) at; on; to

analysieren to analyze

die Anatomie anatomy

*an·bieten (o, o) to offer

*andere other; different

*ändern to change

anders different

anderswo elsewhere

die Änderung, -en alteration, change

an·fahren (ä; u, a) to run into

*der Anfang, ⸚e beginning, start; **am ~** in the beginning

*an·fangen (ä; i, a) to start, to begin; **mit (der Arbeit) ~** to begin ([the] work)

das Angebot, -e offer

angegeben indicated; provided; specified

*angenehm (+ *dat.*) pleasant

angeschwollen swollen

der/die Angestellte (*noun decl. like adj.*) employee; official

*die Angst, ⸚e fright, anxiety; **~ haben vor** (+ *dat.*) to be frightened of

ängstlich (wegen) anxious, uneasy (about)

an·haben to have on, wear

an·halten (ä: ie, a) to stop; to hold

an·hören to listen to, to hear

*an·kommen (kam, [ist] o) to arrive

*an·nehmen (nimmt an; a, angenommen) to accept; to assume

anonym anonymous

an·probieren to try on

*der Anruf, -e phone call

*an·rufen (ie, u) to call up, to telephone

der Anrufer, - caller

anschauen to look at

an·schwellen (i; o, [ist] angeschwollen) to swell

*ansehen (ie; a, e) to look at

die Ansicht, -en view, opinion; **anderer ~ sein** to disagree; **die Ansichtskarte, -n** picture post card

an·sprechen (i; a, o) to speak to

an·springen (a, [ist] u) (motor) to start up

*anstatt (+ *gen.*) instead of; **(an) statt...zu** (+ *inf.*) instead of

anstellen to employ

(sich) an·strengen to strain (to exert oneself); **anstrengend** exhausting

die Anstrengung, -en exertion; effort

*die Antwort, -en answer

*antworten to answer; **antworten auf** (+ *acc.*) to reply to

die Anzeige, -n advertisement, notice; **eine ~ in die Zeitung setzen** to place an ad in the newspaper

*(sich) an·ziehen (zog an, angezogen) to get dressed

*der Anzug, ⸚e suit

*der Apfel, ⸚ apple

der Apfelbaum, ⸚e apple tree

der Apfelkuchen, - apple cake

der Apfelsaft apple juice

*die Apotheke, -n pharmacy

*der Apotheker, -/die Apothekerin, -nen pharmacist

*der Apparat, -e apparatus, appliance

*der Appetit appetite

das Äquivalent, -e equivalent

*die Arbeit, -en work; exam; an die ~ gehen to begin to work; sich an die ~ machen to start working

*arbeiten to work; ~ bei to work at (a company)

*der Arbeiter, -/die Arbeiterin, -nen worker

der/die Artbeitslose (noun decl. like adj.) unemployed worker; die Arbeitslosigkeit unemployment

der Arbeitsplatz, ⸚e place of work, position

das Arbeitszimmer, - study (room)

arbeitslos unemployed

der Architekt, -en, -en/die Architektin, -nen architect

die Architektur architecture

der Ärger vexation, anger

ärgerlich (über + acc.) irritable, angry (about, over)

*ärgern to annoy; sich ~ to become angry

*arm (ä) poor

der Arm, -e arm

arrogant arrogant

*die Art, -en manner; kind, species; die ~ und Weise manner

*der Artikel, - article; goods; der bestimmte~ the definite article

*der Arzt, ⸚e/die Ärztin, -nen medical doctor; zum ~ gehen to go to the doctor; vom ~ kommen to come from the doctor

der Arzthelfer, -/die Arzthelferin, -nen doctor's assistant

asiatisch Asian

der Astronaut, -en, -en/die Astronautin, -nen astronaut

der Atlantik Atlantic Ocean

*atmen to breathe

die Atmosphäre atmosphere

das Atom, -e atom; die Atomenergie atomic energy; das Atomkraftwerk, -e nuclear power plant; der Atomphysiker, -/die Atomphysikerin, -nen nuclear physicist

attraktiv attractive

Attribut: das erweiterte ~ extended modifier

attributiv attributive

aua! ouch!

*auf (+ dat./acc.) on, upon; upward; open

auf·essen (i; a, e) to eat up

auf·fallen (ä, ie, [ist] a) to be noticeable, to attract attention

*die Aufgabe, -n task; assignment

auf·geben (i, a, e) to give up; to deliver

auf·hängen to hang (up), to suspend

*auf·hören to stop, quit; mit etwas ~ to stop something

*auf·machen to open

*aufmerksam (auf + acc.) attentive (to)

*auf·passen (paßte auf; paßt auf, aufgepaßt) to pay attention

auf·räumen to clear away

sich auf·regen to get excited

auf·schreiben (ie, ie) to write down

*auf·stehen (stand auf, [ist] aufgestanden) to get up, to rise

auf·wachen to wake up

auf·wecken to wake (up) (someone)

*das Auge, -n eye

*der Augenblick, -e moment, instant

*aus (+ dat.) out of, from

die Ausbildung, -en education

aus·denken (dachte aus, ausgedacht) to imagine; to make up

*der Ausdruck, ⸚e expression

aus·drücken to express

*Ausflug, ⸚e excursion

aus·füllen to fill out

*aus·geben (i; a, e) to spend; to give out

aus·gehen (ging aus, ist ausgegangen) to go out

*ausgezeichnet excellent

die Auskunft, ⸚e information

*das Ausland foreign country; der Ausländer, -/die Ausländerin, -nen foreigner, alien

aus·packen to unpack

die Ausrede, -n excuse; faule Ausreden lame excuses

der Aussagesatz, ⸚e statement

*aus·sehen (ie; a, e) to look, to appear; aussehend: gut ~ good looking

*außer (+ dat.) except

*außerdem besides, moreover

*außerhalb (+ gen.) outside, beyond

die Äußerung, -en utterance, expression

*aus·steigen (ie, [ist] ie) to get out (of vehicle)

aus·stellen to exhibit

die Ausstellung, -en exhibition

der Austausch exchange; der Austauschstudent, -en, -en/die Austauschstudentin, -nen exchange student

aus·wählen to choose, to select

*(sich) aus·ziehen (zog aus, ausgezogen) to undress

aus·ziehen (zog aus, [ist] ausgezogen) to move out

*das Auto, -s car; *die Autobahn, -en interstate highway, expressway; autofrei without car traffic; der Autofahrer, -/die Autofahrerin, -nen car driver

*der Autobus, -se bus

der Automat, -en, -en vending machine

der Autor, -en/die Autorin, -nen author

*__das Baby, -s__ baby
*__backen (backte, gebacken)__ to bake
*__der Bäcker, -/die Bäckerin, -nen__ baker; **zum ~ gehen** to go to the bakery
__die Bäckerei, -en__ bakery
*__das Bad, ̈er__ bath; **die Badehose, -n** bathing trunks; **die Badewanne, -n** bathtub; *__das Badezimmer, -__ bathroom; **die Badetasche, -n** beach or swimming bag
*__baden__ to bathe; to swim
*__die Bahn, -en__ train; track; road
*__der Bahnhof, ̈e__ train station
*__bald (eher, ehest)__ soon; **~ darauf** a short time later
*__der Ball, ̈e__ ball; dance
__das Ballett, -e__ ballet
__der Ballon, -s__ balloon
__die Band, -s__ band
*__die Bank, ̈e__ bench
*__die Bank, -en__ bank
__die Bar, -s__ bar, pub
__der Bau, -ten__ building; **der Baustil, -e** style of architecture
*__bauen__ to build, to construct
*__der Bauer, -n, -n/die Bäuerin, -nen__ farmer
__das Bauernhaus, ̈er__ farm house
*__der Baum, ̈e__ tree
*__der Beamte (noun decl. like adj.)/die Beamtin, -nen__ official
__beantworten__ to answer
*__bedeuten__ to mean
*__die Bedeutung, -en__ meaning; importance
__bedienen__ to serve
*__sich beeilen__ to hurry
__beenden__ to finish
__der Befehl, -e__ order
__befehlen (ie; a; o)__ (+ dat. of person) to command
__sich befinden (a, u)__ to be located; to feel (health)
*__begegnen ([ist])__ (+ dat.) to meet

__begeistert__ enthusiastic
__der Beginn__ beginning
*__beginnen (a, o)__ to begin; **mit einer Arbeit ~** to begin a job
__begründen__ to justify; to support
__behalten (ä; ie, a)__ to keep, retain
*__behaupten__ to assert; to claim; **sich ~** to assert oneself
*__bei__ (+ dat.) at; near; while, during
*__beide__ both
*__das Bein, -e__ leg
*__das Beispiel, -e__ example; **zum ~** for example
*__bekannt (für)__ familiar; well known (for); **mir ~** known to me
*__der/die Bekannte (noun decl. like adj.)__ acquaintance, friend
__die Bekanntschaft__ acquaintance
*__bekommen (bekam, bekommen)__ to get, to receive
__beliebt__ popular
*__bemerken__ to mention; to notice; to realize
__die Bemerkung, -en__ comment; observation
*__sich benehmen (benimmt sich; a, sich benommen)__ to behave
__das Benehmen__ behavior
__benoten__ to give a grade
*__benutzen/benützen__ to use
*__das Benzin__ gasoline
__beobachten__ to observe
*__bequem__ comfortable
*__bereit (zu)__ ready, prepared (for)
__bereiten__ to prepare
*__der Berg, -e__ mountain
__bergsteigen__ to climb mountains
__der Bericht, -e__ report
*__berichten__ to report
*__der Beruf, -e__ profession; **die Berufsausbildung, -en** education for a profession; **beruflich** professional
__das Berufsleben__ professional life; **die Berufsschule, -n** vocational school

__berufstätig__ employed
__beruhigen__ to comfort, to calm
*__berühmt (wegen)__ famous (for)
*__beschäftigen__ to occupy; **sich beschäftigen (mit)** to occupy oneself (with); **die beschäftigt (mit)** busy (with)
__Beschäftigung, -en__ occupation; pursuit
*__beschließen (beschloß, beschlossen)__ to decide; to conclude
*__beschreiben (ie, ie)__ to describe
__die Beschreibung, -en__ description
__besetzt__ occupied; busy (telephone)
__besonder -(er, es, e)__ special
*__besonders__ especially
*__besser__ better
__best (-er, -es, -e)__ best
*__bestellen__ to order
__besten: am ~__ the best
__bestimmen__ to determine
*__bestimmt__ probably; sure; certain; particular
*__der Besuch, -e__ visit; guest, company; **zu ~ haben** to have a visit from (someone); **zu ~ kommen** to come for a visit; **bei einem ~** on a visit
*__besuchen__ to visit; to attend
__beten__ to pray
__betonen__ to emphasize
__betrachten__ to observe; to regard; to consider
*__das Bett, -en__ bed; **~ machen** to make the bed
__beunruhigen__ to alarm, to worry
*__bevor__ (conj.) before
*__(sich) bewegen__ to move
__die Bewegung, -en__ movement; exercise
*__beweisen (ie, ie)__ to prove
__bewußt__ conscious; aware
*__bezahlen__ to pay
*__die Bibliothek, -en__ library
*__das Bier, -e__ beer
*__bieten (o, o)__ to offer; to show
*__das Bild, -er__ picture
__(sich) bilden__ to form; to educate
*__billig__ cheap

die **Biologie** biology

***bis** (+ *acc.*) until; as far as; by *(time)*; ~ **dann** until then (later)

bisher so far; as yet; till now

***bißchen: ein bißchen** a little

***bitte** please; **wie ~ ?** What did you say?

***bitten (bat, gebeten) (um)** to beg; to ask

blaß (vor + *dat.*) pale (with)

***blau** blue

die **Blechtrommel, -n** tin drum

***bleiben (ie, [ist] ie)** to remain

***der Bleistift, -e** lead pencil

der **Blick, -e** view; glance

blicken (auf + *acc.*) to look (at)

der **Blitz, -e** lightning; flash

blitzen to flash; lightning; **es blitzt** there is lightning

blöd(e) dumb

blond blonde

***die Blume, -n** flower; **der Blumenladen, ⸚** flower shop; die **Blumenvase, -n** flower vase

***die Bluse, -n** blouse

***der Boden, ⸚** ground; floor; attic

***das Boot, -e** boat; **die Bootsfahrt, -en** boat trip

die **Bordkarte, -n** boarding pass

***böse (auf** or **über)** (+ *acc.*) mean; angry (at, about); **mir ~** angry at me

der **Bote, -n, -n** delivery person, messenger

***braten (ä; ie, a)** to fry; to roast

***der Braten, -** roast

brauchbar useful

***brauchen** to need; **nicht ~ zu** to not have to

***braun** brown

***brechen (i; a, o)** to break; to crush

***breit** broad, wide

***brennen (a, a)** to burn; **es brennt** something's burning

***der Brief, -e** letter

der **Brieffreund, -e/die Brieffreundin, -nen** pen pal

***die Briefmarke, -n** stamp

***der Briefträger, -/die Briefträgerin, -nen** mail carrier

***die Brille, -n** eyeglasses

***bringen (brachte, gebracht)** to bring

britisch British

***das Brot, -e** bread; sandwich

***das Brötchen, -** roll

die **Brote** *(pl.)* sandwiches

***die Brücke, -n** bridge

***der Bruder, ⸚** brother

brummen to buzz, ring

brünett brunette

***das Buch, -er** book; **das Bücherregal, -e** bookcase; die **Bückertasche, -n** bookbag; **die Buchhandlung, -en** bookstore

der **Buchstabe, -ns, -n** letter *(of alphabet)*

bügeln to iron

die **Bühne, -n** stage

bummeln to stroll

***die Bundesrepublik Deutschland** Federal Republic of Germany

***bunt** multi-colored

die **Burg, -en** castle

der **Bürgermeister, -/die Bürgermeisterin, -nen** mayor

***das Büro, -s** office; **die Bürokauffrau/der Bürokaufmann, die Bürokaufleute** office clerk

***die Bürste, -n** brush

***der Bus, -se** bus

***die Butter** butter

***das Café, -s** café; **das Studentencafé** a café frequented by students

***das Camping** camping out; ***der Campingplatz, ⸚e** campground

die **CD, -s** CD, compact disc

der **CD-Spieler, -** compact disc player

das **Cello, -s** cello

der **Charakter, -e** character; **die Charaktereigenschaft, -en** character trait

charakteristisch characteristic

***der Chef, -s/die Chefin, -nen** boss

die **Chemie** chemistry

chemisch chemical

chinesisch Chinese

die **Clique, -n** group, set

der **Clown, -s** clown

der **Club, -s** club

das/die **Cola, -s** cola drink

***der Computer, -** computer; **das Computerspiel, -e** computer game

der **Couchtisch, -e** coffee table

***die Cousine, -n** cousin *(f.)*

***da** *(adv.)* there; then; **da drüben** over there

***da** *(conj.)* as; since

dabei thereby; moreover; with it; in the process

***das Dach; ⸚er** roof

dagegen against it; on the other hand

***daher** therefore

***dahin** there; away; gone

dahinter behind (that)

***damals** at that time; then

***damit** in order that; with that

danach after that; accordingly

dank thanks to

***der Dank** reward, thanks

***dankbar (für)** grateful (for); **mir ~** grateful to me

***danken** (+ *dat. of person*) to thank; **(~ für)** to thank (for)

***dann** then

darauf thereupon; afterward

darüber over it; across it; about it

***darum** therefore; around it

***daß** that *(conj.)*

der **Datenverarbeiter, -/die Datenverarbeiterin, -nen** data processor

der **Dativ** dative case

das **Datum, Daten** date

***dauern** to last; **dauernd** continually

***dazu** to this; in addition; for this purpose

die **Debatte, -n** debate

debattieren to debate

***die Decke, -n** blanket; ceiling

decken to cover; **den Tisch ~** to set the table

definieren to define

die Definition, -en definition
dekorieren to decorate
die Delikatesse, -n delicacy
demokratisch democratic
die Demonstration, -en demonstration
das Demonstrativpronomen, - demonstrative pronoun
*__denken (dachte, gedacht)__ to think; **~ an** (+ *acc.*) to think of
*__denn__ (*conj.*) for, because; (*flavoring particle in question*)
dennoch yet, however
deprimiert depressed
*__deren__ whose
*__derselbe/dasselbe/dieselbe__ the same
*__deshalb__ therefore, for that reason
*__dessen__ whose
*__desto: je (mehr)...~ (besser)__ the (more) . . . the (better)
*__deswegen__ for that reason, therefore
das Detail, -s detail
*__deutsch__ (*adj.*) German
*__der/die Deutsche, -n__ (*noun decl. like adj.*) German
das Deutsch (language) German; **ins Deutsche** into German; **auf deutsch** in German
*__(das) Deutschland__ Germany
der Dialekt, -e dialect
der Dialog, -e dialogue
der Dichter, -/die Dichterin, -nen poet, writer
*__dick__ big; thick; fat
dienen (+ *dat.*) to serve
*__dies (-er, -es, -e)__ this, these
diesmal this time
*__diesseits__ (+ *gen.*) on this side (of)
*__das Ding, -e__ thing
direkt direct
*__der Direktor, -en/die Direktorin, -nen__ director
*__die Disco, -s__ dance club
die Diskussion, -en discussion
*__diskutieren über__ (+ *acc.*) to discuss

*__doch__ however; but; still; (*flavoring particle*) after all, indeed; (*response to negative question or statement*) yes, of course
*__der Doktor, -en/die Doktorin, -nen__ medical doctor; Ph.D.
*__der Dom, -e__ cathedral
die Donau Danube River
der Donner thunder
donnern to thunder; **es donnert** it's thundering
doof dumb, stupid
*__das Dorf, ¨er__ village
*__dort__ there; **~ drüben** over there
*__dorther__ from there
*__dorthin__ to that place
die Dose, -n can
*__draußen__ outside
drehen to turn; **einen Film ~** to make a movie
drin inside
drinnen inside
das Drittel, - third
*__drüben__ over there
*__dumm (ü)__ stupid; foolish
*__dunkel__ dark
dünn thin, slender
*__durch__ (+ *acc.*) through, by means of
durchdenken (durchdachte, durchdacht) to think through
*__dürfen__ to be permitted
*__der Durst__ thirst
*__durstig__ thirsty
die Dusche, -n shower
*__(sich) duschen__ to take a shower
*__das Dutzend, -e__ dozen

*__eben__ even, smooth; exactly, precisely; just; (*flavoring particle*)
*__echt__ genuine, real; (*coll.*) very; really
*__die Ecke, -n__ edge; corner; **eckig** square
*__egal__ equal, even; **das ist mir ~** it's all the same to me
egoistisch egotistical
*__ehe__ (*conj.*) before
ehemalig former
eher earlier, sooner; rather

ehesten: am ~ soonest
ehrlich honest, fair
*__das Ei, -er__ egg
*__eigen__ own; individual
die Eigenschaft, -en attribute, trait
*__eigentlich__ actually, really
eilen [ist] to hurry
*__einander__ one another
sich ein·bilden to imagine
*__einfach__ simple; simply
ein·fallen (ä; fiel ein, [ist] eingefallen) to occur to; **es fällt mir ein** it occurs to me, it comes to mind
das Einfamilienhaus, ¨er single family house
der Eingang, ¨e entrance
eingerichtet decorated, furnished
*__einige__ a few, several, some
sich einigen to agree upon
*__ein·kaufen__ to shop
der Einkaufsbummel, - shopping spree
das Einkaufszentrum, -zentren shopping mall
*__einladen (ä; u, a)__ to invite
die Einladung, -en invitation
*__einmal__ once; **nicht ~** not even; **noch ~** once again
ein·packen to pack
(sich) ein·richten to decorate, set up
ein·schlafen (ä; ie, [ist] a) to fall asleep
einseitig unilateral; biased
ein·setzen to insert
einst formerly
*__ein·steigen (ie, [ist] ie)__ to get in, enter
der Eintritt entry; admission; **die Eintrittskarte, -n** ticket; **der Eintrittspreis, -** admission charge
der Einwohner, -/die Einwohnerin, -nen inhabitant
die Einzelheit, -en detail
*__einzeln__ individual, single
ein·ziehen (zog ein, ist eingezogen) to move in
*__einzig__ only; unique
*__das Eis__ ice; ice cream; **eisig** icy

*die Eisenbahn, -en railroad; railroad train

elegant elegant

der Elektriker, -/die Elektrikerin, -nen electrician

*die Eltern *(pl.)* parents

empfehlen (ie; a, o) to recommend

*das Ende, -n end; limit; **letzten Endes** in the final analysis; after all; **zu ~** over

enden to end

*endlich finally

die Energie energy

*eng narrow, tight

*(das) England England; **der Engländer, -/die Engländerin, -nen** English person;

englisch *(adj.)* English

das Englisch (language) English; **auf englisch** in English

das Enkelkind, -er grandchild

entdecken to discover

entfernt distant, removed

entgegen *(dat.)* against; opposite; toward

*entlang (+ acc.) along

entlang·gehen (i, [ist] a) to go along

*entscheiden (ie, ie) to decide

die Entscheidung, -en decision

*(sich) entschuldigen to excuse

*die Entschuldigung, -en excuse

entsetzlich terrible

sich entspannen to relax

die Entspannung reduction of tension; relaxation

*enttäuschen to disappoint

*entweder...oder either . . . or

*(sich) entwickeln to develop

die Entwicklung, -en development

das Erachten: meines Erachtens in my opinion

*die Erde, -n earth; soil

*das Erdgeschoß, Erdgeschosse ground-level floor

*erfahren (ä; u, a) to experience; to hear about

*die Erfahrung, -en experience

erfinden (a, u) to invent

der Erfinder, -/die Erfinderin, -nen inventor

die Erfindung, -en invention

erfolgreich successful

ergänzen to complete

sich erholen to recover

erholsam relaxing

die Erholung recuperation; relaxation; **das Erholungs- programm, -e** entertainment program

*sich erinnern an (+ *acc.*) to remember; **erinnern** to remind

die Erinnerung, -en reminder; recollection

*sich erkälten to catch a cold

*die Erkältung, -en cold

*erkennen (erkannte, erkannt) to recognize; **(an + *dat.*)** to recognize (by)

*erklären to explain; **erklärbar** explainable

*die Erklärung, -en explanation

erlauben to permit; **(+ *dat.* with person)** to permit, allow

die Erlaubnis permit

erleben to experience

das Erlebnis, -se experience

erledigen to deal with; to take care of

*ernst serious

erraten (ä; ie, a) to guess

*erreichen to achieve; to reach

die Errungenschaft, -en accomplishment

*erscheinen (ie, [ist] ie) to seem; to appear; to be published

*erst first; not until; previously

erstaunen to surprise; **erstaunt (über + *acc.*)** surprised (at, by)

erstklassig first-rate

erstmal first

erwachsen grown up

*der/die Erwachsene, -n *(noun decl. like adj.)* adult

*erwarten to expect; to await

die Erwartung, -en expectation

*erzählen (über + *acc.* or von) to tell, report (about)

*die Erzählung, -en story

der or **das Essay, -s** essay

*essen (ißt; aß, gegessen) to eat

*das Essen, - meal; **vor dem ~** before lunch/dinner; **beim ~** at lunch/dinner; **zum ~** for lunch/dinner

*etwa about, nearly

*etwas something; a little

*(das) Europa Europe

*das Examen, - final examination at a university; **~ machen** to take one's finals

explodieren to explode

extravagant extravagant (clothing, eyeglasses); flamboyant, flashy

*die Fabrik, -en factory

*das Fach, ̈er subject; specialty; **der Facharbeiter, - /die Facharbeiterin, -nen** skilled worker; **der Fachmann, ̈er** or **-leute /die Fachfrau, -en** specialist; **die Fachschule, -n** technical school

fähig able, capable

die Fähigkeit, -en capability

*fahren (ä; u, [ist] a) to drive (a vehicle); to go; **mit [dem Zug] ~** to go by (train)

*der Fahrer, -/die Fahrerin, - nen driver

*die Fahrkarte, -n ticket (bus, train)

der Fahrkartenschalter, - ticket counter

der Fahrplan, ̈e schedule (e.g., bus, train)

*das Fahrrad, ̈er bicycle

*die Fahrt, -en tour, trip

der Fall, ̈e case; decline

*fallen (ä; fiel [ist] a) to fall

falls *(conj.)* in case, if

*falsch false; deceitful

familiär family; familiar; intimate

*die Familie, -n family; **das Familienfest, -e** family party; **das Familienmitglied, -er** member of the family

fangen (ä; i, a) to catch

*die Farbe, -n color

*fast almost

faszinieren to fascinate

*faul lazy; rotten

faulenzen to be lazy; to do nothing

*fehlen (+ *dat.*) to miss; to be lacking; fehlend missing

*der Fehler, - mistake; fault

die Feier, -n celebration; *der Feiertag, -e holiday

*feiern to celebrate

*fein fine, delicate, thin; nice

*der Feind, -e enemy

*das Feld, -er field

*das Fenster, - window

*die Ferien *(pl.)* vacation; das Ferienhaus, ‡er vacation home; das Ferienheim, -e camp; der Ferientag, -e vacation day; der Feriengast, ‡e person staying on vacation

*fern far, distant, away

*der Fernsehapparat, -e television set

*fern·sehen (ie; a, e) to watch television

*der Fernseher, - television set

*das Fernsehen television

die Fernsehsendung, -en TV program

*fertig ready, done

*das Fest, -e festival; party; feast

die Fete, -n party

*fest firm; compact, solid

fest·sitzen (saß, gesessen) to be stuck

feucht moist; humid

*das Feuer, - fire; light (cigarette)

das Fieber fever

*der Film, -e film, movie

finanzieren to finance

*finden (a, u) to find, to discover; to think

*der Finger, - finger

finit finite

*die Firma, Firmen firm

*der Fisch, -e fish

fit fit; sich ~ halten to stay in shape

*flach flat; even

*die Flasche, -n bottle

*das Fleisch meat

*fleißig industrious

*fliegen (o, [ist] o) to fly

fliehen (o, [ist] o) (vor + *dat.*) to flee (from); to escape

*fließen (o, [ist] geflossen) to flow

Florenz Florence

die Flöte, -n flute

Flüchtling, -e refugee

*der Flug, ‡e flight; *der Flughafen, ‡ airport; *die Flugkarte, -n plane ticket; der Flugpreis, -e air fare; die Flugangst fear of flying

*das Flugzeug, -e airplane

*der Fluß, Flüsse river

*folgen (+ *dat.*) to follow; to obey; folgend (the) following

die Form, -en form, shape; in ~ bringen to style

*fort away; on, forward

fort·fahren (ä; u, [ist] a) to continue; to drive away

*das Foto, -s photograph; *der Fotoapparat, -e camera

der Fotograf, -en, en/die Fotografin, -nen photographer

die Fotografie, -n photography; photo

fotografieren to take a picture

*die Frage, -n question; eine ~ stellen to ask a question

*fragen to ask; sich ~ to wonder; ~ nach to ask about

die Fragestellung, -en question

fraglich questionable

*(das) Frankreich France

*der Franzose, -n, -n/die Französin, -nen French person; französisch French

*die Frau, -en woman; Mrs., Ms.; wife

*das Fräulein, - Miss (*old-fashioned*)

frech impudent

*frei free; ~ haben to be off from work; ~ sein to be unoccupied

frei·halten (ä; ie, a) to keep free

*die Freiheit, -en freedom; die Freiheitsstatue Statue of Liberty

die Freizeit leisure time

*fremd foreign; strange; das ist mir ~ that is foreign to me; die Fremdsprache, -n foreign language

*fressen (frißt; fraß, e) to eat (*used for animals*)

*die Freude, -n (über + *acc.*) joy (about); voller ~ full of happiness

*sich freuen to rejoice, be glad; sich freuen auf (+ *acc.*) to look forward to; sich freuen über (+ *acc.*) to be happy about

*der Freund, -e/die Freundin, -nen friend; ein fester ~ a steady boyfriend

*freundlich (gegenüber, zu) friendly (to)

die Freundschaft, -en friendship

der Frieden peace

friedlich peaceful

frieren (o, o) to freeze; es friert it's freezing

*frisch fresh; new

*der Friseur, -e barber, hairdresser; *die Friseuse, -n hairdresser

*froh (über + *acc.*) glad (about)

*fröhlich happy, merry

*früh early; früher formerly; earlier

das Frühjahr, -e spring

*der Frühling, -e spring

*das Frühstück, -e breakfast

*frühstücken to eat breakfast

*(sich) fühlen to feel

*führen to lead, to guide

*der Führerschein, -e driver's license

der Funk- und Fernsehtechniker, -/ -technikerin, -nen radio- and television technician

funktionieren to function

*für (+ *acc.*) for

*furchtbar terrible

sich fürchten (vor + *dat.*) to fear

fürchterlich terrible, frightful

*der Fuß, ¨e foot; **zu Fuß** on foot; ***der Fußweg, -e** foot path

*der Fußball, ¨ soccer ball; soccer (the game)

*der Fußgänger, -/die Fuß-gängerin, -nen pedestrian; **die Fußgängerzone, -n** pedestrian zone

füttern to feed

das Futur future tense; **das zweite ~** future perfect tense

*die Gabel, -n fork

*ganz complete, whole; quite

*gar: ~ nicht not at all; **~ kein** none at all

*die Garage, -n garage

die Gardine, -n curtain

*der Garten, ¨ garden; **die Gartenarbeit** gardening; **die Gartenmöbel** (pl.) lawn furniture

das Gas, -e gas

*der Gast, ¨e guest

*das Gasthaus, ¨er inn, hotel

*das Gebäude, - building

*geben (i; a, e) to give; **es gibt** there is/are

*das Gebiet, -e region; subject

gebildet educated, cultured

*das Gebirge, - mountains

*geboren born

*gebrauchen to use

gebraucht second hand, used

*die Geburt, -en birth; **das Geburtshaus, ¨er** birthplace

*der Geburtstag, -e birthday; **zum ~** for one's birthday; **das Geburtstagsgeschenk, -e** birthday present; **die Geburtstagsparty, -s** or **-ies** birthday party

*der Gedanke, -ns, -n thought

das Gedicht, -e poem

*die Gefahr, -en danger

der Gefallen, - favor

*gefallen (ä; ie, a) (+ dat.) to please

*das Gefühl, -e emotion

*gegen (+ acc.) against; about, around

*die Gegend, -en area, region

der Gegenstand, ¨e thing; subject

das Gegenteil, -e opposite

*gegenüber (+ dat.) opposite

die Gegenwart presence; present time; present tense

gegrillt grilled; broiled

*gehen (ging, [ist] gegangen) to go; to walk; **das geht mich nichts an** that doesn't concern me; **das geht nicht** that won't do; **wie geht's?** how are you; **wenn es nach Ralf ginge** if it were up to Ralf

*gehorchen (+ dat.) to obey

*gehören (+ dat.) to belong

gelangweilt bored

gelaunt: schlecht ~ in a (bad) mood

*gelb yellow

*das Geld, -er money

*die Gelegenheit, -en opportunity

*gelingen (a, [ist] u) (+ dat.) to succeed; **es gelingt mir** I succeed

*gelten (i; a, o) to be of value; to be valid; to be in effect; to be regarded as

das Gemälde, - painting

die Gemeinschaft, -en group; community

*das Gemüse, - vegetable

*gemütlich comfortable, cozy; good-natured

*genau exact, accurate; that's right

genießen (o, genossen) to enjoy

der Genitiv genitive case

genügen (+ dat.) to be enough, sufficient

*das Gepäck luggage; **der Gepäckträger, -** porter

*gerade straight; just; **geradeaus** straight ahead

*gern (lieber, liebst-) gladly, with pleasure; **~ haben** to like

*das Geschäft, -e business; store; **die Geschäftsfrau, -en/der Geschäftsmann, ¨er** or **Geschäftsleute** businesswoman/businessman /businesspersons; **die Geschäftszeit, -en** business hours

*geschehen (ie; a, [ist] e) (+ dat.) to happen

*das Geschenk, -e gift

*die Geschichte, -n story; history

*das Geschirr dishes; **die Geschirrspülmaschine, -n** automatic dishwasher

der Geschmack, ¨er taste

die Geschwindigkeitsbegrenz-ung, -en speed limit

die Geschwister (pl.) siblings

geschwollen swollen

*die Gesellschaft, -en society; company

*das Gesicht, -er face

gespannt (auf + acc.) curious (about)

*das Gespräch, -e talk; **ein ~ führen** to converse

*gestern yesterday

*gesund healthy

*die Gesundheit health

das Getränk, -e drink, beverage

die Gewalt, -en power; violence

*gewinnen (a, o) to gain, win

*gewiß sure, certain

das Gewissen conscience; **ein gutes ~ ist ein sanftes Ruhekissen** (Proverb) I just want to be able to sleep nights (i.e. have a clear conscience)

das Gewitter, - thunderstorm

sich gewöhnen an (+ acc.) to get used to; **gewohnt** accustomed

*gewöhnlich normally; common

gießen (o, gegossen) to pour

*die Gitarre, -n guitar

*das Glas, ¨er glass

der Glaube, -ens (no pl.) belief, faith

*glauben (an + acc.) to believe (in); **~** (+ dat. of person) to believe (someone)

*gleich soon; equal; **das ist mir ~** it's all the same to me

gleichfalls likewise

gleichzeitig simultaneous

*das Glück luck, fortune; **zum ~** luckily; **der Glückwunsch, ¨e** congratulations *glücklich (über + *acc.*) happy (about)

die Glühbirne, -n light bulb

*der Gott, ⸚er God; god; ~ Sei dank thank heavens

graben (ä; u, a) to dig

der Grad, -e degree; rank

*das Gramm, -e gram

*das Gras, ⸚er grass

gratulieren (+ *dat.*) to congratulate

*grau gray

(das) Griechenland Greece

grillen to grill; to broil

grob (ö) rude; rough

*groß (ö) great; big; tall

großartig excellent

*die Größe, -n height; size

*die Großeltern (*pl.*) grandparents

*die Großmutter, ⸚ grandmother

die Großstadt, ⸚e city

*der Großvater, ⸚ grandfather

die Grube, -n ditch, pit

*grün green; im Grünen out in nature; ins Grüne into nature

*der Grund, ⸚e reason; bottom

die Grundschule, -n elementary school

die Gruppe, -n group

*der Gruß, ⸚e greeting

*grüßen to greet

*gut (besser, best-) good, well, OK; ~ gegen or zu good to; das Gute the good

*das Gymnasium, Gymnasien high school

*das Haar, -e hair; *der Haartrockner, - hairdryer

*haben to have; to possess

der Hafen, ⸚ harbor, port

*halb half

die Hälfte, -n half

hallo hi, hello

*der Hals, ⸚e neck

*halten (ä; ie, a) to hold; to stop; to keep (a promise); ~ von to think of; ~ für to regard as

*die Haltestelle, -n (bus) stop

*die Hand, ⸚e hand; die ~ geben to extend one's hand

der Handel trade

handeln to act; to treat; sich ~ um to concern; es handelt von it deals with

die Handlung, -en plot; action

*der Handschuh, -e glove

*die Handtasche, -n purse, pocketbook

*das Handtuch, ⸚er towel

hängen to hang

*hängen (i, a) to be hanging

*hart (ä) hard, solid; difficult; stiff

der Haß hate

*hassen to hate

*häßlich ugly

häufig often, frequent

das Haupt, ⸚er head, principal

der Hauptbahnhof, ⸚e main train station

das Hauptfach, ⸚er major subject

die Hauptidee, -n main idea

die Hauptsache, -n main thing

der Hauptsatz, ⸚e independent clause

die Hauptschule, -n classes 5–9(10) for students intending to learn a trade

das Hauptseminar, -e advanced seminar; graduate seminar

*die Hauptstadt, ⸚e capital

die Hauptstraße, -n main street

*das Haus, ⸚er house; nach Hause (to) home; zu Hause at home; die Hausarbeit, -en house work; homework; die Hausaufgabe, -n homework; der Hausmann, ⸚er man who keeps house; die Hausfrau, -en woman who keeps house

der Haushalt, -e household; im ~ helfen to help out around the house

der Haushaltsplan, ⸚e housekeeping schedule

die Haustür, -en front door

*heben (o, o) to lift, raise

*das Heft, -e notebook

das Heim, -e home; institution; heim home(ward); die Heimfahrt trip home; der Heimweg, -e way home; das Heimweh homesickness; Heimweh haben to be homesick

die Heirat, -en marriage

*heiraten to marry

*heiß hot

*heißen (ie, ei) to be called; to mean; es heißt it states

heiter cheerful

*helfen (i; a, o) (+ *dat.*) to help; bei etwas ~ to help with something

*hell bright, light

*das Hemd, -en shirt

*her here

heraus·finden (a, u) to find out

*der Herbst, -e autumn

der Herd, -e (cooking) range

*herein into

her·fahren (ä; u, [ist] a) to drive over

her·kommen (kam, [ist] o) to come over

*der Herr, -n, -en Mr.; gentleman

herrlich magnificent

Hertie name of department store chain

herum around; about

herum·fahren (ä; u, [ist] a) to drive around

herum·führen to show around

herum·laufen (äu; ie [ist] au) to run around

herum·spazieren to walk around

herunter down there

*das Herz, -ens, -en heart; schweren Herzens with a heavy heart; *herzlich cordial

*heute today

*hier here; hierher here

*die Hilfe, -n help

das Hilfsverb, en auxiliary verb

*der Himmel, - heaven; sky

*hin there; away

hinaus out; beyond

hindern to prevent

hinein in; inside; into
hinein·fallen (ä; ie, [ist] a) to fall into
hin·fallen (ä; ie, [ist] a) to fall (down)
hin·legen to put there; **sich ~** to lie down
sich hin·setzen to sit down
*****hinten** in the rear
*****hinter** *(acc./dat.)* behind; back
die Hin- und Rückfahrt, -en round trip
historisch historical
die Hitze heat
*****das Hobby, -s** hobby
*****hoch (höher, höchst-)** high
das Hochdeutsch High (standard) German
die Hochschule, -n university
*****höchst** highest; utmost; **höchstens** at most
die Hochzeit, -en wedding
*****der Hof, ¨e** farm; court
*****hoffen (auf + acc.)** to hope (for)
*****hoffentlich** I (we) hope; hopefully
*****die Hoffnung, -en** hope;
*****höflich (zu)** polite (to)
*****holen** to get
*****das Holz, ¨er** wood
*****hören** to hear; to listen to; **~ auf (+ acc.)** to take advice
*****die Hose, -n** trousers
*****das Hotel, -s** hotel
*****hübsch** pretty
der Hügel, - hill
*****das Huhn, ¨er** chicken
der Humor humor
*****der Hund, -e** dog; **hundemüde** extremely tired
*****hundert** hundred
*****der Hunger** hunger
*****hungrig** hungry
*****husten** to cough
*****der Hut, ¨e** hat
die Hütte, -n cabin, hut
der Hypochonder, - hypochondriac

ideal ideal
*****die Idee, -n** idea
identisch identical
der Idiot, -en, -en idiot
ihretwegen on her (their) account

*****immer** always; **~ mehr** more and more; **~ wieder** again and again
der Imperativ imperative
*****in** *(acc./dat.)* in; at; into; to
indem while; in that
der Indikativ indicative
*****die Industrie, -n** industry
der Infinitiv infinitive
der Infinitivsatz, ¨e infinitive phrase; infinitive clause
der Informatiker, -/die Informatikerin, -nen computer specialist
die Information, -en information
informieren to inform; **informiert** informed
*****der Ingenieur, -e/die Ingenieurin, -nen** engineer
*****der Inhalt, -e** content
initiieren to initiate
*****innerhalb** (+ *gen.*) inside of
die Insel, -n island
insgesamt altogether
intelligent intelligent
*****interessant** interesting
das Interesse, -n (an + *dat.* or für) interest (in)
sich interessieren (für) to be interested (in); **interessiert (an + *dat.*)** interested (in)
international international
das Interrogativpronomen, - interrogative pronoun
das Interview, -s interview
interviewen to interview
inwiefern to what extent; in what way
*****inzwischen** meanwhile
*****irgend** some; any; at all; **irgendein** some; any; **irgendwelch** any (kind)
*****irgendwann** sometime; *****irgendwie** somehow; *****irgendwo** somewhere
sich irren to be mistaken
isolieren to isolate
*****(das) Italien** Italy; **der Italiener, -/die Italienerin, -nen** Italian; **italienisch** Italian

*****ja** yes; *(flavoring particle)* indeed, of course

*****die Jacke, -n** jacket
*****das Jahr, -e** year
die Jahreszeit, -en season
*****das Jahrhundert, -e** century
-jährig years old
der Jazz jazz
*****je** each; for each case; **je...desto** the . . . the; **o ~ !** oh dear!
jed -(-er, -es, -e) each, every; everyone
*****jedermann** everyone, everybody
*****jedesmal** every time
jedoch however, nevertheless
jemals ever
*****jemand** somebody; **~ anders** someone else
*****jen -(-er, -es, -e)** that; the former
*****jenseits** (+ *gen.*) on the other side; beyond
*****jetzt** now
jeweils in each case
*****der Job, -s** job; **auf Jobsuche gehen** to look for a job
joggen to go jogging
das Journal, -e journal
*****der Journalist, -en, -en/die Journalistin, -nen** journalist; **der Journalistenverein** journalist's association
*****die Jugend** youth
*****der/die Jugendliche** *(noun decl. like adj.)* young person
*****jung (ü)** young
*****der Junge, -n, -n** boy
Jura law studies
der Jurist, -en, -en/die Juristin, -nen person with a law degree, jurist
juristisch judicial

*****der Kaffee** coffee; **die Kaffeepause, -n** coffee break
die Kalorie, -n calorie
*****kalt (ä)** cold
*****die Kamera, -s** camera
der Kamin, -e fireplace
*****der Kamm, ¨e** comb
*****(sich) kämmen** to comb one's hair
der Kampf, ¨e fight
*****kämpfen** to fight

(das) **Kanada** Canada; **der Kanadier, -/die Kanadierin, -nen** Canadian; **kanadisch** Canadian

der Kanzler, -/die Kanzlerin, -nen chancellor

*__kaputt__ broken; exhausted; **kaputt·fahren (ä; u, [ist] a)** to drive until worn out; **kaputt·gehen (ging, [ist] gegangen)** to go to pieces; **kaputt·machen** to break

die Karibik Caribbean

*__die Karte, -n__ card; menu; ticket

*__die Kartoffel, -n__ potato; **der Kartoffelsalat, -e** potato salad

*__der Käse, -__ cheese

*__die Kasse, -n__ box office; cashier

*__die Kassette, -n__ cassette; *__der Kassettenrecorder, -__ cassette recorder

katastrophal catastrophic

*__die Katze, -n__ cat

der Kauf, ⸚e purchase

*__kaufen__ to buy

die Kauffrau, -en /der Kaufmann, ⸚er or -leute merchant; **das Kaufhaus, ⸚er** department store

*__kaum__ hardly

*__kein__ no, not a, none, not any; **kein...mehr** no longer; (pronoun) **kein (-er, -es, -e)** no one

*__der Keller, -__ cellar, basement

*__der Kellner, -__ waiter; **die Kellnerin, -nen** waitress

*__kennen (a, a)__ to know; to be acquainted with

*__kennen·lernen__ to meet, become acquainted with

die Kernkraft nuclear power

die Kerze, -n candle

das Kilo, -s kilogram

*__das Kilogramm, -e__ kilogram

*__der Kilometer, -__ kilometer

*__das Kind, -er__ child

das Kindchen, - (diminutive of **Kind**) child

der Kindergarten, ⸚ kindergarten

das Kinderspiel, -e children's game

*__das Kino, -s__ cinema; **im ~** at the movies; **ins ~** to the movies

der Kiosk, -e kiosk

*__die Kirche, -n__ church

das Kissen, - pillow

die Klammer, -n parenthesis

*__klar__ (dat.) clear; certainly

*__die Klasse, -n__ class; **erster ~** first class; **klasse** (coll.) great

klassisch classical

klatschen to applaud; to gossip (coll.)

*__die Klausur, -en__ examination

*__das Klavier, -e__ piano; **die Klavierstunde, -n** piano lesson

*__das Kleid, -er__ dress

kleiden to dress

*__die Kleidung__ clothing

*__klein__ little

klettern [ist] (auf + acc.) to climb (onto, up)

das Klima climate

die Klingel, -n bell

klingeln to ring; **es klingelt** the (door) bell is ringing

*__klopfen__ to knock; **es klopft** there's a knock at the door

*__klug (ü)__ clever, intelligent

knallvoll full to bursting (coll.)

die Kneipe, -n pub

das Knie, - knee

der Koch, ⸚e/die Köchin, -nen cook

*__der Koffer, -__ trunk, suitcase; *__der Kofferraum, ⸚e__ trunk (car)

*__der Kollege, -n, -n/die Kollegin, -nen__ colleague

(das) **Köln** Cologne

die Kombination, -en combination

komfortabel comfortable

komisch funny; strange

das Komitee, -s committee

das Komma, -s comma

*__kommen (kam, [ist] o)__ to come

der Kommilitone, -n, -n/die Kommilitonin, -nen fellow student

die Komparation, -en comparison

der Komparativ comparative form

komplett complete

komplimentieren to compliment

komponieren to compose

der Komponist, -en, -en/die Komponistin, -nen composer

das Kompositum, Komposita compound (word)

*__die Konditorei, -en__ pastry shop; café

die Konjunktion, -en conjunction

der Konjunktiv subjunctive

*__können__ can, to be able to

der Kontakt, -e contact

sich konzentrieren to concentrate

*__das Konzert, -e__ concert, recital

koordinierend coordinating

*__der Kopf, ⸚e__ head; **ihr fällt die Decke auf den ~** she's getting cabin fever; **die Kopfschmerzen** (pl.) headache

*__der Korb, ⸚e__ basket

*__der Körper, -__ body

korrespondieren to correspond

*__korrigieren__ to correct

(das) **Korsika** Corsica

*__kosten__ to cost; to try a food; **das Kotelett, -s** cutlet, chop

das Kraftwerk, -e power station

*__krank (ä)__ ill

der/die Kranke (noun decl. like adj.) patient

*__das Krankenhaus, ⸚er__ hospital

der Krankenpfleger, - nurse (m.)

*__die Krankenschwester, -n__ nurse (f.)

*__der Krankenwagen, -__ ambulance

*__die Krankheit, -en__ illness

*__die Krawatte, -n__ tie

*__die Kreide, -n__ chalk

*__der Krieg, -e__ war

der **Krimi, -s** detective story or film

der **Kriminalroman, -e** detective novel

die **Kritik, -en** criticism

der **Kritiker, -/die Kritikerin, -nen** critic

*__kritisieren__ to criticize

*die **Küche, -n** kitchen; der **Küchenplan, ⁻e** kitchen schedule; der **Küchentisch, -e** kitchen table

*der **Kuchen, -** cake

*der **Kugelschreiber, -** ballpoint pen

*die **Kuh, ⁻e** cow

*__kühl__ cool, chilly

*der **Kühlschrank, ⁻e** refrigerator

der **Kuli, -s** ballpoint pen

die **Kultur, -en** culture; **kulturell** cultural

der **Kummer** sorrow, grief

der **Kunde, -n, -n/die Kundin, -nen** customer

*die **Kunst, ⁻e** art; das **Kunstmuseum, -museen** art museum; das **Kunstwerk, -e** work of art

*die **Künstler, -/die Künstlerin, -nen** artist

*der **Kurs, -e** course

*__kurz (ü)__ short

die **Kurzgeschichte, -n** short story

*die **Kusine, -n** cousin (fem.)

der **Kuß, Küsse** kiss

*__küssen__ to kiss

lächeln (über + acc.) to smile (about)

*__lachen__ (über + acc.) to laugh (about)

*der **Laden, ⁻** store

laden (ä; u, a) to load

*die **Lampe, -n** lamp

*das **Land, ⁻er** land, state, country; **auf dem ~** in the country; **aufs ~** to the country

landen [ist] to land

*die **Landschaft, -en** landscape

*__lang (ä)__ long

*__lange__ a long time

*__langsam__ slow

sich langweilen to be bored

*__langweilig__ boring

*der **Lärm** noise

*__lassen (ä; ließ, a)__ to let; to leave; **(etwas) kommen ~** to order; to have delivered (something)

der **Lastwagen, -** truck

*__laufen (äu; ie, [ist] au)__ to run

*die **Laune, -n** mood; **guter ~ sein** to be in a good mood

*__laut__ noisy, loud

läuten to ring; **es läutet** the (door) bell is ringing

*__leben__ to live

*das **Leben, -** life; **am ~ sein** to be alive; die **Lebensweise, -n** manner of living; life style

*__lebendig__ lively; alive

*die **Lebensmittel** (pl.) food, provisions; das **Lebensmittelgeschäft, -e** grocery store

lecker delicious

das **Leder, -** leather

ledig single, unmarried

*__leer__ empty

legal legal

*__legen__ to lay, put; **sich ~** to lie down

der **Lehnstuhl, ⁻e** armchair

*__lehren__ to teach

*der **Lehrer, -/die Lehrerin, -nen** teacher

*__leicht__ easy; light

das **Leid** pain, suffering, torment

*__leid tun__ (+ dat.) to feel sorry

*__leiden (litt, gelitten)__ (an + dat.) to suffer (from)

*__leider__ unfortunately

leihen (ie, ie) to lend; to borrow

*__leise__ soft, quiet

*__sich leisten__ to afford

leiten to lead

der **Leiter, -/die Leiterin, -nen** leader, director

*__lernen__ to learn

*__lesen (ie; a, e)__ to read

der **Leser, -/die Leserin, -nen** reader

*__letzt__ last

*die **Leute** (pl.) people

liberal liberal

*das **Licht, -er** light

*__lieb__ dear; **~ haben** to be fond of; **~ sein** (+ dat.) to be dear to a person

*die **Liebe** love

*__lieben__ to love

*__lieber__ rather

der **Liebling, -e** darling; favorite

der **Liebeskummer** lovesickness; **~ haben** to be lovesick

liebst favorite

*__liebsten: am ~__ like best, most of all

*das **Lied, -er** song

*__liegen (a, e)__ to lie, be located

*die **Limonade, -n** soft drink

link (adj.) left

*__links__ (adv.) left

die **Liste, -n** list

*der **Liter, -** liter

die **Literatur** literature

das **Loch, ⁻er** hole

*der **Löffel, -** spoon

*__los__ released; loose; **was ist los?** what's up?; what's wrong?; what's the matter?

lösen to solve; to loosen, untie

los·fahren (ä; u, [ist] a) to drive off

los·gehen (ging, ist gegangen) to start; to set off

die **Lösung, -en** solution

los·werden (i; u, [ist] o) to get rid of

*die **Luft** air

die **Lotterie, -n** lottery

*die **Luftpost** airmail

die **Lüge, -n** lie

lügen (o, o) to lie

*die **Lust** pleasure; desire; **~ (an + dat.)** pleasure (in); **~ (auf + acc.)** desire (for); **~ haben** to be in the mood, to feel like

*__lustig__ jolly, amusing; **sich über etwas oder jemanden ~ machen** to make fun of something or somebody

*__machen__ to make; to do

*das **Mädchen, -** girl

*der **Magen, ⁻** stomach

mähen to mow

makaber macabre

***mal** once; **[drei]mal** [three] times; *flavoring particle to soften commands*

***das Mal, -e** time(s)

***malen** to paint

der Maler, -/die Malerin, -nen painter

***man** one *(impersonal pron.)*

der Manager, -/die Managerin, -nen manager

***manch (-er, -es, -e)** many a; some; **manch ein** many a

***manchmal** sometimes

***der Mann, ⸚er** man; husband; **männlich** male, masculine

***der Mantel, ⸚** coat

das Manuskript, -e manuscript

die Mappe, -n briefcase

***das Märchen, -** fairy tale

***die Mark** mark *(German monetary unit)*

***der Markt, ⸚e** market; **die Marktfrau, -en** market woman; **der Marktplatz, ⸚e** marketplace

***die Marmelade, -n** jam

***die Maschine, -n** machine; engine; airplane

massieren to massage; **sich ~ lassen** to get a massage

das Match, ä ⸚e match

***die Mathematik** mathematics

***die Mauer, -n** wall

***der Mechaniker, -/die Mechanikerin, -nen** mechanic

mechanisch mechanical

das Medikament, -e medicine, drug

***die Medizin** medicine; drug; field of medicine

medizinisch medical

***das Meer, -e** sea, ocean; **ans ~ fahren** to go to the sea(side)

***mehr** more; **immer ~** more and more

***mehrere** several

mehrtägig of several days' duration

***meinen** to be of the opinion; to intend; to mean

***meinetwegen** as far as I am concerned

***die Meinung, -en** opinion; **meiner ~ nach** in my opinion; **ich bin deiner ~** I am of your opinion

***meist** most

***meistens** mostly

melden to inform, notify

die Melodie, -n melody

***die Menge, -n** (great) quantity; crowd

***der Mensch, -en, -en** human being; **Mensch!** man!

menschlich human

***merken** to notice; to realize

***merkwürdig** strange; remarkable

***das Messer, -** knife

der Meteorologe, -n, -n/die Meteorologin, -nen weather forecaster

***der Meter, -** meter

***der Metzger, -/die Metzgerin, -nen** butcher; **zum~** to the meat market

***die Metzgerei, -en** butcher shop

***die Miete, -n** rent

***mieten** to rent

der Mieter, -/die Mieterin, -nen tenant

***die Milch** milk

die Milliarde, -n billion

***die Million, -en** million

mindestens at least

***die Minute, -n** minute

mischen to mix

mißverstehen (mißverstand, mißverstanden) to misunderstand

***mit** (+ *dat.*) with; at; by

der Mitarbeiter, -/die Mitarbeiterin, -nen collaborator, coworker

der Mitbewohner, -/die Mitbewohnerin, -nen roommate

mit·bringen (brachte, gebracht) to bring along

***miteinander** together; with each other

mit·fahren (ä; u, [ist] a) to drive along

mit·gehen (ging, [ist] gegangen) to go along

das Mitglied, -er member

mit·haben to have something with one

mit·kommen (kam, [ist] o) to come along

das Mitleid (mit) pity; compassion (for)

mit·machen to go along (with); to join in; **~ bei** to participate in (a group)

mit·nehmen (nimmt; a, genommen) to take along

mit·spielen to join in

***der Mittag, -e** noon; **zu ~ essen** to have lunch/dinner; **morgen mittag** noon tomorrow

***das Mittagessen, -** lunch/dinner

***mittags** at noon; **die Mittagspause, -n** lunch hour

***die Mitte, -n** center

mitten in in the middle (of)

die Mitternacht midnight

***die Möbel** *(pl.)* furniture

möblieren to furnish

das Modalverb, -en modal auxiliary

modern modern

***mögen** to like

***möglich** possible; *(dat.)* **es ist [mir]~** it is possible for (me); **möglichst [bald]** as [soon] as possible

die Möglichkeit, -en possibility

***der Moment, -e** moment

***der Monat, -e** month

***der Mond, -e** moon

das Moped, -s small motorcycle

die Moral morals; moral (of story)

***morgen** tomorrow

***der Morgen, -** morning

morgendlich morning

***morgens** in the morning

***der Motor, -en** motor, engine

***das Motorrad, ⸚er** motorcycle

***müde** tired

die Müdigkeit tiredness

der Müll trash, refuse; **der Mülleimer, -** garbage can

***der Mund, ⸚er** mouth

*das Museum, Museen museum

*die Musik music; musikalisch musical

der Musiker, -/die Musikerin, -nen musician, composer

die Musikhochschule, -n conservatory

der Musiklehrer, -/die Musiklehrerin, -nen music instructor

der Musikprofessor, -en/die Musikprofessorin, -nen music professor

das Musikstück, -e composition

das Musikstunde, -n music lesson

*müssen (muß; mußte, gemußt) to have to; must

der Mut courage, spirit; mutig courageous

*die Mutter, ⸚ mother; der Muttertag Mother's Day

die Mütze, -n hat, cap

na well; come now; what did I tell you

*nach (+ dat.) after; according to

*der Nachbar, -n, -n/die Nachbarin, -nen neighbor

*nachdem afterwards; after

*nachher later

*der Nachmittag, -e afternoon

nachmittags in the afternoon

der Nachname, -ns, -n last name

die Nachricht, -en message; (plural) news; Nachrichten-magazin, -e news magazine

nach·schauen to go and see; to gaze after

*nächst next

*die Nacht, ⸚e night; in der ~ at night

der Nachteil, -e disadvantage

*der Nachtisch, -e dessert

*nahe (näher, nächst-) near, close; ~ der Uni near the university

*nähen to sew

naiv naive

die Naivität naïveté

*der Name, -ns, -n name

*nämlich of course; namely; you see

*die Nase, -n nose

*naß wet

die Nation, -en nation

*die Natur nature; disposition; von ~ aus by nature

*natürlich natural; of course

die Naturwissenschaft, -en natural or physical science

der Nebel, - mist, fog; neblig foggy

*neben (+ acc./dat.) next to, beside; nebenan next door; nebeneinander next to each other

der Nebensatz, ⸚e dependent clause

*der Neffe, -n, -n nephew

negativ negative

*nehmen (nimmt; a, genommen) to take

neidisch (auf + acc.) envious (of)

*nein no

*nennen (nannte, genannt) to call

der Nerv, -en nerve; es geht mir auf die Nerven that gets on my nerves

nervös nervous

*nett nice, kind; pleasant

*neu new

*neugierig (auf + acc.) curious (about)

*nicht not; nicht nur...sondern auch not only...but also

*die Nichte, -n niece

der Nichtraucher, -/die Nichtraucherin, -nen non-smoker

*nichts nothing

*nie never

nieder down

niedrig low

niemals never, ever

*niemand nobody; ~ mehr no one else

Nikolaus Saint Nicholas (brings gifts on Dec. 6)

nimmermehr never

*nirgends nowhere

nö (coll.) no

*noch still, yet; in addition; ~ einmal again; ~ mehr even more

der Nominativ nominative case

(das) Nordamerika North America

*der Norden north; nördich northern

(das) Norwegen Norway

die Note, -n grade; note

*nötig necessary

die Nudel, -n noodle

*die Null, -en zero

*die Nummer, -n number

*nun now

*nur only

nützen (+ dat.) to be of use; nützlich profitable; advantageous; (dat.) du warst [mir] ~ you were helpful to [me]

o oh; ~ je oh dear

*ob if, whether

*oben above; upstairs; nach ~ gehen to go upstairs

*der Ober, - waiter

*oberhalb (+ gen.) above

obgleich (conj.) although, even though

das Objekt, -e object

obschon (conj.) although, even though

*das Obst fruit; die Obsttorte, -n cake with fruit on top

*obwohl (conj.) although

*oder (conj.) or

*der Ofen, ⸚ stove; oven

*offen open; frank

öffentlich public

*öffnen to open

*oft (ö) often

*ohne (+ acc.) without; ohne daß without; *ohne...zu (+ inf.) without

oh oh

*das Ohr, -en ear; der Ohrring, -e earring

ökologisch ecologic

das Öl, -e oil

*die Oma, -s grandma

*der Onkel, - uncle

*der Opa, -s grandpa

die Oper, -n opera

die **Opposition** opposition (party)

der **Optimist, -en, -en**/die **Optimistin, -nen** optimist

optimistisch optimistic

die **Orange, -n** orange; der **Orangensaft, ⁻e** orange juice

das **Orchester, -** orchestra

ordentlich orderly, neat, tidy

die **Ordinalzahl, -en** ordinal number

die **Ordnung, -en** order, regulation; arrangment; **in ~ bringen** to put something in order; to repair

die **Organisation, -en** organization

*der **Ort, -e** place, spot

*der **Osten** east; Orient; **östlich** eastern

(das) **Ostern** (pl.) Easter

(das) **Österreich** Austria

das **Ozonloch** hole in the ozone layer

*das **Paar, -e** pair; couple

*paar: ein ~ a few

das **Päckchen, -** small parcel

*packen to pack (up); to grab

*das **Paket, -e** package; bundle

*das **Papier, -e** paper; document

das **Parfum, -s** perfume

*der **Park, -s** park

*parken to park

das **Parkhaus, ⁻er** parking garage

*der **Parkplatz, ⁻e** parking space

die **Partei, -en** party (political)

die **Partikel, -n** particle

das **Partizip** participle; das ~ **Perfekt** past participle; das ~ **Präsens** present participle

*der **Partner, -**/die **Partnerin, -nen** partner; spouse; die **Partnerarbeit** work in pairs

*die **Party, -s** party; der **Partyservice** caterer

der **Paß, Pässe** passport

*passen (+ dat.) to fit

*passieren [ist] (+ dat.) to happen, to take place

das **Passiv** passive voice

*der **Patient, -en, -en**/die **Patientin, -nen** patient

die **Pension, -en** pension; small hotel

*die **Person, -en** person

das **Personalpronomen** personal pronoun

persönlich personal

die **Persönlichkeit, -en** personality; noted personality

der **Pfeffer** pepper

*der **Pfennig, -e** one hundredth of a mark

*das **Pferd, -e** horse

pflanzen to plant

*die **Pflanze, -n** plant

pflegen to nurse, to take care of

die **Pflicht, -en** duty

*das **Pfund, -e** pound

die **Phantasie, -en** imagination; fantasy

phantastisch fantastic, marvelous

die **Philosophie, -n** philosophy

das **Photo, -s** photograph

die **Photographie, -n** photography; picture

der **Pianist, -en, -en**/die **Pianistin, -nen** pianist

*das **Picknick, -s** or **-e** picnic

die **Pizza, -s** pizza

die **Pizzeria, -s** pizzeria

*der **Plan, ⁻e** plan

planen to plan; to design

*die **Platte, -n** record; *der **Plattenspieler, -** record player

*der **Platz, ⁻e** place; seat

*plötzlich suddenly

das **Plusquamperfekt** past perfect tense

(das) **Polen** Poland

*die **Politik** politics; *der **Politiker, -**/die **Politikerin, -nen** politician; **politisch** political

*die **Polizei** police; police station; das **Polizeiprotokoll, -e** police report

*der **Polizist, -en, -en**/die **Polizistin, -nen** police officer

das **Portemonnaie, -s** billfold, wallet

die **Portion, -en** portion, ration

das **Porträt, -s** portrait

das **Possessivpronomen, -** possessive adjective

*die **Post** post office; mail

*das/der **Poster, -** poster

*die **Postkarte, -n** postcard

die **Postleitzahl, -en** zip code

das **Prädikatnomen, -** predicate noun

das **Präfix, -e** prefix

*praktisch practical

die **Praline, -n** chocolate candy

die **Präposition, -en** preposition

das **Präsens** present tense

der **Präsident, -en, -en**/die **Präsidentin, -nen** president

das **Präteritum** simple past tense

die **Praxis** practice; practice (of a doctor, lawyer)

*der **Preis, -e** price; prize

das **Preisausschreiben** contest

*prima great; first rate

privat private; der **Privathaushalt** residence; das **Privatleben** private life, privacy; der **Privatunterricht** private lessons

*pro per, for

probieren to try out; to taste; to test

*das **Problem, -e** problem

das **Produkt, -e** product; outcome

produktiv productive

produzieren to produce

*der **Professor, -en**/die **Professorin, -nen** professor

*das **Programm, -e** program; schedule; der **Programmleiter, -**/die **Programmleiterin, -nen** director of events

das **Projekt, -e** project

das **Pronomen, Pronomina** pronoun

das **Prozent, -e** percent, percentage

prüfen to test

*die **Prüfung, -en** examination

die **Psychologie** psychology

psychologisch psychological

*das Publikum** audience; public

der Pudding pudding

*der Pullover, -** sweater

der Pulli, -s sweater

der Punkt, -e dot; point; period

*pünktlich** on time; punctual

die Puppe, -n doll

*putzen** to clean; to polish

der Quadratmeter, - square meter

das Quiz quiz; **die Quizsendung, -en** radio or T.V. quiz show

*das Rad, ⁻er** wheel; bicycle; **die Radtour, -en** bicycle tour

*rad·fahren (ä; u, [ist] a)** to ride a bike; **ich fahre Rad** I ride a bicycle

*das Radio, -s** radio

der Rasen, - lawn

*der Rasierapparat, -e** razor; shaver

*sich rasieren** to shave

*der Rat** advice, suggestion; *das Rathaus, ⁻er** town hall

das Rate-Quiz name of quiz show

*raten (ä; ie, a) (+ dat. of person)** to advise (someone); to guess

der Rauch smoke; **der Raucher, -/die Raucherin, -nen** smoker

*rauchen** to smoke

*der Raum, ⁻e** room; space

raus·tragen (ä; u, a) to carry outside

reagieren to react

realisieren to realize; to carry out

rechnen to calculate

die Rechnung, -en bill

*recht** right; just; **einigen Menschen kann man es nie ~ machen** you just can't please some people; **~ haben** to be right; **nichts ~ machen** to do nothing right; **das ist mir ~** it suits me

*das Recht, -e** right; law; justice

*rechts** to or on the right side

*der Rechtsanwalt, ⁻e/die Rechtsanwältin, -nen** lawyer

der Recorder, - recorder

die Rede, -n speech; **eine ~ halten** to give a speech; **indirekte ~** indirect discourse

*reden (über + acc. or von)** to talk (about or of)

der Redner, -/die Rednerin, -nen speaker

*das Referat, -e** report, essay; **ein ~ halten** to give a report

reflexiv reflexive

das Regal, -e shelf

die Regel, -n rule

*der Regen** rain; **der Regenmantel, ⁻** raincoat; *der Regenschirm, -e** umbrella; **der saure Regen** acid rain

*die Regierung, -en** government

der Regisseur, -e/die Regisseurin, -nen director

*regnen** to rain; **regnerisch** rainy

*reich** rich

*die Reihe, -n** row; **du bist an der ~** it's your turn; **die Reihenfolge, -n** sequence

*rein** clear; pure

rein·halten (ä; ie, a) to keep clean

*der Reis** rice

*die Reise, -n** journey, tour; **gute ~** have a good trip!; **das Reisebüro, -s** travel agency; **der Reiseführer, -** travel guide; guidebook; **die Reiseroute, -n** itinerary; **das Reiseziel, -e** destination

*reisen [ist]** to travel

*reiten (ritt, [ist] geritten)** to ride (a horse)

die Reklame, -n advertisement

das Relativpronomen, - relative pronoun

der Relativsatz, ⁻e relative clause

*rennen (rannte [ist] gerannt)** to run; to race

das Rennen, - race

die Renovierung, -en renovation

die Rente, -n pension

der Rentner, -/die Rentnerin, -nen pensioner; **~ sein** to be retired

die Reparatur, -en repair; **in ~** being repaired

*reparieren** to repair

*reservieren** to reserve

*das Restaurant, -s** restaurant

*retten** to save

das Rezept, -e recipe; prescription

*richtig** right

*die Richtung, -en** direction

*riechen (o, o) (nach)** to smell (of)

riesig gigantic, immense

der Ring, -e ring

*der Rock, ⁻e** skirt; coat

*der Rock** rock music; **die Rockband, -s** rock band; **die Rockmusik** rock music; **das Rockkonzert, -e** rock concert

*roh** raw; brutal

*die Rolle, -n** role; **das Rollenspiel, -e** role play

die Rollerblades rollerblades; **~ fahren** to go rollerblading

der Roman, -e novel

der Röntgenstrahl, -en x-ray

*rot (ö)** red

die Routinearbeit, -en routine job

der Rücken, - back

die Rückfahrkarte, -n return ticket

der Rucksack, ⁻e backpack

die Rücksicht, -en discretion; consideration

die Rücksichtslosigkeit inconsiderateness

*rufen (ie, u)** to call

die Ruhe quiet; peace

das Ruhekissen, - bolster; see **Gewissen**

ruhen to rest

*ruhig** quiet, silent

*rund** round

russisch Russian

*die Sache, -n matter; thing;
   die Sachen things (clothes)
der Sack, ⁚e sack, bag
*der Saft, ⁚e juice
*sagen to say, tell
*die Sahne cream
*der Salat, -e salad; lettuce; die
   Salatsauce, -n salad
   dressing
das Salz, -e salt
*sammeln to collect
sanft gentle, easy; smooth
der Sänger, -/die Sängerin, -
   nen singer
*satt satisfied with food or
   drink
*der Satz, ⁚e sentence; der
   Satzteil, -e phrase
*sauber clean; sauber·machen
   to clean
*sauer sour; angry
saufen (äu; soff, gesoffen) to
   drink (excessively or like an
   animal)
saugen to suck; to vacuum
*das Schach chess
*schade (um) what a pity
   (about)
*schaden (+ dat.) to harm, to
   hurt
schädlich harmful
*schaffen to get it done
schaffen (schuf, a) to produce,
   create
schälen to peel
*die Schallplatte, -n record
*scharf (ä) hot; sharp
der Schatten, - shade; shadow
schätzen to value; to guess
schauen to look
das Schauspiel, -e drama,
   play
der Schauspieler, - actor /die
   Schauspielerin, -nen
   actress
der Scheck, -s check
scheiden (ie, ie) to separate;
   sich ~ lassen to get a
   divorce
der Schein, -e gleam, shine;
   appearance; certificate
*scheinen (ie, ie) to shine; to
   appear; es scheint it
   appears, seems
*schenken to give as a present

*schick chic
*schicken to send; ~ nach to
   send for
*schieben (o, o) to push
*schießen (o, geschossen) to
   shoot
*das Schiff, -e ship
schimpfen (auf or über + acc.)
   to complain (about); to scold
*der Schirm, -e umbrella
der Schlaf sleep; der
   Schlafsack, ⁚e sleeping bag;
   *das Schlafzimmer, -
   bedroom
*schlafen (ä; ie, a) to sleep
schläfrig sleepy
der Schlag, ⁚e blow, stroke
*schlagen (ä; u, a) to hit; to
   beat
die Schlagzeile, -n headline
die Schlange, -n snake;
   waiting line, queue
*schlank slender
*schlecht bad; spoiled
*schließen (o, geschlossen) to
   shut
*schließlich finally; after all
*schlimm severe; bad
*das Schloß, Schlösser lock;
   castle
der Schluß, Schlüsse end;
   conclusion; ~ machen to
   finish; to call it a day; am ~
   at the end; Schlüsse ziehen
   to draw conclusions
*der Schlüssel, - key
*schmal narrow; slim, slender
*schmecken to taste; das
   schmeckt mir it tastes good
(sich) schminken to put on
   make-up
der Schmutz dirt
*schmutzig dirty
schnarchen to snore
*der Schnee snow
*schneiden (schnitt,
   geschnitten) to cut
*schneien to snow
*schnell fast, quick
*das Schnitzel, - cutlet
*die Schokolade, -n chocolate;
   der Schokoladenkuchen
   chocolate cake
*schon already
*schön beautiful; nice; OK

*der Schrank, ⁚e closet
schrecklich frightful, horrible;
   very (coll.)
*schreiben (ie, ie) (an + acc.) to
   write (to someone)
die Schreibmaschine, -n
   typewriter
*der Schreibtisch, -e desk
schreien (ie, ie) to scream,
   shout
der Schritt, -e step
schüchtern shy
*der Schuh, -e shoe
die Schularbeit, -en
   homework, home assignment
die Schuld, -en obligation;
   debt; fault; blame; schuld
   sein (an + dat.) to be guilty
   (of)
*schulden to owe
*schuldig guilty; indebted;
   (dat.) er ist mir Geld
   schuldig he owes me money
   schuldlos (an + dat.) blameless
   (of)
*die Schule, -n school; zur ~
   gehen to go to school
*der Schüler, -/die Schülerin, -
   nen pupil
die Schüssel, -n bowl
schützen to protect
*schwach weak
*schwarz black
(das) Schweden Sweden
*das Schwein, -e pig; ~ haben
   to be lucky
*die Schweiz Switzerland; in
   die ~ to Switzerland
*der Schweizer, -/die
   Schweizerin, -nen Swiss
*schwer heavy; difficult
   schwer·fallen (ä; fiel, [ist]
   gefallen) to find difficult
*die Schwester, -n sister
schwierig difficult, hard
die Schwierigkeit, -en
   difficulty
*das Schwimmbad, ⁚er
   swimming pool
das Schwimmbecken, -
   swimming pool
*schwimmen (a [ist] o) to swim
*der See, -n lake
*die See sea

das Segel, - sail; **das
Segelboot, -e** sailboat
*segeln [ist] to sail
*sehen (ie; a, e) to see
die Sehnsucht (nach) longing
(for)
*sehr very, greatly, much
*die Seife, -n soap
*sein to be
seinetwegen on his account
*seit (+ dat.) since
*seit (conj.) since; *seitdem
(conj.) since; (adv.) since
then
*die Seite, -n page; side
*der Sekretär, -e/die
Sekretärin, -nen secretary
der Sekt champagne
*die Sekunde, -n second
*selber oneself
*selbst oneself; **selbständig**
self-supporting, independent;
selbstverständlich obvious;
of course
*selten rare
*das Semester, - semester; **der
Semesterbeginn** beginning
of the semester; **das
Semesterende** end of the
semester
*das Seminar, -e seminar; **die
Seminararbeit, -en** seminar
paper; **der Seminarraum, ¨e**
seminar room
*senden (sandte, gesandt) to
send; **(gesendet)** to
broadcast
die Sendung, -en broadcast,
program (radio, TV)
der Service service
*der Sessel, - armchair
*setzen to set; to place; **sich
setzen** to sit down
*sicher secure; sure; certainly
die Sicherheit security
sicherlich certainly
das Silvester New Year's Eve
*singen (a, u) to sing
der Sinn, -e sense; **aus dem ~**
out of one's mind (forgotten);
sinnlos foolish; meaningless
die Situation, -en situation
*sitzen (saß, gesessen) to sit
skeptisch skeptical,
suspicious

*der Ski, -er ski; **~ laufen, ~
fahren (ich fahre Ski; ich
bin Ski gefahren)** to ski
skrupellos unscrupulous
die Skulptur, -en sculpture
der Smog smog
*so so; **so ein** such as;
*so...wie as...as
*sobald as soon as
*die Socke, -n sock
so daß (conj.) so that
*das Sofa, -s couch, sofa
*sofort immediately
*sogar even
*sogleich at once
*der Sohn, ¨e son
solang(e) (conj.) as long as
*solch (-er, -es, -e) such
*der Soldat, -en, -en/die
Soldatin, -nen soldier
*sollen to be obliged
*der Sommer, - summer
*sondern (conj.) but, on the
contrary
*die Sonne, -n sun; **die
Sonnenbrille, -n** sunglasses
sonnig sunny
*sonst else, otherwise; **~ nach
etwas?** anything else?
sooft (conj.) as often as
*die Sorge, -n sorrow; care;
mach dir keine Sorgen
don't worry; **sich Sorgen um
jemanden machen** to worry
about someone
sorgen für to take care of, look
after
*sorgfältig careful
sortieren to sort
*soviel (adv.) so much; (conj.)
as far as, as much as
*sowieso anyhow
*sowohl...als auch (conj.) not
only . . . but also
die Spaghetti (pl.) spaghetti
(das) Spanien Spain
*sparen to save; **sparsam**
economical
*der Spaß, ¨e fun; joke; **es
macht ~** it's fun; **viel ~ !**
have a good time!
*spät late
später later

der Spatz, -en, -en sparrow;
**besser ein ~ in der Hand als
eine Taube auf dem Dach**
(proverb) a bird in the hand is
worth two in the bush
spazieren·fahren (ä; u, [ist] a)
to go for a drive
spazieren·führen to take on a
walk
*spazieren·gehen (ging, [ist]
gegangen) to go for a walk
*der Spaziergang, ¨e walk,
stroll; **einen ~ machen** to go
for a walk
*die Speise, -n food; meal; **die
Speisekarte, -n** menu
spendieren (+ dat.) to treat (to
a drink, meal, etc.)
*der Spiegel, - mirror; **das
Spiegelbild, -er** reflection
*das Spiel, -e play, game; **die
Spielkarte, -n** playing card;
die Spielregel, -n rules of
the game; **die Spielsache, -n**
toy; **der Spielverderber, -**
spoilsport; **das Spielzeug** toy
*spielen to play
*der Sport sport; **~ treiben** to
engage in sports; **das
Sportgeschäft, -e** sporting
goods store; **der Sportplatz, ¨
e** playing field; **der
Sportschuh, -e** athletic
shoe; **der Sportverein, -e**
sports club; **der Sportler, -
/die Sportlerin, -nen**
athlete
*sportlich athletic
*die Sprache, -n language;
speech; **der Sprachkurs, -e**
language course
*sprechen (i; a, o) (über + acc.
or von) to speak; to talk
(about or of)
das Sprichwort, ¨er proverb
*springen (a, [ist] u) to jump
*spülen to rinse; to wash dishes
*die Spülmaschine, -n
automatic dishwasher
*der Staat, -en state; country;
staatlich government
das Stadion, Stadien stadium

*die Stadt, ⸚e town, city; der Stadtteil, -e district; der Stadtpark, -s city park; das Stadtzentrum town center, downtown; die Stadtrundfahrt, -en city sightseeing tour

stammen to originate

*stark (ä) strong

*statt (+ gen.) instead of; statt dessen instead; *statt...zu instead of

die Statue, -n statue

der Stau, -s traffic jam

der Staub dust; ~ saugen to vacuum; ~ wischen to dust; der Staubsauger, - vacuum cleaner

*stecken to stick; to put

*stehen (stand, gestanden) to stand; to be situated

stehen·bleiben (ie, [ist] ie) to stop; to remain standing

die Stehlampe, -n floor lamp

*stehlen (ie; a, o) to steal

steigen (ie; [ist] ie) to climb

*der Stein, -e stone

*die Stelle, -n place; position, job

*stellen to put; eine Frage ~ to pose a question

die Stellung, -en position

*sterben (i; a, [ist] o) to die; an einer Krankheit ~ to die of an illness

*die Stereoanlage, -n stereo set

das Stichwort, -e cue, catchword

der Stil, -e style

*still calm, silent

*die Stimme, -n voice

*stimmen to be correct, be in order; das ~ that's right

stinken (a, u) (nach) to stink (of)

das Stipendium, die Stipendien scholarship

*der Stock, Stockwerke floor, story (of building)

*der Stoff, -e material; topic

stolz (auf + acc.) proud (of)

stören to disturb, interrupt

*stoßen (ö; ie, o) to push; to hit

*die Strafe, -n punishment; fine

der Strand, ⸚e beach

*die Straße, -n street, road

*die Straßenbahn, -en streetcar; das Straßencafé, -s sidewalk café

streichen (i, i) to paint

der Streit quarrel

(sich) streiten (stritt, gestritten) to quarrel

streng strict; harsh

der Streß stress

stressen to stress

*der Strumpf, ⸚e stocking

*das Stück, -e piece; (theater) play

*der Student, -en, -en/die Studentin, -nen student; das Studentencafé, -s a cafe frequented by students; *das Studenten(wohn)heim, -e dormitory

der Studienalltag everyday life at college

das Studienjahr, -e academic year

*studieren to study; to attend a university; ~ an to study at (a university)

das Studium, die Studien study; university education

die Stufe, -n step; level

*der Stuhl, ⸚e chair

*die Stunde, -n hour; lesson; stundenlang for hours; Stundenkilometer (pl.) kilometers per hour

der Stundenplan, ⸚e class schedule

der Sturm, ⸚e storm

stürzen [ist] to plunge, fall

das Subjekt, -e subject

subordinierend subordinating

das Substantiv, -e noun

die Substanz substance

die Suche search

*suchen (nach) to search (for), look for

*der Süden south; südlich southern

super super

der Superlativ, -e superlative

*der Supermarkt, ⸚e supermarket

*die Suppe, -n soup

surfen to (wind) surf

*süß sweet; cute

der Swimmingpool, -s swimming pool

*die Tablette, -n tablet, pill

*die Tafel, -n blackboard; chart

*der Tag, -e day; am ~ during the day; ~ der Arbeit Labor Day; eines Tages one day; das Tagebuch, ⸚er diary; ~ führen to keep a diary; der Tagesablauf, ⸚e daily routine; das Tageblatt, ⸚er daily newspaper

tagelang for days

*täglich daily

*tanken to refuel, fill up

*die Tankstelle, -n gas station

*die Tante, -n aunt

*der Tanz, ⸚e dance

*tanzen to dance

*die Tasche, -n pocket; bag; das Taschenbuch, ⸚er pocket book, paperback; das Taschentuch, ⸚er handkerchief

*die Tasse, -n cup

*die Tat, -en deed, act

*tätig active, busy

die Tätigkeit, -en activity

tatsächlich indeed, really

die Tatwaffe, -n weapon used in a crime

die Taube, -n dove (see Spatz)

*tausend thousand

*das Taxi, -s cab; *der Taxifahrer, -/die Taxifahrerin, -nen cab driver; der Taxistand cab stand

die Technik technology; technique; technisch technical

*der Tee, -s tea

*der Teenager, - teenager

*der Teil, -e part, section

*teilen to divide

teil·nehmen (nimmt; a, genommen) (an + dat.) to take part (in)

der Teilnehmer, -/die Teilnehmerin, -nen participant

das Team, -s team

*das **Telefon, -e** telephone; **ans
~ gehen** to go to the phone;
das **Telefonbuch, ⸚er**
telephone book; das
Telefongespräch, -e
telephone call; die
Telefonnummer, -n
telephone number
*telefonieren to call; **mit
jemandem ~** to speak to
someone on the phone
die **Telefonzelle, -n** phone
booth
*der **Teller, -** plate
*die **Temperatur, -en**
temperature
*das **Tennis** tennis; das
Tennismatch, -s tennis
match; der **Tennisplatz, ⸚e**
tennis court
*der **Teppich, -e** carpet
der **Termin, -e** date, deadline
der **Test, -s** test
*teuer (dat.) expensive; **das ist
[mir] zu teuer** that is too
expensive for me
der **Text, -e** text
*das **Theater, -** theater; **ins ~**
to the theater; **im ~** at the
theater
das **Thema, Themen** theme;
subject
*das **Ticket, -s** ticket
*tief deep
*das **Tier, -e** animal
der **Tip, -s** advice, tip
tippen to tip; to type
*der **Tisch, -e** table; **den Tisch
decken** to set the table; die
Tischdecke, -n tablecloth
das **Tischtennis** table tennis
der **Titel, -** title
toasten to toast
*die **Tochter, ⸚** daughter
der **Tod, -e** death
todmüde dead tired
*die **Toilette, -n** toilet
*toll marvelous, great,
fantastic; mad
die **Tomate, -n** tomato; die
Tomatensauce tomato sauce
der **Ton, ⸚e** sound
*das **Tor, -e** gate
*die **Torte, -n** cake (in layers)
*tot dead

total total
*töten to kill
*die **Tour, -en** tour, trip
*der **Tourist, -en, -en/die
Touristin, -nen** tourist
*tragen (ä; u, a) to carry, to
bear; to wear
trainieren to train, exercise
*trauen (+ dat.) to trust
der **Traum, ⸚e** dream; der
Traumberuf, -e dream job
träumen (von) to dream (of)
*traurig (über + acc.) sad
(about)
*(sich) **treffen (i; traf, o)** to
meet (with somebody)
*treiben (ie, ie) to push, set
into motion; to occupy oneself
with something
trennbar separable
*trennen to separate
*die **Treppe, -n** stairs
*treten (tritt; a, [ist] e) to step
*treu faithful, loyal
*trinken (a, u) to drink
trivial trivial
*trocken dry
*trotz (+ gen.) in spite of
*trotzdem nevertheless
tschüs so long, good-by (coll.)
*das **Tuch, ⸚er** cloth
*tun (tat, getan) to do
*die **Tür, -en** door
der **Turm, ⸚e** tower
turnen to do gymnastics
*die **Tüte, -n** bag
der **Typ, -en** type; **typisch**
typical

*die **U-Bahn, -en** subway
*üben to practice
*über (+ acc./dat.) over, above,
on top; more; by way of;
across
*überall everywhere
überein·stimmen to agree
with
überhaupt generally; really; at
all
*(sich) **überlegen** to reflect on
*übermorgen the day after
tomorrow
übernachten to stay overnight
überprüfen to verify

*überraschen to surprise;
überrascht (durch)
surprised (by)
die **Überraschung, -en**
surprise
überreden to persuade
übersetzen to translate
übertragen (ä; u, a) to
translate; **ins Deutsch ~** to
translate into German
überwinden (a, u) to overcome
überzeugen to convince;
überzeugt (von) convinced
(of)
*übrigens by the way; moreover
*die **Übung, -en** practice,
exercise
*das **Ufer, -** shore, bank
*die **Uhr, -en** clock, watch; die
~ geht nach/vor the watch
is slow/fast
*um (+ acc.) about; around;
approximately; near;
um...willen (+ gen.) for the
sake of
*um...zu in order to
um·fallen (ä; fiel um, [ist] a)
to fall over
die **Umfrage, -n** inquiry; poll
die **Umwelt, -en** environment
umweltfreundlich
environmentally sound
der **Umweltschutz**
environmental protection
die **Umweltverschmutzung**
pollution
*um·ziehen (zog, [ist] gezogen)
to move
der **Umzug** move, change of
residence
unangenehm unpleasant
unbedingt absolute;
unconditional
unbestimmt vague,
undetermined, indefinite
*und (conj.) and; **~ so weiter**
and so on
*der **Unfall, ⸚e** accident
unfreundlich unfriendly
*ungeduldig impatient
*ungefähr about, approximate
ungefährlich not dangerous
*ungesund unhealthy
ungewöhnlich unusual

*das **Unglück, -e** misfortune; accident

unglücklich unhappy

*unhöflich impolite

*die **Uni, -s** (abbrev. for **Universität**)

*die **Universität, -en** university; **an der ~ studieren** to study at the university; **auf die ~ gehen** to go to a university

unkultiviert uncultivated

unlogisch illogical

*unmöglich impossible

unmotiviert unmotivated

unmusikalisch unmusical

unordentlich disorderly, messy

die **Unordnung, -en** disorder; mess

unpersönlich impersonal

unpünktlich unpunctual

das **Unrecht** injustice; fault

unregelmäßig irregular

unruhig restless

der **Unsinn** nonsense

*unten down; downstairs

*unter (+ acc./dat.) under, below, underneath; **~ uns** between you and me

*unterbrechen (i; a, o) to interrupt

die **Untergrundbahn, -en** subway

*unterhalb (+ gen.) under, beneath, below

*unterhalten (ä; ie, a) to entertain; **sich ~ (über + acc.)** to have a conversation (about)

die **Unterhaltung, -en** entertainment; conversation

unternehmen (unternimmt; a, unternommen) to undertake

die **Unternehmung, -en** undertaking

der **Unterricht** instruction

unterrichten to teach

unterscheiden (ie, ie) to distinguish

der **Unterschied, -e** difference

unterschiedlich different

untersuchen to examine

die **Untersuchung, -en** examination

die **Untertasse, -n** saucer

unwahrscheinlich improbable

unwichtig unimportant

unzufrieden dissatisfied

der **Urgroßvater, ∸** great-grandfather

*der **Urlaub, -e** vacation

*die **USA** (pl.) United States of America

*usw. (abbrev. for **und so weiter**) et cetera

die **Vase, -n** vase

*der **Vater, ∸** father

(sich) verabreden to make a date or appointment; **verabredet sein** to have an appointment or date

die **Verabredung, -en** appointment, date

(sich) verändern to change, transform

die **Veränderung, -en** transformation

verantwortlich (für) responsible (for)

die **Verantwortung, -en** responsibility

das **Verb, -en** verb; die **Verbform, -en** verb form

verbessern to improve; to correct

die **Verbesserung, -en** improvement

*verbieten (o, o) to prohibit

verbinden (a, u) to join, connect

*verbringen (verbrachte, verbracht) to spend time

*verdienen to earn; to deserve

*der **Verein, -e** club

die **Vereinigten Staaten** (pl.) United States

die **Vereinigungen** unification

sich verfahren to get lost (driving)

die **Verfilmung, -en** movie version

die **Vergangenheit, -en** past tense

*vergessen (vergißt; vergaß, e) to forget

der **Vergleich, -e** comparison

vergleichen (i, i) (mit) to compare (with)

das **Vergnügen, -** pleasure, fun; **viel ~ !** have a good time!; **zum ~** for fun

die **Vergnügung, -en** entertainment

das **Verhältnis, -se** relations; situation

verheiratet married

sich verirren to get lost

der **Verkäufer, -/die Verkäuferin, -nen** salesperson

*verkaufen to sell

*der **Verkehr** traffic; das **Verkehrsmittel, -** vehicle, means of transportation

*verlangen to demand; to desire

*verlassen (verläßt; verließ, a) to leave; to abandon

sich verlaufen to get lost (walking)

*(sich) verletzen to injure (oneself)

die **Verletzung, -en** injury

sich verlieben to fall in love

verliebt (in + acc.) in love (with)

*verlieren (o, o) to lose

sich verloben (mit) to become engaged (to)

der/die **Verlobte, -n** (noun decl. like adj.) person engaged to be married

vermieten to rent out

der **Vermieter, -** landlord; die **Vermieterin, -nen** landlady

vermissen to miss; to fail to see

vernünftig reasonable, sensible

verpassen to miss (opportunity, train)

verregnet rained out

*verrückt crazy

*verschieden different

die **Verschmutzung** pollution

verschwinden (a; [ist] u) to vanish, disappear

die **Version, -en** version

sich versöhnen to reconcile

sich verspäten to be late

die **Verspätung, -en** delay

*versprechen (i; a, o) to promise; **sich ~** to misspeak

*verstehen (verstand, verstanden) to understand; es versteht sich that is obvious; sich verstehen to get along

der Versuch, -e attempt; experiment

*versuchen to try

*vertrauen (+ *dat.*) to trust

das Vertrauen trust

vervollständigen to complete

verwandt (mit) related (to)

der/die Verwandte (*noun decl. like adj.*) relative

verwechseln to confuse

die Verwechslung, en mix-up

verwenden to use

verzeihen (ie, ie) (+ *dat.* of person) to pardon, forgive

*die Verzeihung pardon

verzweifeln to despair

*der Vetter, -n cousin (*m.*)

der Videorecorder, - video recorder

*viel a lot, much

*vielleicht perhaps

*das Viertel, - fourth; quarter

das Vitamin, -e vitamin; die Vitamintablette, -n vitamin tablet

*der Vogel, ⸚ bird

die Vokabel, -n word, especially from foreign language

das Vokabular, -e vocabulary

*das Volk, ⸚er people; nation; das Volksbad, ⸚er public swimming pool; *das Volkslied, -er folk song; der Volkswirt, -e economist

*voll (von) full (of); complete

*der Volleyball, ⸚e volleyball

völlig total, entire

volljährig of age

vollkommen complete

voll·packen to pack full

das Vollverb, -en main verb

*von (+ *dat.*) of, from, by; ~ jetzt ab from now on

*vor (+ *acc./dat.*) before, previous; in front of; ~ allem above all; ~ Jahren years ago; ~ kurzem recently

*vorbei over; gone

vorbei·kommen (kam, [ist] gekommen) to come by, drop by

*(sich) vor·bereiten (auf + *acc.*) to prepare (for); vorbereitet prepared

die Vorbereitung, -en preparation

der Vorgang, ⸚e process

*vorgestern the day before yesterday

*vor·haben to intend

*der Vorhang, ⸚e curtain, drape

*vorher before; beforehand

*vorig former, preceding, previous

*die Vorlesung, -en lecture

*der Vormittag, -e morning; vormittags mornings

vorn in front

der Vorname, -ns, -n first name

der Vorschlag, ⸚e proposal

*vorschlagen (ä; u, a) to propose, suggest

vorsichtig cautious, careful

die Vorstadt, ⸚e suburb

*vor·stellen to introduce; sich (*dat.*) vor·stellen to imagine

*die Vorstellung, -en performance; introduction; idea

der Vorteil, -e advantage

vor·werfen (i; a, o) to reproach

der Vorwurf, ⸚e reproach

vor·ziehen (zog vor, vorgezogen) to prefer

*wach awake; alert

*wachsen (ä; u, [ist] a) to grow

die Waffe, -n weapon

*der Wagen, - carriage; car

die Wahl, -en choice

*wählen to choose; to elect

*wahr true; real; correct; nicht ~ isn't that true/right?

*während (+ *gen.*) during, (*conj.*) while

*die Wahrheit, -en truth

*wahrscheinlich probably, likely; plausible

die Wahrscheinlichkeit probability

*der Wald, ⸚er forest, woods

*die Wand, ⸚e wall

der Wanderer, -/die Wanderin, -nen hiker

*wandern [ist] to hike, go on foot

der Wanderschuh, -e walking shoe, hiking boot

*die Wanderung, -en hike

*wann when

*die Ware, -n article; goods (*pl.*)

*warm (ä) warm

Warschau Warsaw

warnen (vor + *dat.*) to warn (of)

*warten (auf + *acc.*) to wait (for)

*warum why

*was what

*was für what sort, what kind

das Waschbecken, - sink

*die Wäsche linen, clothes, laundry

waschen (ä; u, a) to wash

*die Waschmaschine, -n washing machine

*das Wasser, - water; die Wasserflasche, -n water bottle

*das WC toilet

*wecken to wake

der Wecker, - alarm clock

*weder (*conj.*) neither; *weder...noch neither . . . nor

*der Weg, -e way; road; path; direction

*weg gone, away; lost

*wegen (+ *gen.*) because of, owing to

*weg·fahren (ä; u, [ist] a) to drive away, go away

*weg·gehen (ging, ist gegangen) to go away

weg·packen to put away

*weg·werfen (i; a, o) to discard, throw away

*weh tun (+ *dat.*) to hurt

*weich soft

*das Weihnachten, - Christmas; der Weihnachtsbaum, ⸚e Christmas tree; die Weihnachtsferien (*pl.*) Christmas vacation

*weil (*conj.*) because, since

*der Wein, -e wine

*weinen to cry

die Weise, -n manner, way, method; auf diese ~ in this way
*weiß white
*weit wide; far, distant; ~ und breit far and wide
*weiter further; additional
weiter·fahren (ä; u, [ist] a) to drive on, ride on
*welch (-er, -es, -e) which
*die Welt, -en world
*wenden (wandte, gewandt) to turn; sich wenden an (+ acc.) to turn to (someone) for help
*wenig little, slightly, not much
*ein wenig a little bit
*wenigstens at least
*wenn (conj.) when, whenever; if
wer who; whoever
*werden (i; u, [ist] o) to become; was ist aus ihm geworden? what has become of him?
*werfen (i; a, o) to throw
*das Werk, -e work; deed; factory; *die Werkstatt, ⸗en workshop; das Werkzeug, -e tool
*wert (dat.) valued; worth; deine Hilfe ist [mir] viel ~ your help means a lot to me
*weshalb why
*wessen whose
*der Westen west; West; westlich western
*das Wetter weather; der Wetterbericht, -e weather report
*wichtig important
widersprechen (i; a, o) to contradict
*wie how
*wieder again
wiederauf·bauen to rebuild
*wiederholen to repeat
wieder·sehen (ie; a, e) to see again
*das Wiedersehen, - reunion; auf ~ good-by
die Wiese, -n meadow
wieso why, how come
*wieviel how much; wie viele how many
wievielten: den ~ haben wir heute? what's today's date?

*willkommen (dat.) welcome
*der Wind, -e wind
*der Winter, - winter
*wirklich really; true
*die Wirklichkeit, -en reality
das Wirtshaus, ⸗er restaurant
die Wirtschaft, -en restaurant; economy
wischen to wipe
das Wissen knowledge; meines Wissens as far as I know
*wissen (weiß; wußte, gewußt) (über + acc. or von) to know (about)
die Wissenschaft, -en science; knowledge; der Wissenschaftler, -/die Wissenschaftlerin, -nen scientist, scholar; wissenschaftlich scientific
*der Witz, -e joke
witzig funny; witty
*wo where; in which
*die Woche, -n week; in einer ~ in one week, next week; vor einer ~ one week ago, last week; *das Wochenende, -n weekend
*woher where from
*wohin where to, where
*wohl well; probably
*wohnen to live, reside
die Wohngemeinschaft, -en unrelated people sharing an apartment; das Wohnheim, -e dormitory; der Wohnnort, -e place of residence; das Wohnzimmer, - living room
*die Wohnung, -en residence; apartment; die Wohnungsnot housing shortage
das wo-Kompositum wo-compound
der Wolf, ⸗e wolf
*die Wolke, -n cloud
*wollen to want, wish; to intend
*das Wort, ⸗er word; -e (pl.) words (in context); beim ~ nehmen to take someone at his/her word; der Wortschatz vocabulary
*das Wörterbuch, ⸗er dictionary
die Wunde, -n wound

*wunderbar wonderful
*wunderschön very beautiful, very nice
*(sich) wundern (über + acc.) to be surprised (at)
*der Wunsch, ⸗e wish
*wünschen to wish; sich etwas ~ to want or wish for something
*die Wurst, ⸗e sausage; das Wurstbrot, -e cold meat sandwich; das Würstchen, - small sausage
wütend (auf + acc.) furious (with, at)

*z.B. (abbrev. for zum Beispiel) for example
*die Zahl, -en number
das Zahlwort: das unbestimmte ~ indefinite (numeral) adjective
*zahlen to pay
*zählen to count
*der Zahn , ⸗e tooth; *der Zahnarzt, ⸗e/die Zahnärztin, -nen dentist; *die Zahnbürste, -n toothbrush; *die Zahnpaste, -n toothpaste
zeichnen to draw, sketch
die Zeichnung, -en drawing, to sketch
*zeigen to show; (auf + acc.) to point (to)
*die Zeile, -n line
*die Zeit, -en time; era; vor kurzer ~ a short while ago; zur ~ at the moment; die Zeitform, -en tense; der Zeitplan, ⸗e schedule
*die Zeitschrift, -en journal; magazine; der Zeitschriftenartikel, - magazine article
*die Zeitung, -en newspaper; der Zeitungsartikel, - newspaper article
*das Zelt, -e tent
*zelten to camp, tent
der Zeltplatz, ⸗e campground
das Zentrum, Zentren center (of a city)
*zerstören to destroy

der Zeuge, -n, -n; die Zeugin, -nen witness
*ziehen (zog, gezogen) to pull; (zog, [ist] gezogen) to move
das Ziel, -e goal, aim
*ziemlich rather; quite
*die Zigarette, -n cigarette
*das Zimmer, - room; die Zimmersuche room hunting
*zu to; too; shut
*der Zucker sugar
*zuerst first; at first
der Zufall, ̈-e chance
zufällig accidental, incidental
*zufrieden (mit) content, satisfied (with)

*der Zug, ̈-e train
zu·hören to listen
die Zukunft future; zukünftig future
zuletzt at last, finally; the last time
zu·machen to close
*zurück back; backwards; behind
zurückhaltend reserved, restrained
zurück·kommen (a, [ist] o) to come back
*zusammen together
zusammen·fassen to summarize

die Zusammenfassung, -en summary
die Zusammenziehung, -en contraction
zu·stimmen to agree to
zuverlässig reliable
*zuviel too much
*zwar to be sure, of course, indeed
*der Zweck, -e purpose
*der Zweifel, - doubt
zweifeln to doubt; ~ an (+ dat.) to doubt
zweimal twice
zweit (-er, -es, -e) second
der Zwilling, -e twin
*zwischen (+ acc./dat.) between

English-German Vocabulary

The English-German end vocabulary contains the words needed in the grammar exercises that require students to express English sentences in German. The definitions provided are limited to the context of a particular exercise. Strong and irregular weak verbs are indicated with a raised degree mark (°). Their principal parts can be found in the Appendix. Separable-prefix verbs are indicated with a raised dot: **an·fahren°**.

about über
accident der Unfall, ⸚e
acquaintance der/die Bekannte, -n *(noun decl. like adj.)*
across über; **~ the street from us** uns gegenüber
act as if tun, als ob
actually eigentlich
advantage der Vorteil, -e
afraid: be ~ (of) Angst haben (vor)
after nach *(prep.)*; nachdem *(conj.)*
afternoon der Nachmittag, -e; **this ~** heute nachmittag; **afternoons** nachmittags
again wieder
ago: years ~ vor Jahren
agree: I ~ with [you] ich bin [deiner] Meinung
airplane das Flugzeug, -e
all all, alle; **~ day** den ganzen Tag; **~ the same to me** mir gleich; **after ~** letzten Endes; **(not) at ~** gar nicht
alone allein
along entlang; **~ the river** den Fluß entlang; **bring ~** mit·bringen°
already schon
also auch

although obwohl
altogether insgesamt
always immer
amazed: to be amazed (at) sich wundern (über)
American der Amerikaner, -/die Amerikanerin, -nen; amerikanisch *(adj.)*
and und
angry böse; **to make ~** ärgern; **to be ~ (about)** sich ärgern (über + *acc.*)
annoy ärgern
answer antworten; **~ a question** auf eine Frage antworten
anymore: not ~ nicht mehr
anything etwas
apartment die Wohnung, -en
apologize sich entschuldigen
apple der Apfel, ⸚
around um; **~ here** hier
arrive kommen°; an·kommen°
as: ~ if als ob; **as . . . as** so...wie
ask fragen
at [seven] um [sieben]; **~ the movies** im Kino; **~ home** zu Hause; **~ the railroad station** am Bahnhof; **~ the post office** auf der Post
Austria Österreich

back zurück; **come back** zurück·kommen°
bad schlecht; **too ~** schade
basement der Keller, -
be sein°
beach der Strand, ⸚e
beat schlagen°
because weil, da; denn; **~ of** wegen
become werden°; **to ~ of** werden aus...
bed das Bett, -en
beer das Bier, -e
before ehe, bevor
behave sich benehmen°
behind hinter
believe glauben (+ *dat.* of person)
belong gehören (+ *dat.*)
beside neben; **besides** außer
best best-
better besser
bicycle das Fahrrad, ⸚er
biking: to go ~ rad·fahren°; **I go ~** ich fahre Rad
bird der Vogel, ⸚
birthday der Geburtstag, -e; **for [one's] ~** zum Geburtstag
bit: a little ~ ein bißchen
bloom blühen
book das Buch, ⸚er
boring langweilig

bottle die Flasche, -n
box office die Kasse; **at the ~** an der Kasse
boy der Junge, -n, -n; **boyfriend** der Freunde, -e
bread das Brot
bring bringen°; **~ along** mit·bringen°
brother der Bruder, ⸚
brown braun
brush: ~ one's teeth sich die Zähne putzen
burn brennen
bus der Bus, -se
but aber; sondern; doch
buy kaufen
by: ~ the way übrigens; **~ Sunday** bis Sonntag

café das Café, -s; **to a ~** ins Café
cake der Kuchen, -
call up (telephone) an·rufen°
can können; **~not be helped** läßt sich nicht ändern
car das Auto, -s, der Wagen
CD die CD, -s
celebrate feiern
change (sich) ändern
cheap billig
cheese der Käse, -
child das Kind, -er
chocolate die Schokolade
city die Stadt, ⸚e; **in(to) the ~** in die Stadt
city hall das Rathaus, ⸚er
claim: to ~ to be sein wollen
class die Klasse, -n; **to travel [first] ~** [erster] Klasse fahren°
clean putzen
close schließen°, zu·machen
clothes die Kleidung; die Sachen (pl.);
clothing die Kleidung
coat der Mantel, ⸚
coffee der Kaffee
cold kalt; die Erkältung; **to catch a ~** sich erkälten
colleague der Kollege, -n, -n/die Kollegin, -nen
comb der Kamm, ⸚e; sich kämmen

come kommen°; **~ with me** komm doch mit; **~ back** zurück·kommen°
command befehlen°
compare vergleichen°
completely ganz
concern: as far as I'm concerned meinetwegen
concert das Konzert, -e
constantly immer; dauernd
conversation: to have a ~ sich unterhalten°
cook kochen
cost kosten
could (subjunctive) könnte
country das Land, ⸚er; **to the ~** aufs Land
course: of ~ selbstverständlich, natürlich
cream die Sahne
cup die Tasse, -n
curious(ly) neugierig
cut schneiden°

day der Tag, -e; **every ~** jeden Tag; **one ~** eines Tages
dear lieb
describe beschreiben°
different andere, anders; **to be of a ~ opinion** anderer Meinung sein
difficult schwer
dinner das Abendessen, -
dishes das Geschirr, -(e)
do machen, tun°
doctor der Arzt, ⸚e/die Ärztin, -nen
dog der Hund, -e
door die Tür, -en
dozen das Dutzend, -e
dream träumen
drink trinken°
drive fahren°
drugstore die Drogerie, -n; **(pharmacy)** die Apotheke, -n; **to the ~** in die (zur) Drogerie/Apotheke
during während

each jed- (-er, -e, -s); **~ other** einander
easy leicht
eat essen°
educated: well ~ gebildet

either: isn't [bad] ~ auch nicht [schlecht]; **~ . . . or** entweder … oder
electrician der Elektriker, -/die Elektrikerin, -nen
elegant elegant
else sonst
English (person) der Engländer, -/die Engländerin, -nen
enough genug
even sogar
evening der Abend, -e; **this ~** heute abend; **in the ~** am Abend, abends
every jed- (-er, -es, -e)
everything alles
excellent ausgezeichnet
exception die Ausnahme, -n
expensive teuer
experience die Erfahrung, -en; erleben
express aus·drücken

family die Familie, -n
famous berühmt, bekannt
father der Vater, ⸚
feel sich fühlen; **~ sorry for** leid tun; **I ~ better** es geht mir (ich fühle mich) besser
few wenige; **a ~** einige; ein paar
film der Film, -e
find finden°
fine: I'm ~ es geht mir gut
first erst; erst einmal; **to travel ~ class** erster Klasse reisen/fahren°/*fliegen°
fish der Fisch, -e
five fünf
flower die Blume, -n
fly fliegen°
follow folgen (+ dat.)
food das Essen, -
for für; **~ [one's] birthday** zum Geburtstag; **~ a long time** lange; **~ a week** seit einer Woche
foreigner der Ausländer, -; die Ausländerin, -nen
forget vergessen°
France (das) Frankreich
French französisch; **~ (language)** (das) Französisch
freeze frieren°

frequently häufig, oft
Friday der Freitag; **on ~** am Freitag
friend der Freund, -e/die Freundin, -nen; der/die Bekannte *(noun decl. like adj.)* **boy ~** Freund; **girl ~** Freundin
friendly freundlich
from von; aus
fry braten°
funny lustig, komisch
furniture die Möbel *(pl.)*

garden der Garten, ⸚
German der/die Deutsche *(noun decl. like adj.)*; **he is ~** er ist Deutscher; **~ (language)** (das) Deutsch
Germany Deutschland
get bekommen°; **~ from Hamburg to Berlin** von Hamburg nach Berlin kommen; **~ lost** sich verfahren, sich verlaufen, sich verirren; **~ tired** müde werden; **~ off** frei bekommen°; **~ in** ein·steigen°; **~ up** auf·stehen°
gift das Geschenk, -e
girl das Mädchen, -; **girlfriend** die Freundin, -nen
give geben°; *(as present)* schenken; **~ an oral report** ein Referat halten
glass das Glas, ⸚er
go *(on foot)* gehen°; *(by vehicle)* fahren°; **~ back** zurück·gehen°
good gut
gram das Gramm, -e
grandparents die Großeltern (pl.)
great toll
grill grillen
guest der Gast, ⸚e

had: ~ to mußte
hair das Haar, -e
happy froh; glücklich
hard schwer; hart
hardly kaum
hasn't: ~ it? nicht? nicht wahr?

have haben; **~ to** müssen; **I don't ~ to help** ich brauche nicht zu helfen; ich muß nicht helfen; **would ~ to** müßte; **~ [the electrician] come** [den Elektriker] kommen lassen; **~ a party** ein Fest machen, eine Party geben
hear hören
help helfen° (+ *dat.*); **can't be helped** läßt sich nicht ändern
here hier; **around ~** hier
hey! Du (informal)
hi Tag!, Hallo
high hoch
hike wandern
history die Geschichte, -n
hold halten°
home: at ~ zu Hause; **~ (direction)** nach Hause
homework die Hausaufgabe, -n
hope hoffen; **I ~** hoffentlich
hot heiß
hour die Stunde, -n; **in an ~** in einer Stunde
house das Haus, ⸚er
how wie; **~ nice** wie schön
hurry (up) sich beeilen
hurt weh tun° (+ *dat.*); schmerzen
husband der Ehemann, ⸚er

ice water das Eiswasser
idea die Idee, -n
if wenn; *(whether)* ob; **~ only** wenn nur
ill krank
immediately sofort
inform informieren
information die Information, -en
inn das Gasthaus, ⸚er; der Gasthof, ⸚e
instead anstatt; **~ of** anstatt…zu
interest interessieren; **to be interested (in)** sich interessieren (für)
interesting interessant
invite ein·laden°
island die Insel, -n
Italy (das) Italien

jacket die Jacke, -n
juice der Saft, ⸚e
just nur

key der Schlüssel, -
kilo das Kilo, -s
Kilometer der Kilometer, -
knife das Messer, -
know *(to know a fact)* wissen°; *(to be acquainted with)* kennen°

lake der See, -n
last letzt; vorig; **~ night** gestern abend
late spät; **to be ~** sich verspäten
later später
laugh lachen
lawyer der Rechtsanwalt, ⸚e/die Rechtsanwältin, -nen
learn lernen
leave lassen°; weg·gehen°; **~ [the café]** [das Café] verlassen°
leg das Bein, -e
less weniger
let lassen°; **let's** laß(t) uns doch
letter der Brief, -e
lie liegen°
life das Leben, -
lightning: it's ~ es blitzt
like wie; *(prep.)* **speak ~ him** so sprechen wie er; **that's just like him** das sieht ihm ähnlich
like mögen; **would [you] ~** möchten [Sie]; **would ~ to help** würde gern helfen°; **~ something** gefallen° (+ *dat.*); **~ someone** gern haben
listen, Trudi hör mal, Trudi!
liter der Liter, -
live wohnen; leben
long lang (e); **a ~ time** lange
longer: no ~ nicht mehr
look schauen; **~ (at)** an·schauen; an·sehen°; **~ for** suchen; **~ as if** aus·sehen°, als ob…
lose verlieren°
lost: to get ~ sich verfahren, sich verlaufen, sich verirren

lot: a ~ viel; **a ~ of** eine Menge

mad: to be mad sich ärgern
make machen; **made of** aus (+ *dat.*)
make-up: to put on ~ sich schminken
man der Mann, ⁼er
many viele
mark die Mark
married couple das Ehepaar, -e
material der Stoff, -e
may dürfen°; **~ be** es mag sein
maybe vielleicht
mean meinen
meat das Fleisch
meet kennen·lernen; begegnen (+ *dat.*); treffen°, sich treffen° mit
milk die Milch
minute die Minute, -n
miserable: I'm ~ es geht mir schlecht
modern modern
Monday der Montag
money das Geld, -er
month der Monat, -e; **next ~** nächsten Monat
more mehr; **any ~** nicht mehr
morning der Morgen, -de; **in the ~** morgens, am Morgen
most meist; **~ of the time** meistens
mother die Mutter, ⁼
mountain der Berg, -e
move (*change residence*) um·ziehen°
movie der Film, -e
movies das Kino, -s; die Filme; **to the ~** ins Kino; **at the ~** im Kino
much viel
museum das Museum, Museen (*pl.*); **to the ~** ins Museum
musician der Musiker, -/die Musikerin, -nen
must müssen; **it ~ be** es muß sein; **you mustn't** du darfst nicht

natural(ly) natürlich
necktie die Krawatte, -n

need brauchen
neighbor der Nachbar, -n, -n/die Nachbarin, -nen
neither . . . nor weder…noch
new neu
next nächst; **next to** neben
nice nett; schön; **how ~** wie schön
night die Nacht, ⁼e; **one ~** eines Nachts
no nein; kein; **~ thanks** nein, danke
Norway (das) Norwegen
not nicht; **~ at all** gar nicht
nothing nichts
nothing more nichts mehr
notice merken, bemerken
now jetzt

obey gehorchen (+ *dat.*)
o'clock: [ten] ~ [zehn] Uhr
of course natürlich, selbstverständlich
off frei; **get ~** frei bekommen
official der Beamte (*noun decl. like adj.*), die Beamtin, -nen
often oft
oh o; **oh;** ach
okay gut; **is it ~** ist es [Ihnen] recht?
old alt
on an; auf; **~ Sunday** am Sonntag; **~ the street** auf der Straße
once einmal
only nur; **if ~ it** wenn es nur
open öffnen
opera die Oper, -n; **to the ~** in die Oper
opinion die Meinung, -en; **in [my] ~** [meiner] Meinung nach; **to be of a different ~** anderer Meinung sein
or oder
order bestellen; **in ~ to** um…zu
ought sollen; **he ~ to** er müßte
out aus
outside draußen
over über
own (*verb*) besitzen°; (*adj.*) eigen

pack packen; ein·packen

paint streichen°
pants die Hose, -n
paper: [seminar] ~ die [Seminar]-arbeit, -en
parents die Eltern (pl.)
park der Park, -s; parken; **to go for a walk through the ~** im Park spazieren·gehen°
party die Party, -s; das Fest, -e; **to have (give) a ~** ein Fest machen (geben)
patient der Patient, -en, -en/die Patientin, -nen
pay bezahlen
people die Leute (*pl.*)
pharmacist der Apotheker, -/die Apothekerin, -nen
photographer Fotograf, -en, -en/die Fotografin, -nen
piano das Klavier, -e
pick up ab·holen
picture das Bild, -er
piece das Stück, -e
plan der Plan, ⁼e
plant die Pflanze, -n
plate der Teller, -
play spielen
please bitte; gefallen (+ *dat.*)
policeman der Polizist, -en, -en/die Polizistin, -nen
post office die Post; **to the ~** auf die (zur) Post; **at the ~** auf der Post
pound das Pfund, -e
practical praktisch
practice üben
prefer vor·ziehen°; lieber; **~ (to drive)** lieber (fahren)
prepare vor·bereiten
pretty hübsch
price der Preis, -e
probably wohl, wahrscheinlich; **~ is (better)** es dürfte (besser) sein
problem das Problem, -e
professor der Professor, -en/die Professorin, -nen
purchase kaufen
purse die Tasche, -n
pull ziehen°
put stellen; stecken; setzen; legen; **~ on (clothing)** an·ziehen°

question die Frage, -n

quick(ly) schnell
quite ganz; ziemlich

railroad station der Bahnhof, ̈e
rain regnen; der Regen
raincoat der Regenmantel, ̈
rather lieber; **I'd ~ watch TV** ich würde lieber fernsehen
react reagieren
read lesen°
ready fertig
realize merken, bemerken
really wirklich
region die Gegend, -en
relative der/die Verwandte *(noun decl. like adj.)*
remember sich erinnern an (+ *acc.*)
remind erinnern
repair reparieren
report das Referat, -e; **give a ~** ein Referat halten°
reserve reservieren
restaurant das Restaurant, -s; **to a ~** ins Restaurant
rice der Reis
right recht; **to be ~** recht haben
river der Fluß, Flüsse
roast braten°
room das Zimmer, -
run laufen°; *(water)* fließen°

salad der Salat, -e
same gleich; **it's all the ~ to [me]** es ist [mir] gleich
sandwich das Brot, -e; **ham ~** das Schinkenbrot
Saturday der Samstag, -e; **on ~** am Samstag
say sagen
sea das Meer, -e; die See, -n
seat der Platz, ̈e
second zweit-
see sehen°; *(to visit)* besuchen; **come to ~ someone** zu Besuch kommen
sell verkaufen
seminar das Seminar, -e; **to the ~** ins Seminar; **~ paper** die Seminararbeit, -en
send schicken; **~ for** kommen lassen°

several einige; mehrere; ein paar
shop das Geschäft, -e; der Laden, ̈
shopping: go ~ ein·kaufen (gehen)
should sollen; **~ go** sollte gehen; **~ have known** hätte wissen sollen
show zeigen
shower (sich) duschen
shut zu·machen; schließen°
shy schüchtern
sick krank
simply einfach
since seit
sing singen°
singer der Sänger, -/die Sängerin, -nen
sister die Schwester, -n
sit sitzen°
sleep schlafen°
slowly langsam
small klein
smart klug (ü)
smell riechen° (nach)
smile lächeln
snow schweien
so so
some manche
something etwas
sometimes manchmal
son der Sohn, ̈e
soon bald
sorry: I'm ~ es tut mir leid; **I feel ~ for (her)** (sie) tut mir leid
Spain (das) Spanien
speak (to or with) sprechen° (mit); reden (mit)
spend (time) verbringen°
spite: in ~ of trotz
spring der Frühling; das Frühjahr
stamp die Briefmarke, -n
stand stehen°
station (train) der Bahnhof, ̈e
stay bleiben°
still noch
store der Laden, ̈, das Geschäft, -e
story die Geschichte, -n
street die Straße, -n **across the ~ from us** uns gegenüber

study studieren; lernen
stupid dumm; doof
subway die U-Bahn, -en
such solch (-er, -es, -e); **~ a** solch ein, so ein
sudden: all of a ~ plötzlich
suddenly plötzlich
suitcase der Koffer, -
summer der Sommer, -
sun die Sonne, -n
Sunday der Sonntag, -e; **on ~** [am] Sonntag
supermarket der Supermarkt, ̈e
supposed to sollen; **~ to be** sollen sein
sure sicher
surely sicher, bestimmt, wohl
surprise überraschen
Sweden (das) Schweden
sweet süß
swim schwimmen°
Switzerland die Schweiz; **to ~** in die Schweiz; **in ~** in der Schweiz

table der Tisch, -e
take nehmen°; bringen°; **~ along** mit·bringen°; mit·nehmen°
talk (to) reden (mit); sprechen° (mit)
tea der Tee, -s
teacher der Lehrer, -/die Lehrerin-nen
tell erzählen
tennis das Tennis
than als
thanks danke
that das; *(conj.)* daß
theater das Theater, -; **to the ~** *(to buy tickets)* zum Theater; **to the ~** *(to see performance)* ins Theater
then dann
there dort; da; **~ is/are** es gibt
these diese
think denken°; glauben; **think about** nach·denken° (über); überlegen
this dies (-er, -es, -e)
through durch; **to go for a walk ~ the park** im Park spazierengehen°

thunder donnern
thunderstorm das Gewitter, -
ticket die Karte, -n; das
 Ticket, -s
time die Zeit, -en; **every ~**
 jedes Mal; **for a long ~**
 lange; **to have a good ~** sich
 amüsieren
tired müde
to auf; in; nach *(with cities
 and masc. and neut.
 countries)*; zu; **~ the movies**
 ins Kino; **~ the city** in die
 Stadt. **~ the post office** auf
 die Post; **~ the drugstore** in
 die (zur) Drogerie/Apotheke;
 ~ Switzerland in die
 Schweiz; **~ the opera** in die
 Oper
today heute
together zusammen
tomorrow morgen; **~ evening**
 morgen abend
tonight heute abend
too zu; auch; **~ bad** schade
tooth der Zahn, ⁻e
totally ganz
towards gegen; **~ evening**
 gegen Abend
town hall das Rathaus, ⁻er
traffic jam der Stau, -s
train der Zug, ⁻e
train station der Bahnhof, ⁻e;
 from the ~ vom Bahnhof
travel reisen
tree der Baum, ⁻e
TV das Fernsehen; **watch ~**
 fern·sehen°
TV set der Fernseher, -

umbrella der Regenschirm, -e
uncle der Onkel, -
understand verstehen°;
 understood: it's ~ es
 versteht sich
unfortunately leider
university die Universität, -en
until bis
upset: to get ~ sich ärgern
use gebrauchen; benutzen

vacation die Ferien *(pl.)*; der
 Urlaub, -e
very sehr
village das Dorf, ⁻er
visit besuchen; der Besuch, -
 e; **for a ~** zu Besuch; **during
 a ~** bei einem Besuch

wait warten ; **~ for** warten
 auf
waiter der Ober, -; der Kellner
waitress die Kellnerin, -nen
walk zu Fuß gehen°; **to go for
 a ~** spazieren·gehen°
wall die Wand, ⁻e
want wollen
warm warm
was war
watch die Uhr, -en
watch TV fern·sehen°
water das Wasser; **~ bottle**
 die Wasserflasche, -n
way der Weg, -e; **by the ~**
 übrigens
wear an·ziehen°; tragen°
weather das Wetter
week die Woche, -n; **in a ~** in
 einer Woche
weekend das Wochenende, -n

weird seltsam; komisch
well *(health)* gut; wohl; **as ~**
 auch; **well, . . .** na
what was
when als; wenn; wann
where wo; **~ to** wohin;
 ~ from woher
whether ob
which welch, (-er, -es, -e)
whole ganz
why warum; **~ not** warum
 nicht
window das Fenster, -
wine der Wein, -e; **~ glass** das
 Weinglas
winter der Winter, -
wish wünschen; **I ~** ich
 wünschte, ich wollte
with mit
without ohne
woman die Frau, -en
wonderful wunderbar;
 wunderschön
word das Wort, ⁻er
work arbeiten; die Arbeit; **to
 do the ~** die Arbeit machen
would würde; **~ like to help**
 würde gern helfen; **~ have to**
 müßte; **it ~ be nice** es wäre
 schön
write schreiben°
wrong: to be ~ sich irren

year das Jahr, -e
yellow gelb
yes ja
yesterday gestern
yet schon; noch; **not ~** noch
 nicht
you du, Sie; man

Index